D1713418

GRITS
on GUNS

GRITS
on GUNS

By
Grits Gresham

Illustrations by
Greg Bombeck

CANE RIVER
PUBLISHING
P.O. Box 4095
Prescott, Arizona 86302

Published by Cane River Publishing
P.O. Box 4095
Prescott, AZ 86302

Printed in the United States of America
ISBN 0-944438-00-8

Library of Congress Cataloging in Publication Data

Gresham, Grits, 1922 —
Grits on guns.

Includes index.
1. Firearms. 2. Hunting guns. I. Title
TS534.G74   1987 799.2'028'3   87-26786

CONTENTS

CONTENTS

Section Three — Rifles

Section Four — Guns

Section Five — Ammunition

CONTENTS

Section Six — Gun People

Section Seven — Hunting

CONTENTS

Section Eight — Handguns

Section Nine — Optics

FOREWORD

Grits and I have a lot in common. Both of us were raised with guns — me in a little town in West Virginia and Grits in a little town in South Carolina. When we were about six years old we got our first .22 rifles — mine a bolt action and his a little falling block. Mine stayed in the family for a long time, and Grits still has his.

I used to hunt squirrels before going to school (and sometimes forgot school entirely); Grits took his gun to school and hunted on the way home. We both grew up hunting, then joined the Army Air Corps. I stayed in and ended up flying planes for a living; he got out and ended up hunting for a living. And he calls that *work*?

Around home I had rabbits, squirrels, 'coon, 'possums, some quail and, of course, there were always crows. Great sport for a kid with a rifle, and for a shotgun. Squirrels were no problem for me to hunt, or shoot with a .22, because I had good eyes and was a good shot, but the thing I was proudest of shooting with that .22 was a rabbit. A big woods rabbit. You know, they run when you jump 'em, then hesitate just long enough to look back at you. That's when I nailed him.

That was a long time ago. I retired a few years back, and am I having fun! Probably more fun than I've ever had. I love to hunt, and, being in the public eye as I am, I also get a lot of questions as to *why* I hunt. That's easy. Number one — I hunt for recreation. Also, I love game. I love to eat quail; it's better than a rock cornish game hen as far as I'm concerned. And I love elk meat. I love venison.

But, many's the time I've spent a whole day in the field and never fired the gun. Yet, it's the most beautiful time in the world. Today, I hunt primarily for exercise, and that's the reason my favorite hunting is quail and chukar. Man, you walk and run all day, and in great country. Just beautiful.

For more than 30 years I never really had a home, because in the military you're here, there, every couple of years somewhere else in the world. But I sampled all of the hunting opportunities that were offered to me wherever I was.

The best I ever experienced was probably in Germany. That figures, with a name like Yeager, which means "hunter" in German. My ancestors came from there, and they hunted for centuries. The traditions of hunting in Germany are absolutely beautiful. Lay the trophy on its right side and give it the *letzten bissen*, the last bite. And, after a drive, arrange the game in respectful order, and play the last call for each species. We could use a little more such respect for game in this country.

I also really enjoyed hunting in Pakistan, because of the very wildness of the country. The Pakistanis are ardent hunters, were very hospitable, and exposed me to some really primitive areas and to some beautiful hunting.

Now that I'm a bit more settled, I do a lot of handloading. I like accurate rifles, and fool around with different calibers: 270's, 30-06's, 243's and 7mm Remington Magnums. I've about decided to stay with the 7mm mag, my favorite caliber, for everything. One gun to do everything, and then I'll give the rest of my guns to the 12 grandkids.

People who own and use guns should learn to handle and use them properly. Responsibility goes with firearms ownership. I know from personal experience. We had a tragic gun accident in our home when I was very young. But Dad took it upon himself to train us and teach us everything he knew about a gun, and I've been using them ever since.

My son spent a year and a half in Vietnam as the point guy on an ambush team — and survived. He survived because he was raised in a hunting environment. He had the eyes. He knew the land. He was a hunter. He was a real outdoorsman. He was good at it. And he survived because of that.

I believe in the right to own and use guns, and support the National Rifle Association in its efforts to protect that right. My uncle was a gunsmith, naturally a very pro-gun guy, and he bought me my first membership in the NRA about 40 years ago.

When Proposition 15 came up in California, where I settled after retiring, I began to realize that there were actually some strong organized movements against the right to bear arms. I decided that the NRA was the outfit which could best fight such efforts, and that's why I got active. It was just evident that we had to do something or we'd lose that right.

And, of course, I believe in hunting. Hunters are the best conservationists, which is why there's a lot more game in this country, of just about all species — deer, elk, wild turkey, bear because of conservation. Which is amazing since there's obviously much less land available for the animals now than there was then. Two hundred million people take a lot of space, which means there is that much less area as home for wild things.

I don't need to say much about this book or about Grits Gresham. You already know that Grits is the foremost outdoorsman in this country. He knows guns and hunting, he's a damn good writer, and he tells it like it is. You'll enjoy this book. And, if you're like me, you'll learn a helluva lot from it.

GEN. CHUCK YEAGER

ACKNOWLEDGMENTS

Many people have helped foster my love of guns and hunting, my education in the field of shooting, and my incentive and efforts to write about these things. Thanks to a favorite uncle, Leonard Hill, of Weirton, West Virginia, who thought it was a good idea to give his 4 1/2 year old nephew a "BB" gun for Christmas. And who, when the youngster's birthday rolled around six months later, realized that a replacement was needed. Two a year — for quite some time. And to Dad, who supervised those early gunning efforts, and who managed to keep me adequately gunned despite the economic pressures of the depression era.

And I remember with gratitude Roy Ramage, my growing-up, next- door neighbor who shared his guns and bird dogs and hunting; J. Curtis Earl, who taught me about handguns and center-fire rifles and muzzle loaders; Mary Land and Mary Gresham, for their endless encouragement; Ted Kesting and Tom Paugh, for uncanny editorial direction; Bob Brownell, the guru of gunsmithing who is also an accomplished journalist, and who steered me in the right direction on numerous occasions; Pete Brown, my predecessor as Shooting Editor of *Sports Afield* who has been unstinting with his sound advice and support; and all the other gun writers with whom I've enjoyed a warm rapport for decades, and who have contributed immeasurably to my firearms education.

Finally, my thanks to the thousands of you who have written or called, or who took the time to chat a while in hunting camps around the globe, in planes and boats and terminals, on street corners and in gun stores. Your critiques, comments, suggestions and sharing of your experience and expertise have inevitably ended up in this book. So, if you encounter a passage which sounds familiar, it just might be something you told me somewhere along the line.

[Each column followed by a month and year was previously published in that issue of *Sports Afield* Magazine, copyright Hearst Publications.]

INTRODUCTION

What's new! What's important! What's needed! What's interesting! Those are some of the criteria tossed into the selection hopper when the decisions are made as to what my *Sports Afield* shooting columns will be about. The subjects are chosen with care, since for more than a decade I could cover only one topic a month, only a dozen for the entire year. My editors and I choose what we believe gun owners would like to read.

The disadvantage of a magazine column, of course, is that it isn't very permanent. Sure, you and I have hoarded every issue of some magazines for years and years, finally having to stack them up back in the closet, and then out in the garage. We've got 'em, but they aren't really that useful. We can't easily retrieve — find, that is — a particular column we remember reading way back when, one that we particularly wanted to keep.

That's the rationale for collecting these columns into a bound volume. Some of them in this book are just as they appeared in *Sports Afield*, most have been edited to bring them up to date, and others expanded beyond the space restrictions of the magazine. There are also new chapters which have never before been published.

One of the delights of writing about guns and shooting has been the privilege of knowing some of the significant, interesting people involved in this arena of sporting life. Included in this book are chapters about a few of them, the Bill Rugers, John Brownings, Bill Weavers, Roy Weatherbys, John Ambers, Bob Brownells, Bill Steigers and the like who give so much life and color to the gunning scene. I hope you enjoy reading about them as much as I enjoyed the writing.

GRITS GRESHAM

Section One

SHOOTING

BIRDS OF CLAY

There must be something very satisfying about programming a shot charge so that it intercepts a moving clay disk, since that attempt is made more than seven hundred million times each year. Just in the United States, that is. Add the targets smashed — and missed — in the rest of the world, and the total becomes even more impressive.

In 1977 *Sports Afield* tried to get some kind of handle on the magnitude of clay target shooting in the country, and the best criterion seemed to be the number of clay targets manufactured and sold. At that time — about 750,000,000! The total now may be more or less, but I'd tend to guess that it's about the same. And that's a bunch.

How many of those would you think were utilized in organized trap and skeet shooting? Most? Half? Nope, only some 250,000,000 are hurled from the traps of such clubs, which leaves more than half a billion "unaccounted for," more or less. We actually have a pretty good idea where they go. Many are sprung from a simple trap stashed behind barns out on the plains of Kansas and Iowa and the like. Millions are used in the specialized clay target games which are becoming more and more popular throughout the land. And maybe the biggest batch of them all are slung from arm-powered hand traps, brought into play at duck clubs during the non-hunting times, on family picnics, at sessions where dad is teaching son how t'lead 'em, and at sessions where dad himself is trying to find out why he consistently misses that quail quartering to the right.

Why? Why in the world would that many caps be popped each year at an inanimate clay disk that measures 4 5/16 inches in diameter, is 1 1/8 inches high, and weighs just 3 1/2 ounces? Many reasons, of course, but of overwhelming importance is the simple fact that it is FUN. It's a great way for bird hunters to hone their reflexes during the off season; the finest tool to use in teaching a beginning scattergunner; and a powerful lure to the competitive instincts of thousands of shooters.

TRAP and SKEET are the words most people think of when they think of clay target shooting. Trap had its beginning in England, where competitive shotgun shooting began, when live birds were released from a "trap." It came to this country in the same form, again with live birds — usually pigeons, first the passenger pigeon, and then later the domestic pigeon of today. Then came a series of inanimate targets, but none were really successful until a man named George Ligowsky invented the clay target, in essentially the same form as we know it today. The year was 1880, and that was truly a historic event for competitive shotgunning.

Skeet didn't come along for another 40 years, when a group of Massachusetts hunters devised a game to serve as bird shooting practice during the off season. An outdoor magazine conducted a contest to pick a name for this new clay target sport, and from the 10,000 entries came the winner: SKEET — a Scandinavian form of the word "shoot."

What's the difference. In trap the targets are thrown from a single trap, away from the shooters at varying angles but with a fixed elevation. The shooters stand on one of five stations, located in a row 16 yards directly behind the trap house. In skeet the targets are thrown from two houses — high and low, with seven shooting stations set in a semicircle between the houses, and an eighth station positioned midway between the houses. The targets are thrown on a fixed flight path.

Although skeet is better practice for field shooting, trap is more popular for at least a couple of reasons. A trap layout is simple to install — one trap, with a field of fire essentially in one direction. Skeet requires two houses and two traps, and a much broader safe zone, which makes a skeet range more expensive to build. Competitive trap is shot with the 12 gauge, and any modified- or full-choked barrel is fine. If you engage in the full range of skeet competition, you must have guns in 12, 20, 28 and 410 gauges, with skeet-choked (cylinder to improved cylinder) barrels. Again, more expensive.

But, for fun, which is why most of those three quarter of a BILLION targets are used each year, you can shoot trap or skeet with any shotgun you happen to have at hand, no matter what the gauge or choke. It's FUN to try to break a 16-yard target with an open-choked barrel on the trap range, and great practice for getting off a quick one at a grouse in a thicket. It's FUN to shoot a round of skeet with a full-choked gun, and — again — great practice for making sure you're right on.

The epitome of simplicity and low cost when it comes to clay target shooting calls for only a hand trap and a box of clay targets. The trap costs less than 10 bucks, and the targets are inexpensive.

Just pick a safe shooting area and have at it. Just a step up is the use of a portable trap, spring powered, such as those made by Trius, which dominates this field.

Variations on clay target shooting are almost endless, but a few have become quite popular. One is the Crazy Quail layout, in which a single trap is placed in a pit 16 yards from the shooter, with the targets being thrown in ANY DIRECTION at the option of the trap operator. Another is the Duck Tower, where a trap is placed high — on a tower or hill, offering passing and incoming, high angle shots. Riverside Skeet has five stations as in trap, but with a trap house at each end of the line. "Aw, Shucks" was dreamed up (nightmared up?) down at Remington Farms, and involves five shooting stations in a heavily wooded area, with a single trap placed high in a tree. Quail Walks simulate field shooting, with traps hidden near a trail through game habitat, and targets released without warning as the shooter walks along. A new clay target game which includes ingredients from most of the above versions is called Hunters Clays.

The two governing bodies of organized clay target shooting in this country are the Amateur Trapshooting Association and the National Skeet Shooting Association. Each summer they conduct their individual "world series" of their respective sports — The Grand American Trapshooting Championships, held in Vandalia, Ohio, and the National Skeet Shooting Championships in San Antonio, Texas. With the exception of a few of the marathon runs, which are really competitions for only a few of the many thousands who participate in them, the "Grand" attracts more competitors than does any other competition in the nation. Some 5,000 shotgunners from throughout America enjoy a week or 10 days in Vandalia each August, shooting more than three million shotshells at a like number of clay targets.

When you hit a clay target with a shot charge, something happens that is satisfying. It breaks! Like the bottles most of us have popped with sling shot or gun of some sort. You can chip a clay target; you can break it; and you can smoke it. Smoke! That's all that's left when you catch one dead on at decent range, and it's an exhilarating experience.

One day I watched the exuberance of a tryout hopeful on the Olympic skeet range after he broke the last target in a "straight" round, punching the air with clenched fist. It's the "I gotcha!" feeling. You can get the same feeling smoking a clay from a hand trap back in the pasture. Oh, yes — no, he didn't make the Olympic shooting team.

Olympic trap and skeet are very different sports from our conventional American competitions, and are much more difficult. They are of little consequence to most shooters since there are very, very few ranges in the U.S. where they can be shot.

Several films on clay target shooting have been produced by the National Shooting Sports Foundation, with the goal of stimulating interest in this kind of activity. They are shown many times on more than 500 television stations across the country.

There are hundreds of trap and skeet clubs in the U.S., and most of them welcome visitors, with their members delighted to share information about their sport. You can also get information by writing to the National Shooting Sports Foundation, the Amateur Trapshooting Association, and the National Skeet Shooting Association.

National Shooting Sports Foundation
1075 Post Road
Riverside, CT 96870

Amateur Trapshooting Association
1100 Waterway Blvd.
Indianapolis, IN 46202

National Skeet Shooting Association
P. O. Box 28188
San Antonio, TX 78228

November 1984

THE BALLISTIC BOOK

B reathes there a hunter who hasn't paused, gun in hand and game in sight, and wondered: "Where is this bullet gonna end up out there?"

The calculations involved in determining "where" are not insignificant. Cranked into the formula are such factors as velocity, bullet weight and bullet shape, distance to the target, angle from horizontal, height of the scope above the rifle bore, and wind direction and velocity. Even with the mini-marvels called calculators, most of us are hopelessly outgunned by such complex computations.

What I have done is probably what you do: rely on the excellent ballistic charts published by arms and ammunition manufacturers. Those in turn are based on the exterior ballistic tables for centerfire rifle and rimfire cartridges which were recalculated in 1974, using modern computer technology, for the Sporting Arms and Ammunition Manufacturers Institute (S.A.A.M.I.) I still use these very practical tables, which are included each year in the catalogs of Federal, Remington and Winchester, but since 1980 I have also relied increasingly on a modest book which is a gold mine of information for rifle and pistol hunters.

It was shortly after being published that this most unimpressive paperback came to my attention. No pictures; no drawings; no fancy cover! Just a plain brown wrapper with the title and author — *Tables of Bullet Performance,* by Philip Mannes, enclosing 407 pages of nothing except rows of figures. It got my attention largely, I suspect, because I wondered if Dave Wolfe had lost his mind.

Dave is the man behind Wolfe Publishing Co., Inc. of Prescott, Arizona, and since he isn't known for backing losers, I took a second look at this new book. And have been looking at it ever since.

The ballistic tables published by gun and ammo people are necessarily limited in scope. They must, from a practical standpoint, be confined to certain loads and a few distances. Philip Mannes' book contains no such limitations. For comparison, consider that while the current Winchester catalog chart contains cartridge trajectories for each of the 150 varieties of rifle and pistol ammunition they offer, and the Remington catalog just a few less than that, this ballistics book lists more than 22,000 possible combinations. If the gunner has this book, and knows the muzzle velocity and ballistic coefficient of the bullet he's using, he can quickly determine virtually anything he wants to know about the performance of that loading.

How did such a wish book for riflemen and handgunners come into being — and why? And why wasn't it done before?

"I'm a shooter, and want to know all the trajectory data for any range," Philip Mannes answered my questions. "I'm also an engineer, am kinda lazy, and got tired of cranking up the info by hand."

Regardless of Philips' "laziness," and his inclination to make such data more readily available, he couldn't have done it in the era B.C. — before computers. Not only is he a rifleman and an engineer, Mannes also programs digital computers as part of his work in the aerospace industry. And that is the combination of ingredients which brought this ballistic book into being.

"It would take several hours to figure the complete trajectory data for just one bullet," the author answered another question, "if done by hand. You see, the book doesn't give one trajectory for a particular loading, but a complete new trajectory for all distances out to a thousand yards."

Not many of us are very interested in thousand-yard stats, except in an academic way, but from half that on down we can use the data. This book gives it.

Mannes divided the book into two sections. The first deals with bullets having ballistic coefficients between 0.09 and 0.70 with muzzle velocities of from 800 to 1,900 feet per second. The second half covers ballistic coefficients between 0.10 and 0.70 and muzzle velocities from 2000 to 4000 feet per second. For the lower velocities the data is listed out to 500 yards; for the higher velocities, to 1000 yards.

For each ballistic coefficient/muzzle velocity combination there are ten columns of information. The first, range, is the distance of the bullet from the muzzle in yards. The second, velocity, gives the remaining velocity at each distance shown in the first column. The third column lists the midrange height of the trajectory above the line of sight when the gun is sighted in at each distance in the first column.

The next five columns (headed 50 yd to 250 yd in the first section and 100 yd to 300 yd in the second section) give the height of the trajectory above or below the line of sight at each distance in the range column, when the gun is zeroed at the distance designated at the head of any of these five trajectory columns.

By referring to these tables, a hunter can immediately know what the effect will be of zeroing his rifle to be "on" at 100, 150, 200, 250 or 300 yards, where the bullet will strike at any distance out to 1000 yards. Knowing that, he can select the most efficient zero range for his caliber and the game he's after.

There's more. The last two columns list the drift of the bullet at each range distance in inches, in a ten-mile-per-hour crosswind (you can halve it for a five mph wind or double it for a 20 mph wind); and the time of bullet flight, in seconds, from the muzzle out to any distance listed in the range column.

To use the book, as mentioned above, you must know the ballistic coefficient of the bullet and its muzzle velocity. Most bullet manufacturers list the ballistic coefficient in their catalogs, and the muzzle velocities shown in loading manuals are quite reliable. For more precise figures many reloaders use chronographs to check the muzzle velocity of their handloads.

If you use factory ammunition, you'll have to dig a bit to get full value from this book. Ammo manufacturers give the muzzle velocity of their loads (from their test barrels), but not the ballistic coefficients of the bullets. I expect, however, that a note to any of them would bring forth this information.

Even without knowing the exact ballistic coefficient of a factory-loaded bullet, you can get practical results (Mannes says within five percent) by using the ballistic coefficient for a similar bullet. Most 150-grain, .30-caliber, spitzer-type bullets, for instance, will have ballistic coefficients which are close.

Since the tables don't show bullet diameter or bullet weight, Mannes included a separate five-page section by which we can determine the remaining energy in foot-pounds, for bullet weights from 10 to 500 grains and velocities from 500 to 5000 feet per second.

Ken Howell, one of Dave Wolfe's editors, and an excellent ballistician in his own right, wrote the very informative introduction to the *Tables of Bullet Performance*. He summed it up well in his closing lines: "Within the bounds of normal variation, the tables in this book are entirely adequate for use in practical estimation of downrange performance."

That's what this book is about: downrange performance for any rifle or pistol bullet at any range. From the stark rows of figures marching end on end for 400 pages, many of us can conjure up the most vivid shooting scenes imaginable: That perfect bullet placement on a prairie dog at 300 yards, a chuck at 500, or a charging buff at twenty paces. *Tables of Bullet Performance* is obviously not for casual reading, but the production of it was a worthy achievement which is of immense value to the serious rifle and pistol hunter.

February 1982

Y ou've put it all together. More than half a year ago you began making plans for this hunt, and since then you and your buddies have spent weeks pouring over maps, discussing tactics, and getting gear together. Three days ago you four-wheeled your way into the high, back country, set up the camp, and spent the past two days scouting the area. This morning — the season opened.

Right now you've just sprawled into a half-sitting, half- leaning, hasty-sling position on the side of the mountain, with the biggest mulie you've ever seen bouncing his way toward escape. Spooked from the canyon bottom by your partner, the buck chose a route toward the ridge top which made you scramble uphill to get a shot. Now your heart is pounding from excitement, altitude and exertion, and you're finding it tough to make the crosshairs behave.

Have you really put it all together? Will the next few seconds see a record-book trophy collapse 250 yards away, or will they insure that you have one more tale in your repertoire about the biggie that got away?

The answer could well depend upon that little piece of curved metal beneath your finger called a trigger!

When the moment of truth arrives in big game hunting the final act is played by you, your trigger finger and the trigger on your rifle. All else is past history. The only item of any consequence which remains is just a bit more pressure on the trigger.

With stakes that high riding on its performance, it seems reasonable that the trigger on a big game rifle would receive a great deal of attention from its owner. Not so! I would conservatively estimate that most hunters never even think about it, despite the fact that a bit of tender loving care in this direction almost invariably improves shooting performance substantially.

When you buy a production run big game rifle across the counter the trigger pull will usually range from mediocre to atrocious, which calls for an explanation of what a good trigger pull should be. Ideally, for a hunting rifle, it should be moderately light, crisp, smooth, and should have very little movement either before or after the let-off.

Virtually all production rifles are sold with trigger pulls which are too heavy. Match that with one which is creepy, crawly, and rough and you have a combination with which good performance is impossible. This is true, let me emphasize, no matter how good the barrel, action, bedding and cartridge may happen to be.

A trigger which moves in gasps and spurts places an impossible burden on the shooter, since there is simply no way he can achieve a controlled let-off at the moment of his choosing with any consistency. In trying to cope with this problem he soon trades his trigger "squeeze" for a trigger "yank," and yankers don't have much success on big game at any appreciable distance.

In many cases all that's necessary to transform a mediocre to poor trigger pull into a good one is to adjust the trigger — or have it adjusted. And right here let me say that some triggers on factory rifles are very good indeed when they are properly adjusted, and that is true of the leading bolt actions on the market.

Many factory triggers are adjustable, but on most of these the stocks must be removed before the adjustment screws can be reached. Some companies elect to point out the fact that a particular rifle has an adjustable trigger while others don't. The two adjustments possible on most adjustable triggers are for pull weight and for over travel.

At one time Remington included instructions on how to adjust triggers on the Model 700, which is an excellent trigger indeed, but with no fanfare that bit of instruction was dropped from all literature. Product liability is the culprit. Companies have been burned repeatedly by lawsuits, many of them frivolous and unwarranted, making it understandable that they eliminate all potential possible. It's understandable, but it's sad, and costly for the shooter.

Almost all rifle triggers, whether they are the adjustable type or not, can be "adjusted" by a good gunsmith. He can usually smooth out the pull, regulate its weight to a degree, and can often adjust the travel.

Caution! Any prudent gun owner should be able to adjust the trigger pull on his rifle, if the manufacturer says the trigger is adjustable and gives instructions on how to adjust it. Beyond that, unless you are a competent gunsmith, do not mess around on the innards of your trigger mechanism with file, honing stone or whatever. Some trigger assemblies are quite simple, but others are very complex.

(If you'd like to learn a bit more about triggers, get the excellent book by Roy Dunlap titled *Gun Owner's Book Of Care, Repair and Improvement.)*

The pull weight on triggers for most production run bolt action rifles in the big bore calibers generally range from about 6 pounds up to 12 pounds plus. One major manufacturer says that they strive for a four to six pound range, but most check out far beyond that.

It's understandable, of course, that manufacturers must gear their production lines to produce trigger pulls on the heavy side. Safety and liability both enter the picture.

Heavy and light are relative terms when discussing trigger pulls. Light, to a bench rest shooter, could be two ounces. But for the sake of big game hunting rifles my personal "light" range is two to three pounds, and I adjust my bolt actions to the three-pound pull.

So what's the big deal! Three pounds or six. Simply that most shooters are much more accurate with a three-pound pull than with one twice that heavy. The more exertion you must use to pull the trigger, the more difficult it becomes to prevent that exertion from disturbing your sight alignment. Which is why bench rest shooters use extremely light pulls.

Those very light pulls aren't practical for big game hunting rifles. Cold weather and numb fingers, heavy clothing and awkward shooting positions, make a suitable safety margin mandatory in the trigger pull of a hunting rifle. The margin must insure that the firing pin doesn't fall when the bolt is slammed home with force during rapid fire, nor when the rifle gets the sharp rap and jolt which are common on hunting trips.

You obviously need a scale to determine what the pull weight is on your trigger. Any accurate spring-type pull scale will serve the purpose, provided there is enough definition between pound marks. (Keep in mind that a four-pound pull on some "fish scales" may actually be about a two-pound pull.) Just hook the scale on the trigger, pull slowly, and watch the needle until the firing pin falls. Do this several times for a more accurate reading.

Make sure your pull is in the direction it would be if you were actually shooting the rifle. And make sure that the hook on the scales doesn't bind on the trigger guard.

Scales are available which are designed specifically for determining pull weight, with the Ohaus Trigger Pull Gauge a popular one. It reads up to six pounds in one-ounce increments, and is also calibrated in grams. Trigger pull weights, and here we mean actual physical weights in 1/4-pound increments, are more precise, and is the system approved by the NRA. Both are available in some gun stores, or by mail from: Brownells, Rt. 2 Box 1,

Montezuma, Iowa 50171.

You can adjust your trigger without having a scale, of course, relying upon what feels right to you. Use common sense. If you're going to err, do it on the heavy side.

There is one point which should be made, with respect to guesstimating what feels right, on rifles where the stock must be removed before the adjusting screws are accessible. It's simply that you must put the stock back on before dry firing it for feel.

I don't know of any lever action or autoloading big bore rifles which have adjustable triggers, but most of them on the current market can be improved by a competent gunsmith. That also applies to some of the older models, especially the lever actions, some of which have been on the best-seller lists for decades.

It should be obvious that working on the trigger mechanism of an autoloader has a particular potential for danger, and should be done with utmost care and only by someone who knows exactly what he's doing. On my autos, where pull weight is concerned, I want that additional margin of safety which the manufacturers deem necessary.

A number of excellent custom trigger assemblies are available as replacement for those used by the rifle manufacturers. Most of these have good adjustments for pull weight and trigger travel which can be easily made by the gun owner.

These triggers are of three general types. First is a conventional single trigger which has full and precise adjustments. Second is a single set trigger. It can be used as a conventional trigger, but can also be "set" by pushing forward on it to fire at only a few ounces of pressure. Third is the double set trigger. In this the forward trigger can be used to fire the rifle in normal fashion, but it can also be "set" by pulling the rear trigger first.

Some of the best known commercial triggers are made by these companies: M. H. Canjar, 500 E. 45th St., Denver, Colo. 80216; Timney Mfg. Co., 5624 Imperial Highway, South Gate, Ca. 90280; Dayton-Traister, P. O. Box 93, Oak Harbor, Wash. 98277; and Paul Jaeger, Jenkintown, Pa. 19046.

Commercial triggers are very popular for use in hunting rifles built on military actions, since the triggers of the latter usually leave much to be desired. Most military actions have two-stage triggers, the first a quite long trigger travel under little pressure, then a shorter, harder movement to fire. They can often be improved greatly by a good gunsmith, but many hunters prefer to replace the military trigger with a commercial one.

The point of this exercise is simply this: if you're really interested in better shooting performance on big game, don't be content with the store-bought trigger pull which came with your rifle.

June 1976

SOMEBODY'S GOTTA PAY!

I f you bought a gun or ammunition recently, you paid too much. A lion is loose in our land which has manufacturers quaking in their bankbooks. It is the increasingly prevailing philosophy which contends, "If somebody gets hurt, somebody's gotta pay."

Juries imbued with such a belief have awarded astronomical sums to plaintiffs in recent years, with the judgments going against anybody remotely associated with the incident. Responsibility of the injured individual to properly use the product in question, in most cases, does not seem to be a consideration of the jury.

"Ole Joe didn't really mean t'put that 20 gauge shell in his 12 gauge gun and blow off a couple of fingers. He's got a wife and some kids. Let's give him a hundred thou. No, let's make it an even million bucks. Split it between the gun maker, the ammo manufacturer, the distributor, the dealer who sold Joe the stuff, and the insurance companies...Won't hurt anybody...And I know I'd like it if I were Joe."

It won't hurt anybody — nobody except you and me and and the rest of the public.

The consumer should have reasonable protection against products which are defective, but the manufacturer should not be penalized for the stupidity of a few who use his products. Nor should he be penalized because the quality of an item which he manufactured two decades ago is not as high as that of the equivalent product he produces today.

As far-fetched as those two thoughts are, both are a reality today. Manufacturers are being penalized because some consumers misuse their good products, and manufacturers are being penalized because they have improved some of their products over the years.

If somebody gets hurt, somebody's gotta pay.

Huge awards by juries in product liability cases have forced insurance companies to raise liability insurance rates to staggering heights. The product manufacturers simply pass those increased costs of doing business on to their customers — you and me.

If, that is, they can afford to stay in business, which is not always the case.

Not only are we paying more for each item we buy because of the atrocious situation which exists — in all industries, not just with guns and ammo, but we are also having to live with products inferior to those which could be produced with today's technology. Some manufacturers are simply afraid to improve products which they've been selling for years, fearing that juries will penalize them because their earlier products were and are "less safe."

Sound far-fetched? It is reality, a horror story almost without parallel. Consider just a few examples.

Item: a $300,000 settlement by an insurance company for one firearms manufacturer, in a case where a man claimed that he shot his daughter when the rifle malfunctioned and shot out the side of the rifle.

Item: a $1.8 million jury award to a 16-year-old boy injured when sliding headfirst into home plate. The youngster, so the verdict went, should have been warned by the school board that such action was dangerous.

Item: a $138,000 compensatory damage jury award to a man who shot himself in the leg. Then the jury awarded that man $2.8 million additional in punitive damages, arriving at that figure by determining the amount it would have cost the manufacturer to install the latest safety improvement in each older model gun of that type ever sold.

That makes as much sense as would finding Ford Motor Company guilty for not re-calling all Model T's and installing disc brakes in them.

Item: a $1.2 million jury award to a boy who suffered brain damage on a field trip, when he caught his foot on a tree root, fell and struck his head.

Item: a $6.8 million settlement out of court for an injury resulting from massive disregard of the rules for handling guns: loaded rifle in a vehicle, pointing it at a person, fiddling with safety and trigger. The firearms manufacturer wanted to fight this one in court, but its insurance company wanted to settle — said it would not be responsible if the case were tried.

The football season was canceled because of lack of equipment. It could happen. One helmet manufacturer was socked with a SIX

MILLION DOLLAR judgment because of an injury to a high school player. And it was never even proven that the boy was wearing headgear of that manufacture.

Boat makers aren't immune. No manufacturer is. Nobody is. A bass boater injured when as he readily admitted, he took his hand off the steering stick to wave to a friend — almost a hundred grand. Settled out of court. So you pay more for your bass boat.

Perhaps most important and dangerous is that the tool and die makers, who make the tools used to make our products, are feeling the suicidal hand of liability case juries. Put them out of business and we can all return to the stone age.

Sympathy, not responsibility, is the basis for many of the jury awards. Fear of what a jury might do, despite the facts, is the basis for many undeserved out-of-court settlements.

"Much of it is just blackmail," was the way one firearm official put it. They file a suit with little hope of winning it, but with much hope for a settlement to prevent the suit from going to trial.

Such free rides, for plaintiffs and attorneys, may be coming to an end. "We must start defending all suits," another firearms official told me. "We can't afford not to do it."

A manufacturer whose defective product causes injury should be penalized, but reasonably so. The man who improperly uses a sound product, and hurts himself or others in the process, should not be rewarded.

The legal profession gets $ .56 of every liability dollar, and that, in the opinion of many who have studied the system, is the root of much of the evil. Most attorneys who specialize in such cases operate under a contingency fee basis. The injured party doesn't have to bear the trial costs, but in return agrees to pay the lawyer some 30 percent to 50 percent of any settlement or award.

Since the plaintiff is investing nothing, he or she has "nothing to lose." Attorneys who specialize in such cases do all they can to promote that belief, since the attorneys do have much to gain. They know that juries are prone to find for the plaintiff no matter where the responsibility lies, and they know that insurance companies are prone to settle out of court, again regardless of responsibility.

That combination makes the odds great that the trial lawyer will make money on most of these cases. Regardless, once again, of the guilt or innocence of the defendant.

"The loser in one of these cases," one firearms manufacturing

official told me. "should be required to pay all of the expenses for both sides. We settle many cases in which we aren't really involved, simply because that is less expensive than going to court."

The company also raises the prices of its guns for all customers to compensate for those expenses.

Another belief of many is that the amount which lawyers could demand on contingency cases should be limited, and sharply reduced from current levels. Whatever individual measures may be needed, it is obvious that the entire system needs revision.

Two examples of the soaring rates for liability insurance illustrate the problem. The tab for one gun club in recent years was $700 per year, and the following year it was $7,000. In 1976 liability insurance cost the marina operator at a small lake in California $38,000; in 1977 it was $71,000.

The nation cannot afford a continuation of such abuses as have occurred with increasing frequency in the past decade. We need a return to the philosophy of individual responsibility for one's actions, but legislation may be required to bring about such a "philosophy."

As one man put it, "The injured should be treated fairly and equally; and the guilty firmly, but equitably; but the innocent should just be left alone."

July 1978

PSYCH YOUR SHOT HOME

"**B**oss, you sure do confidence that plug," the old paddler swung the boat around ever so slightly, giving me a better angle to cast into a pocket between two cypress trees.

He was referring to the fact that I usually began our fishing day by tying on the same old topwater lure, and that I returned to it time and again when fishing was tough. It had little paint left, courtesy of the many casts which proved more attractive to the tooth-filled jaws of garfish and pickerel than to bass, but what it did have for me was the aura of success.

My paddler was entirely correct. I did have great confidence in that particular lure, but there was an additional ingredient. I was supremely confident that if I tied that plug to my line and fished it I would catch fish.

The difference is subtle, but real. That lure might not be as effective for anybody else, but, paired with my skill, the combination was poison to bass. So I believed, and it usually was.

I use the same type of mental gymnastics in shooting, and I'm a better shot because of it. You can do the same thing.

You can learn to psych your shot home to the target.

The only qualification that voids such a promise is the condition that you've already reached that plateau of confidence. And confidence is what this is all about.

Each area of the country has a few game shots who stand far above the crowd, and I'll bet you can name a couple from your town. These are the hunters who, when the chips are down, seldom miss.

They have one characteristic in common. All have supreme confidence in their shooting ability. When they pull the trigger, they are surprised if nothing falls or breaks.

Such faith in your capability to handle a particular shooting situation results from quite a number of factors, none of which is beyond reach of most shooters. Marksmanship is a prerequisite, of course, and that can be developed.

Acquiring a relatively high degree of shooting skill isn't really all that difficult, but it does require dedication and practice. If a shotgun is involved, shoot skeet, trap, hand- thrown clay targets, crows, barnyard pigeons, and any game birds on which the seasons are open. Keep your pet shotgun within easy reach in your home, and dry fire it at a spot on the wall several times a day. Get to be on intimate terms with your firearm.

Rifle shooters should follow a similar campaign — shooting on the range, shooting at varmints, shooting at a variety of targets under field conditions, and hunting game animals at every opportunity. Practice from practical shooting positions, let me emphasize, which means the steadiest positions possible. Only by practice can a hunter learn to quickly assume such positions, whether it be prone, sitting, slouched against the hillside, uphill, downhill, or propped over a rock. Use any rest available.

Don't neglect offhand practice. It is the least efficient of all, but such a position may be the only one you can use at that trophy of a lifetime.

In all of this practice you will be adding another building block in the confidence structure. You will be assuring yourself that your particular gun is right for you. You will know that the gauge or caliber is adequate, that the choke or scope is right, and that the guns fit you.

Now you have both the right equipment and the skill to use it, so you should be a super game shot. Right? Wrong! There are many hunters who possess both of those qualifications, yet who never rise above mediocrity in the field. They can do so, and so can you, by thinking their way to shooting success.

Psych the shot home.

World class weight lifters indulge in a similar bit of mental hypnosis. Most of them pause momentarily before each effort, psyching themselves to success. So do champions at live pigeon shooting, the toughest shotgun competition of them all, before calling for each bird.

A national pistol champion says that the most important six inches in competitive shooting are those between your ears. That is also true for shooting game, whether it be ducks or deer.

Mental programming is more important in the case of big game hunting than with bird shooting, since success of a trip may depend upon one single opportunity. When a sheep, elk or deer presents that chance, the hunter should be completely confident that he can and will take advantage of it.

I frequently play a game of "pretend" while hunting. What if a buck jumps from that thicket I'm approaching? What if an elk spooks from the bottom of the canyon and starts up the far slope? What if that herd of antelope is just over the ridge?

I am mentally gearing myself to any contingency. What is the animal likely to do, and how should I react. It's a never-ending game which changes as you change locations, and it is uncanny how the characters involved follow the script much of the time.

That includes your role, which is to cope with any situation, to get away a successful shot no matter what your quarry does. If you think you will, you usually do.

At the risk of inviting unflattering comments, I must admit that I talk to myself on occasion. "Gresham, that buck just may cross that opening before crossing the ridge and give you a shot, so put your binoculars down and get into a steady, sitting position. Sling tight. That's about 300 to 400 yards, so hold just below the back line. Just in front of his nose if he's still trotting."

I knew I could kill the deer if those conditions came to pass, since I had mentally adjusted for the situation. The buck, as a matter of fact, stopped in that little opening, and I did kill it.

The power of positive thinking is not infallible, and a dead animal or bird is not always the result of each psychic exercise. No amount of mental programming will make me a Rudy Etchen with the scattergun, but it narrows the gap for me and it can do so for you.

The other side of the coin is equally important. If you think you're going to miss a shot, you probably will.

November 1987

UP AND DOWN: WHERE TO HOLD

I t's true what they say about angles. Whether the shot is uphill or downhill, the rifle will shoot higher than would be the case if the shot were horizontal.

Why? Because the effect of gravity on a bullet is proportional to the *horizontal* distance it travels, which is always less than the rifle-to-target distance on up or down shots.

It is this pull of gravity, of course, which causes bullet "drop." The classic example illustrating this is the comparison of a bullet fired from a rifle barrel which is horizontal, precisely parallel to the ground, and another bullet simply dropped from the same height at the same time. Since gravity acts on both identically, both will touch ground at the same time.

Fire a .30-30 and a .300 mag simultaneously from horizontal rifle barrels and — you guessed it — the bullets will touch ground at the same time. Doesn't sound quite right, does it? And I know television and jet planes can't work, but I watch the tube and fly a lot. Believe.

That .300 mag bullet will hit the ground a lot farther from the muzzle than will the .30-30, of course, which triggers the topic of flat-shooting rifles and cartridges. Flat is fast, nothing more. The quicker a bullet gets from rifle to target, the less time that gravity has to exercise its pull.

Now that we're thinking gravity, let's return to up and down. The effect of gravity's pull in causing bullet drop is greatest in horizontal firing; it is absent when a bullet is shot straight up or straight down. Thus the effect decreases progressively away from the horizontal, as the angle of the shot becomes greater, whether up or down. Which means that your rifle will shoot progressively higher, relative to its horizontal point of impact.

Will it shoot enough higher to be concerned about in hunting situations? Yes, indeed, under some conditions, but it is nothing a bit of care can't cope with. What we must do is determine how much *lower,* if any, we should aim to compensate.

That gets involved, but we're going to uncomplicate it, borrowing from one of my afflictions known as the "about's." My shooting philosophies are just riddled with this disease. I don't shoot "two-inch groups" at 100 yards; I shoot into "about two inches." I guess a buck is "about 250 to 300 yards." I hold "about" a foot down from his back line.

I'm not a "minute of angle" thinker when I'm big game hunting, because there are simply too many variables. I prepare as well as possible in advance, but try to evaluate shooting situations broadly and quickly when they appear. Most of the time the results are "about" right.

Fifteen years ago Pete Brown carried a comprehensive uphill-downhill correction table in the *Sports Afield Shooting Annual,* giving all angles in 10 degree increments, but he cautioned that you can't take a computer in the field. The formula he derived and used is: $C = D (1 - \mathrm{Cos}\ o)$, where C = Correction and D = bullet drop from horizontal for the range.

Figuring your own corrections from Pete's formula is now easy with one of the pocket calculators having trigonometric functions. But down below I've included an "about" table which gets me by.

I've knocked the corners off these correction figures. They are not all exactly right; they are about right. They are good enough for me, fully commensurate with my inability to exactly guesstimate range and angle of shot, and to aim the rifle precisely where I choose under hunting conditions.

These figures work for the four popular caliber-loads listed. For the .30-06, a slower cartridge, the corrections are a bit greater: 30 degrees — 1″, 4″, 7″ and 12″; and for 60 degrees — 5″, 13″, 27″, and 43″.

I've shown only two angles, which split the quadrant into three pieces. On shots which are less than 30 degrees from horizontal, forget any correction. On those between 30 degrees and 60 degrees, or between 60 degrees and 90 degrees, guess.

Let's try an example. From the rim of a canyon I see a buck down below, and guess about 300 yards. A peak at the chart taped to my stock says the 130-grain .270 bullet should hit two inches low at that distance. Forget it, since errors of range estimation and shooting will wipe that out. But a steep angle — let's guess about 60 degrees, which calls for a 10-inch correction.

Where to hold? Low on the broadside buck, probably aiming for the heart, trying to get the bullet into the biggest target area. Never "give away" an animal by aiming completely over it or under it unless such a hold is positively indicated, and that is rare with a properly sighted-in, flat-shooting rifle within 400 yards.

Note that angle correction and holdover for bullet drop may tend to be compensating at long range. At 500 yards my .270 is about 28 inches below point of aim, but if the shot were a 60 degree one the angle correction would be about 30 inches. They cancel each other.

On most of my rifle stocks I tape a simple chart showing point of impact from 100 to 500 yards. By glancing at it regularly during a hunt I program my thinking to those numbers.

If the skeletonized angle correction chart shown here has merit for you, consider taping one like it to your rifle stock. Just keep in mind that these are negative corrections — the amount you should hold *under* to compensate for angle.

Grits' Angle Correction Table

(Which tells about how much to hold under for various angle shots using the following caliber-bullet combinations: .243 — 100 gr)

	Range-Yards			
Angle of Shot	200	300	400	500
30 degrees	−1″	−3″	−5″	−8″
60 degrees	−4″	−10″	−20″	−30″

(The calculations are from Pete Brown's chart in 1963 *Sports Afield Hunting Annual,* and from his mid-range trajectories in 1964 Annual. His formula was detailed in the 1975 Annual.)

April 1978

"Recoil doesn't bother me!"

Sound familiar? Most of us have heard that line a time or two, but it seldom comes from men or women who are top-ranked in their particular brand of gunning. It may be true that recoil does not, indeed, bother these hotshots, but that's most often because they have taken every measure possible to minimize or eliminate the effect of recoil.

It's a matter of degree. The kick of a .22 rimfire doesn't bother anybody, but the guy who says that a .460 Weatherby Magnum doesn't get his attention is either a gorilla or is lying. The few shots that a ruffed grouse hunter fires during the course of a day probably doesn't bother him, but when he toes the line for a 200-target event on the range it's often a different story.

I concede that the recoil of even that .460 WM goes unnoticed if the object of our attention is an oncoming elephant or Cape Buffalo. On occasion I have loosed four quick ones from a .458 Win Mag at these critters and never heard the gun, much less felt it, but in such situations adrenalin shields the body from such trivia.

The traditional methods of minimizing the effects of firearm recoil are well known, with the most popular being a "recoil pad" installed on the butt of the gun. I like them on all of my guns — rifles and shotguns, for several reasons. They do minimize the effect of recoil. They also make the placement of the buttstock on my shoulder seem more secure, although the stock may not slide into place on the shoulder quite as smoothly. And, recoil pads keep my guns from skidding to the floor when I prop them in a corner.

Stock inserts such as the Edwards Recoil Reducer, the C & H Mercury Reducer, Hiram's "Bearcat," the Staub Mercury Inertia unit, and the 2-R Ray Stafford unit are very popular with competition trap, skeet and live bird shooters. Gas-operated semi-automatic rifles and shotguns seem to kick less because the recoil is distributed over a longer time span. At one time the Cutts Compensator muzzle attachment was very popular with skeet shooters (and would have been with trap shooters except that gunners on adjacent stations wouldn't tolerate the increased muzzle blast). It and similar other devices reduce recoil by directing muzzle gases outward and rearward through slots in the attachment, and many shooters believe that they improve patterns as well. The Cutts is still available and retains many faithful users.

Another method of redirecting gases is to cut slots in the barrel of rifle, shotgun or pistol near the muzzle. Placed properly, they reduce muzzle jump and seem to cut down on recoil (about 20 percent less recoil, according to one independent lab, in the case of a magnum rifle). Larry Kelly, of Mag-Na-Port Arms, has popularized this technique. Reducing muzzle jump can, in hunting situations, be as important as actual recoil reduction. Recoil seems less when the gun stays on target, or more nearly so, after that first shot.

Less well known is the fact that certain alterations to shotgun barrels can significantly reduce felt recoil. Stan Baker, the Seattle gunsmith, puts it strongly, "The most effective method of recoil reduction, assuming other factors such as proper stock fit have been attended to, is through proper bore dimensions." By lengthening the forcing cone and/or increasing the inside diameter of the barrel, Stan (and other gunsmiths) decrease recoil by easing the transition of the shot charge from the chamber into the barrel.

All of those things are old hat to knowledgeable shooters, but in the past couple of years three new items have appeared which have impressed me. It was almost two years ago, in fact, when a letter came from Johnny Inman with details about a recoil reducing device called the Counter Coil. Made by MBM Enterprises of Stillwater, Oklahoma, and on the market since July 1982, this is a hydraulic, shock-absorbing buttplate which can be attached to any rifle or shotgun by MBM or any competent gunsmith.

When I finally got around to having Johnny send down a rifle for my testing I was sorry I hadn't done it sooner. He sent his personal rifle, a rather battered Remington M700 in 7mm Rem Mag caliber, which had service scars from duty out west. On the bench it shot beautifully, and the recoil was negligible. I was impressed, and so was veteran gunsmith Ken Eversul when he tried it. Although any such speculation is subjective, the impact against my shoulder and face seemed less than that of a .30-06.

The recoil is still there, of course; it just doesn't reach the shoulder in the same magnitude. The hydraulic action of the Counter Coil acts about like shock absorbers on an auto, where the road bumps are still there but the passenger doesn't feel them.

This unit is adjustable (about ten seconds for the operation) for any caliber or gauge, from the lightest to the heaviest. The object is to take advantage of the full travel of the pistons compressing against the fluid without letting them bottom out. Properly adjusted, the reduction in felt recoil is enormous.

The thorn on this rose is that the Counter Coil, kindly put, ain't no thing of beauty. The pistons are exposed — meaning you can see through the gap between buttpad and the rest of the stock, although I understand MBM now has a covering for that space. But, for my tastes, beauty is as beauty performs where my working firearms are concerned, thus, for me, the utility of this unit far outweighs the aesthetic aspect. One possible negative is that the stock must slide beneath your cheek as the unit functions, but that doesn't bother me. The unit adds four to eight ounces of weight to the gun.

Two other newcomers I've been using with pleasure in the past year or so are pads made of "space age" materials. They're in the form of recoil pads fitted to gunstocks, shoulder pads to attach to your jacket, and cheek pads fitted over the comb of your shotgun or rifle. The two materials are Sorbothane (a "new Polyurethane"), which is used for the recoil pads fitted to your gun; and the second is a polymer or urethane. The first such pads using this material had a label calling them "The Recoil Shock Eliminator," and the second batch I received are labeled "Action Recoil Shock Eliminators."

The Sorbothane pads are called "Sorbocoil," come in three sizes, are attachable to the buttstock of your gun by means of Velcro, or they can be glued directly to the stock. The raw pads have a batch of round protrusions which fit against your shoulder, and which also pick up dirt, gravel and leaves if you aren't careful. Now the company has covers for the pads which eliminate this annoyance.

The Velcro attachment doesn't seem practical for field use, although it has worked for me in bench testing. As for the pads themselves, they are great at taming recoil. By the time this is in print the company should have on the market a new pad, which attaches just as do conventional recoil pads. The Sorbothane in these is in the form of inserts.

The "Eliminator" pads come in several thicknesses, and are designed to be attached to your jacket, or your shirt under your jacket, either with Velcro or with a safety pin. They also fit into the shoulder pocket of Bob Allen shooting vests and jackets. There is also a "Cheek Saver Pad" which is 1/8-inch thick, covered with a soft suede cover, and is Velcro-attached to the comb of your gun. It does wonders toward eliminating recoil jolt to your cheekbone.

These new pads, both the "Eliminator" and the Sorbocoil, are more than gimmicks. They work. Recently I was bird shooting with a friend whose new shotgun was punishing his shoulder severely, with predictable results insofar as his shooting was concerned. After pinning on an Eliminator of mine, both his shooting and his pleasure increased tremendously.

For more information, write:
MBM Enterprises — Counter Coil
715 East 46th St.
Stillwater, OK 74074

La Paloma Marketing — Eliminator Pads
4500 East Speedway #93
Tucson, AZ 85712

Paxton Arms — Sorbocoil
P. O. Box 26245
Dallas, TX 75226

April 1984

USE THE RIGHT AMMO

I t was a crisp, fall afternoon, typical of October in the Colorado Rockies, when Don Kelly snuggled into the rifle sling and began taking up trigger slack. As most of us do, he'd arrived in elk camp early enough for the ritual, essential, sighting-in check, making sure that when the magic moment arrived the gun would perform. But his plans for the next day season opening were abruptly changed the moment he touched off that first shot. Instead of greeting the dawn high on a ridge looking for a bull elk, he spent those hours in the nearest town having metal fragments plucked from his eyes.

He had put a 7mm Express Remington cartridge into his 7mm Remington Magnum rifle.

Ken Eversul fed a live round into the chamber of the Browning BAR he had just finished bore-sighting, nudged the adjustment wheel of the forearm support on the shooting bench, and quickly squeezed off a trial shot. Numbing sound penetrated his ear muffs and hot gases poured into his face.

He had shot a .270 Winchester cartridge in the 7mm Remington Magnum caliber rifle.

Fred Pickett's look was one of disbelief and astonishment when he looked up at me from the shooting bench at the Caddo Rifle and Pistol Club. Flecks of blood began to ooze from his nose and from his face around his glasses.

Like Eversul, Fred had just fired a .270 Winchester cartridge in his 7mm Remington Magnum rifle.

What a bunch of amateurs! Right?

Not quite. Don Kelly is an attorney and member of the Louisiana legislature who began shooting about as soon as he began walking. Ken Eversul is a veteran hunter with experience in Mexico and Europe as well as in the U.S., an excellent trapshot with state titles to his credit, and a fine gunsmith who sights in dozens of rifles each year. Fred Pickett is an administrative law judge, an experienced hunter of many years, and the inventor of the Pickett's Red-i-Rest monopod which he was demonstrating for me when he made his boo-boo.

All three live within an hour's drive of my home here in Louisiana. If the laws of probability hold true, extrapolating this trio of local happenings nationwide can only reveal a huge number of "wrong ammo" accidents each year. My conversations with shooters and guides around the nation indicate that this is indeed a problem. How do such errors happen?

Fred Pickett had taken two of his favorite hunting rifles to the Caddo range, both equipped with his monopods, and we were shooting both the .270 and the 7mm. Open boxes of ammunition for both calibers were on the shooting bench, and Fred just reached into the wrong one. Two weeks earlier he had pulled much the same stunt with the same 7mm Remington Magnum rifle, only that time doing the Don Kelly number — a 7mm Express Remington cartridge in the 7mm mag. At the start of our shooting session he spoke of that mishap, and urged that we not let him do that again. We did.

Ken Eversul keeps his ammo in stacks, according to caliber, down on the second shelf of a workbench. He plucked a box from the right stack of 7mm Rem Mag's, but a box of .270's in that same brand had mysteriously found its way atop the 7mm stack.

"Before heading for Colorado," Don Kelly explained, "I told the boys to buy a couple of boxes of ammo for me. When the clerk handed them over they didn't notice that he'd given them 7mm

Express Remington instead of 7mm Remington Magnum. Neither did I until it was too late."

All of these are cases of shooter error, of course, as are the vast majority of gun "accidents." It's a testimonial to the quality of the guns in use today that there are so few injuries even when the firearms are abused so severely, but those injuries can be severe. Kelly was fortunate not to lose his eyesight, as some have done. Eversul and Pickett were wearing protective glasses, which is highly recommended for all shooters.

In all of these three instances, as is usually the case, the cartridge cases ruptured, spraying powder residue and shell fragments. Kelly took most of the flying metal in his nose, but the ophthalmologist in Craig took five pieces from Don's right eye.

Don's custom, thumbhole stock on his Model 70 was shattered, both in the forearm and behind the pistol grip. The stock on Ken's BAR was chipped and had to be replaced, the trigger guard blew out the bottom, and there was other minor damage. Fred's Remington Model 700 amazingly survived it's first abuse — the 7mm Express Remington fiasco, but the .270 Winchester cartridge ruined the bolt of the 7mm Remington Magnum.

"It was a stupid mistake!"

"I can't believe I did that!"

"You should read all the writing on every box of ammo you use, and then check the cartridges themselves."

Those comments from our three heros about sums it up, with the latter being the *piece de resistance*. You and I must read what the label says — not just glance at the box, simply because there are many similar cartridge designations. And then look at the cartridges themselves. Take nothing for granted.

Loss of eyesight, or even life, can be the penalty for carelessness.

We're saved from some of our errors by the fact that many cartridges won't chamber in a particular "wrong" rifle, but strange things can happen. One such is the case where a bullet is fired through a barrel of smaller diameter, such as a .30 caliber bullet through a .270 bore. It's happened, even without structural damage to the gun.

There are cartridges with different designations which can be interchanged, such as the .244 Rem and the 6mm Rem, or the .280 Rem and the 7mm Express Rem. (Remington, in fact, includes an "interchangeability Chart" in it's guns and ammo catalog.) Most cannot, and confusion is particularly understandable in such categories as the 7mm's and .30 calibers. The clerk filling your order faces stacks of 7X57's, 7mm Mauser, 7mm Express Remington, 7mm Remington Magnum, 7mm-08 Remington, and 7mm Weatherby Magnum. Under the .30 calibers there is the .30-30, the .308, the .30-06, the .30 Carbine, the .30 Rem, the .300 Savage, the .300 Win Mag, the .300 Weatherby Mag, and the .300 H&H Mag.

The bottom line is that it is your responsibility to make sure that the ammo you buy is correct for your gun, and that the ammo you finally slide into the chamber is still the right stuff.

Shotgunners aren't immune to mismatching, and one combination is especially dangerous. A 20-gauge shell placed in a 12-gauge gun will slide partway down the barrel and lodge right there, out of sight. If a 12-gauge shell is fired with that 20gauge obstruction in place, the result is almost inevitably a ruptured barrel, usually with injury to the gunner. Such mishaps are less frequent now than once was the case, since manufacturers now color code 20-gauge shells yellow to distinguish them from other sizes.

Safety Hints

1. Always read the label on the cartridge box before using that ammo.
2. Read the caliber designation on the cartridge head, especially if that ammunition isn't from a fresh box.
3. Never have more than one box of ammunition on the shooting bench at any one time.
4. Read the label on the cartridge box when the gunshop clerk sells it to you.
5. Don't mix loose cartridges of different calibers.
6. Each time you leave camp to hunt, re-check to make sure you have the right caliber ammo.
7. Wear protective glasses when shooting.

December 1982

SMART SHOOTERS USE GUN SLINGS

The short strip of leather known as a gun sling can be the difference between a good hunting trip and a bad one. It can be the bridge between comfort and discomfort, between convenience and inconvenience, and — most important of all — between success and failure. Why many hunters never use slings, or don't use them properly, is a mystery in this era of the sophisticated sportsman.

Many of us were first introduced to rifle slings through courtesy of the U. S. armed forces, where we quickly learned that the "military" sling on our firearm was there because it provided two functions. We discovered that we could shoot more accurately, in some shooting positions, using the sling. And it became obvious that the use of a sling as a carrying strap was quite desirable on the long strolls which the army allowed basic trainees to take.

Draping a rifle over the shoulder, using a sling as a carrying strap, is the most convenient and comfortable way to tote a gun. Most big game hunters in the western part of the country do just that, and it makes sense. It places the weight of the rifle where it's least noticed, and it leaves the hands free to help in negotiating rough terrain or to use binoculars.

Eastern and southern big game (deer) hunters aren't that consistent in the use of slings. Many use them, but many don't, although the trend is upward. In the South, the use of slings may be going up partly because the hunters are going up — up into tree stands in increasing numbers. It's easier and safer to take your rifle along, slung, when climbing up into a tree stand, than to pull the rifle up with a rope after you get there.

As an aid to accurate shooting, slings are most useful when the shooting is from prone or sitting positions. They help least (some say not at all) when you're shooting offhand, standing.

How much does a sling help? In my case, a tremendous amount, and I invariably use it when shooting if the situation permits. It can give almost benchrest stability when used properly.

Despite that, I'd guess that most big game hunters don't use their slings when shooting, even when their guns are sling- equipped. Some say they don't need it; others say it's too much trouble and too slow; but most of them who neglect the sling just aren't familiar enough with its use.

Sling use is simple. In the military version, an adjustable loop about mid-point of the sling is snugged up around the shooter's upper left arm. He then makes one wrap around the lower part of his arm before grasping the forearm of the rifle. When properly adjusted, there is tension on the strap when the rifle is shouldered.

A technique more suited to hunting involves the "hasty sling" position. The shooter just puts his left arm between sling and rifle, makes that one wrap, and shoulders the rifle. It is almost as effective as is the adjustable loop, and it's the method I use. Most hunting slings made today, in fact, have no adjustable loop, and must be used as a hasty sling.

Using a gun sling when shooting is fast, not slow. With only a minimal amount of practice, which can be done in your den or out in the backyard, you'll find yourself able to dampen those wobbling sights and get the shot off quicker than you ever could before. Then, take to the woods or range with live ammo and shoot a few targets in both the prone and sitting positions. And be amazed at how much your shooting has improved.

Slings on shotguns don't look quite right to me. They seem out of place, but despite that, I love 'em. My affection is greatest when I'm slogging across a boggy marsh in hip boots, carrying a load of decoys or a limit of ducks or geese, or both.

After the walking, when the time comes to swing that smoothbore on a fast-flying game bird, a sling becomes excess baggage. The answer is a sling light and compact enough to carry in the pocket, and one that is easily attached or detached as the occasion requires. There are several nylon or leather models which simply slip over the barrel at one end and the buttstock at the other.

Shotguns can also be equipped with swivels, or with swivel bases to accept quick-detachable swivels. That has long been a trademark of many European shotguns, and is gaining a few fans in this country.

More handguns are being used for hunting today than ever before, with the emphasis on big game hunting. Years ago a few handgunners decided that the best way to carry their heavy, long-barreled pistols was by a strap or sling, and manufacturers have moved to meet that need. In use they drape the sling over head and one shoulder, letting the pistol hang beneath one arm.

A pistol sling is also an aid to shooting. When properly adjusted, with handgun in the extended shooting position and sling over the head and shoulder, it provides tension on the strap that gives substantial stability.

Sling swivels are not really swivels. They're metal loops which are attached to stock and forearm of the rifle to hold the sling strap. They can be permanently attached or quick detachable (QD), with the QD having a great edge in utility. By using the QD style, a hunter can use the same sling for several rifles, needing only a set of swivel bases for each rifle and one set of swivel loops for the sling. Michaels of Oregon makes swivels and bases to fit just about any gun.

Slings are available in a smorgasbord of materials, shapes, colors and designs. Shooters can choose the traditional full grain leather, or suede, or one of the synthetics which are very strong and extremely light. From Michaels of Oregon they can pick a white sling for snow conditions or a camouflage one for non-snow use. Many manufacturers offer slings with wide, padded sections where the sling meets the shoulder, and Torel adds full- color embossing of your favorite game animal or bird.

Sling designs run the gamut from the traditional military type to a simple one-piece leather strap. One of my favorites is the Latigo Conway, marketed by Brownells Incorporated. With a tug on a hardwood "pull" this strap instantly moves from the slack shooting or carrying position to a tight, neat configuration which makes it easy to slip into saddle scabbard or gun rack. A simple push on the strap and it's ready for use again.

Anderson Designs promises that its unusual new sling places the gun weight on the waist, won't slide off the shoulder, is quick drawing, and steadies either rifle or shotgun for better shooting. Using a waist belt as well as an over-the-shoulder sling, this one straps the shooter to the gun.

A handy sling that stays in my duck hunting coat is nylon, weighs one ounce, and costs $4.00 postpaid from Sports Accessories.

One use for a gun sling seldom gets much consideration when discussing a sling's advantages, yet just about everybody uses a sling in this fashion. A sling is a great way to hang the gun up: from a nail in tent or cabin; from a tree limb outside the tent; from a limb when you're up in a tree stand; from a limb when you're knee-deep in water hunting ducks — Stuttgart fashion; or from the frame of a duck or goose blind, to keep the gun butt out of the muddy goo which seems to always accumulate in the bottom of the blind.

Just as you should periodically check your scope mounts when you're hunting, do the same with sling swivels and buckles. If one or the other does fail when you're carrying your rifle, odds are good that the scope will take the brunt of any fall.

Rifle slings aren't for everyone. Most African professional hunters never use them on their heavy rifles. In a pinch, as they put it, they can't afford the time required to free a sling caught on brush.

For most hunters, though, a sling is a worthwhile accessory of which we haven't taken full advantage.

SLING MANUFACTURERS

Torel, Box 592, Yoakum, TX 77995
Roy's Custom Leather Goods, Box G, Magnolia, Ark. 71753
Anderson Designs, Box 287, Gladstone, N.J. 07934
Bianchi, 100 Calle Cortez, Temecula, CA 92390
Brownells, Inc., Montezuma, IA 50171
Kolpin Mfg., Inc., Box 231, Berlin, WI 54923
Nocona, Box 57, Nocona, TX 76255
Boyt, Box 220/E, Iowa Falls, IA 50126
Brauer Bros., 2012 Washington, St. Louis, Mo 63103
Chace Leather, 507 Alden St., Fall River, MA 02722
John's Custom Leather, 525 So. Liberty, Blairsville, PA 15717
Sports Accessories, 2113 West 2300 South, West Valley, Utah 84119

November 1982

KEN OEHLER AND HIS CHRONOGRAPH

H ow fast is it!
As a nation, Americans are intensely interested in speed, in knowing how quickly an event occurs. We live with highway speed limits; are fascinated by Indy 500 and NASCAR lap times and average records; assaulted by auto manufacturers' 0-to-60 mph performance claims; and take for granted the amazingly brief trip times which are routine with modern jet airliners.

Most such performance figures are handed us on a platter, as it were, with no need on our part to wonder how they were derived. For our auto speed we need only glance down at the speedometer, and most of us can casually understand how those things work: the faster the car wheels turn, the faster the speed indication on the dial.

Until relatively recent, however, such was not the case with shooters wanting to know the muzzle velocity of their rifles. Or shotguns. Or how fast the BB's or pellets were leaving their air rifles. Or the arrows from their bows. Devices to measure such things were cumbersome and expensive, and not particularly reliable.

Then along came Ken Oehler.

"I'm a shooter and a hunter," Ken explained how he got into the chronograph business 20 years ago, "and just wanted one for myself. The timing was right, in that integrated circuits were just becoming available, which meant that we could produce a chronograph which was much smaller, simpler and more reliable."

It didn't hurt that Ken Oehler (pronounced A-LER) also had, in addition to a shooting background and a desire for a better instrument, a Ph.D. in electrical engineering and considerable experience in the field. He was director of engineering, for instance, for one company which produced digital cardiotachometers used to measure the heart rate of astronauts.

But, I can hear some of you thinking, ammo manufacturers will tell me the muzzle velocity of their products, so there's no need for me to measure it myself. And they will, and do, and most shooters who use factory ammunition really don't need to chronograph their loads. Those ballistic tables in ammo catalogs give a tremendous amount of information — velocity and energy figures at the muzzle and at various distances downrange, plus approximate impact points high or low for various sighting-in distances. The tables even guide us to adjust their figures to our rifles when the length of the test barrel differs from ours. But, even with factory ammo, chronographing is fun, interesting, and at times very revealing.

Chronographs are most useful to those of us who handload. Despite the excellent reloading manuals available which give a selection of formulas for each caliber, only by testing your particular loadings can you get the most from them. Variations in powders, cases, primers, bullets, and your particular reloading routine can cause variations in performance in your particular rifle.

"Our business continues to increase," Ken told me, "and it's because shooters are now much more knowledgeable than they were when I began in 1966. Handloaders are now experts. Many shooters spend 50 weeks a year trying to get better performance from their guns and maybe two weeks in actual hunting."

Better performance in rifles or pistols usually refers to better accuracy, and the name of the game toward better accuracy is consistency. The muzzle velocity within a single box of factory ammo varies from round to round, as much as 100 fps or more, which is insignificant to most big game hunters but important to those who like tack-driving rifles. By using a chronograph, a handloader can experiment with various recipes to get greatest consistency, which results in accuracy.

The Oehler Research, Inc. Model 33 Chronotach, now the only model Ken manufactures which is of interest to non-commercial shooters, measures a piddlin' 2"x6"x10" and weighs less than three pounds. What this tiny unit does, however, is giant-size.

When in use, two sensors (Skyscreens) are attached to this base unit by cables and positioned a precise distance apart just in front of the shooting position. The shadow of a bullet (or shot charge or arrow) passing over the sensors starts and stops a timing process in the Model 33. It does the rest.

After each shot the velocity of the bullet passing between those sensors is automatically displayed, and the figure remains visible until the next shot is fired, but the unit is re-set for another round within 0.6 seconds. You can continue to shoot as many as 255 shots in a series without touching the Chronotach, which will retain the data in its memory. You can delete from memory any round which is obviously a bad reading just by pushing the "FORGET" button.

Here's what the Model 33 will tell you when you've finished shooting. With successive touches of the SUMMARY button it will display: 1. the lowest velocity (LO) in the series; 2. the highest velocity (HI); 3. the extreme spread in velocities between high and low in the series (ES); 4. the average velocity (A); and 5. the standard deviation of the velocities (Sd). By continuing to push the button you can cycle through and review the data again, as many times as you like. You can fire additional shots, and they automatically will be programmed into the earlier ones. Turn the unit off and back on and the memory is erased: you're ready for a new series.

Standard deviation is one of the most important figures, since it provides the most reliable indication of uniformity. The smaller the deviation, the more likely that batch of ammunition is to be accurate.

Chronographing your ammo is interesting whether it's of factory loads or reloads, but it's especially important when reloading for maximum loads. When the handloader is striving for high, safe muzzle velocities, the chronograph will tell him when he's approaching the point of diminishing returns — not much velocity increase for an additional grain (or half-grain) of powder. That's frequently the point, too, where the limits of safety have been reached.

Ken Oehler's first chronograph sold for less than $100 when introduced in 1966. Now, the very sophisticated Model 33 lists for

$300, probably comparable when adjusted for inflation. The Deluxe M33, with a new, more sensitive, less critical Skyscreen III System and including the stands to hold them, costs $380, with all prices including shipping.

If you own an Oehler product, you're in good company. Oehler Research makes units for the U.S. (Army, Navy, Air Force, Dept. of Justice, Dept. of the Treasury, and Los Alamos Scientific Armaments Div.), for Federal, Winchester and Remington, for Activ and Estate Cartridge, for Hornady, Sierra, Speer, Hercules, Smith & Wesson, Lyman, Crossman, the H. P. White Lab, and for General Electric. A recent instrument for G.E. is interesting. It will measure, in 1,500-round bursts, shots from a 10,000 round-per-minute machine gun, automatically giving the muzzle velocity of each shot, time to target of each, location on the target where each bullet strikes, and the accuracy within 0.1 inch.

'No, we don't have much repair problem," Ken answered my final question, "despite the fact that guys take them out of their car trunks at super high temperatures in Arizona or below freezing in Alaska. Less than one percent ever come back. That's a must for us, since it probably costs us more to handle a repair job than to build the unit in the first place.

Oehler Research sells direct to consumers, and the address is P. O. Box 9135, Austin, TX 78766. Telephone 800-531-5125.

February 1986

GUNS DO NEED CLEANING

"**D**o I what?" My buddy looked as if I'd hit him with a wet dishrag.

"Do you ever clean your rifle barrel?" I repeated the question.

For some weeks we had been talking, now and then, about his accuracy problem with a pet rifle. Over the last few years it had seemed to go sour on him, with his annual sighting-in groups becoming larger and larger.

"My old gun just won't shoot like it used to," was the way he first broached the subject, and the statement was made with an air of resignation. He was accepting the inevitable, that as guns get old they become less accurate, but he hedged his bet by adding,

"But maybe I don't shoot it as well."

We finally got around to examining the problem. We eliminated the obvious — loose scope mounts; and the semi-obvious — bedding problems. Neither seemed to be a factor. And the barrel itself? They can be shot out, of course, but not in this case since my friend seldom shot more than 20 rounds a year.

Then, from out of my past, came a thought: "Do you ever clean the barrel?"

Certainly not! Didn't everybody know that modern non-corrosive primers and powders make scrubbing a rifle barrel unnecessary? Even undesirable? Just squirt a little LPS or WD-40 or something similar down the tube now and then and you're home free. Maybe cleaning the barrel is okay for competition shooters, but not necessary for hunters.

Whew!

He was right about one thing. Competition rifle shooters are meticulous about their barrel cleaning chores.

Years of neglect had affected the accuracy of his rifle barrel, but not to the extent which might be expected. His "squirt" down the barrel now and then wasn't all bad.

Even after a thorough cleaning, the rifle didn't group quite as well as it had done years earlier, but the improvement over the pre-cleaning groups was substantial.

Yes, hunters, you should clean your rifle barrels now and then.

The incident brought back memories. Years ago I left a favorite 7mm Rem Mag with Kenneth Eversul, a gunsmith friend of mine, to have him switch scopes and sight it in. When I stopped by his shop to pick it up, and to make any minor sighting adjustments which might be necessary with me doing the shooting, Ken had a question.

"When was the last time you cleaned that gun?"

I was embarrassed to say that I couldn't even remember. It had been several years since I last shot it, and on that last occasion — whenever it was — I had even neglected to clean it before stashing it in the gun rack.

"My groups were terrible," Ken continued, "but then I saw how dirty the barrel was. It took some scrubbing, but it's okay now. You'd be surprised at how often we run into this."

Eversul, whose gunshop midway between Boyce and Alexandria, Louisiana is headquarters for shooters throughout the central part of the state, and who is the only factory-authorized gunsmith for the superb Italian Fabbri shotguns, estimates that 85 percent of the rifles which pass through his hands have fouling problems. Copper fouling, build-up from the copper bullet jackets, is the big culprit insofar as accuracy is concerned.

"It can make the difference between a two-inch group and an eight-inch group," was the way Ken put it.

Okay, we're convinced we should clean rifle barrels, preferably after each shooting outing. How do we go about it?

Your cleaning equipment should include a cleaning rod and the proper tips (a brass brush of the proper size, and a tip for patches), cleaning patches of the proper size, a powder solvent such as Hoppe's #9 (or others such as made by Gunslick and Rusteprufe), and a rust preventive such as Rig, LPS or WD-40. It isn't necessary to have a vise to hold the rifle while you clean it, of course, but that piece of equipment is a tremendous aid. A break-down cleaning rod is handy for trips, but for best results day-to-day buy the best one-piece rod you can find. Those made by Durango and by Parker-Hale are excellent. The former is of stainless steel, and the latter is steel coated with plastic. Both have ball bearing, rotating handles.

If you can clean your rifle from the chamber end, which is preferable, it's best to use some sort of bore guide. This keeps the rod centered in the bore, and prevents accuracy-damaging injury to the throat of the chamber.

Commercial bore guides are available, are inexpensive, and keep the gook from the cleaning operation from getting down into the magazine. Except for this latter advantage, however, an empty shotshell does about as well. Punch the old primer from a 20- or 12-gauge empty, depending upon the size of your rifle chamber, and slide it in place of the bolt.

If the cleaning rod is too big for the primer hole, drill that hole out to fit.

Once you have your cleaning items assembled, the actual task of properly cleaning the barrel is simple and takes little time. First, soak the brass brush in a good powder solvent and run it back and forth at least 10 times. Replace the brush with your patch tip, and push a dry cleaning patch through the bore. Follow it with one saturated with the powder solvent. Then, another dry patch which should tell you how clean the barrel is.

Don't worry if that final patch comes out a bit stained, since it's virtually impossible to end up with one that's lily white. As the last step, slowly push through the bore a patch which has been coated with some rust preventive, and it's ready for the rack. Before you shoot it again you might want to run one dry patch through the barrel.

Most competitive shooters fire no more than 10 shots before cleaning their rifles again, but such diligence isn't necessary for hunting accuracy. The best policy is to acquire the habit of going through the above procedure after each shooting session.

If copper fouling has accumulated over a long period of time, normal cleaning may not get the job done. In that case try something like J-B Bore Cleaner, following the directions on the label. If that still doesn't get the fouling out to your satisfaction, let your local gunsmith take over. He'll likely use some type of ammonia formula.

A clean, slick barrel minimizes copper fouling, but with neglect that build-up progresses in geometric fashion. The dirtier the barrel, in short, the more copper is abraded away as each bullet passes by.

Keep in mind, too, that powder residue in a barrel collects and holds moisture, which triggers rust. This might be the place to emphasize that stainless steel is not rustproof, although it is very rust resistant.

If you're one of the many who haven't touched their rifle with cleaning rod in years, do me a favor. Take it out and shoot the best group you can. Then, give it a good cleaning, then shoot another group.

That scrubbing just may slice your group size in half, or more, and might even cut your winter meat bill as much.

In planning gun cleaning in the field, adapt your gun cleaning gear to conditions in transit and/or in the hunting camp. A one-piece rod is no problem if you're taking a rigid, full-length gun case to camp. Otherwise, a good jointed rod of steel, such as the stainless one made by Belding and Mull, P.O. Box 428, Phillipsburg, Pa. 16866, is a fine choice for camp use. A pull-through cleaner is a useful pocket item when you're actually hunting, or in camp. They're available from K.W. Kleindorst, Taylor Town Rd., Montville, N.J. 07045 (a steel cable unit); from Schultea's Gun String, 67 Burress, Houston, Tx. 77022 (nylon string); and from Brownells (U.S. Government cleaner, available only in .22 and .30 caliber, with both brush and slotted tip). A neat item for emergency use (snow or mud in the barrel, for instance) which I carry in a full-length jointed rod of aluminum, which, in its leather case, is seven inches long and weighs three ounces (Butler Creek Corp., Box GG, Jackson Hole, Wy 83001).

So you can't find the gun cleaning supplies you need in your local sporting goods store? In the little town of Montezuma, Iowa there exists an institution which has been coming to the rescue of guys like you for more than 40 years. Bob Brownell and his son, Frank, preside over an operation which has been and is the mother lode for gunsmiths.

Nobody who is an avid shooter should be without a catalog from Brownells, Inc., Rt. 2, Box 1, Montezuma, Iowa 50171. It'll cost you $2.50 [now $3.50], refunded with your first order of $25.00 or more, and the 145 slick pages contain a hundred bucks of browsing pleasure. If it has to do with gunsmithing, shooting and reloading, it's in the catalog. Do yourself a favor. Get a copy.

October 1978

HUNTER'S CLAYS: NEW SHOTGUN GAME

In the fall of 1986 I carefully wound my way through a gorgeous pine-hardwood forest on Maryland's Eastern Shore which seemed to shout "birds," and my shotgun and nerve endings were appropriately at attention. Then it happened. From a thicket to my right came the sound. I twisted in that direction, began to mount the gun, then saw a blur of orange streaking through the trees, heading left. Zipping behind and through trees, it blended in and out with the colorful fall foliage. Now you see it; now you don't. I stabbed the muzzle out front and touched off the shot.

Hunter's Clays! That's the clay target game I was enjoying, and it may well prove to be the best thing to happen to shotgun shooting since the breech loader, if you'll excuse the real thing — bird shooting itself. Why such high hopes for a newcomer most Americans haven't yet heard of, let alone tried? Simply because this new kid on the block is the next best thing to shooting at feathers.

Trap and skeet and casual clay target shooting are all great activities for the shotgunner, as their long and illustrious backgrounds prove. Skeet is a rather new game, originating here in America in the 1930's, but trap began in England more than a century ago. That's well and good, but the fact remains that these formal competitive game have never found a place in the hearts of most shotgunners in this country. Registered trap and skeet shooters may number in the hundreds of thousands, but such numbers pale in comparison to the millions of bird shooters who eagerly venture afield each fall.

Each fall, that is, which emphasizes that bird seasons are all too brief. No shotgun activity has yet come along which will stimulate most of these gunners to unlimber 'ole Betsy with frequency year-round.

Until now! Hunter's Clays may well be the key that turns shotgunning in America into a twelve-month-long sport for great numbers of shooters. What is it about the game which has such potential? In fact, just what is this game?

It is simply a shooting sport using clay targets which closely simulate the flight of upland game birds and waterfowl, often in a setting which is identical to actual field hunting habitat. Most targets are thrown from traps hidden in cover, with unpredictable timing, and at varying angles and elevations. Just as is the case in actual hunting, the shooter must not have his gun mounted before the "bird" appears.

Even on the stations where the shooter can signal for the target, there's a variable delay between the call and the release, just as was true in skeet for many years. And, again as was true in skeet, the low gun position is mandatory.

Most of us have enjoyed at least one of several interesting, challenging clay target games in recent years — Crazy Quail, Riverside Skeet, 'Aw Shucks, plus training layouts such as the Duck Tower. Hunter's Clays adopts portions of these and adds more, keeping all as hunter-oriented as possible.

As was true for trap shooting, this new game originated in England. There, called Sporting Clays, it is intensely competitive, and has become the leading shooting sport.

Many in this country use the names Hunter's Clays or Sporting Clays interchangeably, but the National Shooting Sports Foundation chose the former. "Hunter's Clays" seems to appeal to a wider audience, but in practice there isn't a great deal of difference in the physical layouts of the ranges in America. Relatively few in number at this embryonic stage, such ranges are multiplying at an encouraging rate.

Ranges for these games are constructed to take advantage of the natural terrain that's available, whatever it may be. The emphasis is on simulating actual field shooting conditions, giving "flushing quail," "springing teal," "driving doves," or "passing mallards."

Fields can be designed so targets will simulate almost any kind of moving game bird, or even running rabbits. Shooting from an authentic duck blind on lake or marsh, you may get a "bluebill" screaming out over the decoys just feet above the water, a crossing "pintail" high out front, or a sneaky "wood duck" powering past from behind. Walking through grouse cover you get a "ruff" exploding from a thicket to the right and then, at the sound of your gun, a "woodcock" climbing almost vertically from that alder patch on the left. When you shoot the single "quail" quartering left from the lespedeza you're apt to get a whole "covey" going in all directions.

Realism! That's the name of this game, and it's fun.

Unlike trap and skeet ranges, which have precise, exact dimensions, no two ranges for Hunter's Clays are alike. In that respect they are like golf courses, each a separate challenge unto itself. The degree of difficulty can be adjusted simply by changing the position of either the shooter or the trap.

Hunter's Clays has a number of pluses going for it in addition to being interesting and challenging: 1. It's great practice for field shooting; 2. Nobody breaks them all, which means that there's no stigma attached to missing one, which in turn encourages novices to try the game; 3. The field shot, the hunter, can frequently do as well or better than can an expert skeet or trap shot; and 4. The ammunition cost is less because an "event" consists of fewer targets than in skeet and trap (the First Annual North American Sporting Clays Championships, for instance, held in June of 1986, consisted of only 100 targets shot over a two-day period).

The range I shot that same fall on the Eastern Shore was The Fairfield Shooting Grounds at Chestertown, where we were filming a television show on shooting for the NSSF. The manager told me that they have a steady and growing list of participants, from several states around, who regularly attend each of their meets. That same tale of success was repeated at most of the other clubs I contacted.

Houston, Texas has been the hotspot for Hunter's/Sporting Clays in this country, and is home for the headquarters of the: U.S. Sporting Clays Association, 111 North Post Oak Lane, Suite 130, Houston, TX 77024. For more information, including the location of the ranges nearest you, drop a note to that Association, and to: NSSF, P.O. Box 1075, Riverside, CT 06878.

September 1987

F rom all points of the compass the armed troops headed south. In dribbles and droves they arrived by plane, train and auto, assembling over a period of days in the city on the banks of the Red River. Clans and packs and family groups, under a wide variety of banners, wearing colorful and imaginative uniforms, they came with widely divergent backgrounds but with a common goal.

From more than 700,000, in the beginning, this dedicated contingent had dwindled down to these precious few.

This non-tattered remnant of some 375 young boys and girls, which arrived in Shreveport, Louisiana for the Fourth of July festivities, were the cream of the crop where BB shooters are concerned. Having survived eliminations which brought them to the surface from among almost three quarters of a million other 7- to 14-year olds, they had gathered to compete in the 11th annual Daisy/U.S. Jaycees International BB Gun Championship Matches.

The program in which this huge number of youngsters participated is a Shooting Education Program. Developed by Daisy and co-sponsored by local Jaycee chapters, it is without doubt one of the most significant in the nation in its influence on the future of shooting and hunting. Through it millions of future voters have been exposed to the recreational pleasures of shooting, and have been trained in safe and proper gun handling, in marksmanship, and in safe and ethical methods of hunting.

It would be difficult to overestimate the progressive and cumulaive impact of this program in blunting the thrusts of anti-gun, anti-shooting and anti-hunting trends in the United States. The favorable fallout extends far beyond the 700,000 actual participants each year, influencing parents, brothers, sisters and members of the 3,000 local Jaycee chapters which serve as co-sponsors.

The United States Jaycees Shooting Education Program is no token operation. Using local Jaycees as instructors, with cooperation from Daisy, state fish and game departments and local conservation organizations, it gives to the 700,000 boys and girls each year a comprehensive course of instruction.

In 10 one-hour lessons they learn about the different types of guns and ammunition, the rules for proper gun handling, the rules for sale hunting, the parts of guns, how to aim a gun, how to shoot, and the rules for firing a gun on a rifle range. They not only learn about these things, they practice them. During the 10 weeks of the course they have both written tests and shooting matches, and the results of both are used in selecting a competition team to represent that chapter.

The youngsters who have qualified for the team tryout are announced during the seventh lesson, which is Parent's Night. During the course of that hour the students demonstrate to their parents what they've learned in the previous six weeks, and the Jaycees emphasize to the mothers and fathers present that shooting is a lifetime sport with no sex barrier, age barrier or physical ability barrier. And, especially, that shooting is fun.

A competition team of five firing members and two alternates is selected by each chapter at the end of the course, and that team is the representative in regional and state competition to determine the team which will advance to the finals — the "world series" of B.B. shooting.

The matches are shot from 15 feet in the four positions: prone, sitting, kneeling and standing. Ten shots are fired from each position, making a possible total score of 400X400 if each shot makes the ten ring. The difficulty is apparent when we consider that the ten ring is only slightly larger than a single BB shot, which measures .177 inches.

Only spring-powered BB guns are permitted, with the official guns being the Jaycee Target Special Model 299 or the Daisy Target Special Model 99. Iron sights only, and only un-altered Daisy Match BBs are allowed.

American ingenuity being what it is, winning BB scores are seldom shot with off-the-line air rifles. Over the 11 years of the International B.B. Championship the instructors and team coaches of the teams have done what shooters in all forms of competition have done: experimented with ways to improve performance.

They've done just that! Winning scores, both team and individual, have risen steadily. In the 1966 inaugural of the matches, held in Dayton, Ohio, the winning team was Joplin, Missouri with a score of 1676X2000. Last year, in Clarksville, Tennessee that same Joplin team won it again, but this time with a record-breaking score of 1920-16X.

To score an "X" the hole made by the BB must be entirely inside that tiny ten-ring.

There is no doubt that the ability of the shooters has improved tremendously because of better coaching and more effective training programs. But the customizing of the guns by some coaches has been of great significance.

Two techniques seem to have helped the most, with the greatest aid being a reduction in muzzle velocity effected by weakening the spring. A round BB pellet is a relatively inefficient shape from a ballistic standpoint, and the faster it is driven the greater the "knuckle-ball" effect. Conversely, reduction in velocity reduces the tendency for erratic flight.

The other alteration is to weight the guns up to the maximum six pounds by adding lead in stock and forearm.

Other customizing involved replacing the standard peep sight with a more efficient, micrometer rear peep; reducing the trigger pull weight and smoothing out the pull; and roughing or checkering the stock butt and forearm to provide a non-slip surface.

Recognizing the improved performance with the customized air rifles, Daisy incorporated some of the alterations — including reduced muzzle velocity and an optional micrometer rear sight — into a new Model 499 Target Air Rifle which will be the official gun for the Jaycee program from now on. Although the new gun met with widespread approval when introduced during the latest Championship matches, you can bet that coaches and instructors will continue to search for improvements.

Since 1970 a written test, based on material covered in the Shooting Education course, has been an integral part of the International competition. The 100-point examination has equal weight with each of the shooting positions in determining the team championship.

In both 1973 and 1974 it did just that! In 1973 Trenton, Michigan had the highest shooting score, but lost out to Joplin because of lower test scores. But the following year the Trenton team came back with a perfect 500 written test aggregate for its five shooters, winning the team championship over that same Joplin team although having lower shooting scores.

The individual championship is based only on the shooting, and in 1975 Joplin's Butch English set the record which still stands with a remarkable 394X400, with 8X. Which means that he let only six shots out of the 40 stray away from that tiny 10-ring.

The weaker sex? Don't you believe it when BB shooting is the event. In 1973 girls took both first and second places in the individual aggregate (shooting plus the written test) competition at the International Matches. And the following year a pretty lass named Jill Spry was the individual shooting champ, with a 389-4X. She also had a perfect test score of 100 to set a new aggregate record of 489-4X.

This 14-year old Jill Spry appeared on the Johnny Carson television program not long after winning the championship, and captivated both studio and television audience with her poise, impeccable gun handling, and her marksmanship.

When the "smoke" cleared from that Fourth of July shoot-out in Shreveport, Joplin had done it again. For the second consecutive year, and the fourth time since the Championships began, the entry from this Missouri city won the team championship.

And Mike English followed in brother Butch's footsteps by winning the individual championship with 392X400, only two points shy of his brother's record score of 394.

The team victory didn't come easily. Norton, Kansas, a three-time winner of this event, finished only three points behind Joplin's winning aggregate of 2,363.

This 1976 Championship was a record-breaker in that, for the first time in a single match, all 50 states were entered in the event. Plus another team from the District of Columbia, and a Canadian entry sponsored by the Kitchener, Ontario Jaycees.

It is interesting to note a sad commentary on our times: that the District of Columbia team was forced to leave the District in order to practice because of the gun laws in effect in Washington.

But what a marvelous event this 1976 Championship was! The more than 350 youngsters, housed on the campus of Centenary College, participated in an array of activities other than the shooting events. They made friends from throughout the nation, swapped souvenirs at a Barter Bar, visited Barksdale Air Force Base, and were a major part of Shreveport's giant Riverfront Bicentennial Celebration.

Most of the contestants won't return for the 12th Annual International Match on July 1, 2 and 3, 1977, which will be held at Sioux Falls, South Dakota, because the shooting members of a team cannot compete two years in a row. Many of the alternates will — if their team is again their state champion.

For the first time, that 1976 event was sanctioned by the National Rifle Association, and all winning scores were entered on the books as national records. Mike English held the first national shooting aggregate with his 390X400. The new individual event record holders were: Prone — David Wiltfong, Norton, Kansas, with

100X100; Sitting — Marty Cocking, Trenton, Michigan and Mike English, each with 99X100; Kneeling — Bryan Fields, Pleasant Garden, N.C. and Mike English, each with 99X100; and Standing — Bryan Fields, 99X100.

David Wiltfong, an 11-year-old sixth grader, was required to continue shooting after his 100X100 in the prone position in order to establish his record. All he did, under the watchful eye of Referee and Olympic Gold Medal winner Gary Anderson, was to shoot 10 more bullseyes — 20 straight in all — before letting a shot slip from the 10-ring.

November 1976

TIPS ON SIGHTING IN THAT RIFLE

S ighting in a rifle isn't all that difficult, but there are certain procedures and precautions which *must* be observed. The penalty for not doing so can be to duplicate the semi-tragedy acted out with frequency each fall, those many occasions when a hunter burns up a couple of boxes of high-priced ammo and still ends us swearing, "I still don't know where th' hell it's shootin'!"

There are rules: 1. You *must* shoot from a solid rest position, preferably a shooting bench; 2. All the screws on your gun and scope must be tight; 3. You cannot sight in a rifle while the barrel is hot.

Ignoring one or more of those three things is the primary cause of most of the "sighting in" grief experienced by shooters. Leaning over the hood of a pickup won't get it done as a solid rest position, and I've even seen guys try to sight in offhand. A good percentage of the rifles I inspect from casual hunters have one or more screw loose, and I'm skipping the one between the ears. Stock screws need not be super tight, but they must be firm — and stay that way. If the screws holding scope mount bases to a rifle barrel are not dead solid tight, forget trying to sight it in. Same is true for the screws or clips or levers which attach the scope to the scope mount rings, or the rings to the bases. Dead solid tight! For a variety of reasons, any or all of those points of attachments can loosen from year to year, so don't take them for granted when you head for the range.

It is typical and normal for most rifle barrels, especially those of hunter weight, to "walk" their bullets on the target as the barrel heats up. The point of impact often begins to rise, but it can be wildly erratic.

When the barrel gets hot, you *must* let it cool before continuing the sighting-in process. That usually takes time, so allow plenty of time for it. Don't be in a hurry.

For hunters, three-shot groups are much more sensible than are the five-shot groups so many shooters attempt. Gear your efforts in that direction.

Okay, so you want to sight in your new rifle on which you have just mounted a scope. First, from the scope literature find out what the adjustment increments indicate. How much change in the bullet impact out at 100 yards will one increment (or click) of scope adjustment make. Depending upon the scope, that will usually be 1 inch, 1/2 inch or 1/4 inch. Now let's sight it in.

1. Although we'll sight in at 100 yards, make your first shot, at a regular rifle sighting-in target, at one-fourth that distance — at 25 yards. At that distance you'll probably hit the target somewhere, which might not be the case at 100 yards if the adjustments are appreciably off.

After that one shot, make horizontal and vertical adjustments to bring the point of impact to the center of the target. REMEMBER: at 25 yards it will require four times as many "clicks" to move the impact an inch as would be the case at 100 yards. After making those adjustments, fire one more shot. If it's anywhere close to the bullseye, and it should be, move back to the 100-yard firing point.

2. Let the barrel cool.

3. Fire three well-aimed shots, and note the location of the center of the triangle formed by those three bullet holes.

4. Make horizontal and vertical adjustments to move that "center" to the bullseye.

5. Let the barrel cool.

6. Fire three more shots. The rifle should be sighted in but, if more fine tuning is necessary, continue the adjustments and the firing. And, letting the barrel cool.

After those first two three-shot groups, the fine tuning can usually be done one shot at a time if you are confident of your solid rest and trigger release. Depending upon your rifle and your hunting needs, of course, you can sight in so that the point of bullet impact is some distance above the bullseye, that is, above the point of aim.

The "two-shot" sighting in technique is a simple, quickie method of getting your rifle pretty much on target. You must be able to hold the rifle steady, and it helps to have a buddy make the adjustments. Here's how. Aim at the bullseye and fire one shot. No matter where the bullet hole is, aim at the bullseye again and, while you hold the rifle rock steady in that position, make horizontal and vertical adjustments which will move the crosshairs from their position on the bullseye to a position on the bullet hole. That's it!

You can ignore the number of clicks or increments. While looking through the scope just tell your buddy which way to move the crosshair and how far. The rifle *must* not move, of course, while the adjustments are being made. Although this two-shot version isn't as definitive as that outlined earlier, it's a very handy procedure to know.

POINT BLANK ZERO: A SIGHTING-IN ALTERNATIVE

For openers, let's outline a few facts. All bullets fired from a horizontal barrel begin to drop as soon as they leave the muzzle. The laws of gravity are inexorable, and act upon a speeding projectile just as they do on any other unsupported object.

Consider the often-told classic example — that a bullet fired from a horizontal barrel, and one dropped from the same height at the same time, will both touch ground at the same time. An obvious difference is that the bullet fired from a rifle or pistol will touch ground farther away, the exact distance depending largely upon muzzle velocity. The higher the muzzle velocity, the farther the bullet will travel in that "X" time required for gravity to pull the bullet to the ground.

Got it? That one fact of physics is of paramount importance when we consider sighting in a rifle. From this, it's obvious that the rifle barrel must be pointed above the desired point of impact (bullseye) if it is to strike dead center. There is no such thing as a caliber so flat shooting that "it don't drop at all," as we've all heard said on occasion.

Okay, so we adjust the sights so that the barrel is pointing sufficiently above the target that the pull of gravity brings the bullet right down into the bullseye. But now for the $64 question. At what range? At 100 yards?

Not if you want to take full advantage of the ballistic capability of your cartridge, and here's why. Let's use the modest-performing .30-30 as an example. If we sight it in to shoot dead on at 100 yards, the bullet is about 1/2 inches high at midrange — at the 50-yard mark. That's no problem hunting deer, or just about anything else. But out at 200 yards the bullet has dropped about 9 inches below the point of aim, and that is a problem.

The sure-kill vital area of a deer is usually described as being about 12 inches — a circle with a 12-inch diameter, or a square which is 12 inches to the side, and that's probably about right. At the 200-yard range? The above example, with a dead-on hold at the center of that circle, the bullet would drop out of that vital zone. Not so good.

Suppose we sight in, however, so that the bullet strikes two inches high at 100 yards. That puts it dead on at 150 yards, maybe three inches to four inches high at 75 yards — no problem in deer hunting, but look what happened out there at 200 yards. Now the bullet drops a bit less than five inches below the line of sight, well within that vital, killing zone. Sight in for three inches high at 100 yards, and that's even better, since you would be less than three inches low at 200.

The principle is the same no matter what the caliber. With a 7mm Remington Magnum caliber using the factory 150-grain bullet, for instance, a "three-inch high" setting will give you a 350- yard-plus point-blank range for deer. Which means, to repeat, that at any range within that distance you can sight directly "on" the deer without the bullet rising or falling more than six inches — half the vertical span of that vital killing zone.

That three-inch-high sighting-in figure is a broad, widely- quoted number, and it's a perfectly workable premise which many hunters can use to advantage. To get maximum efficiency from any caliber, of course, study the ballistics tables, and then sight in your rifle to achieve best results for your situation.

Studying those ballistics tables, incidentally, includes concern that your bullet-caliber combination retains sufficient energy out at "maximum point blank" range to be efficient on deer.

May 1981

A DIFFERENT VIEW OF SIGHTING IN

Years ago I was admonished, as a writer, to be judicious with the use of a couple of words — always and never. It was good advice which I've tended to follow, comfortable with the feeling that hedging one's bet isn't all bad. Adopting such a philosophy isn't dishonest, perish the thought, since there are indeed few absolutes in the realm of the outdoors.

Despite those good intentions, avoiding most references to the "best" in various categories — deer rifles, duck guns, loads, there was one area where I backslid a bit. In sighting in a rifle, of course, everybody who is somebody knows that it *is* proper and right to zero for maximum point-blank range. For any particular caliber and loading, that is, the scope should be adjusted to take full advantage of that trajectory.

At the 100-yard distance at which most of us sight in our rifles, such a procedure would place the bullet above the point of aim — usually two to three inches for most calibers. The technique can be fine tuned depending upon the size of your quarry.

It's a good system, and I've flirted with saying that it is indeed the best system. But best for everybody?

Last year, twice in the space of one month, I had it brought home to me that, indeed, it is not best for all. In both instances, one from the mountains and one from the flatlands, the preferred method is to sight in dead on at 100 yards.

From Alan Creed, in Idaho, came a letter: "Most of the bear and elk hunters I've hunted with zero in three or four inches high at 100 yards, and say just perfect. I think this is perfectly wrong."

His experience in the steep mountains of Idaho convinces Alan that, "as a rule, we are shooting downhill at long range, and there's an updraft. A hunter with a magnum sighted in four inches high might as well be shooting blanks. The bullets lift up and out of that canyon like an airplane, and I swear I've seen some shots several feet high. The hunters think the rifle is defective. I'm a backwoodsman and am not about to tell some of these dudes they are wrong (about sighting in), and I also learned not to say I told you so. Guides may appear awkward, but most can tell you how to zero in a rifle, and tell you where to put the crosshair on a target that's 200 yards downhill — if the rifle is zeroed on the 'X' at 100 yards."

Alan's point is that there is a vast difference between shooting conditions on a rifle range and those in the rugged mountains he hunts. Not only does he think that updrafts, downdrafts and sharp shooting angles complicate the shooting, but that accuracy is also affected by altitude, temperature and humidity.

A Canadian guide arrived at the same policy of sighting in directly on at 100 yards, but for completely different hunting conditions. One fall I hunted whitetail deer with him in the flatlands of eastern Alberta, and he explained his system.

"It's been my experience that most misses are high. As you know, most people sight in a little high at a hundred and maybe dead-on at 250 yards. If you can keep that in mind, theoretically you'll never miss. But when our hunters get into a snapshot situation they shoot instinctively, and it's instinctive to shoot at a deer when it's close and to hold high when it's far away.

"When visibility is poor you see a buck at 275 yards, think it's 350, hold just over his back and shoot. And miss — just over his back. With our guns sighted in to be on at 100 yards, we aim on if a buck is about that distance. But if he's on out there — out to about 400 yards, we hold on the top of the back line."

What he is doing is *using* the bullet drop below the point of aim. "I'll hit him even if I'm not sure how far away he is," he emphasized. "Most hunters can't tell whether a deer is 250 or 350, especially when they don't have much time. Much of our shooting is hurried, and the method works for us and our hunters."

Let's examine a bit more closely this "system." For practical purposes he divides opportunities at deer into two categories: short and long range. As he put it, the "short" range is about a hundred yards, but in reality that shakes out to a max of about twice that. Hold right where you want to hit. At 100 yards — bingo, you're right on. At twice that the bullet he shoots is less than two inches low, and most of us can't shoot within two inches at 200 yards.

His "long" range begins somewhere on out there, and for these he and his clients aim at the *back line* of the deer. At 300 yards their bullets drop seven inches from the point of aim, which would put them into the deer seven inches below the back line. At 400 yards the drop is almost eighteen inches, enough to completely (or almost) miss a Texas hill country whitetail. But the whitetails of eastern Alberta are extremely large, with that particular sub-species characterized by deer experts as reaching the maximum size of any whitetails in North America. The target, in short, is a bigger one than most of us have to work with in our deer hunting.

"Another advantage," this guide pointed out, "is that at long range it is much easier to align the horizontal hair in the scope with the horizontal line of a deer's back than it is to hold at a particular point down in the deer's body. It's an easier reference point."

Attempting long range shots at deer, and I consider 300 yards very long, should not be done lightly. Only those hunters who know their rifle/cartridge capability well, and who are confident in their own ability to make the shot, should consider doing so. Game animals deserve no less.

The two examples, one from Idaho and one from Canada, have given me food for thought, two more reasons not to become too complacent in my views. If you'd like to explore just where your bullets would be striking on out beyond, when they're dead on at 100 yards, you can do so by referring to ballistic tables. Good ones are in the Hornady Handbook of Cartridge Reloading (Hornady Mfg. Co., Box 1848, Grand Island, NE 68801...$11.95), and in Tables of Bullet Performance (Wolfe Pub. Co., Box 30-30, Prescott, AZ 86302...$17.50).

July 1983

EYES: YOUR WINDOWS TO SHOOTING

W ithout the ability to see, we wouldn't do much hunting or shooting. That's belaboring the obvious, of course, especially when measured against the overall ramifications of the loss of sight, but too few hunters and shooters give proper consideration to this very important topic.

How well can you see? Pretty good? Very good? Not so hot? The answer may be that you really don't know. And that's very important, since hunters decide when to squeeze the trigger based primarily on what they see. Or, what they think they see.

The truth probably is that you don't really know how well you can see. Deterioration in vision is usually gradual, and only a competent eye examination will tell the tale. Such checks at regular intervals are, again obviously, a good idea. And the good part of that good idea is that most vision defects can be corrected, but they won't be if you don't know they're there.

Good vision enables a hunter to distinguish detail against a variety of backgrounds, focus clearly on either near or distant objects and switch focus quickly, judge distance, detect objects and movement on either side of the target, identify colors, and do all these under varying light and weather conditions. If you need prescription glasses or contacts to accomplish these tasks in your everyday life, then you need them for hunting.

Long ago my Dad's shooting improved tremendously when he began using my Mossberg bolt action rimfire which had a flat-topped blade front sight and an aperture rear sight. Back then I really didn't understand why, but — now I do. Older eyes can't handle the range of focusing demanded by open sights, a problem virtually cured by that rear "peep." Odds are good that a massive number of deer hunters across the land who are now using open sights would benefit greatly from switching to an aperture rear sight, but such a system has fallen from favor and most such sights suitable for hunting have disappeared from the scene.

Enter the scope sight, by all odds the most efficient of them all for most hunting conditions. It is great for two reasons: it helps you to SEE better; and, the single sighting plane eliminates the need to align anything except the crosshair and the target. Most efficient for most hunting conditions, that is. Pouring rain? Snowstorm? A moving target at 20 feet in a thicket? Love those open sights.

I have a few friends who have a particular appreciation of the fact that eyes are precious. Early in 1985 Chet Brown squeezed the trigger on one of his fiberglass-stocked rifle creations and almost bought the farm. The 20-grain overload in his handload virtually took apart a super-strong action. Among the other goodies, one lens of his glasses was blown from its frame back into Chet's eye, and two months later he was thankful that the side effects — flashes of light and blurred vision — were finally easing off.

Just down the road my gunsmith Ken Eversul slipped the wrong ammo into a rifle he was sighting in. So did Fred Pickett when we were testing his Red-i-Rest. And my buddy, Sen. Don Kelly, who lives just across town, while checking his rifle in a Colorado elk camp the day before the season opened. Ken and Fred were wearing shooting glasses, which protected their eyes from the metal fragments that sprayed the rest of their faces. Don wasn't, and spent opening day having pieces of metal dug from his eyes.

Can't happen to you? These four guys are "pros" in the shooting and hunting arena, and it did happen to them. There have been thousands of similar happenings, many with much more tragic results. The moral is obvious, especially the advisability of using shooting glasses.

I don't always wear such glasses. I frequently leave 'em off when big game hunting if I'm using binoculars and/or camera often, which is usually the case. But a big game hunt is a one- shot proposition, we hope, so the odds against an accident of that kind are great.

If my shooting activity of the moment involves more than a shot or two, on the other hand, I always wear shooting glasses! Sighting a gun in, checking a zero, plinking, varmint shooting, ducks or doves, trap, skeet, casual clay target bustin'...always wear glasses. The more you shoot, the greater the possibility that something can go wrong.

I wear shooting glasses to guard against eventualities such as those above, but also for other reasons. They protect the eyes from twigs and limbs when I'm plowing through thickets, and from stray shot when bird hunting; they cut the glare of sun, particularly from water or snow; and they sharpen the image of clay target or bullseye.

Bud Decot is the guru of shooting glasses, with his Decot Hy-Wyd's decorating many competitive skeet, trap and live bird gunners. He's a fixture around the shooting circuit. For 35 years he has been wrestling with problems of gunning vision, and when this Phoenix entrepreneur speaks, it pays to listen.

"Deteriorating vision," Bud told me recently, "is usually self-inflicted. The general public hasn't been adequately informed that the eyes need nutrients and exercise to maintain their sparkle and accuracy. Not many understand that vision is a mental process and eyesight is physical. Mind and eye must operate as one to perform at top efficiency. You look with your eyes, but you see with your mind."

Bud has contributed to and benefited from the current interest and research in sport vision, a rather new field in which there is understandably some difference of opinion on particular aspects of various programs. There seems to be no disagreement that exercise and proper nutrition contribute enormously to better vision.

Shooting glasses have been improved tremendously in the past few decades, and there are now a number of excellent brands available. (There are also some "sunglasses" which are harmful, and which should be avoided.) As is true with regular prescription glasses, plastic lenses have been a boon to shooters because of their light weight and strength. They're made in a wide array of colors, with some of the more exotic ones favored by skeet and trap shooters for certain conditions. One of the more useful "colors" is the clear glass, which simply gives protection.

The newer synthetic lens material is amazing. Dennis Burns recently sent me a pair of his Gargoyles sports glasses which had been shot with a trap load at close range, in which test the pellets scarcely dented the lenses. Bud Decot showed me a new lens material which had gone through the same kind of shooting test, with equally excellent results. The good glass shooting lenses also give good protection from stray shot. No matter what you have to pay for them, a pair of good shooting glasses could be one of your best investments.

"Hunting and Vision" is a pamphlet which is available free to anyone who sends a self-addressed, stamped envelope to: American Optometric Asso., Communications Div., 243 North Lindbergh Blvd., St. Louis, MO 63141.

"Bragg System to Better Eye-Sight," $1.00 from: Health Science, Box 310, Burbank, CA 91503.

"Sports-Vision," by Dr. Leon Revien and Mark Gabor, $4.95 from: Workman Publishing, 1 West 39th, New York, N.Y. 10018.

"An Insight to Sports: Featuring Trapshooting," by Dr. Wayne F. Martin, from: Creative Communications, 330 Dayton St. — Suite 6, Edmonds, WA 98020.

Information on shooting glasses from: Bausch & Lomb, 42 East Ave., Rochester, N.Y. 14603; Bilsom International, 11800 Sunrise Valley Dr., Reston, VA 22091; Bushnell/Bausch & Lomb, 300 North Lone Hill Ave., San Dimas, CA 91773; Carl Zeiss, Inc., P. O. Box 2010, Petersburg, VA 23803; Decoy Hy-Wyd, Box 10355, Phoenix, AZ 85064; Gargoyles, Inc., 11108 Northrup Way, Bellevue, WA 98004; Simmons, 14205 S.W. 119 Ave., Miami, FL 33186; Tasco, Box 520080, Miami, FL 33152.

June 1985

PROTECT YOUR HEARING

I f gun writers had a password, it probably would be something like, "EH? WHAT'S THAT? WHAT DID YA SAY?" The reason is simple. Many of them have damaged their hearing by too much shooting without ear protection. Not by too much shooting, please note, but by shooting too much *without proper ear protection.*

Avid shooters throughout the world face a common hazard each time they pop a cap. It's simply that, if they shoot a lot, the potential for loss of their hearing is great.

"Everybody knows that!" I can hear in the background, "Gun writers, of all people, should certainly know."

Maybe. but that wasn't always the case. In those years of gun writing lore when guys named O'Conner and Page and Brown and Keith were dominant, public knowledge of the nature and extent of this phenomenon was minimal. All of these gun writing legends, and many more, suffered significant loss of hearing. So did many members of the shooting fraternity who used their gunning tools for competition and/or business, and especially the Bill Jordans and Charley Askins who specialized in handgunning.

Incremental; accumulative; irreversible! Those are the words to keep in mind when thinking about hearing loss caused by loud noise. Incremental — it happens one step at a time. Accumulative — each step builds on the previous one. Irreversible — the damage is permanent.

And it's insidious, which may be the most cruel adjective of all. Most hearing damage occurs so slowly that the shooter rarely knows it's taking place.

Normal conversation is at a sound level of 50 to 70 decibels, the accepted unit of measure in this field, and the softest sound which the average person can hear is about 1 decibel. Hearing loss will result from continuous exposure to sound levels of about 130 decibels, and most gunfire is louder than this. Handguns, as we know, are worse offenders than are long guns in this respect. While a .22 Long Rifle rimfire rifle just reaches that 130 decibel level, a pistol of that caliber tops the 150 decibel mark.

Dr. Jon Liland is a Boston hearing specialist/surgeon who is also an avid shooter and hunter, and during a recent hunting trip he explained for me some of the intricacies of the problem. "There are two kinds of hearing problems," he emphasized. "Mechanical ones, such as wax build-up, eardrum perforation and stirrup bone deficiencies, can often be cured or helped greatly. Nerve damage to the inner ear, the result of exposure to gun shots or other loud noises, cannot be cured, since nerve cells do not regenerate once they are damaged or destroyed."

Hearing is of two types, according to Jon. One is the perception of sound — you hear something. The other is discrimination — the difference between hearing "goodbye" or "hello," for instance. Long time shooters who suffer hearing loss can frequently hear but can't understand.

"It's too bad," Jon made a significant point, "that there is no pain associated with the gradual loss of hearing. There's no warning, except for a ringing if a gun is fired very near the ear."

It is a bit ironic that Jon, who studied at the Harvard Medical School and also teaches there, has some high frequency loss of hearing caused by shooting. He is a native of Norway, and was a member of the Norwegian rifle shooting team before going to med school — before learning of the hazards of not using ear protection.

Continuous noise of a high level is worse than intermittent noise. Guinea pigs exposed to six hours in a disco suffered temporary deterioration in hearing (TTS — Temporary Threshold Shift); when exposed six hours a night for one week there was permanent loss of some hearing (PTS). In such a situation the ears do not have opportunity to recover. Trap and skeet shooters face similar conditions, although not as severe, getting pounded by noise from adjacent gunners as well as from their own shots.

The solution is prevention! If you already have some hearing loss, and many veteran shooters do, begin using ear protection to prevent additional damage. Make sure your youngsters realize at an early age the value of proper protection.

Ideally, we should wear ear plugs or muffs any time we pull the trigger, but there is a practical limitation. When shooting trap or skeet, shooting pistols, sighting in rifles or competing in silhouette matches — always use protection. Most of us won't when we're roaming the woods after deer or elk, or pheasants or grouse, where shots are infrequent; but there are other hunting situations where good judgment calls for protection.

Keep in mind that spectators can also suffer hearing damage from the sound of gunfire.

Most good ear plugs and ear muffs offer sufficient protection to prevent ear damage if they fit properly. Using both plugs and muffs at the same time has merit under some severe conditions. Ear plugs range from the soft "foam" disposable ones (I keep a batch of them in each hunting and shooting coat) to complex ones which are designed to allow passage of harmless, low-level sounds such as conversation, while blocking sharp jolts of noise such as gunshots.

There are also plastic plugs, formed to the individual ear, which are popular with many clay target competitors.

Muff-type protectors, such as those worn by many airline ground crew personnel, are available in a wide array of size and shape. Not as convenient as ear plugs, they are the most effective, according to the National Shooting Sports Foundation (a booklet on hearing protection and firearms safety is available for 25 cents from the NSSF, 1075 Post Road, Riverside, CT 06878).

If you already have hearing loss, consult a hearing specialist to determine what kind of loss it is, and if help is available for your particular problem. Hearing aids may help, especially if they are designed to amplify the high frequency sounds which are first lost to shooting noise, but only a competent doctor in this field can make that determination.

If you haven't been using ear protection, start doing so. And, make sure that beginning shooters realize the importance of this easy and inexpensive route to a lifetime of good hearing along with a lifetime of gunning.

Hearing Protector Manufacturers:

AO Safety Products, 14 Mechanic St., Southbridge, MA 01550
Bausch & Lomb, 635 St. Paul St., Rochester, NY 14602
Bilsom International, 11800 Sunrise Valley Drive, Reston, VA 22091
David Clark Co., Worcester, MA 01604
E.A.R., Inc., Box 2146, Boulder, CO 80306
Marble Arms, Box 111, Gladstone, MI 49837
Norton Company, P.O. Box 7500, Cerritos, CA 90701
Penguin Industries, Airport Industrial Mall, Coatesville, PA 19320
Silencio/Safety Direct, 23 Snider Way, Sparks, NV 89431
Sportmuff, Inc., 37 Tripps Lane, East Providence, RI 02915
Tico International, 339 World Trade Center, San Francisco, CA 94111
Action Products Company, P. O. Box 100, Odessa, Mo. 64076

March 1985

Section Two

SHOTGUNS

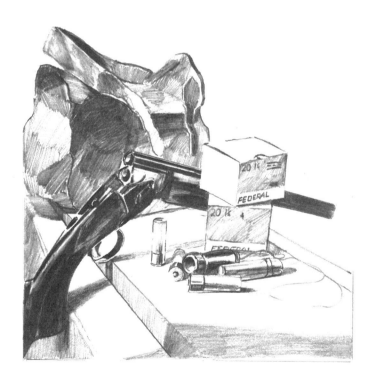

TIGHT CHOKES MEAN FEWER KILLS

Y ou can become a better wingshot — overnight.
Choke is the key. Nash Buckingham said it about duck calls, but the crux of our particular situation is succinctly stated by paraphrasing his remark, to wit: "A full-choked shotgun in the hands of the unskilled is conservation's greatest asset."

I would unhesitatingly expand that to include the semi-skilled wing shot; yea, even the average good shot. For anyone short of the expert, moving to a full choke boring is a move past the point of diminishing return. If you prefer to leave more birds out there for me, use a full choke. But if you'd like to put more birds in the bag with fewer shots, read on!

First, let's jot down three facts of shotgunning life which we should commit to memory, and to which we should cling with tenacity: 1. shotguns are short-range tools; 2. the average range at which most game birds are killed, regardless of species, is short; and 3. hunters routinely overestimate distances of kills.

Hitting a flying game bird with a shotgun is not an easy task, which will come as no surprise. It becomes progressively more difficult as the size of the shot pattern with which we work decreases, which in turn occurs as we move to tighter and tighter chokes. Visualize your shotgun as a paint brush with which you intend to "paint out" that flying bird, and it's elementary to note that you can do so more easily with a six inch brush than with one only half that width.

The goal in selecting the proper shotgun choke, therefore, should be to arrive at the one which will give you the biggest paint brush — the largest pattern, while still retaining sufficient pattern density for effective kills *at the distance most kills are made.*

Distance is the ingredient which permeates all discussion of shotgun efficiency and wing shooting skill, yet a majority of hunters are inept at estimating range with any degree of accuracy. This is unfortunate from two standpoints. Most serious is the widespread tendency to shoot at birds out of range, frequently far out of range. Second is the overestimation of the range at which birds are killed.

The latter is less damaging to the resource, but it misleads the gunner insofar as the shotgun requirements for his particular sport is concerned. If he believes most of his ducks are being killed at 45 yards, then he opts for a choke/shotshell combination which will do the job out there at 45 yards.

If he is actually killing his birds at 30 to 35 yards, he could immediately become a more "skilled" wing shot by switching to a choke adequate for that distance. He would have a much bigger paintbrush at the range where it counts, the range where the birds are killed.

Forty yards? Few hunters have much conception as to just how very far that is. A good example is the friend of mine who helped shoot the hundred-odd patterns shot while researching this article. After measuring off 40 yards, putting up a pattern sheet and returning to the firing point, he went back and measured it again. "I just couldn't believe," he told me later, "that 40 yards was that far."

It is! It's almost half the length of a football field, and you might use that readily-available piece of real estate to establish some perspective regarding distance. Put a half-gallon milk carton on the 40-yard line and another on the midfield stripe, then retire to the goal line to contemplate what a drake mallard looks like at 40 and 50 yards. Move one of them over to your opponent's 40-yard line... and dream of that 60-yard shot.

That half-gallon carton approximates the vital area of a drake mallard or a cock pheasant. Now, to really get your attention on this distance bit, replace those cartons with a regular size beer can, which is about the vital size of a teal. Or twice the size of the vital area of a dove.

One of the most important ways in which we judge distance is the apparent size of a known object. Our binocular vision permits us to estimate the distance to an auto down the street by comparing how big the auto "appears" with how big we actually know it is. That capability works pretty well in a horizontal plane, but fails miserably as we approach the vertical.

An example is a full moon hanging just above the horizon, where it appears huge — and near. But when it is directly overhead it seems small and very far away, despite the fact that neither its size nor distance from the earth have changed.

I'll bet the farthest kills on flying game you've ever seen were on passing birds directly overhead. Man, I recall a few doves and ducks and geese I pulled down out of the stratosphere that took five minutes to fall. Must have been 70 yards up, at least.

Not likely! Like that moon, they just appear a long, long distance away when they're up in the sky.

Killing range for ducks over decoys: 33 yards. That is the mean distance at which 241 hunters in Michigan, shooting over decoys, dropped ducks cleanly. Even then, eight percent of those birds were unretrieved.

The mean distance at which they hit ducks which fell at a distance ("sailers") was 39 yards, and more than half of those were not retrieved. The six additional yards of mean distance — from 33 to 39, obviously made a tremendous difference in the ability of hunters to kill birds.

For mourning doves: how about 25 yards...or 33 yards.

In a two-year study conducted in Oklahoma (Oberfell and Thompson — "The Mysteries of Shotgun Patterns") the average estimated distance at which doves were bagged "dead" (dead when retrievced) was 25 yards. Average for those bagged "alive" (alive when retrieved) was 33 yards.

Ducks and doves are killed at ranges much greater than this, of course, but what concerns us in our quest for greater wing shooting efficiency are the distances at which most birds are killed. I believe, from gunning experience in a variety of situations over too many years, that the ranges shown above are completely reasonable.

And how about pass shooting at ducks and pheasants and chukars and western quail? Well, all of these bring forth a goodly bit of long-ranged shooting, but the average distance of a kill on these won't miss 33 yards by enough to write home about.

All of which boils down to this: if you're killing 30-yard birds, you don't need 40-yard capability in your shotgun. If you insist on it then you do so at the expense of killing efficiency, in terms of pattern size, at the distance at which you kill most of your birds.

Put aside any notion you may have that a shotgun choke is a precise thing. The degrees of choke constitute an arbitrary, but useful, system of measurement based on the percentage of any given shot charge which can be enclosed by a 30-inch diameter circle on a pattern fired at 40 yards.

Full, Modified, Improved Cylinder, Cylinder: what do they mean? Well, it depends upon whose list you're checking, as witness these four authoritative sources:

Choke Designation	List A	List B	List C	List D
		Percentages		
Full Choke	70	70-80	65-75	65-75
Improved Modified	65-70	65-70	55-65	55-65
Modified	60	55-65	45-55	45-55

Choke Designation	List A	List B	List C	List D
		Percentages		
#2 Skeet	—	55-65	—	50-55
Improved Cylinder	45	45-50	35-45	35-45
Skeet	45	35-40	30-35	35-40
Cylinder	35-40	35-40	25-35	25-35

There is obviously a considerable variation in the designated percentages, from list to list, for the same choke. That's a bit confusing, but not fatal, and stems from the fact that there is a considerable variation in percentages from shot to shot from the same barrel, especially when different shotshells are used.

Consider these consecutive patterns from one barrel, with heavy loads of 7 1/2 shot: 35, 45, 39, 41 and 46 percent — an average of 41 percent. But switch to heavy loads of 8's in the same barrel and we get 29, 31, 40, 30 and 39 percent — for an average of 33 percent. Again with the same barrel, with light loads of 7 1/2 shot, the patterns jumped to 58, 51, 57, 47 and 53 percent. The average — 53 percent.

Is this barrel a 33 percent choke or a 53 percent choke? Or a 41 percent choke? Depending upon which load you're using and which list you choose, it could be Cylinder, Skeet, Improved Cylinder or Modified.

All of which should graphically bring home this fact: that you have no idea what's spewing forth from the muzzle of your favorite scattergun until you shoot a batch of patterns with it. With the exact loads you use in hunting.

The fickleness of shotgun barrels in digesting various shotshells obviously makes it impossible for gun manufacturers to be precise in the choke markings for production run firearms. Custom barrels can be tailored by some manufacturers and some gunsmiths with greater pattern percentage preciseness, but for only one particular shotshell loading.

That very fickleness can be an advantage to the one-gun hunter. If he has done enough patterning he can, within the range of the fluctuation, select the brand, shot size and loading to give the "choke" he needs at the moment.

What's the best combo?

For my money — 35 to 40 percent in the first barrel; and 60 to 65 percent in the second barrel. For the single barrel man — as close to 50-percent patterning as possible.

Such a combination in a double, or a boring in a single barrel, could only make "better" wing shots out of most hunters who are gunning ducks, doves, pheasants, western quail, chukar, and the like.

Over-the-counter choke combinations for doubles and O&U's are limited, with most brands, to Skeet/Skeet; Improved Cylinder/ Modified; and Modified/Full. (The Browning Superposed is available with any combination of Full, Improved Modified, Modified, Improved Cylinder, Skeet or Cylinder.) An IC/M boring on a stock shotgun would come as near as anything to my favorite combination in most brands, but the Skeet/Improved Modified just about hits it on the nose.

But keep in mind, of course, that barrels marked "Skeet" and those marked "Improved Cylinder" can throw patterns which overlap, as can the Modified and Improved Modified. Arbitrary choke designations aside, let's just say that most gunners would do better with an "open" first barrel and a "fairly tight" second barrel. For the single barrel enthusiast: a tight improved cylinder or a weak modified, which we can translate into a "fairly open" choke.

Here's the key! A cylinder bore shotgun is just as efficient a killer at 30 yards as a full choke is at 40 yards.

That means our 35 to 40 percent first barrel will kill anything within that 25- to 35-yard range where a vast majority of the birds are killed, and give us an economy-sized pattern with which to work. The 50-percent boring on the single barrel is a compromise.

Some gunsmiths can open up a choke by reaming it out, and some can — with more difficulty — put more choke into a barrel. The patterns listed above are for the lower barrel of a Winchester 101 which Byron Dugat, gunsmith in Beeville, Texas, opened up for me. Originally "modified," the 41-percent average pattern with heavy loads of 7 1/2's is about what I wanted. Although the top barrel is marked "full," we found it wasn't necessary to alter it since its patterns with the same load averaged 62 percent.

That is not, of course, a full-choke pattern with that particular load, no matter how the barrel is marked. Only with heavy loads of 4's does this barrel reach the 70-percent figure.

Two factors militate against the use of a true 70 to 80 percent full-choke pattern by most shotgunners. First is that such a tight boring gives much smaller patterns at normal killing ranges. Second is the fact that a very high proportion of that 70 to 80 percent is concentrated in the center of that 30-inch circle at 40 yards — within a 20-inch circle, let us say. While all patterns thrown by any choke become progressively less dense as we move away from the center, a true full choke accentuates this.

At the risk of damage to shooting egos, few of us have the skill to hit a flying bird with a 20-inch pattern at over 40 yards.

Some few do! Live pigeon shooters, the best of whom may well be the very best wing shots in the world, usually prefer the tightest pattern possible for their second barrel, and the better box bird shooters want that for both tubes. But their skill is exceptional, and their requirements — to drop the bird in a restricted area — unusual.

The favorite combination for those who shoot thrown birds, which more closely approximates much hunting, is improved cylinder and full.

Shotgun chokes for woodcock, grouse and bobwhite quail should be open — cylinder, skeet, or certainly no tighter than a weak improved cylinder. For geese, and "long range" pass shooting at ducks — modified or full.

For everything else: improved cylinder in a single barrel; improved cylinder and modified for a double or over & under.

And remember, the proof is on the pattern sheet. Here's how to pattern your shotgun.

At a measured range of 40 yards, shoot at the middle of a sheet of paper which is at least four feet by four feet. Draw a 30-inch diameter circle which will include the greatest number of shot holes, no matter where on the paper that happens to be. Count the number of holes within the circle, and divide that by the total number of shot in the load you're using. The answer is your pattern percentage.

$$\frac{\text{Number of Shot in Circle}}{\text{Number of Shot in Load}} = \text{Pattern Percentage}$$

Shoot at least five patterns with each load and average the five results. Ten would be better. Arms and ammo companies usually average the results of 100 patterns.

Approximate Number of Pellets Per Load

Oz. of Shot to the Shell	Shot Size						
	2	4	5	6	71/2	8	9
1 7/8	168	252	318				
1 5/8	146	219	276	366			
1 1/2	135	256	337	525			
1 3/8	124	186		309			

Oz. of Shot				Shot Size			
to the Shell	2	4	5	6	71/2	8	9
1 1/4	113	169	213	281	438	513	731
1 1/8	101	152	191	253	394	461	658
1 oz.	90	135	170	225	350	410	585
7/8		118	149	197		359	512
3/4		101	128	169	263		439
1/2		68	85	113	175		293

February 1976

THE SIXTEEN GAUGE SHOTGUN: MR. IN-BETWEEN

During my early teen years in South Carolina, our next-door neighbor had a Yankee friend who came down to bird hunt with him each fall. In fact, that fellow from up north left one of his bird dogs, a big black and white setter, with Roy year-round, and we hunted him along with our batch of pointers.

He also left a shotgun there year-round, and when he wasn't down for a hunt I kinda took care of his gun. What I really did was use it all the time, and was it something. It was a Parker double! Not a real fancy-grade Parker, but compared to my own shotgun it was a dandy. I'm sure the barrels were open choked, since the owner hunted bobwhite quail with it, but, no matter; I worked the quail and doves over with it pretty good for a couple of years. I hated to see it go back north.

I don't recall the choke borings, but what I do remember well is the gauge. It was a 16 gauge. Since then I have never hunted with another sixteen, and never owned one at all until last year. Now I've got a couple. Last fall John Bailey, out in Livingston, Montana, showed me a pair I couldn't live without, and since then I've thought a lot about just why the sixteen hasn't been very important in my decades of gunning. And, more important, why it has so fallen from grace throughout this country.

And that's a fact! The 16 gauge isn't sweet any longer in the United States. Across the board, our domestic ammunition and firearms manufacturers report a steady and continuing decline in sales of this number for the past few decades. The reaction on their part to this trend was predictable: reduced production of shotguns chambered for this gauge, and of shotshells for it. That reaction, understandable and probably justified, has nonetheless triggered what is virtually a self-fulfilling prophesy. With few 16-gauge guns on the shelves and a limited range of shotshells from which to choose, bulwarked by an almost complete absence of any promotion of this number, it is a bit far-fetched to imagine any substantial renewed surge of popularity for Mr. In-between.

And that's a shame, since the 16 could well be the most versatile and practical of them all. Could be, that is, IF the improvements which have enhanced 20-, 12- and 10-gauge guns and shells in the recent past were lavished on the forgotten 16. Remember the "Sweet Sixteen" — and we're still talking guns! In the days of yore that Belgium Browning autoloader was perhaps the single most respected tool of the hunter in this country. If you owned a "Sweet Sixteen" you were the envy of the whole town, not just the block. Any "Browning" was the prestige shotgun, but if it were a "Sweet Sixteen' — even better.

I have news for you. Browning doesn't sell the "Sweet Sixteen" anymore. Fact is, Browning doesn't market a 16-gauge shotgun at all, of any kind. What's more, neither does Winchester. Nor Marlin. Nor Mossberg. Nor Weatherby. Nor Ruger. And Remington? Surely, Remington makes the M1100 and M870 in 16 gauge. Sorry. All 16's disappeared from the Remington catalogs between 1980 and 1981. Gone!

Harrington & Richardson and Savage (Stevens) are your only bets these days for a 16 gauge made in this country, if my casual perusal of the catalogs didn't miss others. Both still make and sell a single barrel which is available in 16 gauge. There are also a few other foreign-manufactured 16-gauge single barrels which are imported and sold here.

"This brings us to the 16 bore," wrote Elmer Keith, who shot a 16 all his life and used it more than he did any other shotgun, "perhaps the nicest of all upland guns and a very useful gun for average range duck shooting."

"The 16, running lighter than the average 12, throwing patterns on a par with the best of the big guns, capable of ranging out with all but the heaviest 12's, beautifully balanced, fast handling, with less recoil and lighter fodder to tote, has plenty of stuff on the ball." So wrote Col. Charles Askins a quarter of a century ago, but he also added that the 16 "seems to be slipping from the picture."

"Perhaps the Europeans are right and the 16 is the best

compromise," was the way Jack O'Conner summed it up a couple of decades ago. What Jack referred to is the fact that the 16 gauge is the gauge on the continent of Europe, the most popular gauge of them all. It still is today, often in the form of a drilling, the gun which has a pair of side-by-side shotgun barrels atop a rifled barrel in an appropriate caliber. In such countries as Germany, all game seasons are often open at the same time, and in one outing the gunner may have chances at birds, deer or boar. For such mixed-bag hunting a drilling works well, and in such a firearm 16-gauge barrels seem to be a perfect blend of balance and capability.

There are a couple of "clay target" reasons which undoubtedly contributed to the decline in popularity of the 16 gauge in this country. Obvious is the fact that all trapshooting is done with 12-gauge guns. You can use smaller gauges if you wish, but such selections would handicap the competitor. Organized skeet competition involves four gauges — 12, 20, 28, and 410 — no 16 gauge. Again, you could use a 16 in the all-gauge matches, where most use the 12 gauge, and it's a bit surprising that few people (if any) do, since some do use the 20 gauge in these events. It's surprising, that is, until you consider that none of the ammunition companies makes a 16 gauge "target" load, which is superior to all other shotshells in excellence and consistency of patterns.

The three major ammo companies still list a reasonable assortment of 16 gauge loadings, but finding them on the shelves of your local gun dealer is often a problem. Sales just don't justify maintaining much 16 gauge inventory.

If you're required to shoot steel shot, forget your 16 gauge unless you're prepared to reload. Nobody makes 16-gauge shotshells loaded with steel shot. (Federal makes 20, 12 and 10 gauge; Winchester offers 12 and 10 gauge; Remington — only 12 gauge.) The specialty shells aren't made in 16 gauge — the Premium, the "Nitro Magnum," the Super Pigeon, nor the Super Double X Mark 5. Nor the specialized clay target loads, as pointed out earlier.

Here are the 16-gauge offerings which are being manufactured by our three major companies. Winchester: Super-X Game Load (3 1/4, 1 1/8, 4-5-6-7 1/2-8-9); Super-X Magnum Game Load (3 1/4, 1 1/4, 2-4-6); Upland Field Load (2 3/4, 1 1/8, 4-5-6-7 1/8-8-9); Value Pack Game Load (2 1/2, 1, 8; and Max, 1 1/8, 6). Remington: "Express" Magnum (Max, 1 1/4, 2-4-6); "Express" Extra Long Range (3 1/4, 1 1/8, 4-5-6-7 1/2-9); "Surshot" Field Load (2 3/4, 1 1/8, 4-6-7 1/2-8-9). Federal: Super Magnum (3 1/4, 1 1/4, 2-4-6);

Hi-Power (3 1/4, 1 1/8, 4-5-6-7 1/2); Field Load (2 3/4, 1 1/8, 6-7 1/2-8); Game Loads (3 1/4, 1 1/8, 4-6-7 1/2; and 2 1/2, 1, 6-7 1/2-8). All three manufacturers market a 16-gauge rifled slug (4/5 ounce) loading, and a buckshot loading with #1 buck.

My two "new" 16-gauge guns are both doubles, but there the similarity ends. One is a Winchester Model 21 "Skeet" gun, oddly enough since there is no 16-gauge event in skeet competition, and I intend to have fun with it this fall on doves, quail and woodcock. The other is a well-used Lebeau-Courally made in Leige, Belgium in 1958 for a Mr. J.E.A. Dorhout. One of a pair, choked full and half-choke, it was apparently his waterfowl gun, and saw substantial duty in Europe. I'm betting it will smoke a mallard over decoys in a Cajun marsh just as it did on the Continent.

Realistically, I know that the days are dwindling down for the 16 gauge in America. Shotshells will continue to be available for a long time, perhaps always, but probably in a reduced selection as the years pass. But no more 16-gauge guns are being offered shooters on this side of the big pond, if you'll excuse the few "single barrel" exceptions, and that's significant.

But, despite that, I'm going to give some attention to this in-between gauge in the coming years. It may just be a nostalgic trip, evoking memories of that Parker of by-gone days. But, then again, it may well be that I'm just returning to a gauge which is, as many shotgunners have maintained over the years, the best compromise of them all as the all-round shotgun.

Shotshell reloading is enjoying great popularity these days, and it holds much attraction for 16-gauge enthusiasts who can't get the particular loadings they want over the counter. One problem with this is that 16-gauge components are also difficult to find. Dave Fackler maintains a good supply at his Minnesota mail-order house, and tells me that he will probably be importing new 16-gauge hulls from Europe next year. Write: Ballistic Products, Box 488, Long Lake, MN 55356.

January 1985

[ADDENDUM: This column, published in January 1985, generated a tremendous outpouring of letters from shooters around the country, most of whom own and use 16-gauge guns and the rest of whom would like to. Whether the column was in any way influential in the decision or not, and we're vain enough to think "maybe,"

Browning Arms Company brought back into its line two 16-gauge shotguns in 1987: the venerable "Sweet Sixteen" autoloader, and the Citori O&U. *June 1987]*

ANATOMY OF A DUCK GUN

It was the fall of 1944, and a Fort Lauderdale bicycle/gun shop owner had taken under his wing a shavetail from nearby Boca Raton Air Base who persisted in making a nuisance of himself with questions about Florida hunting. Following a near-midnight departure, we greeted the dawn of the first day of the duck season in the marshes south of Lake Okeechobee, and shortly thereafter I pulled the trigger on my first shot at waterfowl.

The string of ducks poured past our boat at fly-rod height, and the bark of my 20-gauge was lost in the boom-boom of my companion's black powder 10-gauge double. "Good shot," he grinned and tossed me a canvasback. I neglected to tell him that the unfortunate hen was the third or fourth duck in line, and that I'd been aiming at the leader.

Factory shotshells were scarce in those war years, and my mentor had taken from retirement his old black powder double. In the days before the season opened, I watched in fascination as he hand loaded his sleek brass cases. Memory dims after 40 years, but I can still recall the satisfying "thunk" when he dropped one of those big hulls into the chamber.

Now, that was a duck gun. I never knew the brand name, but I've not forgotten those imposing hammers and those long, huge twin tubes. Probably 34 or 36 inches long, and odds are great they were bored full and full.

What's a duck gun! What are the ingredients which come together in the firearm that triggers the comment that "this is my duck gun," a line I've heard countless times from hunters in many places. The line is the same; only the guns are different.

It was an Ithaca field-grade double choked modified and full which I used to kill that first duck, and the experience was new for the shotgun as well as for me. I'd used it in the Piedmont section of South Carolina for whatever was available in my growing-up years, mostly doves (I worked them over pretty good), rabbits, squirrels and quail (mod & full? no wonder quail were hard to hit).

It's leaning over in the corner now, probably frowning because I don't use it for ducks anymore. With a 5 1/2-inch down pitch on the stock — and no, I don't know how it got that way — it isn't the perfect pointer. I'm much more sophisticated about stock design now than I once was, back in the days when I creamed just about anything I shot at with the Ithaca — because I didn't know any better.

As fond of it as I am, however, I don't pick up that little Ithaca and say, "This is my duck gun." Neither would that kind gent in Florida, methinks, when referring to his 10-gauge double. Both were simply compromises of the moment: mine, the only shotgun I had; and his, because he had powder and shot for reloading.

When I think of classic duck guns I sometimes think of the glory days of duck gunning, of market hunting, and of the sport hunting era when daily limits of 25 and 50 ducks were the norm. What kind of shotguns did those guys use, hunters who had more opportunity for evaluating a "duck gun" in one season than most have nowadays in a lifetime.

We'll keep this on a reasonably modern basis, but it's also fun to look back a bit to the favorite duck guns of bygone eras. For me, such a glance to the rear gives a much better perspective of just how far we've come since that time. Or, perhaps, just how far we haven't come.

A century ago Fred Kimble killed 57 straight bluebills with his muzzleloader. He often used a combination of one double barrel muzzleloader and another single barrel when duck hunting, usually in gauges ranging from a 6-gauge down to a 10-gauge. He killed 122 wood ducks one morning before nine o'clock using a single barrel muzzleloader, and 128 mallards another time with his 9-gauge single to win a match. Before you get too shook up about these super magnum killers, let me add that Kimble was loading only one and a quarter ounces of shot in that 9-gauge at the time, which is what we shoot now in our standard 12-gauge express loadings. Less than in the 12-gauge magnums.

Kimble, incidentally, thought that one of his hunting partners was the best duck shot he ever saw. Bob Hinman recounts these tales, and more, in his most interesting book, "The Golden Age of Shotgunning," published by Winchester Press in 1971.

Muzzle loading shotguns might have been old timey, but they weren't (and aren't) all that primitive. They have the advantage over "modern" guns, in fact, in that no forcing cone is necessary, eliminating the pattern-damaging crush as pellets from our shotshells move from chamber to barrel. Black powders give lower pressures, another aid to better patterns.

Most of the first breech-loading shotguns used by duck hunters were doubles made in England, and those hand-crafted shotguns were expensive. But American manufacturing ingenuity addressed that, and during the last quarter of the 19th century hunters had a wide array of made-in-America shotguns from which to choose, as well as an assortment of imports of varying quality and price. But it was the last gasp of the century which saw the introduction of the shotgun which was to change waterfowling forever.

The Winchester Model 1897 really *was* a duck gun. That exposed hammer pump from the fertile mind of John Browning was on the scene for little more than a decade before market hunting was made illegal, but it became a favorite tool of that trade. It was in its heyday during the height of the waterfowl sport gunning era, and I'm sure that a batch of M97's are still being shucked in duck blinds today.

Years ago I interviewed a former Louisiana market hunter who showed me his well-worn, 16-gauge Model 97 with which he had plied his trade. From his album I looked at a photo of him just returning from a morning hunt, piroque filled with the fruits of his efforts, a quartet of live decoys perched on the forward gunnels, and that M97 lying atop the heap.

Pumps and autoloaders dominate duck hunting today, with good reason. They are reliable, reasonably priced, and well suited to the requirements of the game. And, where the marketplace was once dominated by Winchester's Model 12 pump, Remington's Model 11 automatic, and Browning's Auto 5, there are now many such shotguns of various brand names adorning gun shop shelves.

Side-by-side doubles crafted in America have a long duck blind tradition, of course, with such names as Parker, Ithaca, L.C. Smith, Fox and Winchester most prominent. Doubles lost ground in the years before and after World War II, but in the past couple of decades the vertically-stacked twin tubes have made their move. Over-and-unders are popular not only with trap and skeet shooters, but also with a significant minority of duck hunters.

Doubles have two obvious advantages. One is a choice of two chokes, and the other is the compactness made possible by the absence of any receiver loading system as is present in pumps and autos. They're four to six inches shorter than is a "repeater," even with the same length barrel.

Repeaters repeat. The firepower advantage of pumps and autos isn't as great as in pre-three-shot-limit days, but it's still present to the tune of 50 percent. An additional shot isn't really significant for killing more ducks, not in this era of reduced limits, but it can be for anchoring cripples quickly.

Doubles are at a disadvantage in a duck blind when it comes to reloading, simply because it's awkward to break and load them in a confined space. The magazine of pumps and autos, on the other hand, can be stuffed full with ease and convenience from just about any position. Doubles have the advantage, of course, when you need to quickly replace those 7 1/2's with 4's for that flock of geese. You pay your money and take your choice.

What's a "duck gun"! Consider those in my rack which have done most time in duck blinds over the years. There are a couple of pumps, a 20-gauge built 45 years ago and a 12-gauge magnum which is only 30 years old; a couple of O&U's, again a 20-gauge with three-inch chambers and 26-inch barrels bored IC&M, and a 12- gauge, again with three-inch chambers and 28-inch barrels with choke tubes. Then there's that plain Jane 12-gauge auto, no magnum, with a choke tube system installed in a 25-inch barrel, which has done yeoman duty on many occasions.

Quite a variety, come to think of it, and I guess that's what this "duck gun" business is all about. A duck gun shakes out to be whatever makes you happy and, hopefully, effective. If I must make a choice, for what it's worth, I prefer to be simpatico with the gun I'm shooting and a bit less effective, than to smoke every duck with a shotgun I don't enjoy shooting — if there is such a thing. For most of us, fortunately, we can have the best of both worlds.

Without being specific, there are parameters which I place upon a gun being bought for duck hunting. Gauge — 20 to 12, with nothing smaller than the latter if you shoot steel shot. Barrel length — 26 to 28 inches in doubles; not over 26 inches in autos and pumps. Choke — modified for a single barrel; IC&M for a double; and, if an interchangeable choke tube system is available, even better. Stock — an inch or two shorter than the length which feels perfect to you in the gun store. Feed and water your new partner with regularity — and enjoy.

October 1984

N ow and then, infrequently, there comes along a happening in the world of shooting which changes the face of that facet of the gunning game. Smokeless powder, breechloaders, scope sights, shot protectors and the shotgun choke itself. These, among others, were milestones along the path of our quest for greater shooting efficiency. Now we can add "screw-in choke tubes."

In 1975 I wrote: ("Variable Chokes You Can't See," SA Aug. 1975) "the screw-in choke concept is a striking breakthrough in variable choke devices." I added that they had received little fanfare, despite being around for quite a while; that few hunters knew about them; and that they weren't generally available.

Scratch all that! If you scratch anything these days, another screw-in choke falls out. They're the hottest item on the shotgun agenda. Most gun manufacturers have several models which feature screw-ins. Stan Baker, the man who began custom installation of screw-ins on his customers' barrels in 1975, is still doing a big business in such conversions. Jess Briley has carved out a significant niche with his own screw-in version. Many gunsmiths around the nation will install one of the many "name brand" conversions which have made the scene.

Winchester started it all in 1961 with its "Versalite Choke," an option on the ill-fated, glass-barreled Model 59 automatic. Both quickly disappeared, but Winchester refined and revived the choke tube concept in 1969, calling it the Winchoke, which is still available (and popular) on the M1200 and M1400 domestic Winchesters (U.S. Repeating Arms Co.), and on the Japanese-made doubles (M101 over and unders and M23 side-by's) marketed by Winchester/Olin.

Winchoke tubes are relatively thick (and strong), and to accommodate them Winchester tapered the barrels to give more metal out at the muzzle. Stan Baker developed a system of swelling the last few inches of a barrel to provide room for his choke on barrels not designed for such an addition. His is essentially the Winchoke, and most of the time Baker tubes and Winchoke tubes will interchange.

"They're basically the same," Stan Baker told me, "except for the tolerances. We hold a very close tolerance, and our chokes are a little oversized. They're tight. We do that so the choke itself can't move around. For mass production they make everything a little bit looser so that there's no possibility that you'll get one which doesn't fit."

On the Winchoke and Baker choke tubes a small knurled ring protrudes beyond the barrel, as it does on the Italian-made Perazzi and on some of the other domestic chokes. Now, there are also a host of choke systems in which the tubes are concealed entirely within the muzzle. These tubes are very thin, and can be fitted into most barrels without "swelling" them as Baker does. They are undoubtedly more aesthetically pleasing than are the slightly bulged Baker muzzles, as are those which are manufactured with an unnoticeable taper to permit installation of the thick tubes.

"That's the way to put in screw-in chokes," Baker emphasized. 'You should build the barrel to take the choke tubes, tapering it out. You wouldn't make it like our conversion; you wouldn't have an expansion at the muzzle, and you wouldn't have it thin like these other conversions."

The conversions are popular because shooters already have barrels which they want converted, and because some factory guns still don't offer the screw-in chokes. Remington was a major holdout, and many, many M1100s and M870s (and some M3200s) have received the treatment from Baker, Briley and others. Then, in 1985, the Du Pont firm came out with its "REM-CHOKE."

Stan is concerned about the proliferation of installation operations: "They're advertising no expansion, and they don't have any because they're making everything thin — thin barrels, thin chokes, thin threads. They aren't as strong, and most have no control over the point of impact. They just go in the front with a brace and bit, ream it out and put threads in it. No way they're going to get it in line with the bore. They can just ruin the gun.

"I mentioned Briley. His tubes are super thin, but it's a good job, a precision installation. He uses good, tough material. Some do a good job, and some don't."

Jess Briley, who has been making his chokes for half a dozen years or so, echoed the concern about poor installation. "When some of these guys have to start shooting steel shot," he said, "I'm afraid the tube is going to leave with the shot."

Briley tubes don't interchange with Winchoke. He uses a coarser thread (20 pitch) and a long choke, which he believes provides a better pattern across the range of choke constrictions.

Various choke tubes also differ in the placement of the threads — some near the muzzle end of the tube and others toward the receiver end (Perazzi started with front threads but has now changed to rear threads); and in the threads themselves — some metric and some domestic. Some chokes are of conical design, and some are conical/parallel. Each manufacturer using one of the options tends to claim his is the best.

The Winchoke system is used by both "Winchesters," and by Stan Baker, Mossberg (Accu-Choke), Smith & Wesson — now marketed by Mossberg (MultiChoke), Weatherby (MultiChoke), Excel Arms, and Savage. Browning (Invector) chokes, made in Japan, fit completely inside the barrel, but have Winchoke-compatible threads. Beretta has an Invector-type system on some of its O/U shotguns, and the current system on the Beretta autoloader (technically not a "screw-in" since the drop-in tube is held in place by a separate retaining collar) was changed to the invisible, screw-in type in 1986. Weatherby has switched the choke tube systems on all its shotguns — auto, pump and O&U's — from the Winchoke-type with exposed knurled ring to invisible tubes which Weatherby calls the Integral Multi-Choke (IMC). Walker Arms Company uses several systems, some of which are Winchoke-compatible and some which aren't. Ithaca, before closing its doors, had "inside" tubes available on the Model 37 slide action. Tru-Choke, distributed by La Paloma Marketing, is another "inside" choke, with threads that do not interchange with Winchoke threads.

Some of the arms companies offer both 12 and 20 gauge screw-in chokes, some 12 gauge only, but some of the custom choke makers also market 16 and 10-gauge chokes. While the gun company "chokes" are generally limited to Full, Modified, Improved Cylinder and Skeet tubes (Perazzi has a greater range), some of the custom tube makers offer choke constrictions in increments of be removed in order to see the marking), i.e. .690, .710, .725; while various other makers use code numbers on each tube (1, 2, 3 etc.), or just mark each tube with the "name" of the choke — Mod, Full, Sk 1, etc., while some don't mark the tubes at all (Walker Arms doesn't, but does include a choke gauge which works well if you have it with you). Most of the Winchoke-type tubes having the external, knurled ring protruding from the barrel have markings on the tubes so that they can be read with the tubes in place.

"Some guys don't wanna be bothered by the details," Stan Baker laughed. "They tell us to just mark the tube 'Full' instead of .690, and one trap shooter didn't even want that. He wanted one tube marked 'Singles' and the other marked 'Handicap,' so we did that.

We offer a wide range for the guy who likes to tinker, to fine tune his gun's performance. No one choke constriction works the same in all guns with all shot sizes, of course, and only experimenting will tell a shooter what's best for him."

As with any product which meets with success, the screw-in choke system has attracted quite a number of entrepreneurs, some good and some not-so-good. You'll find few problems with manufacturer-installed systems, but if you elect to have the chokes added to your present gun barrel, use the caution you should exhibit when buying any product. Inexpensive isn't always "cheap," but it sometimes is. It isn't always easy, or even possible, to ascertain the reliability of an operator, but try. Make sure they guarantee your choke installation, including no shift in the point of impact of your shot pattern (unless you want it changed, which can be done with some installations).

A decade ago I wrote, "I can only believe that these Winchoke-type changeable choke tubes are one of the great ideas to evolve in shotguns in recent decades...," and my experiences since that time have only enhanced that belief. In 1975 I finished that line with, "...and the unfortunate aspect is that they're not generally available." Now they are.

Some gun shops that install chokes

Briley Mfg., Inc., 1085 Gessner, Houston, TX 77055.
Reed-Chokes, 30016 S. River Rd., Mt. Clemens. MI 48045.
Stan Baker Chokes, 10,000 Lake City Way, Seattle, WA 98125.
Tru-Choke, La Paloma Marketing, 4500 E. Speedway Blvd, Suite 93, Tucson, AZ 85712.
Walker Arms Co., Hwy. Rt. 2, Box 73, Selma, AL 36701.

October 1985

THE REMINGTON 3200

In 1932 Remington Arms Company introduced to America's shooting public the first over-and-under shotgun produced in this country. It was the Model 32, presumably so labeled for the year of introduction. One short decade later, faced with the realities of a war-time 1942, the Bridgeport firm ended production of this model.

The Model 32 was an excellent shotgun and enjoyed reasonable popularity, and its demise triggered many a lament. It was resurrected in 1948 as the Krieghoff Model 32, made in West Germany, and it's still in production, and still popular.

The success of that imported near-duplicate could have been the catalyst which caused Remington to re-introduce the Model 32 after a thirty year absence, but the growing popularity of over-and-unders in general was a more likely stimulus. Whatever the reason, in 1973 a completely modernized Model 3200 made its appearance on dealer shelves across the country.

The fanfare which accompanied the debut of the M3200 was more than just sales talk. It was a "new and completely modern over-and-under shotgun design". Many of the features of the old Model 32 were retained, notably the separated barrels and the sliding top lock which serves as a shield over the entire breech, but three decades of advancement in gun design and technology added changes to the new shotgun.

Least apparent, and perhaps most important, of the new innovations was the exceptionally fast lock time of just 1.4 to 1.8 milliseconds. That means, as the Remington release of the moment put it, that "the shot will be out of the barrel of a Remington 3200 and on the way to the target before it even pops the shell crimp in most shotguns."

Most apparent was the new three-position combination safety and barrel selector, which deserves more acclaim than it has received. The teardrop-shaped safety pivots rather than slides. Flicked to the left, the safety is off and the lower barrel fires first. To the right, the upper barrel first. It is simple and positive. It's greatest value is for the hunter rather than for the competitive shooter, which is a bit ironic since the Model 3200 has enjoyed minimal popularity as a field gun.

The new M3200 incorporated subtle improvements. The design eliminated danger of firing pin breakage from dry firing. The center of gravity was lowered, meaning faster recovery for the second shot because of reduced muzzle jump. The entire construction was beefed up to increase durability.

It isn't fair to say that the M3200 fell on its face when introduced in 1973, but it is accurate to say that it didn't set the world on fire. It came out with a full house of models — field grade, skeet, trap with both regular and monte carlo stocks, a "Special Trap" grade with better wood, and a "One of 1000" Trap gun. The latter, commemorating the introduction, was limited to 1000 consecutively serial numbered (1-1000) guns. It was available only in 1973, featuring the finest wood, engraving, and gold inlay and grip cap.

Remington maintained the same line-up of models for year two, and also issued a Skeet grade run of "One of 1000," but then in 1975 brought out a model which I felt would be a winner. It was a gun with a beefed-up muzzle to cope with steel shot, and chambered for 3″ magnum shells. It was the only "double," at the time, either over-and-under or side-by-side, approved by the manufacturer for use with steel shot. My guess that waterfowlers would find it attractive didn't prove true.

In 1976, Remington added "Competition" grades of skeet and trap guns to the array. These featured selected wood and an optional satin finish which is more in keeping with a high quality shotgun, and they have become among the most popular models in the line-up.

The men from Ilion and Bridgeport made no changes in the Model 3200 line in 1977, but it must have been a year of soul-searching. By this time, after four years of marketing the O&U, it had obviously become apparent that although the M3200 was gaining some enthusiasts among trap shooters, and to a lesser degree among skeet shooters, it was finding little favor with hunters. The result was that in 1978 Remington dropped both the field grade and the Magnum models from the line, retaining only the trap and skeet configurations.

Perhaps you've noticed that I haven't mentioned gauge, a key word in the life and times of the M3200. It was available only in 12 gauge, which mitigated against it becoming popular with upland hunters who prefer smaller gauges, and with skeet shooters who compete in all four gauges.

The beefy proportions of this fine gun provide extreme durability and reliability, both of great importance in competitive shooting, but they resulted in guns weighing from 7 3/4 pounds in the field grade to 8 3/4 pounds in that ill-fated Magnum. Those are good numbers for waterfowlers and for competitive shooters, but don't find much favor with upland gunners.

We gun-writer types speculated for years that Remington might have in the works a scaled-down, lightweight O&U M3200 in 20 gauge on the drawing board. Maybe, but if so that drawing board was as far as the idea progressed. Instead, it brightened the scene for skeet shooters with the unveiling of a superb new Skeet Set featuring a single stock and receiver, and four individual barrel sets in 410, 28, 20, and 12 gauges. No matter which set of barrels is attached, the weight and balance of the gun is the same.

For 1979 Remington also introduced a Live Bird gun in the Competition grade. Identical to the Competition Skeet model with 28″ barrels, except for choke borings of improved modified and full rather than skeet, this beautiful number should have proved attractive to the duck and dove hunter as well as to the competition flyer shooter.

After half a dozen years of life it seemed that the M3200 had found a niche for itself among the ranks of competition clay target shooters, one which should have been solidified with the new skeet set and the Live Bird model. It's an excellent, high grade, American-made shotgun. For years I wouldn't have bet against a lighter weight 20 gauge M3200 being placed on the market, nor against it becoming a winner.

The sad fact is that none of the M3200's were winners in the Remington scheme of things, and no models appeared in the 1983 Remington catalog. All had been discontinued.

If you can find one of those discontinued Magnum models, you might consider adding it to your collection. Not only is it a superb waterfowl gun which will handle any 12-gauge shotshell made — lead shot or steel shot, but odds are good that it will become quite a collector's item.

That's probably true for any M3200, for that matter, an excellent, American-made shotgun which never quite got off the ground.

November 1979

IF THE STOCK FITS

I've never seen a gorilla cuddle a yardstick, but a reasonable facsimile of that action takes place each time a friend of mine shoots a production line shotgun. Not that he's awkward, since he is class "AA" in any kind of scattergunning, but when he makes his move it reminds me of a preying mantis attacking a fly.

Bill Jordan can't help it if he's six feet, seven inches tall, wears 36-inch sleeve shirts, and can palm a watermelon in each hand.

If he could, I'm sure he wouldn't. And, since he is also one of the fastest guns in the world with a pistol, I like him just as he is.

But my long, lanky buddy will admit that contortions are in order when he adapts his frame to a factory-stocked, assembly-line shotgun. He just doesn't fit that mythical "average" for which mass-produced products are designed.

Neither does my wife, Mary, who nudges five-two if she stretches.

Therein lies a problem for both manufacturers and for shooters. Standard dimensions, whether for gun stocks or other products, can't be perfect for everybody.

Matching a rifle stock to the shooter is nice, and could make a difference on those rare snapshot opportunities, but it is of minimal importance when compared to the proper dimensions of a shotgun stock. In the latter case, if the stock fits, you'll shoot much better.

Thus we make the case for proper shotgun fit quite simply. Now let us explore what this means and how to achieve it, after first confiding that I really don't understand all I know about this subject. More about that later.

The most important stock dimensions are for length of pull, drop at the comb, drop at the heel, and pitch. For the first three a typical factory field stock will measure 14 inches, 1 1/2 inches and 2 1/2 inches. Length of pull is the distance from the trigger (front trigger in the case of a double having two triggers) to the center of the butt. Drop at comb and heel are the measurements from a line extended from the top of the barrel down to the stock at the comb (where your cheek touches when in shooting position) and at the heel (top of the butt).

Pitch is really the angle of the butt relative to a line drawn through the barrels. It should be so measured (a 90-degrees angle would be zero pitch) but isn't. It is generally referred to in inches of pitch, either up or down, and is the distance from vertical of the muzzle when the shotgun is stood upright on its butt. Which makes little sense, since that figure will vary depending upon barrel length.

If you will imagine trying to shoot a rifle without a rear sight, you can readily understand the importance of proper stock fit in a shotgun. For the scattergunner, the stock *is* his rear sight, and ideally will place the gunner's eye in the same (correct) position for each shot.

Let me emphasize that shooters do a marvelous job of adapting to factory stocks. The point to be made is simply that many of them could shoot even better if the stock fit.

The king of the stock fiddlers is the live pigeon shooter, and with reason. He knows that in his game, where the races are short, any slight advantage means much. Trapshooters aren't far behind, if any, in their quest for the no-miss combination.

Length of Pull: For hunting use, under field conditions, most stocks are too long. I'm convinced most hunters shoot better with stocks just long enough to prevent recoil from jamming their hand into their nose.

A point which should be obvious, but which frequently is overlooked, is that one length of pull can't be perfect for fall gunning in shirt sleeves and also perfect for winter waterfowling in a heavy down coat.

Keep in mind that a little change goes a long way, and that it is much easier to remove wood than to replace it. Years ago, however, I overdid that caution when I shortened the stocks on Mary's shotguns from 14 inches down to 13 inches — quite drastic, but it wasn't enough. Years later we finally discovered that she shoots best with a 12-inch length of pull.

Despite that, proceed slowly with any changes. Experiment without permanent alteration, when possible. Add a slip-on recoil pad to try more length. Remove a buttplate or recoil pad to try a shorter stock.

Drop At The Comb: The rule with rifles is to adjust the rear sight in the direction you want the bullet to move, and with a shotgun the comb is the rear sight. The higher the comb, the higher the pattern will print. It helps to understand that a higher comb means less drop means a straighter stock.

A trap stock is "straighter" than is a field stock, to place the pattern high so it will intercept the rising clay target. Skeet and field stocks, essentially the same dimensions, have a low comb with a comb-drop of 1 1/2 or 1 5/8 inches. A typical trap comb-drop is 1 3/8 inches, not much difference, but that 1/8 or 1/4 inch changes the point of impact of a shot pattern a great deal.

Factory field stocks are low enough for most hunters, and seldom need wood removal for proper eye placement. Going in the other direction, it is easy to slowly add comb height, temporarily, checking as you proceed. Just add layers of moleskin (Dr. Scholl's) which is available at most drug stores.

English shooting instructors use the following technique for determining whether or not your gun shoots where you look, which is what this is all about. At hunting distance, they have you repeatedly mount the gun and shoot at a target on the pattern board, firing the instant the butt settles on your shoulder. It is interesting that the point of impact from shot to shot is so consistent, and amazing that it is often off target.

The Holland & Holland shooting school in London which I sampled used a try gun, a double with a fully adjustable stock that can be quickly adapted to any individual. By changing the dimensions, the proper combination to give best shooting results can be determined.

You can make your own impact test. Just make sure that you shoot as soon as the gun is mounted, without making aim corrections, and that you look at the target rather than the gun. If your patterns are consistently off the mark, changes in stock dimensions may be indicated.

Among the hunters who might benefit from a stock somewhat straighter than normal field configuration are those who gun quail, woodcock and grouse, where quick shots at rising birds are the rule. If you're one of these, a layer of the doctor's moleskin on your comb might be the prescription for your next hunt.

There is a direct relationship between stock length and drop at the comb on the normal field gun. When the stock is shortened, drop at the comb is decreased. The shooter's cheek contacts the comb farther forward, consequently higher, which raises the point of impact of the patterns.

The opposite is true, of course, with the gun tending to shoot a bit lower when the stock is lengthened. In either case, if the alteration is slight, then the change in the point of impact probably isn't significant.

Drop at the Heel: The 2 1/2-inch heel-drop on most standard field guns works for a vast majority of us, which makes this perhaps the least important of our stock measurements. It determines the position of the butt on the gunner's shoulder when he is in proper shooting position, and a change in it usually necessitates major stock surgery.

There is at least one butt plate on the market which is adjustable, and some trap shooters use it to effectively change the heel-drop.

Pitch: If your stock tends to slip down off your shoulder, then it probably has little down pitch, none at all, or even an up pitch. Too much down pitch may make it impossible to look down the top of the barrels when your head is firmly on the stock.

Most modern field guns have a down pitch of 2 to 2 1/2 inches, but I grew up shooting a 20-gauge Ithaca double which has a down pitch of five inches and a comb-drop a bit over two inches. Since I didn't know any better, I shot it quite well, but admit I developed a rather high head gunning position. If I cheek that stock firmly, all I can see is the back of my right hand.

The amount of pitch is determined by the angle of the buttplate relative to the plane of the barrels, and it is not unusual for that pitch to be inadvertently changed when a stock is shortened or a recoil pad installed. If you want to try a different degree of pitch, you can easily make a temporary alteration by using shims between the butt plate at either the toe or the heel.

Remember that shortening a stock substantially may raise the point of impact of the pattern. That can be compensated for, if necessary, by changing the pitch very slightly at the same time. More down pitch will make the gun shoot lower.

The most important function of pitch, however, is to insure that the butt of the stock snuggles securely and comfortably into the shoulder pocket. Alterations in point of impact are ideally achieved by changes in other stock dimensions.

Grip: I like the sleek, racy look of a straight (English) grip on a shotgun, but I shoot better with a pistol grip or a semi-pistol grip. And I suspect that most people do. The straight grip is an advantage, however, when shooting a double-trigger shotgun, making it easier to slide the hand when switching from one barrel to the other.

The size and shape of the grip is important to me. The superb Perazzi O&U has a grip which is too fat for my tastes, but those on such examples as the Remington 1100, the Winchester 101, Ruger O&U, and the Beretta give me a feeling of confidence and control.

Cast — Off and On: When the plane of the stock isn't the same as for the barrels, it has cast. Cast-off if the stock angles away from the shooter's face; cast-on if it angles toward the shooter.

Cast is simply one more control toward building a shotgun which will shoot where the gunner looks, no matter what his physical dimensions are. Many European gun makers, who charge enough for their products to make such detailed treatment practical, will give the customer any cast he desires. So will many custom stock makers in this country.

Even old stocks can be "bent" to change the point of impact, left or right, up or down. Just make sure you entrust your gun to a reliable gunsmith who knows what he's doing.

Custom Stocks: Two firms from the "show me" state have done just that when it comes to providing shooters with "custom" stocks. I doubt that sportsmen can get any greater value received for their dollars than from Reinhart Fajen (Box 338) or E. C. Bishop (Box 7), both doing business in Warsaw, Missouri 65355.

Fajen and Bishop can supply just about anything needed in the way of stock wood, from the rough blank to the customized finished product. A $5.00 blank from Bishop which I bought about 25 years ago still graces one of my favorite sporters, and a Fajen-stocked Springfield rebarreled to 7mm Rem. Mag. by Walter Womack has taken more big game for me than has anything else on my rack.

The cost of restocking a gun can be modest or tremendous, and the range is justified. Choice walnut is scarce and, understandably, expensive. I drooled a bit when Frank Pachmayr showed me his hoard of superb wood stashed away at Pachmayr Gun Works, one of the finest such collections in the world.

The Orvis Company (Manchester, Vt. 05254) will order for you a custom side-by-side double, and have the stock tailored to your specific dimensions. There are many excellent stock makers in this country who can produce anything you need or desire.

Most custom stock makers make use of a try-gun. If one isn't available to you, a reasonable substitute is to just try as many different guns as practical. Trap and skeet ranges, pigeon shoots and sporting goods stores offer such opportunities. When you find one that fits you, buy it or measure it.

One of the things I know about stocks, which I don't understand, is that two with identical dimensions can feel and fit completely different. It probably has to do with the mating of stock dimensions with weight, balance, barrel length and type of action.

Whatever the secret that produces the magic brew, now and then we happen upon a shotgun which is just right. One which we shoot beautifully.

When that happens to you, make an unreasonable effort to acquire that shotgun by any method necessary. And when it's yours, never change it.

May 1978

CHOOSING A SHOTGUN

I f you're in the market for a shotgun, allow plenty of time for your shopping. Best time is probably when the hunting seasons are closed. Then you need not be rushed. You have months in which to shop at your leisure — to study the catalogs and visit the gun shops. And, once you make a decision, you'll have time to get to know your new gun before the bird seasons begin.

A number of decisions must be made when shopping for a shotgun. First of all, what will it be used for. What you want your shotgun-to-be to *do* is virtually a prerequisite for other decisions that follow. Must it be able to handle waterfowl, or will the demands upon it lean more toward gunning grouse? Do you want an all-around tool for a variety of field-gunning chores?

Beyond the consideration of function, there are quite a number of variables which will require your attention. Among them are: 1. type of action; 2. gauge; 3. barrel length; and 4. choke. Those are not necessarily listed in the order of importance, but the sequence is generally practical.

Action: In this choice beauty does indeed lie in the eye of the beholder. I know gunners who wouldn't be caught with a semi-automatic in hand, yet many others who think that the efficient, gas-operated self-loaders are the end in all. You pay your money.

The single barrel shotgun deserves consideration because it fills a decided need. It is inexpensive, lightweight and the safest action of all. With those attributes, it's often the best choice for the beginning shooter, especially the youngster.

If you select a single barrel with an exposed hammer for your youngster, make sure that he has strength enough to safely cock the hammer. And to let it down into the "safe" position from a cocked position. There are single barrels available which have internal hammers and tang safeties. In these you trade off the visual advantage of the exposed hammer (you know at a glance whether or not the gun is cocked) for the convenience and ease of operation of the tang safety. Which is best for your needs must be your decision.

Another situation where the single barrel comes into play is in the specialty gun, and at opposite ends of the spectrum. One is the single barrel trap gun, and the other is the turkey/goose single bored for the 10-gauge magnum. In turkey hunting, particularly, one shot is usually all you need (or get), and the increased efficiency of 10-gauge shotshells now available make a single barrel in this gauge particularly attractive to the gobbler gunner.

Most inexpensive single barrels suffer from poor handling qualities, but there are some decent ones available. Shop around.

Bolt actions are modestly priced, offer ample shell capacity, but their handling characteristics generally range from poor to fair.

The "double" barrel, both over-under and side-by-side, has two valuable attributes. It usually offers excellent handling qualities and the choice of two choke borings. Whether you choose the conventional double or the over-under is a matter of personal preference, but there is a greater selection available in the latter.

The side-by-side has a slimmer profile, and requires less break in order to expose the chambers for loading, but the single sighting plane of the stacked barrels seems to work best for most shooters.

Pumps and autos — these are the shotguns which have been the favorites with Americans for decades. Both offer the advantage (over doubles) of greater shell capacity. They have the single sighting plane, and both have a well-deserved reputation for delivering reliability and efficiency at modest prices.

Slide actions once were thought to be more reliable than autos, but that gap has narrowed or disappeared with the improvements which have been made to autoloaders. Marathon races in both trap and skeet, which test the endurance and reliability of shotguns, are regularly won with autos.

Some people believe that pumps are inherently "safer" than are autos, since they require a physical action between successive shots, but I don't think this should be a consideration for experienced shooters. If autos are more "unsafe" because of the autoloading feature, then so are single-trigger doubles.

Most hunters have little trouble learning to shuck a pump gun, and with practice can fire aimed shots as quickly as with an auto. Second and third shots are easier with an auto than with a pump in some situations — cramped blinds, awkward shooting positions, or when the hunter is bundled in heavy clothing.

A decided advantage of the gas-operated autos is recoil reduction. The total recoil on a shell-to-gun weight ratio remains the same, since the laws of physics are inflexible, but by distributing that recoil over a longer period of time the apparent recoil on the shooter is reduced. The effect is the same — less kick.

Gauge: Confine your gauge selection to either 20 or 12, unless there are unusual requirements involved. The 410 is not a good choice for the beginner simply because it isn't very effective. A 28 gauge would make more sense, but shells are often more expensive, difficult to find, and the selection of loads is very limited. The 16 gauge? Nothing wrong with it, except that it is a fading number, probably destined for much the same fate as the 28 gauge as a hunting gun.

As to the 12 or 20 choice, your particular needs must prevail. For all around use, go with the 12. Particularly in a gun with three-inch chambers. For most upland game bird gunning, I prefer the 20 gauge.

One more time: the 20 gauge will not kill as far as will the 12, simply because the payloads of shot delivered by the latter is greater and it's delivered more efficiently. That point is not a prime consideration in most instances, since the range at which most game birds are killed (not shot at) is quite modest.

If you have need for a speciality gun such as the 10 gauge, by all means buy one. With the superb shell loadings finally available in this biggie, it offers the ultimate in long-range capability for such game as waterfowl and turkey.

In a pump or auto, there is no need for a barrel length of greater than 26 inches for hunting use, but you may not be able to find one that short in the choke you desire. Do your best. For doubles, select either 26-inch or 28-inch tubes.

Most hunters would be more effective with less choke than they're using. That's always been true, but it's even more so with the vastly more efficient shot shells with which we are now blessed.

It's obviously impossible to pick one choke boring as being best for most gunners, but if I had to try I'd go with improved cylinder.

Never handicap yourself with a full choke unless your needs are specific in that direction, and even then only if your gunning ability is competent to take advantage of such a tight boring.

My personal choke preferences would run something like this: ducks, pheasants, chukars, and Western quail — modified; bobwhite, woodcock, and grouse — cylinder or skeet; doves — improved cylinder. In a double the best all-around choke combination that's generally available in a factory gun is improved cylinder and modified.

Most factory shotguns are now available with interchangeable, screw-in choke tubes, and such a system can be added to any shotgun. It makes for a very versatile gun.

Those are some guidelines to shotgun selection. Use them as just that — guidelines, and adapt my suggestions to your own personal requirements.

May 1980

THE PERFECT DOVE GUN

M ourning doves have made the scene! I can remember the time when popping a cap or two at the elusive gray ghosts was a casual thing. In most communities the number of dedicated dove devotees could be counted on one man's fingers. Organized dove hunts were rare.

Color that era long gone! For years now the number of doves harvested by hunters each year has exceeded that for any other game bird. More doves than pheasants or quail or woodcock or grouse or ducks or geese.

The last figure which I can recall for total kill was in the heady range of 50 million doves for the season, and keep in mind that some few states do not permit the hunting of this bird. When he learned that hunters had killed such a huge number of doves one hunter, who had experienced a particularly frustrating day on a shoot, voiced the sentiments of many of us: "Durned if I see how!"

And it's a fact that the mourning dove can be one of the most difficult of all wingshooting targets. When he turns it on this streamlined bird is fast, erratic and prone to take violent evasion action at the hint of danger. Under the "right" conditions doves can be almost impossible.

Such as the cold winter day when a strong north wind was spitting a trace of rain and sleet, and doves were riding it into the cornfield as if jet propelled. After an hour or so a friend came past my stand, heading out, and delivered the perfect bottom line: "I'm quittin' while I'm still straight! Four boxes of shells and four birds!"

Dove shooting isn't always that difficult, of course, and is more often associated with warm to hot weather and shirt sleeves. When they come loafing in to a feeding field on a warm, windless September afternoon, in fact, doves can be relatively easy targets — until the first shot is fired.

Much of the attractiveness of dove hunting lies in its variety. You can walk them up, take a stand within or around a feeding field, shoot over a water hole, or pass shoot doves traveling to and from feeding area, watering area, rest area or roost.

What shotgun and shotshell combination is best for doves? That very variety of shooting conditions complicates the choice, but an examination of the basic requirements involved will narrow the selection. Let's look at what we have.

First, the target involved is quite small. A dove on the wing or perched on a power line appears rather large, but strip away the feathers — especially the long tail — and there isn't a great deal left. Although the bird measures about a foot in each direction (beak to tip of tail and wingtip to wingtip), it weighs only four or five ounces.

Okay, the target is small; the pattern should be dense.

How about quickness? How important is it that our ideal dove gun should be a quick gun? Well, with due acknowledgment that no good shotgun should be ponderous, not very. A hunter usually sees the dove coming and can be prepared, thus he can place less premium on getting into action with lightning speed than can a man after the explosive ruffed grouse, for instance.

Firepower? Again, not very important. There is nothing wrong with using a pump or auto having the three-shot maximum capacity permitted under federal regulations, and I frequently do, but if the truth be known that third shot at a flock (or single) is usually an exercise in futility. Except under ideal conditions, or when using a retriever, trying to knock down two or three doves from a single flock can lead to many cripples and lost birds.

Recoil can be more of a factor in dove shooting than in most other forms of gunning, for two reasons. First is that it's far from unusual for a hunter to burn several boxes of shells in a very short time on a dove hunt, which is almost unheard of with any other game bird species. And most dove hunting takes place in warm weather, so the hunters are lightly clad, with little or no padding on the shoulder. Some shoulders and upper arms I've seen following dove shoots would put a peacock to shame, resplendent with hues of blue, purple, green and yellow.

One of my favorite woodcock guns is a 20 gauge which weighs just 5 1/4 pounds, and that semi-auto is docile enough and most effective at the now-and-then shots in the thickets of mid-winter. But on a September dove shoot it lost much of its charm after a dozen or so quick shots.

Small, fast, erratic and evasive, the dove is a most challenging wing target. The general estimate is that four shells are fired for each dove killed, which at that conservative figure (I have many times seen 25 to 50 shots fired without effect at a lone dove streaking a field) would mean some 200,000,000 shotshells used to harvest the 40 million plus doves taken annually. Taking all of this into consideration, what can we do in the selection of gun and shell to improve our odds.

On our side is the fact that doves are not very tenacious of life. They're easy to knock down — if you can hit them. They do not, in short, require a lot of killing. What we're looking for in our ideal dove gun is a combination which will place a dense pattern of small shot into the path of this bird.

Gauge: Either the 20 or the 12. The 16-gauge will obviously do the job, and in 1987 Browning breathed new life into "Mr. In-between" by bringing back two shotguns for the gauge: the legendary "Sweet Sixteen" autoloader, and the Citori O&U. The .410 and 28 gauge are delightful to shoot, and can be efficient for the proficient at modest ranges, but neither fits our "ideal" parameter.

Weight: Not less than six pounds in the 20 gauge or seven pounds in the 12 gauge.

Action: Pump, automatic, over-and-under or side-by-side double, whichever makes you the happiest. The slide actions still offer the most gun for the money; nothing touches the two-barrels for pointing and handling qualities; and the gas-operated auto should be considered if you're recoil-shy.

Shotshells: Although there are dove shooters who do well with #6 shot, and even larger, in maximum loads, my vote is for the pattern density delivered by size 7 1/2 or 8 shot. Under all except the most extreme conditions I prefer "light" loads insofar as the powder end of the shell is concerned, but with a relatively heavy shot charge.

Example. The typical 12-gauge field load contains 1 1/8 oz. of shot and a 3 1/4 drams equivalent powder charge. But Federal, Remington and Winchester all have available a 3 1/4 dram 12-gauge load containing 1 1/4 ounces of shot. The extra 1/8 ounce of shot gives a more dense pattern, of course, and that makes it a better dove load.

Ditto for the 20 gauge. A light (2 1/2 drams) load here with 1 ounce of shot is a better dove load than the number with 7/8 ounce.

Why not go to #9 shot, you ask, if greater pattern density is the object. Fair question, and the answer is that #9 shot does make for a very potent dove load, but the efficiency of such light shot decreases rapidly beyond modest ranges. Use #9 shot if you prefer, but keep in mind that the point of diminishing return is reached rather quickly as the distance of the shot increases. That's particularly true under windy conditions.

It's obvious, of course, that we can get a heavier payload of shot, hence greater pattern density, by going to express loads. Some occasions call for doing just that, but they're the exceptions which prove that light loads are right most of the time. The additional recoil from express loads, when fired in numbers during a brief period, reduces the efficiency of most shooters.

Choke: I deliberately separated this item from other physical shotgun considerations, and placed it after the discussion of shotshells, because here is the meat of the whole thing. Memorize it!

The paramount reason for wanting the most shot possible in our dove load is this. It permits us to use a more open boring while still giving sufficient pattern density for clean kills at moderate ranges.

When we spread the pattern by opening the choke we reduce the maximum effective killing range, of course, but few hunters are skillful enough to hit doves at maximum range with any consistency.

Most of us will kill far more birds by virtue of the bigger pattern at close and moderate ranges than we will lose from being unable to scratch one down now and then way out yonder.

The full-choked shotgun is just about the best friend a dove has.

So, if you prefer to be a "conservationist" and save more doves for the rest of us, use a full choke. But if you care to kill more doves with fewer shots, remember that a washtub-size pattern at 25 to 35 yards, where most doves are killed, will compensate for a lot of aim error.

It's obvious that no particular degree of choke is best for all dove hunting situations. A skeet gun, a wide open boring, can be poison over a water hole where the average shot is 20 to 30 yards. Improved cylinder or modified chokes are probably best for most dove hunting conditions. The over-and-under or side-by-side bored IC&M is perhaps the nearest approach to our ideal.

The key point is to use the most open choke compatible with most of the shots in a particular situation, and then to use restraint in passing up shots beyond your effective range. Only you can determine what that effective range is. Do it by testing your shotgun with various shotshell loads on a dove-sized target. (You needn't be a Rembrandt to draw, with a marker pen, a crude silhouette of a dove in the middle of a sheet of newspaper.)

Suppose we have a shotgun with a particular choke, and don't care to open that choke a bit, buy another barrel, or add an adjustable muzzle attachment. We can still open our patterns somewhat by the proper choice of shotshells.

Remington has a "Scatter Load" (3-1 1/8-#8) which has a special wad column. Federal has a new "Special" 12 gauge target load (3-1 1/8-#7 1/2, 8, 9), which has no protective shot sleeve and gives about five percent greater shot dispersion. Winchester has a new International Skeet Load which has no protective shot sleeve, very soft shot (1/2 percent antimony), and a muzzle velocity of 1300 feet per second compared to 1200 fps for the normal skeet load. It is a 1 1/8 ounce load of #9 (2mm) shot, and the powder charge is the equivalent of about 3 1/2 drams. The soft shot, high velocity and omission of the shot sleeve combine to give about 10 percent greater shot dispersion than with a normal, shot-protected skeet load. Most of the offerings which give bigger patterns are available only in 12 gauge, and keep in mind that some of these loadings may have passed from the scene by the time you're reading this. Odds are good, however, that one or more ammo maker will have similar numbers.

There is obviously no one shotgun which is perfect for all hunters in all dove shooting situations, but here's my pick for the one which most nearly approaches it. Perhaps it's not your cup of tea or mine, but for most shooters — men, women and youngsters, under most dove hunting conditions, my vote goes to the gas-operated semi-automatic with a 24-inch barrel bored improved cylinder. Twenty or twelve gauge? Your choice!

September 1975

THE MAG TEN GROWS UP

P intails shake me up! When a flock swings toward my decoys and begins to circle, the whole world is just a better place to live. They are the epitome of the artistry and grace of the waterfowl world.

But, man, can they be contrary! Time and again they'll circle your decoys just out of range, and circle again, and again and again. About a decade and a half ago, however, I got just a bit of revenge. I shook up more than one drake sprig that suddenly found he was circling five or ten yards nearer the blind than he should have been.

What the pintails didn't realize was that my 12-gauge magnum had suddenly become substantially more effective, courtesy of a rather insignificant looking item called a shot protector.

It's the nature of the human beast that we grow accustomed to situations, that we tend to take things for granted after a period of time. "What odor?" is the usual answer from people who live in the vicinity of a paper mill. Whether the aroma is from a paper mill or political shenanigans, our olfactory senses tire easily.

So it is with the vast improvements which have been made in shotshells during the past two decades. We forget what it was like back when, but I was reminded quite vividly recently when running pattern tests with Remington's new 10-gauge magnum shells. In the process it became obvious that the mag 10 has now reached maturity.

The 10-gauge shotgun has suffered declining popularity in the past half century, probably for a number of reasons. Essentially a waterfowl number, the era of progressively more restricted seasons and bag limits on ducks and geese gave little incentive for hunters to buy the big bore. U.S. gun manufacturers virtually gave up the 10-gauge market, with foreign-made doubles soon becoming about the only 10 gauge guns available.

With such a situation it is understandable that the ammunition manufacturers ignored this gauge when the shotshell improvements evolved. Sales of 10 gauge shells didn't warrant making the changes to improved crimps, wads and shot protectors. Now they apparently do, or have prospects of doing, since Remington recently placed on the dealer shelves new 10-gauge and 10-gauge magnum shells incorporating the Power Piston wad and shot cup. What influenced the Bridgeport firm to make the belated improvement? Again, a number of factors, all of which added up to an about-face in interest in the 10 gauge on the part of the hunting public. For the past few years that interest has been increasing, not decreasing.

Improved waterfowl populations, with more liberal seasons and limits, played a part. The nation's goose flocks, in particular, are in especially good condition, and many hunters think of the 10 gauge as a "goose gun." Open seasons on sandhill cranes are now routine in several states, providing hunters with another goose-sized bird which is tough to kill and which is routinely gunned at the longer ranges.

And the third "big bird" on the agenda which is influencing interest in the biggest legal bore is the wild turkey, for which hunting opportunities around the nation have mushroomed in the past few years.

But I would wager that the coup de grace which finally crumpled resistance to improving the 10 gauge shotshells was the introduction two years ago by Ithaca of its "Mag 10." This excellent, gas-operated automatic chambered for the 10 gauge magnum has far exceeded most predictions as to popularity and sales.

Although I had shot a box or two through the Mag-10 early last year at targets — on a trap range, yet, last fall was my first opportunity to hunt with it. More on that later, but in passing I'll say that the gun performed flawlessly. Ten gauge magnum shells are available only with #2 shot, not my favorite duck size, but even so, the combination was moderately impressive on high pintails.

I was shooting Remington's old timey shells back in November, the only kind available at the time, but what I didn't suspect is that I was getting only 54-percent patterns from that 32-inch "full choke" barrel on the Ithaca. The fact is, of course, that I hadn't bothered to pattern the combination before hunting with it. And as we gun writers try to tell you readers, the only way you (and I) can know is to put it on paper.

Last month I did just that with the old and the new shells, and the results are striking.

Shells with no shot protectors: 40 yard patterns averaged 54 percent. Shells with "Power Piston" wad and shot cup: 40 yard patterns averaged 75.5 percent.

If percentages don't grab you, consider that these new 10 gauge magnum shells are putting an average of 38 more big #2 shot into a 30-inch circle at 40 yards than will the old ones. And that's almost a 40-percent improvement in performance.

Comparable improvement for a four-minute miler would be to do his thing in 2:34. For a .400 hitter in baseball it would require lifting his batting average to .560. Reflecting on such comparisons helps keep me from becoming blase about the accomplishments of the ammo manufacturers.

Moving on out to 60 yards the performance improvement of the new over the old 10 gauge magnum shells was equally impressive, or more so. This time there was a 50-percent improvement from the old to the new.

With the old shells: 24-percent patterns at 60 yards.

With the new shells: 36-percent patterns at 60 yards.

The 10-gauge magnum is loaded with 2 oz. of #2 shot, with the average shell having 180 pellets. Thus the old shells placed 43 #2 shot in a 30-inch circle out at 60 yards, while the new ones with "Power Piston" shot protectors placed 65 pellets in that same circle. In terms of killing efficiency the vast improvement is obvious.

At 40 yards: 97 pellets in the 30-inch circle without the shot protector; 136 pellets with the shot protector.

As I mentioned earlier, this whole exercise reminded me of the improvements which we have enjoyed in the other gauges for the past 15 years or so, and which we now tend to take for granted. The value of a shot protector in "tightening" patterns, in fact, increases as the bore diameter decreases, since a greater percentage of the shot charge is in contact with the barrel with the smaller gauges.

All shotgun patterns become progressively less dense away from the center, with this concentration of shot in the middle accentuated in full-choked barrels. With that in mind it's interesting to examine 20-inch patterns as well as the 30-inch patterns.

The 20-inch inner core patterns in our tests averaged, at 40 yards, 30 percent for the old shells and 50 percent for the new ones, for a 64-percent improvement. At 60 yards the figures were 12 percent for the old shells and 20 percent for the new, an improvement of 59 percent.

Always keep in mind that shotgun patterns are imprecise. They vary, sometimes substantially, from shot to shot with the same gun-shotshell combination. In these tests we fired 10 patterns at each range with both old and new shells, and an examination of the variations is revealing.

Looking at the 30-inch patterns at 40 yards, we see that the old-style, no-shot-protector shells varied from a low of 36 percent to a high of 66 percent, a tremendous differential. Even with the "Power Piston" wads the variation within the ten-shot string was from 62 to 84 percent.

But averages are the best we have to work from, and, despite the obvious variations from shot to shot, the message which cuts through the chaff is the great improvement in 10-gauge magnum performance brought about by these new shells.

Remington's new 10-gauge magnum shell has a plastic hull which contains the powder, the "Power Piston" wad, and 2 ounces of #2 shot. The wad is too short to hold the entire shot charge, since this same wad is used in the shorter 10-gauge ammo. Remington's Neil Oldridge says this has negligible effect on patterns. The shell has the top wad and roll crimp of the old shells.

The 10 gauge magnum shells is listed as a "3 1/2 inch" shell, which is about right in the fired hull configuration, although the loaded shell is a shade less than 3 1/4 inches long. The "three-inch" 12 and 20 gauge shells, by the same token, are actually just a bit over 2 1/2 inches long before being fired.

Even with the major improvement in performance which we've outlined, it's apparent that some additional gains are still possible by going to the modern crimp, which eliminates the top wad, and by using a shot protector which protects the entire shot string from possible deformation. I see no reason why it should not be possible, too, to add another 1/8 or even 1/4 ounce of shot.

Remember that a full 1/4 ounce of additional shot was added to the standard express load 12 gauge when the ammo companies brought forth the baby magnum.

Remember, too, that the 10-gauge magnum is a specialty item, and that the ammunition manufacturers must carefully evaluate the costs of improvements in a number which has such relatively low sales. Accountability to stock holders does play a role.

But I'm going to guess that additional improvements to this biggie are in the cards in the next year or two, and that Remington will also see fit to offer this shotshell with #4 shot. And it wouldn't surprise me to see Remington and/or Winchester offer the 10 mag incorporating the granulated polyethylene powder into the shot column as in the superb Winchester Super-X Double X 12 gauge magnums.

I'll make no attempt to compare effectiveness of the 10 gauge magnum with smaller gauges, except to say that it has the same potential advantage vis-a-vis the 12 gauge as the 12 does to the 16 gauge. With one proviso: that the shooter has the ability to take advantage of the potential.

It is interesting to note that, when I was gunning ducks with the old style 10 gauge magnum shells giving only a 54-percent pattern, I still had more shot in the pattern than would have been true with a 75-percent pattern in a standard express load 12 gauge. It should also be pointed out that the present 10-gauge magnum load with

2 ounces of shot contains only 11 more #2 pellets than does the 12-gauge three-inch magnum shotshell with 1 7/8 ounces of shot.

Some 10 gauge magnum buffs, let me say, have evolved excellent handloads giving patterns in the 90-percent range, using shot protector sleeves and a buffering agent. They have also worked up loads with 2 1/8 and 2 1/4 ounces of shot.

If present plans aren't changed, steel shot will be required for waterfowl in selected areas of the Atlantic Flyway this fall, progressing in the same "hot spot" fashion to the Mississippi in 1977 and to the remainder of the nation the following year. Since ammo manufacturers have been unable to cram more than 1 1/8 oz. of steel shot into a conventional 2 3/4 inch 12-gauge hull, it's understandable that some waterfowlers — especially goose hunters — have been casting eyes at that big 10 gauge case.

I doubt that factory loads of 10 gauge magnum with steel shot are in the picture for the foreseeable future, although such a shell with #1 shot could well be the very best possible in a non-toxic load for big geese. The cost of these big shells with lead shot is very high, and with steel, even higher! But odds are good that 12-gauge three-inch mags will be on the steel shot agenda before serious consideration is given to steel 10's.

Handloaders will undoubtedly experiment with steel in the 10 magnums, despite the fact that I know of no current source of steel shot for reloaders. Extreme caution is advised when reloading with steel shot, since this is a whole new ball game. Many of the rules applicable to lead shot just don't hold true with steel.

The magnum 10 gauge isn't a 100-yard goose gun, as has been bandied about. It's a whale of a good 60-yard goose gun, and — especially with #4 shot — could be a super 60-yard gun for big ducks.

I'm not prepared to guess at how far beyond 60 yards this combination will kill a goose, crane or turkey. One reason is that I cringe a bit when considering the stats on a 70 yard goose moving 50 mph at right angles to the gunner, the key of which calls for a lead of about 24 feet. The shot will drop two to three feet at that distance, and a modest 14 mph wind can cause shot drift of another 2 1/2 feet at that 70 yards.

But then there are those times when a flock of Canadas or sandhill cranes will hang up there high, high above the decoys, almost motionless. And not much lead is required on a turkey gobbler walking in toward the call.

The Ithaca "Mag 10" is in a class by itself when it comes to shotguns readily available today for the 10-gauge magnum. It is beautifully made, and the design is so good that handling qualities are excellent despite the 11 1/2 pounds it weighs.

The gas-operated recoil system tames the recoil in a fashion which must be experienced to be believed. The effect on the shooter is comparable to a 12-gauge magnum in a double or over-and-under. It performed flawlessly with plastic hulls, although I understand that feeding and ejection problems occur with paper hulls.

Stock and fore-end are semi-fancy (and better) American walnut with very good hand checkering. One model only: 32-inch ventilated, full-choke barrel. With the excellent Pachmayr recoil pad, which is standard, the suggested price is about $500.

This "Mag-10" is really Ithaca's re-entry into the 10-gauge magnum field. More than 40 years ago, when Western Cartridge Company developed the 3 1/2-inch magnum from the standard 10 gauge shotshell, Ithaca began chambering a beefed up N.I.D. (New Ithaca Double) model for it, and continued to manufacture them until 1942.

Marlin now offers its bolt action "Super Goose Gun" in the 10 gauge magnum for about $150. This three-shot repeater has a 34-inch, full-choke barrel.

Other than these, the only 10's available to my knowledge are a few imported numbers in side-by-side doubles, single barrels, and at least one over-and-under.

July 1976

[Addendum: Since 1976, when this was written, the 10-gauge magnum has indeed come of age. Now most of the ammunition companies offer mag 10 ammo which is state of the art, replete with all of the goodies which make modern ammo superb. Steel shot in the mag ten is also available from most companies, and both lead and steel come in a wide array of shot sizes in this biggest of the shotshell ammunition.

Ithaca gun company closed its doors in 1986, but before doing so it had offered its fine MAG-10 in a number of models in response to growing popularity. Now Remington has bought some of the assets of the firm, including the MAG-10. My latest report is that Remington will offer an autoloader in the 10-gauge magnum gauge for the 1988 season, although it may not be an exact replica for the Ithaca MAG-10. *June 1987]*

BROWNING B-80 IN BOTSWANA

The mores of American shotgunners over the past century or so have reflected definitive preferences, and changes, in the scatterguns most hunters prefer. Skipping lightly over the single barrels, both muzzle loaders and breech loaders, we find that the side-by-side double was the shotgun for decades. In addition to the lofty niches occupied by those superbly crafted English side-by's of that era, the gun racks of the bird-shooting aficionados came to be dominated by the Parker, the Fox Sterlingworth, the Ithaca, the L.C. Smith and the LaFever.

Intruding into this near-monopoly crept the slide action, the pump, affectionately known as the corn sheller. Winchester was dominate, first with the venerable Model 97 with its classic exposed hammer, and then with the superb Model 12 which even today commands a premium price beyond reason. On trap field and hunting field, the "shuck-shuck" sound of pumps was ever-present.

Enter the autoloader, the semi-automatic, the gun designed by John Browning around the turn of the century, and the first to bear the Browning name. Controversial to the extreme, decried by many as the instrument which would eradicate game populations, the autoloader was slow in catching the fancy of the public. But it did, and the Browning Automatic became the most popular shotgun in America. Then Remington came along with its Model 1100, a streamlined, soft-recoiling, gas-operated gun which continues to dominate the marketplace.

Success stimulates imitation, and in the past decade a veritable rash of gas-operated semi-auto's have appeared. Most of them are quite good, but I recently put a relative newcomer through a field test which can only be described as super-rigorous, and this Browning B-80 performed superbly.

In September of 1982 I spent a week bird shooting in the Lake Ngami area of northwest Botswana, and as a shotgun battery for the safari I took along a B-80 with 26-inch I.C. barrel, and an old favorite Winchester Model 101 with tubes. Both in 12 gauge. The M101 was used almost exclusively by another member of the party, whose own guns failed to arrive, and gave a customary fine performance.

Before leaving for Africa, I test fired the new B-80 with a mixture of ammo — light and heavy hunting loads, magnum steel shot load, and trap and skeet loads. It digested all, in any combination, without a hiccup.

In Botswana, the four members of our hunting party, plus both professional hunters, combined to give the B-80 a workout. In all, we fired more than 1,000 rounds through it in the week of shooting. The shells we used were manufactured in South Africa and in Czechoslovakia, and included both light and heavy hunting loads, international trap loads and international skeet loads.

Gas-operated automatics have a reputation for being finicky about being kept clean. As the story goes, and it's largely true, an automatic will malfunction unless you keep the gas ejection system clean. The B-80 performed flawlessly during our first few days of shooting, despite the fact that I had not cleaned it at all. With that in mind, I decided to give the shotgun the full treatment — no cleaning at all until necessary. That point never came. The gun operated as beautifully at the end of the week, without cleaning, as it did at the beginning. During the entire week of shooting there was only one "failure to feed," possibly caused by a faulty shell, or to sand and dust in the action.

Making the record all the more remarkable is the fact that we were shooting under some of the "dirtiest" conditions I've ever encountered. Botswana was suffering from an extreme drought, with four inches of rainfall in the previous year rather than the normal 14. Dust and dirt were the names of the game.

I would characterize the B-80 as a semi-humpback auto, perhaps midway between the abruptly-shouldered Browning Auto-5 and the streamlined Remington Model 1100. The wood in my sample is better than average, and the gun has the overall quality look of a Browning. Checkering is quite good.

One of the prime advantages of the "gas gun" is the ease of recoil compared to recoil-operated autos of the same gauge and weight. My B-80 was as pleasant to shoot as any I've ever handled, even when firing several hundred rounds of express loads at a sitting. All who used it had the same impression.

The Browning B-80 is manufactured in Portugal for Browning by FN HERSTAL, and the barrel carries a "Patent PB Italy" patent number. It is essentially the same shotgun — inside — as the Beretta A-302, and uses the proven Beretta gas system.

All gas-operated automatic shotguns are basically similar in that a measured amount of gas is bled downward from the barrel into the cylinder below. With a system of ports, baffles and pistons, that gas is directed rearward to operate the mechanism which ejects the fired empty and loads a fresh shell into the chamber.

Browning introduced the B-80 in 1981, only in 12 gauge, but last year added a 20 gauge and a Superlight 12 to the line-up. Both gauges are also available in the Buck Special configuration, which has rifle sights and is bored for use with rifled slug or buckshot. All of the B-80's, with the lone exception of the Superlight, are offered with either standard length or three-inch chambers.

Barrels are interchangeable by the owner, with no fitting required. Simply by swapping barrels you can switch from standard to three-inch magnum capability. The gas ports on the magnum barrel are different from those on the standard barrels, and standard-length shells used in a magnum may or may not cycle the action (short magnums will).

As for the physical dimensions, the standard B-80 I used in Botswana weighs 7 pounds 12 ounces. Stock dimensions on all versions are the same: 14 1/4 inch length of pull; 1 5/8 inch drop at the comb; and 2 1/2 inch drop at the heel.

Weights of the other models range up to a shade over eight pounds for the three-inch Magnum version of the 12 gauge with a 32-inch barrel (also available with either 28- or 30-inch barrels). In the other direction, the 12 gauge Superlight weighs only 7 pounds, courtesy of an alloy receiver instead of the all-steel receiver on all other models. The 20 gauge is a true, scaled-down little brother of the 12, and with the 26-inch barrel tips the scales at a delightful 6 1/2 pounds.

Browning says there should be no problem with this gun for those who use steel shot. The barrels are drilled and bored from Nickel-Chromium-Molybdenum bars, and are chrome plated internally.

Shotguns either have or don't have a somewhat indefinable quality which gunners call "life". Those which have it come alive when they're brought to the shoulder, while the ones which don't just lie there. This Browning B-80 has it. Suggested retail price is $529.95.

For more information about the B-80, drop a note to: Browning, Route One, Morgan, Utah 84050.

February 1983

Section Three

RIFLES

A GUN FOR DEER

"Johnny wants a deer rifle and I promised him one for Christmas. I've never hunted deer and have no idea what to buy."

Deja vue. I get letters and phone calls. But I just wrote that column, discussing why such questions arise more frequently now than was the case when I was young (there are deer *everywhere* now; there weren't back then), why you don't need a cannon to kill a buck (most of 'em really aren't all that big), and why early emphasis should be placed on safety.

Well, not "just wrote it," exactly, since that last column on choosing a deer gun was published more than eight years ago. The 12-year-old who can legally hunt big game for the first time this year was only four years old at that time. Not only was he not too interested in reading *Sports Afield* back then, but his non-big game hunting Dad probably skipped that column, too.

One consequence of the dramatic increase in deer numbers from coast to coast is that huge numbers of hunters are systematically confronted with a decision: what gun shall I get for deer hunting. Many are youngsters just entering the age at which, legally or physically, they can hunt big game. Others may have hunted for years, but not for deer. Still others: non-hunting adults who have decided that they've been missing out on a good thing.

Depending upon where you hunt, some of the "deer gun" decisions have been made for you. In Pennsylvania, one of the top deer states in the nation, you cannot use a semi-automatic rifle. In other states or portions of states, you can't use a rifle at all.

Selecting a deer rifle can be especially confusing for those without any exposure to center-fire calibers. The array of options is bewildering. Any gun catalog offers a smorgasbord of possibilities: a variety of actions and calibers, of bullet weights and barrel lengths, of iron sights and scopes. Sorting it all out isn't easy without competent advice.

Ah, competent advice. In the days of yore, before the advent of chain discount houses that frequently sell guns at below *dealer* cost, and of the thousands of "gun dealers" whose only inventory is an FFL and a mailing address, there were places where competent advice about buying a gun was readily available. They were called gun stores, may they rest in peace.

There still *are* great gun stores sprinkled around the country, establishments staffed by clerks and managers and gunsmiths who do know guns and hunting and who are competent to advise customers, but they are few and dwindling in number. The money-takers in most chain discount stores seldom know much about the guns or the ammo they sell. Some of the FFL-maildrop dealers, to be fair, are avid shooters, but in many instances their expertise is limited to a very narrow brand of gunning.

Caliber: This is where selection of a rifle begins. Back in 1979 I lumped deer calibers into two practical categories: short range and long range. That's still useful. As short range numbers consider the .30-30, the .30 Remington, .30-40 Krag, .35 Remington, .444 Marlin, .44 Rem Mag, .375 Winchester, and the .45-70. Long range, those with consistent deer taking capability beyond 150 yards; almost all other calibers, including the good oldies such as the .250-3000, .300 Savage and .257 Roberts.

Two new calibers are now available in the long range class which weren't around eight years ago: the .307 Win, developed for the beefed-up, "Angle-Eject" Model 94 lever action; and the 7mm-08 Rem, a 7mm based on the 7.62 NATO case. Another very good oldie, this time a short range caliber, got a shot of new life this year when Browning re-introduced the Model 71 lever action in the .348 Win caliber.

Unless there is a compelling reason to buy one of the short-range calibers, and an addiction to the .30-30 in a lever action is an excellent example with which I identify, buy one from the long-range group. They will obviously anchor deer at eyeball distance even better than they do beyond 150 yards.

For virtually all beginning deer hunters the choice of caliber should be on the conservative side. Choose one of these five: .243 Win, 6mm Rem, .25-06 Win, 7mm-08 Rem, or .30-30 Winchester, but this latter only where shots will be limited to 150 yards.

There are many other calibers in this same power range, such as the .250-3000, .257 Roberts, 7X57mm, .300 Savage, and .307 Win, but if you're buying a new gun you should choose a caliber that is alive and well, one that figures to be around for many decades. It's arguable that the 7X57 has been with us forever, but don't count on your corner grocer to stock that ammo. Nor that for the others listed here. And the .307 Win, a good caliber which I've used on deer with pleasure and success, is unlikely to ever become a household word, more's the pity for lever action fans.

For the deer hunter who is a more experienced *shooter*, who can handle a bit more recoil, add these four to our initial five: .270 Win, .280 Rem, .308 Win, and .30-06. The .30-06, it should be emphasized, deserves its reputation as one of the best, most effective all-around big game calibers ever developed.

My choice of them all for any beginner: .243 Win or 6mm Rem.

Shotguns: If you use rifled slugs, the most important consideration facing you in selecting a shotgun is that it must have good sights...or you must add them. Decent accuracy isn't possible with "shotgun type" beads. Fortunately, most manufacturers now offer slug barrels equipped with rifle sights, which is a giant step ahead in slug shooting efficiency. As with rifles, a scope is even better.

Rifled slug barrels are also available that will usually give even better accuracy than factory smoothbore barrels.

Whether a shotgun will be used with rifled slugs or with buckshot, it's imperative that you experiment with a variety of shell brands and loadings, and with various choke tubes if the gun is so equipped. Only this will reveal which combination performs best in your shotgun.

As for gauge, select the 12 gauge unless there are concrete reasons not to do so. In any event, nothing smaller than 20 gauge should be considered, and that only for very modest ranges with either buckshot or slug. The 10-gauge magnum, obviously, carries a much heavier payload of buckshot for those who can handle the weight and recoil.

Action: Any action is "right" for deer hunting — in some places in some hands. Good rifles are available in lever, bolt, semi-auto, slide action and single shot; shotguns, in semi-auto, slide action, single shot and doubles. Although I don't usually recommend a semi-auto for beginners, I hedge just a bit. A gas-operated autoloader is less punishing in recoil, making it particularly attractive to small people: youngsters and ladies. A practical safety solution is to use it *as a single shot* until the novice is more experienced.

So, understanding that vacillation, don't buy a semi-auto for a *beginner*, but don't hesitate to pick any of the other actions. And, for those who are experienced shooters, the semi-auto may be perfect.

My choice for a beginner: rifle — a lightweight bolt action, or a lever action; shotgun — a slide action, or an autoloader used as a single shot.

A double barrel shotgun isn't a good choice for shooting rifled slugs, since few of them will shoot to the same point of aim with each barrel.

Sights: The open sights on most factory rifles aren't bad, and the bead sight on a shotgun is adequate for wingshooting, but they suffer terribly when compared to either aperture (peep) sights or to scope sights for rifle or rifled slug accuracy.

Aperture sights are very efficient if they are of hunting design (a big aperture, primarily), are properly installed (quite near the eye when in shooting position), and if the user practices sufficiently to become comfortable with them. But, for most deer hunters, a telescopic sight is the best. Contrary to some beliefs, it is fast and easy to use.

My choice for the beginner as sighting equipment for either rifle or rifled slugs: a fixed power scope of not more than 4X power.

November 1987

GUNS FOR BLACK BEAR

My five-foot, two-inch wife isn't what you would call the "scary" type. For many years she has followed (led?) me around the world in pursuit of whatever we seek, shooting her share of game, catching a disproportionate share of fish, and taking a batch of photographs. She doesn't like snakes, but in that she has much company. She isn't too fond of alligators, despite the fact that she took — at snapping distance — the photo of the big gator which graced the July *Sports Afield* cover.

But when the two of us are roaming the woods alone together, and I feel that two's a crowd, all I have to do is whisper "bear." She's gone! It's not that she doesn't like bears; it's simply that she is afraid of them. Afraid, hell, she is scared to death, as the saying goes, of bruin!

As is true for most hunters, I don't get too shook up about these critters. I'm considerate of grizzlies, but black bears? Naw. But, the funny part is, Mary's right; we're wrong.

Those comical black bears roaming the campsites of our nation's parks contributed greatly to the public's perception of them being relatively harmless. How could such a lovable creature, standing on his hind legs begging for a handout, be dangerous! Easy, that's how. There is probably no animal its size that is stronger than the black bear. It can break the neck of a full grown cow with one swipe of the paw, which means that to duplicate the feat with a puny, 200-pound man would require merely a wave of that wand.

Black bear in the wild are normally shy, fleeing at any presence of man, but there are times. While I was in Alaska a few years ago a geologist landed on a remote lake, taxied his float plane to shore, and walked a hundred yards or so to make an observation. He and his wife saw, and ignored, a black bear feeding on the hillside nearby. The bear attacked and mauled the man, who escaped only by running back into the lake, where he was picked up by his wife who had stayed in the plane.

Another incident which happened in Alaska during the same time frame had an uglier ending. A black bear killed and partially ate a solitary hiker. These creatures are omnivorous, will eat almost anything, and love freshly-killed meat.

Some two years ago a party of Arizona hunters were camped up in the Rim country, and had stashed away in their vehicle all food and remnants of the evening meal before going to bed. Despite those precautions, a black bear entered the tent in the middle of the night, grabbed one of the men and began to drag him away. Awakened by the screams, another hunter shot the bear several times with his handgun, forcing it to drop the man and flee. The medium-sized bear was found later not far away, and the man survived with a severely mauled and bitten arm.

The odds against an outdoorsman being attacked by bear are huge, but the above incidents are related to emphasize that selecting a gun to use in hunting black bear has an ingredient which is missing in the selection of a deer rifle. Bucks don't bite; bears do!

Black bear in the wild aren't all that big, despite the impression millions of people got from Gentle Ben of TV series fame. Neither are they that docile and cuddly, again those presumed qualities fostered upon the public by the writers of that series, and by such "humanizations" as Yogi Bear and Smoky Bear.

The size of the animal in question is a significant consideration when it comes to selecting a gun to use in the hunt, which makes it appropriate that we look realistically at the vital statistics of the black bear. They are just about what an NFL scout would have in mind for the perfect pulling guard. Not very tall — a maximum of about 36 inches high at the shoulder, down to some 30 inches and even 27 inches for more normal adults. From nose to tail — 50 to 65 inches, with now and then a rare "six footer" measured horizontally. Weighing in at 200 to 400 pounds, the black bear has a very low center of gravity. Very fast, and very, very maneuverable. Sign him up.

There are bigger black bruins, and I think the record is something more than 700 pounds. Two very big blacks, 500 to 600 pounds or so, were taken in Arkansas a few years ago, which only means that some exceptions are still out there.

Any gun that will kill a deer will kill a black bear — most of the time, under good conditions. In shooting a bear at a bait, or one which has been treed or bayed with dogs, I would have no hesitation in using any such "deer" rifle, or a shotgun/rifled slug combination at the appropriate short range. That would include two of my favorite light deer calibers — the 6mm Remington and .243 Winchester; and, of course, anything with more punch.

The key to using such modest rounds is proper bullet placement, which is relatively easy to accomplish under baiting or baying conditions. But not always possible, which is why I would recommend something more powerful when selecting a gun specifically for black bear. It makes sense to use a gun which will properly kill under less than ideal conditions, both from humane and success standpoints.

There are occasions when a more powerful rifle might protect the hunter himself from injury, or even death, at the hands of a black bear. It should be emphasized, however, that most such injuries — and they are rather numerous — happen to non-hunters, to campers, hikers, bird watchers, and to just plain tourists in parks of various kinds. Hunters are more aware of what might happen, and are more careful.

The methods used in bear hunting vary greatly from state to state, and among the Canadian provinces. In some areas hunters may take bear while hunting other species, but in others there are specific bear seasons — fall, spring or both. The legality of dogs and baiting follows the same mishmash pattern from area to area, legal here and illegal there.

If you hunt deer with a legal firearm, no matter where you live, you need not make a change when you get an opportunity at black bear. With one exception: buckshot. That is illegal in most states (perhaps all), and isn't practical anywhere. Not only is your deer rifle adequate for bear, but it is likely to be very good for the area you're hunting. The lever-action .30-30 which is a favorite deer gun for woods hunting in much of the eastern half of the country is a very decent black bear choice for that same kind of habitat.

The .30-06 autoloader, another very popular deer rifle combination, is even better for black bear (the autoloader is illegal in Pennsylvania). The scope-sighted bolt actions which most western hunters use for deer, on the other hand, are perfect for bear, particularly well-suited for cross-canyon opportunities which are frequent. Under such long range conditions, of course, that .30-30 would be out of place.

Let's consider choosing a rifle as a black bear gun, and it should be a rifle, not a shotgun. I would select a caliber in the .270 Winchester, .280 Remington, .308 Winchester or .30-06 range, all of which are modest in recoil, and which will cleanly kill bear under just about any conditions. For all of these there is a wide array of excellent bullets available for reloading, and an adequate variety of factory loadings.

Choose a bullet weighing from 130 grains to 180 grains. It should be strongly constructed, despite the fact that the black bear is relatively "thin skinned" as big game animals go.

As for the rifle action, select one appropriate to the area you hunt and the technique you use. One or all of the above calibers, and similar ones, are available in lever action, pump, autoloader, single shot and bolt action.

Magnums? Obviously more than adequate. On a sheep hunt several years ago I shot a black bear with a 7mm Rem Mag, the caliber I had chosen because of the possibility of unpleasant encounter with a grizzly. It was a short-range shot under ideal conditions, and just about any caliber would have done the job. On another hunt, this time for brown bear, I shot a big black bear with the .375 H&H I was carrying. Enough gun, needless to say. For black bear you don't need a magnum, but if you have one and shoot it well, why not.

Handguns are adequate for black bear, provided the caliber is proper and the hunter competent. This is particularly true for such "controlled" conditions as hunting with hounds, and in shooting over bait. The .41 Magnum and .44 Magnum are good choices, as is the .357 Maximum. Nothing smaller should be used, and there are even more potent numbers which do a better job, provided the shooter can handle them.

The black bear is an interesting animal with a secure niche in American history. Once extremely abundant in many parts of its range (some 3600 were killed by one Louisiana man, according to research done by federal game agent Dave Hall), it has bounced back in many states under more aggressive game management. One of the management tactics was restocking, which has led to some bizarre events.

Several states got their bear for restocking from Minnesota, most coming from "garbage pit" populations, and Louisiana released a batch of these in the Atchafalaya Basin. Homesick, many of them began a trek back north, with interesting results. One wandered into the middle of my hometown, 150 miles north of the release site. Others showed up in Mississippi, and a few misguided bruins went west into Texas, more than 100 miles away. But a sizable number of the replants took, and hunting seasons have been held for the past 10 years.

Habits die hard. When fall came the transplants which stayed began to hibernate on their old Minnesota time clock, despite Louisiana temperatures in the seventies.

Trapping of black bear is still permitted in some of the Canadian provinces, and it hasn't been very long since there was a bounty on them in Nova Scotia, where they were classed as vermin until 1969. Timber growers in the northwest deplore tree damage by bears, as do beekeepers in many parts of the range. Despite such problems, the black bear is a fine game animal, with future hunting opportunities limited only by the preservation of suitable habitat.

September 1984

THE ALPHA CUSTOM RIFLE

I n 1979 I reported in this column the pending birth of a new center-fire rifle. In due course — the fall of 1982 — the Alpha I finally made its appearance on dealer shelves, and the trim, quick big-game and varmint bolt action soon garnered a modest following. It weighed 6 1/4 pounds or less, shot well, and was not expensive.

In 1984 I began enjoying a second generation "Alpha," the Alpha Custom. As the name indicates, this is an upscale version of that first offering, which was intended to be and was a plain Jane, inexpensive rifle which would be a joy to tote and effective to shoot. Since its introduction, interestingly enough, the Custom has far outsold the much less expensive Alpha I which it replaced.

The Custom is a beautiful rifle. Like its predecessor, this one has a walnut stock which is of excellent design, but there the similarity ends. The plain (and lightweight) semi-gloss wood of the Alpha I was replaced with figured California Claro having a hand-rubbed oil finish. From no checkering to very good hand checkering on both forearm and pistol grip. From no fore-end tip to one of black Gaboon ebony. The thin, attractive rubber butt pad is made by Pachmayr for Alpha Arms.

This Alpha rifle, designed by Homer Koon, features a bolt having a very short (60 degree) lift, and very short lock time. The barrel is made by E. R. Shaw, and the trigger group is one designed and manufactured by Alpha Arms. Although the trigger is fully adjustable, instructions recommend that this be done only by a competent gunsmith. My sample, as it came from the factory, had a crisp pull of 2 3/4 pounds.

The magazine box deserves mention. It holds three cartridges and has a solid bottom, but since the safety does not lock the bolt handle, both the magazine and chamber can be emptied with the safety "on." It is the feeding system, however, which is unique, and patented. Cartridge travel is controlled by lips formed into the magazine box instead of by receiver rails.

"Cartridges are fed straight up and pushed into the chamber by the bolt face," explained Jim Hill, Chairman of the Board of Alpha Arms, Inc.. "No loading ramp is necessary. Shoulders in the magazine box hold the cartridges to the rear of the box, preventing bullet point damage from recoil. Then, too, the box is a full three inches inside, so you can seat the bullets out to increase powder capacity."

The safety is a two-position one similar to that on the Remington Model 700 and positioned in the same place, but on the Alpha it is recessed into the wood of the stock to minimize the possibility of moving it to the off position accidentally. In addition to the red indicator spot which is revealed when the safety is off, there is also a red spot which appears just behind the bolt shroud when the bolt is cocked. (In later models the safety was replaced by a three-position "Model 70" type which Alpha makes.)

I like the bluing. It's attractive yet not shiny, and Alpha describes it as "lightly bead blasted and blued to achieve a rust-blued type of finish."

With "better" walnut, you're going to get a bit more weight, but I can live with the Custom I'm shooting. With mount bases (Buehler) installed, my rifle weighed 6 1/2 pounds when it arrived. With a Leupold 1 1/2X-5X scope attached with Buehler rings, and a sling in place, the weight in 7 1/4 pounds. It's in .284 Win caliber, and shoots 1 1/2 inch groups with factory ammo (the sample target which comes with each rifle had a 1 1/8-inch group with Winchester 150-grain Power Point ammo).

My rifle has a 21-inch barrel, as do those in .257 Roberts and .25-284; while the other calibers available — .243 Win, 7mm-08 Rem, and .308 Win — have 20-inch barrels. A hard case is supplied with each rifle. The suggested retail price is $1275.00.

"The feel of wood and the stability of glass," was the way Homer Koon describes yet another version of his latest offspring called the Alpha Grand Slam. "It's a laminated stock made from thin layers of hardwood veneers which are vacuum impregnated with resins under high pressure. It looks good, feels like wood, is quiet where fiberglass is noisy, and weather just doesn't affect it at all."

Other than the stock, the specs for the Grand Slam are the same as for the Alpha Custom. The bolt is fluted to reduce weight, and an optional aluminum floor plate and trigger guard is recommended to save three ounces. The Grand Slam weighs about 6 1/2 pounds, about 8 ounces more than the Custom.

I'm much impressed with the Alpha Custom and it has proven itself in the field. I also hunted with Jim down in Mexico, on Ralph Donaho's "Operation Whitetail," using one of the Grand Slam's in that same .284 Win caliber. Luck was the name of that game, since I brought back a spectacular 5X7 buck with a double drop tine, killing him with one shot from the Grand Slam so far away I won't even write it down. And I like the company's attitude. As Jim Hill put it, "We want total customer satisfaction. If a customer has a problem he can ship his gun to us freight collect, and we'll make any necessary repairs at no cost if it hasn't been altered or misused."

For more information, write: Alpha Arms, Inc., 1000 Spinks Drive, Flower Mound, TX 76051.

More Lightweight Rifles

Lightweight center-fire rifles are having their moment in the sun, and 1984 may go down as the "light" year. Most gun companies now have one or more versions of such bolt actions in their line-up, and the popularity of such rifles is understandable. Most hunters do much more carrying of a rifle than they do shooting it, and some of us are willing to sacrifice some measure of performance to gain greater ease of carrying. As a general rule, most of us can hold a heavier rifle a bit steadier when shooting it, but the difference is slight and might be negated by added fatigue.

Another flyweight I've been shooting with pleasure of late is the Weatherby Vanguard VGL. This one is listed at 6 1/2 pounds, and it's available only in two conventional calibers — .243 Win and .308 Win — no Weatherby calibers. My test gun is in the .30 caliber, and with 2X-7X Weatherby scope in Buehler rings and bases, plus sling, it weighs 7 1/2 pounds.

This Vanguard has a satin, oil finished walnut stock with hand checkering, rubber butt pad, and a streamlined 20-inch barrel. The suggested retail price is a modest $389.00.

Shortly after we wrote about lightweight rifles in our Sept. 1982 issue (the re-introduction of the M70 Featherweight, and the then new Ruger International), Remington unveiled its new Model Seven. I hunted with it in Canada that fall and was much impressed, and I still am. With an 18 1/2-inch barrel, the overall length is only 37 1/2 inches and the weight a delightful 6 1/4 pounds. In .222 Rem, .223 Rem, .243 Win, 6mm Rem, 7mm-08 Rem and .308 Winchester.

Since then: Ruger with a M-77RL ultra light bolt action in both short and long action, about six pounds in a full range of calibers; and U.S. Repeating Arms with a short-action M70 Featherweight, and a new M70 Lightweight (20-inch barrel) at 6 to 6 1/4 pounds.

For more info, write: Weatherby, 2781 Firestone Blvd., South Gate, CA 90280; Sturm Ruger, Lacey Place, Southport, CT 06490; Remington, 1007 Market St., Wilmington, DE 19898; and USRA-Winchester, Box 30-300, New Haven, CT 06511.

February 1985

KENNY JARRETT'S SUPER-ACCURATE RIFLES

"**S**hoots good enough t'kill a deer!"
It's a saying which isn't uncommon where hunters gather, and it's a line which tends to make the hackles rise on the neck of one James Kennedy Jarrett. "If 'good enough' is all they want," he emphasizes, "they don't need one of my rifles."

Kenny Jarrett is understandably biased in the direction of accurate rifles. Within the past five years he has held half a dozen world benchrest records, and half of them still stand. All were shot with a rifle he built.

"How accurate is Kenny and his rifle?" Try a five-shot group measuring just .750 inches. But, you say, that's very good but really not spectacular. You're right, but I neglected to say that the range wasn't 100 yards; it was 300 yards.

His best 100-yard, five-shot group in competition was .320 inches, but he did have a 100-yard sighting-in group, witnessed and signed, which was .150 inches. The one group I shot with Kenny's "world record" rifle (fired in the rain by a rank amateur), was a one-hole .321 inches. In benchrest circles that won't get you a cup of coffee.

All of the above performances were played with a wildcat, benchrest caliber, the 6mm PPC. For some of his records Kenny used a custom 62 1/2-grain Watson bullet at 3300 fps, and for others a custom 68-grain Allie Euber bullet at 3100 fps. Although either load would get a buck's attention, they certainly aren't for big game.

But the .280 Ackley Improved, delivering a 140-grain Nosler Ballistic Tip bullet at 3200 fps plus, definitely is. And can Jarrett build a rifle for such a caliber which will shoot? The last group I saw fired while visiting Kenny's Jackson, South Carolina shop last December measured .240 inches. It was shot by Bob Keen, of Columbia, with his Jarrett rifle in .280 Ack Imp — his deer rifle. With another Jarrett-built rifle in the same caliber, Kenny's assistant recently put three shots into .206 inches. Definitely not shabby. That's a wildcat caliber, true, but other Jarrett rifles in factory calibers shoot as well.

Reports from several of Jarrett's enthusiastic customers, including Bob O'Conner (Greensboro, N.C., who has two Jarrett rifles) and Sport Holland (Barnwell, S. C., who has four), made me curious as to just what makes Kenny run. Specifically, how has he managed to transfer the rifle building techniques which produce one-hole, benchrest accuracy to hunting rifles. After spending five days with him I think I now know.

Fanatical dedication and devotion to detail and principles best describes, perhaps, the Jarrett success at building super accurate rifles. "Good enough" is not in the vocabulary when describing the care which Kenny and his assistant, John Lewis, lavish on each operation when building a rifle. It's either right, or it's wrong. It's either done right — or it isn't done at all.

On his custom hunting rifles Jarrett prefers to use a Remington Model 700 action, a McMillan fiberglass or graphite stock, a Hart stainless steel, custom barrel, and a Shilen trigger. He also uses Schneider and Shilen barrels, and can tune a M700 trigger beautifully.

Kenny also makes extra barrels for his rifles in different, compatible calibers. They can be switched in less than a minute by simply unscrewing one, with a small barrel wrench which Kenny makes, and screwing the other barrel in place. (He admitted that a "pipe wrench" would work, but his expression was a pained one.)

Jarrett believes that the accuracy factors in building a rifle, in no particular order, are: 1. Glass stock ("Don't consider wood."); 2. Proper pillar bedding; 3. Squared-up fit for barrel/receiver threads ("Most factory guns aren't."); 4. Barrel ("No factory barrel can possibly be as accurate as the best custom barrels."); 5. Hand-lapped lugs connecting the bolt and receiver ("Improper fit sets up metal stress which affects accuracy."); and 6. a few special Jarrett techniques which were taught to him in confidence, and which he plans to pass on only to his son Jay, now age nine.

Keep in mind the parameters within which Kenny Jarrett's mind works. "Good enough" just isn't.

As do most benchrest competitors, Jarrett has a fetish about cleaning a rifle, both "how" and "how often." Clean a hunting rifle at least every 15 shots. And very, very carefully...if you hope to maintain the accuracy built into your rifle, especially if it's a Jarrett rifle. Use a bore guide to prevent damage to the chamber throat from the cleaning rod, which should be one-piece, preferably coated, and which itself should be cleaned each time, before being used, to remove any possible grit.

His cleaning procedure: run a patch saturated with solvent through the barrel; next, scrub with a good, brass brush wet with solvent, one round-trip stroke for each shot that's been fired ("Brush must be full size or over-size so it will follow the rifling. After pushing it out the muzzle, rotate it a quarter-turn before pulling it back through. Replace the brass brush often."); use a dry patch for the final cleaning ("Never shoot a wet barrel — wet from rain or solvent — if you can help it."), then swab out the chamber area.

Copper fouling can destroy accuracy. If any is suspected, Kenny pushes a patch soaked with Sweets Solvent through the barrel, lets it soak for 30 to 60 minutes, then cleans it with dry patches. If the patches are still green, he repeats the process.

"Hunters should also remember to shoot one or two fouling shots before hunting," Kenny added, "since the first shot or two from a clean barrel may be fliers."

As part of the TLC accorded each offspring by Kenny and John, they work up loading data for that particular rifle, and along with the new gun furnish the owner a handloading recipe, a target shot with the rifle, and a box of ammo. It is the time-consuming, detail-intensive operations such as this which will probably insure that Jarrett never gets rich at building rifles.

The basic price of a Jarrett hunting rifle is $1400, less $200 if you supply the receiver. As expected with a custom operation, you can get just about anything you're willing to pay for, but the only thing really essential which isn't provided in the package is a scope. Rings and bases are included and installed, and Jarrett keeps in stock Leupold, Kahles, and Schmidt & Bender scopes. You can select barrel contour and rifle weight as you choose. Jarrett prefers heavier barrels and rifles, saying that "lighter isn't more accurate," but one of his .243 Ackley Improved rifles owned by Sport Holland weighs 7 1/4 pounds complete and shoots half-inch groups. Good enough for deer!

The Buckland Gun Shop will do most gunsmithing chores, and for $180 Kenny will dust his accuracy magic over your bolt action rifle. The work includes bedding, crowning ("Hunters are too careless about damaging the crowns."), lapping the locking lugs, and adjusting the trigger.

Kenny's rifles have immigrated to most parts of the nation, including Alaska, but he really has a fan club of good 'ole boys (and girls) in the Carolinas and Georgia who think that a Jarrett Rifle is the best thing since sliced bread. And, although many of the benchrest records in the southeast are held with "Jarretts," most of these guys use their rifles for varmints and big game. Five or six dozen of 'em belong to the Buckland Tackdrivers Club, Kenny's loose-knit shooting group, and they aren't happy when there's more than one big hole on the target after they've shot a group. They kill many deer (no limit in parts of S. C.), and pride themselves on precise bullet placement — at any distance.

The delivery time for a complete Jarrett rifle, at the moment, is only a few months, and that tab is $1400. As the word spreads, however, expect both the wait and the price to escalate, since in the world of shooting that better mousetrap doesn't remain undiscovered very long. Jarrett Custom Rifles, Rt. 1, Cowden Plantation, Jackson, SC 29831. Phone 803-471-3616 or 471-3313.

June 1986

TAKE-DOWN BIG GAME RIFLES

Traveling with a big game rifle is no hassle at all — if you do it by auto. Just slip the gun into a good soft case, or a hard one, if you prefer, and stash it in the trunk. But an increasing number of hunters are making the trek through the friendly skies, and then it does become a bit of a problem.

In the days before skyjacking, even going by air was relatively easy. Back then pilots would place your cased gun in the cockpit, from which you could retrieve it on deplaning. Remember?

Now, when traveling by commercial plane, you must transport your gun in a hard case, since it must be placed in the luggage compartment. Most of them arrive at the destination on time, usually in shootable condition. But, since a long, rigid gun case looks like nothing else but a gun case, sometimes your checked firearm doesn't get there at all. Somebody along the way decides he needs it more than you do.

Shotguns don't present as great a problem for one reason: they can be broken down so they'll fit into a much shorter gun case which doesn't necessarily look like a gun case. Perhaps it encloses tennis rackets, or whatever.

Another beef against the long, hard case is that it is very cumbersome. It doesn't really fit well in revolving doors, hotel elevators, taxis (especially the tiny ones used in most countries of the world, and increasingly abundant in the U.S.), jeeps, small bush planes and the like. For several years I've occasionally detoured around this annoyance by disassembling my rifle for transit: just remove the barrel and action from the stock. That helps. The two pieces can be accommodated in a shorter gun case, and the zeroing isn't usually far off when you put the rifle back together in hunting camp.

A couple of years ago I was discussing this topic with Dick Mellen, who has been associated with the gun industry for many years, and he told me about a rifle he owns that is a better solution. It's a bolt action which Gus Pachmayr converted into a prototype take down several decades ago. He even brought the rifle to the Dallas airport when I had a brief layover there so I could take a look.

Now, all of a sudden, or so it seems, there are two companies making such conversions in this country on a commercial basis, and I recently had each of them chop one of my bolt actions in two. That, in a word, is what the conversions involve.

The Custom Gun Guild, of Doraville, Georgia performed the operation on a Remington Model 700 in .25-06 caliber, scoped with a 2 1/2X-8X Bushnell with Bushnell mounts. In this conversion, as Guild President Frank Wood explained, the receiver is not altered. A receiver bushing made of 4350 monochrome steel is hand fitted to each gun. The barrel threading is altered to interrupted threads, and a separate hanger system is attached to the bottom of the barrel. The hanger system acts as a detent locking system and also supports the forearm. With four interruptions in the threads, the barrel can be removed by rotating it only 1/8 of a turn after the detent button is pushed.

Such an interrupted thread system makes taking the rifle apart and putting it back together quick and easy. It also has the added advantage of making it unnecessary to remove the scope.

When Frank returned my gun he reported that their test groups with the rifle, after the conversion, ran about one inch. I've not been able to do quite that well — but almost. With 100-grain Remington ammo, all of my groups have been under two inches; and, in one 1 3/4-inch five-shot group, four of the shots were into 3/4 of an inch. When I switched to 120-grain Winchester ammo, group sizes were less than 1 1/2 inches, and the point of impact moved only 1/2 inch with that change of bullet weight. I expected more.

Of even more importance than the precise accuracy, to me, was comparing the performance before and after taking the rifle apart and putting it back together. There was no change in accuracy, and the point of impact shift was no more than 1 1/2 inches, and often less. Impressive.

The Custom Gun Guild conversion separates the rifle immediately in front of the receiver. With the 24-inch barrel on my M700, that made the barrel end of the take down 23 inches long; the stock end — 21 inches, or 24 inches with the scope still mounted.

S K GUNS, Inc., of Fargo, N.D., began making take down guns to fulfill a need of the company President, Tom Smith. "While fishing in Canada several years ago," Tom told me, "one of the finest black bears I'd seen in a long time came down and joined us while we were stern-trolling for walleyes. Having no gun along got us to thinking and, after looking at pictures of the old time take down Winchesters, we decided we could do the same thing."

The take down .30-30 lever actions which Tom has been producing have been popular as camp guns, with bush pilots as survival guns for the aircraft, boaters, backpackers and cycling groups. Now he's converting bolt actions as well as lever actions, and the rifle he converted for me is a Winchester Model 70A in .300 Win Mag caliber. It's topped with a 2X-7X Redfield scope in Redfield mounts.

Here's how Tom explained his conversion to me: "The conversion is done by removing the original barrel from the action, carefully marking it in order to maintain the factory headspace. The barrel is then turned down at the threaded end and a half inch thick steel block is pressed over the turned down portion using about 15 tons of pressure. After this block is installed, the barrel is again set up on a lathe and machined so that it fits back against the receiver and comes to the exact headspace as when it left the factory. The block itself is drilled and has adjustment screws mounted in it, so that after the barrel has been removed and reinstalled a number of times, any movement that occurs because of wear can be adjusted."

To take the S K conversion apart, you must first remove the front sling swivel, which allows the forearm to be slid forward about an inch and removed. Then the barrel is unscrewed, which is simple if the rifle has no scope. If there is a scope which extends beyond the receiver, which most do, the scope must be removed before the barrel can be rotated the necessary 360 degrees.

Range tests with the S K Guns conversion showed good to excellent accuracy, before and after takedown and reassembly. Using Federal 150-grain ammo, group sizes averaged less than two inches, and one three-shot group was only 3/4 inch. Again, even more impressive was the fact that the point of impact shifted only one inch before and after, even with scope removal and replacement.

Switching bullet weight, to a 180-grain Winchester loading, continued to give good accuracy, but this time I did get a change in point of impact of about five inches. This isn't unusual, of course, with any rifle.

The amazing thing about Tom's conversion is the price — about $125 to do the job on your Marlin or Winchester lever action, $140 for a Savage M99, and $150 for a Browning BLR. The tab to convert your Winchester M70 is only $125, and for a Remington M700, M788, or M7 is $140. Quite a value.

"We've been rather careful of the options we offer on these guns," Tom said, "simply because we've attempted to maintain a price that is affordable to the average hunter."

Another advantage of these take down rifles is that extra barrels in different calibers can be used with the same receiver and scope.

Both S K Guns and Custom Gun Guild will furnish such additional barrels and forearms.

Frank Wood, at Custom Gun Guild, will either convert your own bolt action to take down for $550, or sell you a complete gun which has been converted. An extra barrel assembly in a different caliber costs $550, and Frank will guarantee both to shoot to the same point of impact — IF you specify what loads you will be using. His conversion involves much handwork to make sure the rifle is an accurate one before as well as after the conversion, and the Gun Guild is able to do just about any custom work you might desire.

[Frank's take downs no longer use the detent button. Instead, there is a new ball locking system, and you simply twist the forearm and barrel to make it release. He says it gives even better accuracy than before.

His newest rifle offering is either a Remington M700 or M7 with a fiberglass stock, which in the take down version lists for $975. With an extra barrel in another caliber — $1449; with two extra barrels — $1923.]

For more information on these take down rifles, write: Thomas T. Smith, Pres., S K GUNS, Inc., 1001 23rd St. South, Fargo, N.D. 58103, or Frank S. Wood, Pres., Custom Gun Guild, 5091-F Buford Hwy., Doraville, GA 30340.

December 1984

THE BLASER "ULTIMATE" RIFLE

After years of attending trade shows and firearms seminars, seeking out the latest developments, the "new" often seems to run together. That's particularly true when it comes to center-fire, bolt-action rifles. A stock design change here, a new finish there, a new caliber! A bolt-action rifle is a bolt-action rifle, right? And, if the truth be known, the state of the art of such rifle making in this country has reached an extremely high plateau. There are many excellent bolt actions available which perform beautifully, so why fix something that isn't broken. Right?

Early in 1985, at a trade show, I listened to an intense, intelligent man named Gerhard Blenk tell me about a new bolt action rifle which *is* very different. And each difference is for a reason. In due time a sample arrived from West Germany, where Gerhard is owner of BLASER-Jagdwaffenfabrik, which makes the rifle. It is called the "ULTIMATE."

What's new about the "ULTIMATE?" First, it can be taken apart in take-down fashion in seconds, in nearly equal "halves" about two feet long. It can be transformed from one caliber to another, even from a standard caliber to a magnum or vice versa, in minutes, simply by changing the barrel and/or bolt head. The "safety" actually cocks and uncocks the bolt. The bolt locks directly into the barrel. The action is a very short one, about three inches shorter than that of most bolt-action rifles. The barrel is completely free-floating.

Since the receiver is made of aluminum, the rifle is light in weight. The solid steel bolt face, locked into the barrel itself, gives the strength. With a 4X scope in place, my sample in .270 Win caliber weighs 7 1/4 pounds, unloaded. With the interchangeable .375 H&H Magnum barrel and bolt which came with it, it weighs very little more.

"The bolt and the barrel, both made of high tempered steel, lock together," Gerhard Blenk explained to me, "and they cope with the gas pressures. Everything else on the rifle we just design to cope with recoil forces, which is why the rifle can be very light in weight."

The rifle was designed by the Blaser design team. In addition to the two basics — the simple takedown and the interchangeable caliber features — they have incorporated other very innovative features.

The safety system is unique. The "hammer" on the "ULTIMATE" isn't a hammer at all. It's a safety lever with which the rifle is cocked, by pushing the lever forward until it engages. When the lever is in the rear position the rifle is completely safe, making it practical to hunt with a live cartridge in the chamber itself. After the first shot is fired, the lever remains forward, the bolt being cocked when it is operated to eject the fired case and load a fresh cartridge.

The safety lever can be returned to the rear (safe and uncocked) position by simply depressing a button on the right side of the bolt assembly. Just forward of that button is a rocker switch with which you can manually lock the bolt to prevent it being lifted accidentally while hunting. It is unlocked automatically by recoil from the first shot.

The bolt handle is of the flat design, preferred by most Europeans, which tends to grow on you with use. The bolt has a very short 55-degree lift. The handle is positioned farther forward than is true on most rifles, making for a slightly longer "reach" to operate the action.

The excellent trigger can be used as a normal trigger or as a set trigger. The "normal" mode is not adjustable, and mine came from the factory at a crisp 40 ounces. The "set trigger" mode is easily adjustable with a small Allen wrench, and my sample was at eight ounces when it arrived. The trigger is "set" by pushing it forward.

Each "ULTIMATE" barrel is machined with integral scope mount bases, the front base of the typical pivot design, and the rear a pair of grooves cut into the barrel. Blaser makes QD rings which fit this system. When a particular scope is zeroed for one barrel, it will return to zero when the scope is removed and then replaced.

Left handed? Any of these rifles becomes a left-handed model simply by installation of a left-handed bolt, which is a dream situation for gun dealers. With both port and starboard bolts, standard and magnum bolt heads, a stock and a forearm, and a selection of barrels in various calibers in stock, he can "build" an "ULTIMATE" to a customer's specifications.

The action on this rifle is the smoothest of any I've ever handled, reflecting both good gun design and superb workmanship. The gun is a quality product in every respect, and even my "production" model (the low end, with a suggested retail price of about $1,200 with one barrel) has a very attractive stock with good checkering. Custom models are available in three grades.

This ingenious rifle is short and handy, it's accurate, and I look forward to using it on big game. In a lightweight firearm, of course, recoil is substantial with the heavy calibers, particularly the .375 H&H Magnum.

On the debit side, from a personal standpoint, I think the stock design could be improved a bit for American tastes. A higher comb would place the eye more in line with the scope. The Blaser mount system, a very good one, places the scope higher (two inches above the bore) than I prefer, although Europeans find no fault with this.

The force required to push the safety lever forward to cock the bolt is substantial, and I doubt that most youngsters or women would have thumb strength enough to do it. I find it difficult. And it's virtually impossible if the scope extends back over the lever, which prevents thumb placement at the top of the lever where leverage is greatest. It's necessary to cock the gun in this manner only once on each shooting occasion, of course, since working the bolt cocks it for subsequent shots. I wouldn't be surprised that the Blaser design team improves this on down the line, perhaps with a lever spur similar to those used to facilitate the cocking of hammers on scope-mounted lever-actions and T/C Contenders.

The "ULTIMATE" is available in these calibers: .22-250, .243, .25-06, .270, .308, .30-06, .264 Win Mag, 7mm Rem Mag, .300 Win Mag, .338 Win Mag and .375 H&H Mag. Extra barrels are $331.00 each. A pair of barrels in the calibers of your choice has obvious possibilities for a battery of two. Mine fits into the factory, briefcase-style case (27"x14"x4"), and weighs less than 20 pounds complete with scopes. All magazines hold two cartridges, which makes the rifle a three-shot since a live round can be carried safely in the chamber. Cartridges are held in the magazine at their shoulder and fed in a straight line, so there's never any damage to bullet points from recoil.

All magnum barrels are 23 1/2-inches long, as are .22-250 and .30-06 calibers. The rest are 22 inches in length, except for a 19-inch carbine with a full-length stock (in .243 and .308 only). Brown Precision will fit the "ULTIMATE" with a fiberglass stock, making the package even lighter, which should make a fabulous backpack rifle.

For a brochure, write: Blaser U.S.A., 308 Leisure Lane, Victoria, TX 77904 (Phone 512-576-4350), the U.S. factory outlet. Or, contact the Canadian importer: H. W. Imports, P. O. Box 695, Winnipeg, Manitoba R3C 2K3 204/334-2481.

July 1986

RIFLES FOR LITTLE PEOPLE

Big folks often find it difficult to understand the optimum gun dimensions for little folks. I got the message in spades some years ago when Mary took her already-cut-down Model 12 to a gunsmith and had him chop *another* inch off the buttstock, after which she smoked doves, ducks and quail with much more regularity.

In recent years there has been more attention given to youth firearms, shortened on both ends to better accommodate the physical stature of youngsters and ladies. Winchester (U.S. Repeating Arms) has both shotguns and center-fire rifles in this category, the excellent Ranger Youth bolt action carbine in .243 Winchester caliber, and the Ranger Youth pump shotgun in 20 gauge. Mossberg has its Model 712 Junior autoloader in 12 gauge, and the Model 500 pump in 20 gauge. Both have removable plugs which make them single shots, and come with coupons which let the buyer purchase a full-sized replacement stock for only $9.95. Browning offers its BPS pump shotgun in a "Youth and Ladies" model, and Remington has its Model 1100 in an LT-20 (20 gauge) Youth Model.

This is a most welcome gift from the gun manufacturers, but those are really for semi-little people. Where guns are scarce is in very small .22 rimfire rifles. Air gun manufacturers have long offered a stair-step array of models to fit youngsters as they grow, but the line-up for graduation to a "22" was meager. There just weren't many downsized .22 rifles which fit those small bodies.

Three which do fit are the Chipmunk, by Chipmunk Mfg., Inc. of Medford, Oregon; Marlin's "Little Buckaroo;" and Iver Johnson's "Li'l Champ." All are single-shot bolt actions in .22 rimfire caliber (Short, Long or Long Rifle), but that's where the similarities end.

The Chipmunk gets the nod as the cutest of the lot, and it's the smallest. With an oil-finished walnut stock, pistol grip and Monte Carlo, a stainless steel bolt handle and a fully-adjustable aperture rear sight, this rifle has an excellent look and feel. At the time of "researching" this column my seven-year-old grandson, Ryan, was visiting, and I persuaded him to help, although his previous experience at gun testing had been limited to the "BB" variety.

He fell in love with the Chipmunk, as most little people do, probably because it fit his slight frame. No, he won't really be old enough for a "22" for some time, but he served a purpose and enjoyed the work. Especially when he put 10 shots into one big hole at a modest 20-foot range, which demonstrated the efficiency of the "peep" sight as well as the rifle.

Slightly bigger and heavier is the "Li'l Champ" from Iver Johnson, another bolt action with a very classy appearance, contributed to in no small measure by a black synthetic stock trimmed with white spacers at buttstock and pistol grip. It has a solid feel, and is equipped with very good open iron sights (a clean, square notch and a flat-topped front blade).

Moving up a bit, from America's largest rifle maker we have

the Marlin "Little Buckaroo," which is a shortened version of Marlin's larger bolt action rimfire rifles. Although heavier than the "Li'l Champ," courtesy of an adult-sized receiver section and bolt, a solid walnut stock, and a husky, micro-grooved steel barrel, it has a shorter length of pull. It also has good open sights, and a solid, crisp trigger pull.

The barrel lengths on all three of these little rifles are 16″ plus a fraction. The length of pull on the Chipmunk and the Marlin is essentially the same — 11 1/4″ and 11 1/2″ respectively; while on the Iver Johnson it's 13 1/4″. Overall length: Chipmunk — 30″; Iver Johnson — 32 1/2″; Marlin — 33 1/4″. Weight: Chipmunk — 2 1/2 lbs.; Iver Johnson — 3 lbs. 2 oz.; Marlin — 4 1/4 pounds.

Chipmunk offers an optional scope mount base, while the other two have receivers which are grooved to accept tip-off mounts.

One significant difference between the the rifles is the safety/cocking design. To cock the Chipmunk and the "Li'l Champ" the bolt knob must be pulled back manually, after which they are ready to fire. There is no separate safety. The Marlin is cocked when the bolt handle is lifted, similar to most modern bolt action center fires, and there is a separate safety. The safety is a thumb button on the right side, similar in looks and operation to that on the Remington M700 rifle, but with this difference. The "Safe" position on the Remington is the rear position; on the Marlin, "Safe" is the forward position.

Pulling the bolt knob back to cock the rifle can be difficult for very small youngsters, and it is more difficult for them to "uncock" it if they don't fire the round in the chamber. Uncocking requires holding the bolt firmly with one hand, and easing it down (forward) when the trigger is pulled with the other hand. As the warning on the "Li'l Champ" reads: "THE RIFLE COULD DISCHARGE IF THE COCKING KNOB IS ACCIDENTALLY RELEASED BEFORE IT IS ALLOWED TO TRAVEL FORWARD SLOWLY." When the Chipmunk and the Iver Johnson are cocked, the bolt cannot be opened. The Marlin bolt can be opened for loading or unloading whether the safety is on or off.

In loading the Chipmunk and the Iver Johnson, the round must be inserted into the chamber and then the bolt closed. The easy-load feed throat on the Marlin lets you drop a round into the opening, after which the bolt will feed it into the chamber on closing.

These three little .22's offer an excellent choice for Dad looking for Junior's first firearm, and odds are great that many of them will end up beneath "the tree" later at Christmas time.

Examining and shooting these three bolt actions brought back memories of my first .22, so I plucked it from the closet for a comparison. This half-century oldie is a single shot, falling block Remington Improved Model 6. It, and the similar Hamilton and Stevens rifles, were extremely popular, which makes me wonder why nobody builds one today. The exposed hammer on them is easier to cock than is a pull-knob on a bolt action, and easier to uncock. The falling block action is simple, sure, and easy to check for safety sake. For comparison, this venerable Model 6 is 33 1/2 inches long with a 21-inch barrel, has a 12 1/2-inch pull, and weighs 3 3/4 pounds.

For more information on the Chipmunk, "L'il Champ," and "Little Buckaroo," write: Chipmunk Mfg. Inc., 114 E. Jackson, Medford, OR 97501; Iver Johnson Arms, 2202 Redmond Rd., Jacksonville, AR 72076; and Marlin Firearms Co., 100 Kenna Dr., North Haven, CT 06473.

December 1986

THE LIGHT RIFLE

T he hills do get steeper, and the guns I carry do get heavier, as the years go by. There was a time when I tended to scoff at such notions voiced by my elders and, although I do not admit to now being one of 'em, I have come around to their point of view.

It is not, I am quick to point out, a case of being unable to cope with arduous hunting situations. The truth is that as my years of experience have stacked themselves atop each other I have become more amenable to accomplishing the same goals with less effort.

The case is much more one of increasing intelligence than it is one of deteriorating physical condition.

Whatever. In recent times I have been carrying with me less and less of more and more when hunting. I choose the lighter boots and lighter clothing, smaller cameras, and some of my backpack items once considered essential now stay at home.

Where a hunter's take-along weight is concerned, however, the big item is his gun. Years ago that fact began to make brownie points in my thinking, not coincidentally with my planning for a sheep hunt which promised to be physically demanding. So, in 1977 I decided to put together a lightweight sheep rifle for that hunt, and it was one of the better decisions I ever made. I should have done it sooner.

One of the greatest areas for saving weight in a rifle is in the stock, and the use of fiberglass for sporting rifle stocks was a giant step in the right direction. Walnut gun stocks vary in density and therefore in weight, and selection of other wood species can reduce stock weight even farther. No wood stock, at that time, approached the weight reduction afforded by fiberglass. My choice was obvious.

A call to Chet Brown put things in motion. Yes, he would kindly rush the assembly of one of his Brown Precision fiberglass stocks to the ingredients of my choosing.

Now for the choosing, and the choice of caliber was the most difficult. I quickly narrowed my options to these numbers: .25-06, .270, .280, .308, .30-06, 7X57, and 7mm Remington Magnum. After a bit of soul-searching I decided upon the .270 Winchester.

Introduced by Winchester half a century ago, this necked-down version of the .30-06 has a long track record of superior perform-ance on medium-size game. Its great accuracy, modest recoil, and long-range capability combined to give the end product I wanted in this particular rifle.

What action? Although the Ruger M77 and Winchester M70 are two of my favorites, Chet recommended the Remington M700, so I had a barreled M700 ADL action in .270 Win caliber sent to him at his California shop. Using the ADL action rather than the BDL eliminated the stock cut for a hinged floorplate, saving a bit of weight and making for a bit more strength in the finished package.

The Model 700 trigger is very good, and is still adjustable by the owner (no matter what the new instruction manuals say as a concession to product liability), but I had Mat Canjar send Chet Brown one of his superb custom triggers, the 2S/1 Deluxe Trigger, for installation. Not only is it crisp and stable, but it is externally adjustable, an important consideration since I had decided to have the action glued to the stock.

What scope? In few fields of interest to shooters has there been greater overall improvement in quality than has been true with rifle scopes, and I poured over the specs of the product lines of Bushnell, Redfield, Weaver, Burris, Tasco and Leupold. In the end I picked the 1.5x5 Leupold variable, weighing 9.8 ounces, and Jack Slack soon had one of these traveling from Beaverton, Oregon down to Chet.

I must admit that there is a kinfolk advantage to being a shooting writer when it comes to relations with manufacturers.

Why a variable rather than a fixed power? In this case going to a 4X would have saved only half an ounce in weight, and in my particular situation I intend for that 1.5X setting to be useful for other hunts I have in mind.

Chet put it all together. We left the barrel length at 22 inches for better performance with the .270 Win., although chopping it to 20 inches would shave a few ounces. He saved three or four ounces by turning the barrel down, and mounted the scope with the light and strong Redfield FR rings and bases. A trim Pachmayr recoil pad and sling swivels completed the job.

Unloaded, but complete with a sling, the rifle weighs 6 3/4 pounds. Another M700 of mine, with the same scope, weighs a shade over nine pounds.

The proof is in the shooting. With 130-grain, over-the-counter Remington Core-Lokt ammo, it put four consecutive shots into less than two inches at 100 yards, with no waiting between shots to cool the barrel. That is excellent hunting accuracy, and surprising consistency for that many back-to-back shots from such a thin barrel.

The advantage of fiberglass stocks, in addition to weight reduction, is stability. The warping and swelling which can afflict wood is eliminated, and change in impact from one climate to another is rare. Benchrest competitors have proved this superiority by using fiberglass stocks to take most of the top honors in recent years.

My new rifle pet is a handsome thing, but not even Chet Brown could call a fiberglass stock pretty — much less beautiful. Skillfully crafted gunstocks of dense, figured walnut win that contest easily.

Scratches on my fiberglass stock stand out, removing paint which reveals the white below. Another minus is that the stock gets very hot when exposed to the direct rays of a summer sun, to the point that it is difficult to handle without gloves.

But I love it!

I blessed it each foot of the hundred miles or so I carried it on its first sheep hunt. The bottom line is that it did its job, helping me take a great desert bighorn ram at long range down on the Baja Peninsula. In the decade since that time the lightweight, big game rifle has come of age. It is the "in" thing of the moment, and virtually all manufacturers have versions of it. Fiberglass stocks are no longer a novelty in the hunting field, and I've added several more to my collection since that first one. Lee Six put together a virtual duplicate of that first one, with just a couple of changes: it's in 7mm Rem Mag caliber rather than .270, and it's topped with a 3X-9X Zeiss scope. I've shot it six times with malice aforethought, tagging an elk on the Mescalera Apache Indian Reservation in New Mexico; a black bear in the Alaska Range near Rainey Pass; two antelope in Wyoming; a Dall sheep in the Wrangells in Alaska hunting with Bill Ellis, and a Stone ram in the Yukon hunting with Dave Coleman. I can't ask for better than that.

In the mid-1980's Weatherby placed on the market the first factory rifle with a synthetic stock, and it was an immediate winner. Within a couple of years most manufacturers followed suit, with a variety of synthetic materials — fiberglass, Kevlar, combinations of the two, and some others cooked up by Remington's parent company — Dupont. Alpha Arms unveiled a fine, stable stock made of laminated wood which has been impregnated with resin under pressure, and that type of stock has attracted some imitators. The bottom line is that hunters now have a wide range of stable stocks, in factory rifles, from which to choose.

Another fall-out of the "glass stock" phenomena has been an array of *lightweight* factory rifles, both with wood stocks and with synthetic stocks. The reaction of hunters to lightweight custom rifles pointed to a need, and firearms manufacturers moved to fill it.

My latest rifle featuring a glass stock is a .280 Ackley Improved built for me by gunmaker Kenny Jarrett, of Jackson, SC, and does it shoot. Coming from a benchrest background as Kenny does, he didn't build this one as a lightweight. It's about nine pounds, compete with 3X-9X Zeiss scope, Hart barrel, and McMillan stock. My last three-shot group, using handloads of 150-grain Nosler Partitions, went into .015 inches, which is better than I can shoot.

That's straying a tad from the topic of lightweight rifles, but the good news is that Kenny is now applying his benchrest knowledge to building rifles that are easy on the scales. Don't miss the chapter in this book that tells how Kenny crafts his firearms.

February 1987

"Use an automatic on deer? What kind of a meat hunter are you, anyway?"

"No, I wouldn't use an automatic. If you're shootin' an auto and the deer is over a hundred yards away you might as well forget it. They spray shots everywhere."

"An automatic? No, man. Just when you need another shot they'll jam every time."

Ethics, accuracy, reliability — the automatic big-game rifle has enjoyed mixed reviews in this country during the past three-quarters of a century. Throughout all these decades shooters have been exposed to a continuing controversy over these and other aspects of the use of this type of firearm.

For all practical purposes, the era of the self-loading, autoloading or semi-automatic big-game rifle — which is what our "automatics" really are — began in 1905 when Winchester introduced its M/05 and in 1906 when Remington introduced its Model 8. The Winchester was chambered for the .32 Winchester and .35 Winchester calibers; and was followed by the Model 1907 in .351 Winchester caliber and the Model 1910 for the .451 Winchester cartridge. That first Remington was chambered for four Remington calibers: .25, .30, .32, and .35 Remington.

All of these were low velocity cartridges, and the design of the rifles themselves, while a quantum leap forward in the evolution of sporting firearms, did not lend itself to very good accuracy. It was during the heyday of those early autos that such rifles acquired their "inaccurate" reputation, a reputation that lingers on in the minds of many hunters.

The motion that it isn't "sporting" to use an autoloader on big game is a puzzling phenomenon, and one that has evolved only in recent years. I doubt that such a thought ever crossed the minds of men prior to World War II, but of late most of the nation has become a bit obsessed with the bolt action for big game. And with that love affair came an equal bit of prejudice against the automatic.

One region of the country was largely immune to this trend. Deer hunters of the South took the Remington Model 740, and later the Model 742, to their bosoms with gusto. And, despite a significant increase in use of other actions in recent years, the autoloading big-game rifle is still the tool of choice for most hunters in this region of the country. The same was and is true, to a lesser extent, for deer hunters in the East. Except in Pennsylvania, which prohibits the use of autoloaders for big-game hunting.

That the automatic deer rifle has been tinged with the unsporting label is rather curious, particularly when such criticism comes from hunters who regularly gun quail or ducks with automatic shotguns. Perhaps the notion that big game hunters should "make one shot count" rather than spraying a volley around is partly responsible, but the same philosophy should also be the norm for bird shooters. Looking at it from the other side, I expect a duck or a quail would think it deserves the same consideration given a buck.

In truth, there isn't nearly as much anti-sporting sentiment toward automatic big-game rifles as there are charges that they are inaccurate and unreliable. Although I've used automatics for deer hunting now and then for some 20 years, I must admit that all of it — with one exception — was in the South. When I headed west or north I used bolt actions.

That exception was a Remington seminar held on the Mescalera Indian Reservation in New Mexico, where gun writers used the new Remington Model 4 semi-auto for hunting mule deer. Mine was in 7mm Express Remington caliber (now the .280 Remington) and, although I needed three shots to do it, I killed a buck — at more than 400 yards.

About two dozen of the new Remington automatics were used on that New Mexico seminar, and were sighted in there on the Mescalera rifle range. With no fine tuning, groups ranged from a bit more than three inches at 100 yards down to less than an inch.

Last week I performed a seat-of-the-pants accuracy test on three autoloaders I happened to have in the house at the time: a Remington Model 4 in 7mm Express Remington (.280 Remington) caliber; a Browning BAR in .30-06; and a Winchester Model 100 (discontinued in 1974) in .243 Win caliber. With Louisiana temperatures crowding the century mark, I took the batch down to gunsmith Ken Eversul in Alexandria, where I could shoot from the air conditioned confines of his shop, and explained my project to Ken.

"I can answer that accuracy question pretty quick", he came right back. "The answer is not very!"

Several hours later he shook his head, "You've only got one bad group (3 1/2″) on the whole row of targets. The only way I can explain that last group is that the gun was pointing in the direction of the target."

That last group, which Ken shot, was with the M100. All shots went into one ragged hole that measured one-half inch. The "bad" group? It was one I shot — with a bolt action I was sighting in for an elk hunt.

The average size of the groups shot with the three autoloading rifles was less than two inches. The best group with the Model 4 was a 1.6 inches; with the BAR, an even one inch; and with the Model 100, of course, that "miracle" one-half incher.

The Model 100 was equipped with a 6X Burris scope, and tested with 100-grain Winchester Power Point ammunition; the BAR — a 3X-9X Bausch & Lomb scope, using 150-grain Federal Premium ammo; the Model 4 — a 3X-9X Leupold scope and 150-grain Remington Core-Lokt ammunition. All the groups were three-shot groups, which I consider "hunting" groups.

This obviously was not an extensive test of the accuracy of even these three automatics, much less of all big-game autoloaders. To get the maximum potential from any rifle it's usually necessary to experiment with a variety of ammunition, both brand and bullet weight. What this test did duplicate, I feel, is the kind of test most deer hunters give their rifle. They buy one box of ammunition and use that for sighting in. Period.

I have always felt that modern autoloaders have taken a bum rap on the "inaccurate" business. Despite that, I was as surprised as was Ken Eversul at the performance of these three rifles. No, I don't think the Model 100 is a "half-inch" rifle, and the BAR might not be a minute-of-angle gun. I would guess that all will shoot three-inch groups day in and day out. Any way you slice it, that is very decent big-game accuracy.

How about reliability? With rare exceptions, autoloaders are just as dependable as other repeating actions. My only "jam" in a hunting situation was my fault, an improperly resized case in a handload. Poor handloads are the principal cause of autoloader malfunction.

Pluses and minuses of automatics? On the good side, they are by all odds the fastest in getting off a second or third aimed shot, and there are occasions when that is important. They don't "kick" as much, courtesy of the gas-operated action found in most of today's autoloaders, as does a bolt, pump or lever action in the same caliber and having the same weight.

On the debit side, some people are bothered by the slamming action of the mechanism, as is equally true for auto shotguns.

Autoloaders are less than ideal for reloaders. The vigorous ejection system makes the empties hard to find and also deforms the cases. Triggers on most autoloaders are poor, although the BAR and the new Remingtons are much improved over prior models.

There aren't many automatics currently on the market which are of interest to big-game hunters. Remington's Model 4 and Model 7400, which replaced the all-time best seller Model 742, is available in 6mm, .243, .270, .280, .308 and .30-06. The Browning BAR is the only auto available in magnum calibers — 7mm Rem Mag and .300 Win Mag, as well as in .243, .270, .308, and .30-06. Heckler & Koch has an autoloader which uses a delayed roller-locked bolt system, in .308 and .30-06. And Sturm Ruger has its Model 44, a lightweight in .44 Rem Mag caliber, a combination which is adequate for deer within 100 yards. There are many of the discontinued Remington Model 742's on the used gun market, and quite a few new ones still on dealer shelves.

If the semi-automatic rifle appeals to you, don't be deterred by the scare tales. You might not end up with a tack-driver that can drill a prairie dog way out yonder, but when it comes to deer and the other big stuff you'll be in good hands.

December 1983

A PAIR OF PLINKERS

It is quite a coincidence, and perhaps a bit ironic, that two of the most useful utility rifles for the outdoorsman are — or were — being marketed by "handgun" companies. They are the Explorer, from Charter Arms Corporation, a relatively young and very aggressive company which has a well-deserved reputation for building excellent revolvers, and the Backpacker, from Sterling Arms Corporation, another young company which made good automatic pistols, but which disappeared from the gun manufacturing scene in the early 1980's.

Both the Explorer, often called by the designation AR-7, and the Backpacker are rifles chambered for the .22 rimfire cartridge, and both break down into astonishingly small packages for transport or storage, but beyond that they are as different as night and day. One thing they do have in common, too, is that both are extremely practical in a wide range of situations. Both are also great fun to shoot.

I am quite a skeptic, as a general rule, when it comes to outdoor products which fringe upon gadgetry. That's not to say that I can resist taking a look at just about everything new that makes the scene, because I can't, but simply that most such items prove to be impractical, badly designed or poorly constructed.

Insofar as the AR-7 and the Backpacker are concerned, I was fully prepared to be disappointed once again — or twice again. What a pleasant surprise, then, to find both of these rifles to be soundly put together and eminently practical.

Don't let my enthusiasm mislead you. These are not finely-tuned examples of the gun craftsman's art. They are exactly what they purport to be: well designed and built firearms for utility use.

The Backpacker is the more conventional of the two. It breaks down into two "halves" of approximately equal length. The barrel section locks into the receiver-stock part with a simple 180 degree turn of a slotted pin.

This is a single shot which accepts any 22 rimfire ammunition — short, long or long rifle. Loading is simple. The barrel section is rotated 90 degrees, exposing the chamber, and a single round is inserted. When that section is rotated back to firing position, it snaps into place with a ball detent.

Pulling the forearm slightly to the rear, when the barrel is in the load or unload position, lifts the fired case or unfired cartridge up so it can be easily removed manually. It's a simple and positive extractor.

To cock the rifle, you pull back on a knob which protrudes from the right side. Once the rifle is cocked, the cross bolt safety behind the trigger can be placed in the "safe" position.

When fully assembled the Backpacker is 39 inches long, but when broken down the package measures only 19 inches. It weighs 3 1/4 pounds. Suggested list price was $49.95.

Now to the AR-7 Explorer. This is a really amazing autoloading, clip-fed rifle, but when you see it in the knocked down configuration you seem to have nothing but a stock. Twist the butt cap off the stock, however, and you'll find a barrel, receiver and clip magazine, all nestled in their respective niches. It's an ingenious arrangement.

The receiver is attached to the stock by a thumbscrew in the pistol grip, and the barrel is fastened to the receiver by a knurled ring. The magazine just snaps into place, and the clip release is in the front of the trigger guard.

And it floats. Yep, put together or stowed away, the rifle will float, which could be quite an advantage in some situations.

The AR-7 is 35 inches long when assembled; 16 1/2 inches long when disassembled, which is the length of the stock; and it weighs 2 1/2 pounds. Suggested list price is about $100.

The stocks on both rifles are plastic, tough and durable as befitting utility arms. The Backpacker has open sights, and the Explorer has an aperture receiver sight. Both are adjustable for elevation, and point of aim on the Explorer could be changed right or left by tapping the front sight in its slot.

Trigger pulls on both were very heavy, but then that's a condition now found on most expensive sporting center fires now that product liability suits have become so popular. The pull on the AR-7 was smooth and consistent, even if heavy, but that on the Backpacker is creaky and heavy.

The Explorer Survival Rifle is also available in the AR-7S version, which features a silvertone, anti-corrosion finish, and in handgun versions called the Explorer II and SII Survival Pistols. An interesting feature of these pistols is that interchangeable 6-, 8-, and 10-inch barrels are available.

Obviously not intended to be tack drivers, both of these rifles are still fully accurate enough for their intended purposes. Right out of the boxes, with heavy trigger pulls and no tuning at all, I got quite decent groups at about 25 yards.

With the Backpacker, leaning over the hood of the car, my first 5-shot string measured 1 3/8 inches, but the horizontal spread was less than 1/2 ". Even at that, three of the five shots were in the black and in less than half an inch.

With the AR-7 — aperture sight and smoother trigger, the first 5-shot group measured one inch, but printed a bit high. Just for kicks, without adjusting the sight, I held low and shot another group at almost rapid fire. The size stretched a tad to 1 1/8 inches, but three of the five were in the bull in 3/8 inches. Not too shabby.

When I consider the uses these unusual guns are suited for, and the people who could use 'em, the list gets to be long: camper, fisherman, hunter, boater, private pilot, backpacker, skimobiler, RV'er — for small game, survival, plinking, varmints, targets and protection. They'll fit into a backpack, and one or the other often fit into my duffle bag when I pack for big game outings. They're awfully handy for potting grouse, rabbits or squirrels to change the menu.

The Details

Backpacker: Weight — 3 1/4 pounds; Length assembled — 34 ";
Length Broken Down — 19"; Action — Single Shot; Caliber —
.22 rimfire Short, Long or Long Rifle; List Price was $49.95, but
the manufacturer — Sterling Arms — went out of business in the
early 1980's.

AR-7 Explorer: Weight — 2 1/2 pounds; Length assembled — 35 ";
Length Broken Down — 16 1/2 "; Action — Autoloading; Magazine
Capacity — 8; Caliber — .22 rimfire Long Rifle only; List Price
— less than $100.00. For more info write: Charter Arms, 500
Sniffens Lane, Stratford, Conn. 06497.

August 1979

SEMI-MAGNUMS FOR HUNTERS

"Magnum" is a word whose time has come, apparently, insofar as rifle calibers are concerned. It is in.

And what's a magnum? Nothing more than a cartridge which
is loaded to higher velocities, with consequently higher chamber
pressures, than is normal for the bullet diameter involved. What's
"normal?" A rather imprecise adjective.

But difficult as it may be to define precisely magnum rifle cali-
bers, all big game hunters know what they are. They are the hot
7mm's and .30 calibers of Remington, Winchester, Weatherby,
H&H, and Norma: 7mm Remington Magnum, 7mm Weatherby
Magnum; .300 Winchester Magnum, .308 Norma Magnum, .300
Weatherby Magnum, and .300 H&H Magnum.

There are others, but they aren't as important in the general big
game hunting picture. The .257 Weatherby Magnum is an excellent
caliber, but its maximum bullet weight leaves a bit to be desired
for elk-sized game. The .338 Winchester Magnum, the .375 H&H
Magnum, the .458 Winchester Magnum, and the Weatherbys of
like persuasion are impressive and effective, but are unnecessarily
powerful for most North American big game, although the .338
Win. Mag. could approach being the very best number for *everything*
on this continent if we were forced to choose just one.

So the 7mm's and .300's are the magnums in the spotlight in the U.S. as of the past decade or so, and no hunter worth his salt would think of gunning our more exotic big game with anything less. Deer and antelope, perhaps, but heaven forbid not elk, moose, sheep, goats or bear.

Let the record show that the 7mm Remington Magnum and the .300 Winchester Magnum are two of my favorite calibers, with which I have killed more big game than with any other half dozen calibers. But let the record also show that most of you would be more efficient hunters with rifles a bit less potent.

The semi-magnums, to make the point plain, are best for most.

My definition for this coined term is simple. I refer to that superb array of calibers whose ballistics fall just below those of the magnums. It includes, among others, the .270, the .280, the 7x57, the .30-06, the .308, and the 8mm Mauser.

Our perspective has a way of being distorted, and I think that has happened in the case of big game calibers. The distortion, as is frequently true, came about slowly. But suddenly that creeping change became a common belief: the powerhouse rifles of yesterday were no longer adequate for today's big game. Long live the magnums.

Consider that W.D.M. Bell, that fabled African hunter, killed more than 1,000 elephants with a 7mm Mauser (7x57), which is substantially less powerful than the .30-06. He killed many, many others with a 6.5mm.

His performance does not make the 7x57 ideal for elephants, but it does lend a certain credence to my argument that such tools are adequate for most North American game animals. But aren't the magnums in question even more adequate, more than adequate, unquestionably adequate for all North American big game?

In my hands, yes. In your hands, maybe. In the hands of the average big game hunter, no.

The difference lies in the ability to handle the magnums confidently, to shoot them accurately. If you are average, I would give odds that you cannot do so. The reason is that you don't practice.

Mr. Average Hunter shoots his big game rifle once a year — during the hunting season, or maybe it's twice: once the day before the season opens, at a rock on a hillside to "see if it's still sighted in," and the other at a deer, elk, antelope or other trophy.

Few hunters can learn to cope with magnum recoil with such limited practice, and the recoil of the 7mm's and .30-caliber magnums is what this is all about. In short, they belt you around right smartly.

A typical case finds Mr. Average buying a magnum, and after one session of sighting in across the car hood he is sore of shoulder and cheekbone, fearful of heart, and he probably has a half-moon crescent over his right eye from the scope. From then on he will shoot his new toy as infrequently as possible, and when his moment of truth does arrive his finger approaches the trigger as if it were a snake.

Pride is a powerful emotion. Most hunters would rather roll over and die than admit they are sensitive to recoil.

Well, recoil bothers *me*. I have a lot more fun shooting my favorite whitetail caliber, a 6mm Remington, than I do my two favorite biggies — the 7mm Remington Magnum and the .300 Winchester Magnum. But the difference between me and Mr. Average is that I shoot the year 'round, and have learned to handle the magnums. I may not relish long shooting sessions with them on the bench, but when game appears their recoil is not a factor.

Not only does the recoil not bother me physically when I am hunting, but, most important, the fear of it does not interrupt my concentration nor interfere with my accuracy.

The semi-magnums are no patsies when it comes to recoil, as most soldiers who shot the .308 and .30-06 will testify, but the magnums are simply in another class. They are more potent on both ends of the rifle.

I'm not immune to magnumitis. It had been years since I had plucked from the rack anything other than a magnum for a hunt of any significance, but on an elk hunt Ithaca asked me to try their LSA bolt action sporter in a .30-06 caliber. With this "obsolete" number I shot a decent 5-point bull through the lungs and he went down within 30 yards.

Magnums are better but only if you can handle them. If you can't, dust off that semi-magnum and be confident that you are using enough gun.

August 1977

In 1968 the small New Hampshire gun firm called Thompson/ Center Arms unveiled a single-shot pistol of a somewhat radical design. Bucking the odds, and the advice of the experts, designer Warren Center brought to the marketplace the Thompson/Contender, a firearm which has since become our most popular hunting handgun, and one of the most popular in the growing sport of silhouette shooting. In 1981 while visiting with Warren Center and discussing his handgun, I was shown the prototype of his then current project.

It was a single-shot rifle in the same vein as the Contender, and the plan was to have the same interchangeable barrel/caliber feature which has contributed so greatly to the popularity of the handgun. That was indeed the case when that new rifle reached dealer shelves a year or so later. The rifle offered to the public in 1982 is called the Thompson/Center Single-Shot Rifle (T/C Single Shot), and was initially available in five calibers: .30-06, 7mm Rem Mag, .243 Win, .22-250 Rem, and .223 Remington. Odds are good that additional calibers will become available over the counter, probably by the time this is in print.

Why would anybody want a single-shot hunting rifle in this era of slick feeding, magazine bolt actions and fast-firing pumps and autos? That was the reaction way back in 1967, when Bill Ruger introduced his Ruger Number One single shot, the first such critter to come along in decades. But want them the public did, and the success of that Ruger and the models which followed is history. With that background, the ground having been broken by the Number One and the Browning Model 78 which followed, there probably wasn't a single "why" murmured when the T/C Single Shot made its appearance.

The new T/C is a top-break action along the same line as the Contender handgun (and single and double barrel shotguns), completely different from the falling block actions of the Ruger and Browning (which is no longer available). It is this "simple" design which makes interchangeability of the barrels, and calibers, practical. For $425 (list price) you could buy the basic T/C rifle in the caliber of your choice — say the 7mm Rem Mag with which you plan to pot an elk. Then, for another $140 you could buy a .223 Rem barrel for varmints or turkeys, or a .243 barrel for deer and antelope. You can literally interchange them in seconds.

The appearance of my test rifle was what we have come to expect from Thompson/Center, a look of quality. The classic stock of American walnut is good grade, wood-to-metal fit is good, the simple cut checkering pattern on pistol grip and forearm is nice and functional, and the metal finish is excellent, although a bit shiny for my tastes. The stock has a trim, rubber recoil pad and a right-hand cheekpiece. It does not come with sling swivels, which is a bit surprising.

All T/C rifles come equipped with open sights, which may be easily removed for scope mounting if desired. The stock design positions the eye a bit high for easy use of the open sights, but in good position for scope use, and I can't foresee much reason for ever using such a rifle as this without a scope. Offering the barrels without sights, in fact, would seem to make sense. As would offering it with sling swivels.

This single-shot rifle weighs about seven pounds, varying a bit depending upon caliber. Even with a 23-inch barrel, the overall length is a compact 39 1/2 inches, making this a pleasingly quick-handling gun, a trademark of this type of action.

The first TCR'83, as T/C labeled the rifle, was equipped with "adjustable double set triggers," which was 50 percent accurate. The "set" trigger was adjustable. The single stage trigger was not adjustable and was very bad. In my August 1984 *Sports Afield* column reporting on my first test rifle, I wrote, " I think both T/C and shooters would be better served if the TCR'83 came with a quality, adjustable single-stage trigger such as the custom Canjar, leaving the double set triggers to the Europeans." Thompson/Center Arms listened to the criticism, and the following year had a single trigger model (the Hunter) as well as the double trigger Aristocrat. By 1986 the double trigger model had been dropped completely, leaving only the Hunter with a very good adjustable single trigger.

The cross-bolt safety, located in the forward portion of the trigger guard, is a bit of an oddity. There is a lock button on the front of the trigger guard which must be depressed and held there while the safety is switched to the "off" (shooting) position. The objective is to prevent the safety from being switched off inadvertently, and it certainly does that.

Some of the design features of the TCR'83, and the entire tone of the instruction booklet, are obviously a result of the insane product liability awards which have plagued gun manufacturers (all manufacturers, for that matter) in the past decade. The public is reaping, in the form of less functional products, what it sowed.

I should add that T/C is not the only gun manufacturer to walk softly. Several years ago Remington changed the instruction booklet for the M700 rifle, replacing the trigger adjustment instructions of previous booklets (for their excellent adjustable trigger) with a warning that "all adjustments to the trigger must be made by the factory or a Remington recommended gunsmith."

My first TCR rifle shot well, even with little experimenting with various loadings. The .22-250 barrel gave a 1 1/4-inch, three-shot group for its best performance, using Remington 55-grain Power Lokt ammunition. A 7mm Rem Mag interchangeable barrel had a best five-shot group of two inches with 125-grain Remington Core-Lokt ammo.

To be expected, there were a few problems with the early rifles. There was no structural "stop" for the barrel assembly on opening, and, as a consequence the rear of the forearm iron hit the bottom of the receiver when the action was fully open. The action was difficult to open after firing, especially with the 7mm Rem Mag barrel. And with that 7mm, with some brands of ammo, the "belt" on the cartridge would hang up on the edge of the extractor during loading. Loading could be accomplished after a bit of fiddling around with the extractor, which isn't satisfactory.

T/C solved those problems down the line, and the rifle now being marketed is excellent. It is very accurate, and is now available in both standard weight and silhouette/varmint weight barrels. The 1987 caliber listing for standard weight: .22 Hornet, .222 Rem, .223 Rem, .22-250 Rem, .243 Win, .270 Win, .308 Win, and .30-06. In the silhouette/varmint weight: .223 Rem, .22-250 Rem, 7mm-08 Rem, .308 Win, and .32-40 Win.

And...the price went down. Suggested retail for the rifle and one barrel is now $395, and additional barrels only $155.

Warren Center came up with another winner.

For more information, write to: Thompson/Center Arms, Box 2426, Rochester, NH 03867.

August 1984

O ne glance was all I got at the mule deer buck. He wasn't there, and suddenly he was, disappearing over the rim into one of the countless Missouri River breaks. Alvin Grassrope, my Sioux guide on the Lower Brule reservation near Chamberlain, South Dakota, made a dash toward a point on the rim obliquely away from the deer, stopped 20 yards from the edge, and motioned me on. When I eased over the edge the mulie was standing on the far side of the canyon, watching his back-trail, giving me time to sit and steady the crosshairs behind his shoulder.

Hey, wait a minute! Something's wrong. This doesn't seem right. What are you doing hunting mule deer in wide open country with a Winchester Model 94 lever action? The gun that won the west! At spittin' distances, that is.

Late in 1982 the U.S. Repeating Arms Company announced a new version of the venerable "94" which it called the Winchester Model 94 XTR Angle Eject carbine. It is chambered for the .375 Winchester cartridge, and for two new, more powerful calibers: the .307 Winchester and the .356 Winchester. I was in South Dakota at the invitation of USRAC to try one of the new calibers in the field.

As the ranges get longer, most hunters — especially those of us with "mature" eyes — use telescopic sights. Use of a scope on the old Model 94 isn't impossible, but it's most awkward due to the top-opening, top-ejecting system of the M94. You can't mount a scope directly over the receiver because the ejected empties would hit the scope. Enter "Angle Eject."

The ejection system of this new carbine has been modified to throw the empties to the side, at about a 45 degree angle up and away. It's a major design change which allowed top mounting of a 1.5X-5X Leupold on the .307 Winchester I was using, and the system worked flawlessly for me.

Just as the top ejection of the M94 has been a minus factor insofar as scopes are concerned, it is a plus when it comes to easy visual inspection of magazine and chamber. The new Angle Eject rifles, of course, retain that "plus" feature.

The two new calibers were developed for the Angle Eject by the Winchester Group, Olin Corporation. In essence, they are rimmed versions of the .308 Winchester and the .358 Winchester cartridges, with only slightly reduced performance figures from these rimless numbers. To be more specific, let's compare muzzle velocities, all from 24-inch barrels (the carbine has a 20-inch barrel).

With 150-grain bullets, the .308 Win has 2820 fps while the new .307 Win gives 2764 fps. With 180-grain bullets it's 2620 fps vs. 2506 fps.

Comparing the two .35 calibers, we find the .358 Win with 200-grain bullet gives 2490 fps at the muzzle; the .356 Win, 2455 fps. With 250-grain bullets the figures are 2230 fps vs. 2162 fps.

It's interesting, from an academic standpoint, to compare the performances of the new calibers with that of those from which they were spawned. But, since neither the .308 Win, or .358 Win is available in the M94, it's even more useful to gauge the new ones against the .30-30 Win, the most popular caliber in the M94. With a 150-grain bullet the .30-30 has 2390 fps muzzle velocity — almost 400 fps less than the .307 Win, and with the 170 grain it's 2200 fps. It is obvious that the new calibers are, indeed, substantially more powerful than any calibers previously available in this traditional Winchester. How was it accomplished?

"Basically," said Ed Vartian, Director of Product Development for USRAC, "the bolt is the biggest change we made. We put the action into the .375 Winchester receiver, which has heavier walls. The extractor was moved from the top of the bolt to the right upper quadrant, to give the angle ejection, and the right side of the receiver was dropped a bit to give room for the ejection. Barrel diameter is the same at the chamber but a bit larger at the muzzle, to give added weight.

"My biggest concern with this whole project," continued Ed, "was whether the system would be strong enough. Most people said there was no way we could put that cartridge into the M94 system, that the receiver would come apart, and we'd have hard opening. We worked at both problems, and I'm satisfied with the safety. Pressures with the factory loadings of these new calibers are in the 48,000 to 50,000 psi ranges. At double those pressures, in test loads, the gun was still functional, although the extractor bent slightly."

The stocks on the samples I used were classy looking. Of American walnut with the XTR satin finish, the straight grip stock is Monte Carlo style to position the eye for a scope. It has cut checkering, a rubber recoil pad, and detachable sling swivels.

When I sighted in my Angle Eject M94 prior to our South Dakota deer hunt I was surprised at the accuracy. From a "kneeling" bench rest, on a bitter cold windy morning, I got three-inch groups at 100 yards, and am confident the rifle would have done better had it been better directed. But, with that confidence-building session under my belt, I had few qualms at touching one off at the mulie buck at some 225 to 250 yards. Lung shot, the deer went only about 30 yards before going down.

Later in the season I shot another buck with the same rifle, this time a whitetail that required two shots to keep him down. The first, at about 200 yards or a bit less, penetrated the chest cavity and flattened against the shoulder bone on the off side. The second, at about 75 yards, angled forward through the chest cavity, exiting midway the rib cage. The exit hole was huge, as big as I've ever seen in a deer. The one shot on the mulie went completely through the chest cavity, leaving such a small exit hole that it might indicate lack of expansion. The same 150-grain bullets were used on both deer.

I go into some detail about bullet performance with the new calibers for a reason. In a tubular feed magazine gun such as the Model 94, pointed tip bullets cannot be used. The reason is the danger of the pointed bullet of one cartridge striking the primer of the cartridge ahead of it and causing it to fire in the magazine. Thus the ammunition loaded (by Winchester Group, Olin) for the two new Angle Eject calibers has a blunt-nosed bullet similar to that in .30-30 ammo. This non-streamlined configuration gives excellent expansion at moderate ranges, provided that the velocity is sufficient, but it does not retain velocity downrange as well as do the spitzer types. Take my experience with the load on just two deer for what it's worth: interesting, but too limited to draw from it any firm conclusions about downrange performance.

I'm favorably impressed with the Angle Eject edition of the M94, despite my initial "ho hum" reaction to news of the introduction. The prototype I used had a couple of bugs — some difficulty in loading cartridges into the magazine, and a very hard, creepy trigger pull — but those were eliminated in the production rifles. Although the Angle Eject certainly won't replace bolt-action rifles for long range, pinpoint performance, it does mark a significant advance in the performance of the Model 94. This new model is now a solid 200-yard, deer rifle, courtesy of both the increased power of the new cartridges and the new compatibility with scope sights. It should be a winner.

Suggested retail price of the Winchester Model 94 XTR Angle

Eject, complete with bases and rings for scope mounting, is $399.95. For more information, write: U.S. Repeating Arms Co., 275 Winchester Ave., New Haven, Conn. 06511.

U.S. Repeating Arms Co.: Since July of 1981 all domestic production of Winchester firearms has been under a new corporation — the U. S. Repeating Arms Company. At that time Olin granted to USRAC an exclusive license to use the trademark "Winchester" on firearms approved by Olin. The O & U and side-by-side "Winchester" shotguns manufactured in Japan continue to be marketed by Olin/Winchester.

Bob Morrison, a Vice-President of USRAC, was on the South Dakota hunt, and outlined for me some of the goals of USRAC President Hugh Fletcher and Executive V-P Dick Pelton. In essence, and predictable, it was to bring domestic Winchester firearms back to the esteem they once held in the hearts of hunters.

"We are dedicated to quality," Bob emphasized, "and for the last 18 months I've been concentrating on improved rifle accuracy. It's back to basics, and it's paying off. I think our Winchesters are now more accurate than they've ever been, and you see the results of our program in this Angle Eject model. We know the Model 70's are more accurate than they've ever been — we've got all the old records. Some of the accuracy we're getting now is startling. Our Ultra Grade Featherweight, for instance, with .270 handloads, will shoot into less than an inch at 100 yards. And all of that tightening up is finding its way into our regular production runs."

April 1983

GUNS

PROTECT YOUR GUNS

If firearms aren't No. 1 on the thieves' "hit" parade, they rank mighty high. Survey a batch of hunters around any hot stove, and odds are one or more will have had personal experience in losing a gun to theft.

Pardon a bit of digression, but this whole subject opens an old wound that I'd like to share with you. It's simply my biased belief that theft of any item of hunting or fishing gear should be a capital crime. Take my auto, television set or other nonessential, but don't touch my guns.

Notwithstanding my feelings in this regard, punishment for such crimes is seldom much of a deterrent. Theft of firearms is widespread, of epidemic proportions, leaving the gun owner with this question: How do I protect myself?

Two ways: Protect your guns against theft to the best of your ability, and protect yourself against financial loss with insurance. Let's examine both.

A written description of your guns is important, let me emphasize, whether you have few or many. Keep a copy of the list at home, but place another copy in a safe-deposit box, with your attorney, or in some other place safe from loss.

Describe each gun completely, including such things as barrel length, finish, sights and any custom work that might have been done. You'll record the serial number, of course, but criminals often obliterate such numbers on stolen guns. If so, and in the event that your stolen gun is recovered, you may need all possible items of identification to prove that the gun is yours.

Your gun-record file should include such data as invoices or bills of sale plus a current estimate of each gun's value. These descriptions and estimates are necessary ingredients when you seek insurance, or when you file a claim under your homeowner or automobile insurance policy. Photographs of your firearms can be very helpful indeed, especially if the guns are quite valuable.

No gun is immune to theft, regardless of its location, but most vulnerable are those in homes and vehicles. Most homeowner insurance policies, and some auto policies, will cover loss of guns by theft or fire, but with limitations.

A homeowner policy, in any event, will not cover guns to a greater total amount than the "contents" coverage. Most such policies, however, *have a limit of $500 on firearms.* A few years ago I suddenly discovered that my policy had been changed from "no limit" up to the contents coverage, down to a very low limit, without any notification to me. Sure, the change was in the policy, but who reads all the fine print? I do — now!

If the loss of your guns takes place away from your home, keep in mind that your coverage under most homeowner policies is limited to 10 percent of the unscheduled personal-property coverage.

Automobile policies usually have a very limited coverage of contents, often a maximum of $500. If theft is involved, the vehicle must show evidence of forcible entry.

Examine your particular policies in detail to make certain exactly what they do cover. Question your agent closely and, if possible, get his answers in writing.

If the coverage under your homeowner policy isn't adequate, you can insure your guns individually with some companies.

Perhaps the best gun insurance now available is a new membership benefit of the National Rifle Association, available only to active NRA members for their personal gun collections. Each member can receive $300 worth of free coverage, but can also get additional coverage up to $9700 (a maximum of $10,000) at the extremely low cost of $1.05 per $100 of coverage.

These premiums are based on three years' coverage, payable in advance, with rates guaranteed for the three years. For more information, write: NRA Firearms Insurance Program, 2100 M. Street, N.W., Washington, DC 20037.

Better than collecting insurance, of course, is preventing the theft of your guns in the first place. A good beginning toward this is to keep a low profile as to your gun ownership. One of the delights of gun ownership is the simple pride in owning firearms, but to share that delight with others by displaying your guns invites theft.

Lock your home and your automobile. Despite the fact that skilled thieves can open either about as quickly as you can do so with a key, such a precaution can save you from an amateur.

Burglar-alarm systems are well worthwhile, and they're getting better. Miniaturization and sophistication of electrical components have brought the cost of such systems down and the efficiency up.

Most security systems are triggered by one of three things — noise, motion, or disruption of an electrical circuit. Those based on noise or motion are becoming increasingly popular, and installation of them is simple.

Steel security chests provide excellent protection for guns and other valuables, and are available in various models that will hold as many as a dozen firearms. Tread Corporation (Box 5497, Roanoke, VA 24012) also has a clever storage unit that replaces the back seat in recreational vehicles such as the Chevy Blazer and comparable models manufactured by GMC, Dodge, Plymouth and others. It has locked space in both seat and in back for guns and other equipment.

Hidden storage areas inside the home are becoming more popular. One of the easiest to install is a false back in a closet, creating a shallow, between-the-walls space that will house a number of guns. There are also roll-down steel doors which will turn a closet into a semi-safe.

Don't leave your guns in your auto overnight when you are traveling. Take them into the motel or hotel with you. A dozen or so gunners attending a shoot not long ago, and staying in the same motel, were ripped off the same night.

Inventory and insurance are high on the priority list for protecting your guns. But beyond that, make it as difficult as you possibly can for a thief to steal them.

The Complete Guide to House, Apartment, and Property Protection is a helpful book available for $4.95 if you write to: Brownells, Rt. 2 Box 1, Montezuma, IA 50171.

August 1978

FAJEN: THE KING OF GUNSTOCKS

"Y ou're more popular than the preacher," Dr. Shepardson whispered as I sat down after being introduced by my host, Reinhart Fajen. We were in the basement of the United Methodist Church for the weekly Lions Club luncheon. "A shooting editor gets attention around here."

That's understandable. I was in Warsaw, Missouri, home of Reinhart Fajen, Inc., which is the largest producer of gunstocks for sporting firearms in the country, and an economic mainstay in the picturesque village of 1500 people. The ladies of the Church kept bringing delectable dishes, the likes of which most civic clubs only dream of, finally ending the orgy with a square of orange sherbert frozen on a cracker crumb base, topped with a sprinkling of brown sugar granules. "If you make stocks as good as this," I turned to Reinhart, "you're a winner."

"I told you the food was good," he grinned.

Thirty-five years ago I sent a check for $5.00 to Warsaw, and soon received in return a semi-finished stock blank for a war surplus Springfield. The "sporterized" .30-06 that resulted, largely through the expertise of a friend named Curtis Earl, still has a prominent place on my gun rack.

That was a "Bishop" stock, a product of E. C. Bishop & Son, the first gunstock making operation to set up shop in Warsaw, and the place where Reinhart Fajen honed his skills as a stockmaker. It's a far-fetched possibility that he handled my order, since most of his work was making custom stocks, and it was also about that time that he left Bishop and established Reinhart Fajen, Inc., which has become the pre-eminent producer of stock blanks and custom stocks in the nation.

You need a stock for your gun? Shotgun? Rifle? Handgun? Muzzle loader? Gunstock for a camera? Rough blank? Semi-finished? Finished? Super-finished? Off-set? Cross-over? Adjustable trap stock? Silhouette stock? Walnut…in half a dozen varieties and that many grades? Maple? Curly or birdseye or silver? Laminated?

Fajen's got it!

But the old shotgun with the stock you cracked last season is old — I mean, really old. No sweat, most probably, since Reinhart *can fit about 800 different models* with routine ease. If your keepsake Betsy isn't among them, Fajen can still duplicate your old broken stock, although it'll cost you a bit more.

How about the cost? Some of the prices even make Reinhart shake his head, but there's a market out there for finished stocks from Fajen at several thousand dollars a pop. But, you can also get a "Utility" grade semi-finished stock for a bolt action rifle for $37, $180 if custom fitted to your gun, and $300 fully finished and checkered. In AAA Fancy Walnut those tabs jump to $198, $358, and $498.

Fajen also offers low-cost replacement stocks for a large number of older, low-cost shotguns and rifles for which there's no longer a replacement supply from the gun manufacturer, many of whom are no longer in business. Price: $32. And for most of the popular pump and auto shotguns of the past half century made by Remington, Winchester, Browning, Ithaca, Marlin, Savage, and Stevens, at a semi-finished low end cost of $27.

The key to the Fajen success, in addition to the talent, foresight and drive of Reinhart himself, lies in no small measure in the excellent craftsmen who build the stocks. Most joined the firm right out of high school, and many have been there for 20 years and more. Fred Wenig, the plant manager and a master stockmaker: more than 30 years with Fajen. To watch Elbert Smith and his brother, Darrel, and Duane Kendall and Donnie Gemes and the others skillfully contour a cheekpiece, file a comb down, inlet a blank or checker a gorgeous piece of English walnut is to watch talent at work, men who obviously like what they do and are proud of the results.

Reinhart sold the two-million dollar operation last year, having had it cruising smoothly on auto-pilot for a long time. His daughter-in-law, Marty Fajen, vice president and office manager, runs the day-to-day business with skill and tact. She supervises contact with the 6,000 gun shops which buy Fajen blanks, and with the thousands of individuals who call and write to specify just what they want in a stock.

Some shooters are going directly to the source: they're going right to Warsaw. One big reason is the stock fitting service which Reinhart instituted a few years back, following his development of a Fajen version of a "try-stock" which enables him and Fred to determine exactly what stock dimensions are best for the customer. For months an average of two such fittings a week were on the agenda, with many of shooters flying in by private plane. One arrived in a helicopter.

I flew a commercial flight into Springfield, Missouri, then drove north for a couple of hours on U.S. Highway 65. Warsaw is nestled between two excellent fishing lakes — Lake of the Ozarks and Truman Reservoir, which tempts many Fajen customers to use a rod and reel while waiting for a stock to be roughed out. Following the "roughing-out," Fred will take you out back and have you shoot your gun for a point-of-impact check. Corrections are made on the spot.

John Beringer is the new owner and president of Reinhart Fajen, Inc., and the businessman from Akron, Ohio has some good ideas. One of the best is to resist fixing what isn't broken.

"I don't intend to change the best stock-making operation in the country. There are other avenues which we're getting into that will diversify the business."

One of those moves was to form another company, with American Walnut, Inc., that's called Fajen American. Based in Cameron, Missouri, it will build stocks on contract for various gunmakers.

How did Reinhart Fajen end up dominating the stock making business of the nation?

"My timing was good," Reinhart's eyes twinkled as he reminisced. "During World War II I worked for Pratt & Whitney building aircraft engines, and when the war ended there was a great demand for stocks to sporterize the military rifles brought home by the G.I.'s — Springfields, Enfields, Mausers and the rifles of the Japanese. Not long after that most of the armies of the world began replacing bolt-action repeaters with semi-auto's, and those surplus bolt actions began to flood the country. That called for more stocks to sporterize the guns.

"Before the demand for rifle stocks could taper off, shooters began wanting them for shotguns. Years ago it required a very skilled stockmaker to restock a fine old double, but the semi-finished stocks we now make for Parkers, Lefevers, Ithacas, L.C. Smiths and all the rest are so close to finished dimensions that many do-it-yourself shooters can build a first-class stock.

"I wish more shooters realized the importance of proper stock fit, especially the big game rifle shooters. If you've got time to get down into a benchrest position, fit doesn't make much difference. But if you've got only seconds to get off the shot, and the trophy is moving, the man with an ill-fitting stock doesn't have much chance."

On the last day of July, 1987, two days after our Lions Club lunch feast, Reinhart Fajen walked away from Reinhart Fajen, Inc. for the last time, his year as a consultant, following the sale of the business, having ended. The personable 76-year old did so with a springy step and an optimistic outlook toward more leisure time to enjoy the vacation land in which he lives. He can also bask in the knowledge that his gunstocks will play an effective, pleasurable role in all kinds of gunning for decades to come.

(For a 52-page color catalog of the stocks and services offered by Fajen, send $5.00 to: Reinhart Fajen, Inc., P.O. Box 338, Warsaw, MO 65355)

December 1987

T he price of most things have soared in recent decades, and firearms haven't escaped the increases. Despite this, guns remain one of the best buys in today's market in terms of value received per dollar spent.

But good value or not, the sportsman plagued with increased financial pressures from the necessities of life may wonder whether he can or should spring for the price of a new shotgun or rifle. (He probably considers the new gun a "necessity," but others in the family might disagree.) Could he solve the situation by buying a used gun?

Maybe. And maybe not. A used firearm can be a good buy or it can be a bad bargain. Let's examine a few considerations which could make it one or the other.

Price, of course, is a dominating factor in deciding whether a second-hand gun is right for you at a particular time. If the price approaches that of a new gun, pass it up and buy the new one, even if you must strain a bit to do it. I would question the wisdom of a used gun buy, in general, if it doesn't save the buyer at least 20 percent over the cost of a new one. There are exceptions, of course: a pre-1964 Model 70 may bring more as a used gun than does a new one; out-of-production numbers such as the Winchester Model 42 and the Remington Model 32 sell for more now than they did when new.

But the mill-run, used firearm will usually sport a price tag averaging from 45 to 75 percent of the cost of a new one. It's logical to think that a gun at about half price would be a good buy and one at 75 percent of new list might not be, but it is also true that one which sells for only 45 percent of list could be a bad buy while one at 75 percent could be a good one. Condition of the gun, caliber and degree of obsolescence are factors other than price which should be considered.

I discussed the general question of buying used guns with several gun dealers and gunsmiths, especially Jack Alexander, of Shreveport (La.) and Kenneth Eversul, of Alexandria, (La.), and several points of agreement were evident. One is that you're better off most of the time if you buy from an individual rather than from a gun store, a thought which was rather surprising since it came from owners of gun stores.

"Many of the guns we buy or take in trade," one shop owner told me, "are in need of repair. That's often why we get 'em — they won't work. Which means we must examine, repair and guarantee them to be shootable before we can offer them for sale, all of which boosts the price we must get to make handling used guns profitable. Tell your readers to check the classified ads of their newspapers first."

Another consensus is that buying an old "army" rifle — Springfield, Enfield or Krag — and sporterizing it, is a no-no since the finished product will probably cost as much or more than a new factory sporter. The exception: if you can do the work yourself and elect to devote the time and effort necessary.

It can make sense and cents if you buy one of these to use it "as is," if you buy at the right price. All are acceptable big game calibers, of course, even if your rifle won't look as slick as a new factory number.

Availability of ammunition for an old gun should be part of your consideration in buying second hand. Does it matter to you that the crossroads store down the road doesn't carry .30-40 or .32-20 ammo, or whatever the case may be, while they always have .30-06 and .30-30 cartridges? Only you can make that decision.

Another second hand consideration: are repair parts available for the gun? If not, then repairs will be either impossible or quite expensive. You must weigh the gamble.

Many "broken" guns, according to the gunsmiths, have little or nothing wrong with them, which is a point sportsmen should take to heart when looking for used guns. A very common case is the gas-operated autoloading shotgun which "won't work" because the owner has never, ever cleaned the gas mechanism. Some gas systems are more prone to clogging from powder residues than are others, but all need tender loving care now and then. TLC, in this case, means clean and dry.

Squirting the gas mechanism with oil, let me emphasize, is worse than doing nothing, yet that's exactly what gunsmiths frequently find when they check a gas auto which won't function. (All instruction manuals caution against doing that, of course, but reading the instructions is a last resort for some people.)

Okay, let's run down some random observations and recommendations from gunsmiths and gun dealers relative to buying used guns.

Minor pitting and rusting in the barrel of a shotgun doesn't usually affect patterns greatly. In a rifle, however, it could be critical. Check lands and grooves to make sure they're sharp. Best bet is to shoot any gun for functioning reliability, and any rifle for accuracy.

In the case of rifles, either center-fire or .22, the used bolt actions are the best buys. Lever action Winchesters (94's and 64's) and Marlins (336 and 39A) are usually good.

If possible, examine a fired cartridge case from a rifle you're considering. Swelling indicates excessive headspace.

Cracked stocks on doubles which are no longer being manufactured can indicate a bad buy, since a custom stock will cost $100 to $150 and more. Only in the case of the high grade oldies (Parker, Fox, etc.) would this usually be worthwhile.

On old Winchester Model 12 pumps make sure the serial numbers match. If not, make sure the replaced barrel was fitted properly.

Used Model 1100 Remington autoloaders: "Usually good buys if price is right, since repair parts are readily available and relatively inexpensive."

Browning autoloading shotguns (long recoil): check pre-WW II 16 gauges to make sure chamber length is 2 3/4 inches rather than 2 and 9/6 inches. Conversion of the short chamber to standard length is easily done by a good gunsmith, but that adds to the cost.

Check used revolvers for side play in the cylinder, by cocking hammer and trying to roll cylinder back and forth. Should be no more than about 1/32 of an inch play.

Revolvers: "S&W" on the barrel doesn't necessarily mean it was made by Smith & Wesson. The S&W could be the designation of the caliber (.32 S&W, .38 S&W, etc.), and the pistol may or may not have been manufactured by Smith & Wesson.

In 1975 a spot check with a gun store in Phoenix, Arizona revealed these used guns available, all in good to excellent condition: Browning O&U — $500; Browning Sweet 16 — $289; Remington 870 with rib barrel, 12 gauge — $119; another 870, rib, 20 gauge — $159; Mossberg 500A — $90; Winchester 37A, excellent condition — $59; Winchester Model 94 in .30-30, excellent — $75; Browning lever action .308 — $200; Remington Model 700 in .30-06 — $139; Ruger 77 in .243 — $160; Remington 742 in $300.

On the same day that the above check was made, a Louisiana gun store was advertising these discount prices for new guns: Browning autoloaders — plain $289.50, vent rib $309.50; Winchester Model 94 — $79.95; Remington Model 700 — $144.95; Remington Model 742 — $169.95; Mossberg Model 500 — $69.95; Winchester Model 1200 — $95.

The important thing to note is that some of the used gun prices are as high as the discount prices, or even higher in some instances. The obvious moral is to shop carefully, checking both new and used gun prices.

May 1975

TRAVELING WITH GUNS

F ew of us do our shooting in the backyard, which means that guns must be moved from home to the site of the shoot. We must transport them in some fashion to a nearby field or woods, to another state or country, and the act deserves thought and care.

Grown men don't usually cry, but Stan Fagerstrom was near tears some years ago at an airport in South America. His fishing rod cases which just came off the baggage conveyor had a new shape. The last foot or so was at right angles to the rest of the case.

Two very strong aluminum tubes, taped together for added strength, had been bent 90 degrees as if they were match sticks. Prized rods inside followed the same contour.

Cartoons to the contrary notwithstanding, most airline baggage personnel are moderately careful in handling luggage. It is the nature of the operation, however, that anything checked as airline baggage may be in for a very rough trip. The rod cases probably got the crush from a mechanized conveyor belt.

If the case in question happened to contain your finely tuned rifle, arriving with you for the big game hunt of a lifetime, it would have ruined your whole day. Depending upon where you happened to be, you might have been able to borrow a gun, but that's a most unsatisfactory "solution." Odds are good that you had spent months getting *your* rifle ready: deciding which one to take, fitting it with the right scope, and making sure you and it were properly tuned. And you had chosen just the proper ammo, and odds are slim it would fit whatever rifle you were able to borrow.

The point is that you should protect your guns when transporting them, whether it is to the nearby skeet range or to another country. Not only does common sense dictate it, the law often requires it.

In the good ole "BS" days — Before Skyjacking — it was usual for the airline to accommodatingly stash your soft-cased gun inside the cabin, the ultimate protection from the ravages of luggage handling procedures. That neighborly gesture is no more, of course, doubtless gone for good.

Now the oblong case made of hard plastic or rigid aluminum is the standard for carrying firearms on planes, and many of us use them in autos and boats as well. They are often awkward to handle, but they provide the best possible protection for guns.

Rigid cases come in a variety of sizes which hold one or two guns in either take-down or full-length configuration. Most brands are fairly good, but some are better than others. Those with full-length, piano hinges are strongest, but make sure those hinges are tamperproof. In some the hinge pin can be slipped out easily, providing ready entry via the back door.

Latches are important, and there should be at least four along a full-length case. Manufacturers should consider adding one at each end, since most cases suffer gaposis at those points when the top is cinched down over two guns, permitting dust to sift in.

But the best ones are very tough, and I've never had a gun damaged in transit while in one.

When you take along a gun on a commercial airliner the Federal Aviation Administration requires: 1. that it go as checked baggage; 2. that it be unloaded; 3. that the airline be notified that you are checking a firearm; and 4. that the luggage containing the gun be locked if it contains a handgun. Nobody would check a loaded gun, right? Wrong. It isn't rare for airlines to find loaded guns, and there have been several instances of accidental discharge during handling. One baggage handler was killed when a pistol in a duffle bag went off.

Some airlines may furnish hard cases for transporting guns, usually at a moderate rental fee.

Make sure your name and address is *inside* the gun case as well as outside. Another good precaution is to tape all of the latches shut, even those with locks.

Theft of firearms is an increasing danger, including those checked as baggage. A few loops of tough duct tape around the case in several places may discourage a thief even more than would a lock.

Removing the bolt from a rifle, carrying it separately in your other luggage, could influence a criminal into leaving your gun even if he gets into the case. Few will want the trouble and danger of replacing that missing part.

A friend of mine taking several gun cases to Africa used another ploy. He fastened all of them together with steel bands, making the total package so heavy that only a well-muscled thief could walk off with it. I'll skip this idea, since it makes my back ache to even think about it.

Although rigid cases are a necessity on commercial carriers, they are often a nuisance at the other end of the trip. They just don't fit in a small bush plane, jeep, or on a horse. Take along soft cases in your luggage, or strapped to the hard cases, and make the switch at the appropriate time. An item I've found very handy is a nylon stretch sock which can be pulled on over shotgun or rifle. Available from the Orvis Company.

Kolpin makes an unusual hard case of molded polyethylene which is padded inside, is shaped like a gun, and can be used as a shipping case or as a scabbard.

A word of caution is in order if you take guns to other countries, most of which are less casual than is the U.S. regarding firearms. In virtually all of them you must obtain permits to possess and transport your particular gun(s) but, in addition, make sure you have those permits and your passport on your person at all times those guns are in your possession. Federals of most nationalities are disinclined to accept explanations about permits "back at the hotel." I recall with no joy a few hours I spent under interrogation at the Buenos Aires airport explaining one round of 7mm mag ammo that a thief had found in my camera bag after he stole it. When the culprit found that single cartridge he feared it was a setup, a trap, and since the penalty at that time for ownership of such ammo could be a firing squad he turned the bag in to the police, saying he had found it.

The epilogue to that little tale is a commentary on the old adage that it's not what you know, it's who. Despite having all my "papers" intact and correct, I was having no success in getting either me or my cameras released...until I remembered a business card in my wallet that had been given me by an Argentine Air Force general at a party a month earlier. On it he had penned his home telephone number, inviting me to call if he could ever be of help. After showing the card and demanding that the security police call the GENERAL — it was 3:00 A.M. by that time — I discovered that the federales had no further interest in either calling my friend or detaining me any longer.

When it comes to transporting your gun via auto, the rules of common sense and the laws of the state involved apply. Inviolate, from my point of view, however, is the axiom that no sporting firearm should be placed in a vehicle with a round in the chamber.

Gun racks are available in wide variety for cars and trucks which will hold guns safely, yet readily accessible. They fit along the dash, vertically or horizontally; along the front or the backs of the seats; and across the back window of pickups. Security chests are also available which replace the back seat in such rec vehicles as the Chevy Blazer, and comparable models manufactured by GMC, Plymouth, Dodge and others. Both the back and bottom of these padded chests have locked and concealed storage space for guns, and similar chests are available for installation in pickup beds.

But most hunters merely toss their guns into the car trunk or on the back seat. Various state laws may require that firearms be carried inside the trunk, cased, and/or unloaded. Some permit cartridges or shells in the magazine but not in the chamber.

Soft padded cases are usually protection enough for a car-carried gun if care is used. If you carry one uncased, either in the trunk (if bumps and scratches don't shake you up) or inside the vehicle, make it a practice to keep the action open. Not only is it an excellent safety practice, but it also makes your companions much more comfortable.

Duck hunters should keep their guns cased enroute to the blind (an obvious exception are those actually hunting from canoes or sneak boats). Here, and in the blind, hard cases are impractical. Since a gun case used for waterfowling is apt to get wet, make sure it has a full-length zipper to facilitate drying. A case I've found useful for any situation where rain, spray or other moisture is a problem is a very simple one made of waterproof "plastic," a synthetic of some sort with no padding inside to get soaked. They aren't easy to find, but L. L. Bean carries a good one that's not expensive.

An excellent idea for boats used to transport hunters is to install gun racks similar to those used in autos, adapted for the space available.

Two precautions which traveling hunters can take are: 1. insure checked guns with airlines for a greater amount than that afforded by normal airline coverage; and 2. register firearms being taken out of the country on U.S. Customs Form 4457. The added insurance premium is quite low and is available from the airlines at the counter (some airline desk clerks may not even know that this is possible, and many of them resent the added time such a procedure requires, so make sure you get to the airport with time to spare). Listing guns on Form 4457 (along with any foreign-made cameras, binoculars, tape recorders, etc.), which can be quickly done at the international airport of your departure, and can help you avoid trouble getting them back in on your return.

Remember that you must take these items to the customs office at the airport, which may be some distance from your departure gate, so allow plenty of time for this.

Theft of firearms from some airports is quite a problem, with the three New York airports being among the worst. There are a couple of things you can do to lessen the risk. Airlines now require each gun case to be tagged with a red "FIREARM" tag which you have signed to swear the gun isn't loaded. That tag is an advertisement to one and all that the case contains a FIREARM. In most instances you will be permitted to tuck that tag inside the case where it's not visible, and that's worth the time and effort, especially if your luggage will be going through one of the bigger airports. The other tip is to use short "take-down" gun cases where possible, since they don't *look* as much like a gun case as do the full-length one.

January 1978

GRITS' GUN BATTERY

Y ou might not *need* "all those guns," as the keeper of the budget is wont to say, but some are certainly indispensable to the well-armed hunter. How many do most of us really need if we hunt most of the game in this country — or intend to hunt some day. Better yet, how few? What's the least number of firearms that will adequately serve as a complete battery for the average man? And what would they be?

Sorting out such a selection is a tremendously enjoyable pastime, whether done on an esoteric, imaginative plane or on a purely practical one. I've done both. Often, some of my lists were a bit beyond the pale, replete with names like Rigby and Fabbri and Parker. But I have one for-real array which wouldn't leave me pleading that I'm under-gunned. Or poorly-gunned. It may apply to your situation, or it might not, but considering the options I chose should help you define yours.

Most of us, if the truth be known, can get by quite nicely with just *three* long guns. Here are the ones I'd choose for my gun rack, and my reasons for doing so.

#1. Rifle — .22 Rimfire: Fun to shoot; inexpensive ammo; perfect for learning to shoot and for maintaining your shooting skill; excellent for small game, and for varmints of modest size at moderate ranges; a good survival gun. Another reason for including this one, of course, is that it borders on being un-American *not* to own a "22." If I could have only one, it would be an autoloader with open sights.

#2. Rifle — 7mm Rem Mag caliber. This is one of the most versatile big game calibers on the market. Superb choice for deer, antelope, black bear, sheep, goats, caribou and, with well-constructed bullets, for elk and moose. Trajectory characteristics make this an excellent long-range caliber. Because of the popularity of this caliber, there is available an excellent array of factory ammunition and good bullets for reloading. Recoil is sharp but not overpowering, which encourages practice. I'd choose a bolt action with a synthetic stock, weighing not more than 7 1/2 pounds with scope.

#3. Shotgun — 12 gauge O&U, 28-inch barrels with three-inch chambers and a screw-in choke system, weighing less than eight pounds. This is a compromise, of course, for the guy who likes to shoot both upland birds and waterfowl. I don't prefer to tote a gun that heavy after quail, but it isn't all that bad, and I certainly don't like to push three-inch magnums at geese through a lightweight. There are now available superb light loads which, with the appropriate tubes installed, make such an O&U as this a most adequate upland gun, yet it is still excellent on waterfowl with the right combinations.

Actions: Choose the type of action that suits you and your shooting conditions. For my center-fire rifle I chose a bolt action. This is largely a personal preference, although the bolt is generally more accurate and more reliable that most other actions. Having said that, I urge you not to dismiss semi-auto's and lever actions as always being inaccurate, which tends to be a relative term when you're shooting at a deer at less than a hundred yards, as is often the case in much of the country. Some autoloaders, in fact, are very accurate.

Single shots and double rifles are specialty items, and can be desirable if they fit the temperament and needs of an individual hunter. Semi-auto's are *usually* reliable in function, but that wee doubt rules them out for me for hunts where trophy opportunities may be scarce.

For my .22 rimfire, on the other hand, I select the autoloader. It's my favorite plinking gun, and is great fun on squirrels, and on running cottontails and jack rabbits.

Options — You say you live and hunt in the East, the Midwest or the South, are wrapped up in deer hunting and never care whether you go west or not? The center-fire rifle that's best for you may be that lever-action .30-30 or autoloader .30-06, both of them solid favorites, and solid performers. That auto '06, in addition, shouldn't be discounted for *anything* in North America's big game line, with the probable exception of the big bears.

Many who hunt in "short range" deer country, we should keep in mind, do so with flat-shooting, scoped bolt actions which have a lot of muscle. My 7 Mag is just as proficient in such conditions as it is in the western mountains.

The idea, of course, is to tailor your choices to the kinds of gunning you prefer and the kinds of terrain in which you do them. The possibilities and variations are endless, but the categories themselves can be fairly well defined. Let's see how that shakes down.

#1. A plinker/small game/survival firearm. Caliber: .22 rimfire or .22 rimfire magnum.

#2. Varmint Rifle. Bolt action or single shot rifle in one of these calibers: .22-250, .222, .223, or .220 Swift.

#3. Deer Rifle. For "eastern" hunting, one of these calibers in an appropriate action: .30-30, .375 Win, 6mm Rem, .243 Win, .270 Win, .280 Rem, 7mm-08 Rem, .308 Win, .30-06, 7mm Rem Mag, .300 Win Mag. For "western" hunting (including antelope, sheep, goats, caribou) a bolt action in any of these calibers except the .30-30 and .375 Win. All are adequate for black bear.

#4. Elk Rifle. Bolt action in .30-06, 7mm Rem Mag, .300 Win Mag, .338 Win Mag, 8mm Rem Mag. (All excellent for moose, with the latter pair good choices for brown bear and grizzly). The comparable Weatherby calibers, it should be emphasized, are excellent in all big game rifles, with the .270 W.M., .300 W.M., and .340 W.M. being especially effective.

#5. Africa — heavy rifle. .458 Win Mag has become the standard big rifle for dangerous game, but the .375 H&H hangs on as a close second and an even better all-around caliber. Get a bolt action.

#6. Shotgun — For waterfowl, a 12-gauge pump or auto

chambered for three-inch shells and with screw-in choke tubes. Although I prefer the feel and balance of doubles, they are awkward to reload in the cramped confines of a duck blind or goose pit, and the third shot of pump and auto is frequently an advantage in quickly anchoring crippled birds. It should weigh in the 8 to 8 1/2 pound range. The advent of required steel shot makes the selection of any gauge smaller than a "twelve" virtually academic, since they presently can't carry sufficient payload to be effective except at short ranges.

#7. Shotgun — For upland birds. 12 or 20 gauge, in the action of your choice. I prefer an O&U weighing not more than 7 1/4 pounds in either gauge. There are many pumps and autos in this weight range so, again, your choice. Again, screw-in chokes are an advantage in coping with various field conditions. Although a three-inch chamber isn't necessary in the 12 gauge, it can be an advantage in the 20 gauge under some conditions.

#8. Shotgun — for goose shooting, particularly where steel shot is required and where ranges are apt to be long: 10 gauge magnum. Although the recoil is heavy, especially in double barrels, nothing approaches this number in effectiveness on geese with steel shot. The Ithaca Mag 10 autoloader is excellent, one of a kind, and its gas-operated system makes recoil tolerable.

Three long guns we could live with, but I'd be more comfortable with five. If four were the magic number, I'd add a 20 gauge shotgun (#7). Five would also let me spring for a heavy rifle (#5), and it would be in .375 H&H Magnum caliber. Although this one is more than half a century old, it remains one of the very best, even today, for really big game. It's an excellent choice for African dangerous game at close range, but it is also sufficiently flat-shooting for 200 to 300 yard shots on smaller game, which makes it superb for elk and moose in North America. It could well be the very best of all for brown bear and grizzly, if the shooter can handle the considerable recoil.

March 1987

T he phenomenon around which the life and times of most gun companies revolve is an annual gathering, a trade show, at which manufacturers can show their products to gun dealers around the country. And, they hope, to sell their firearms. For many years that big event was the NSGA, the National Sporting Goods Association trade show, which was held each February in Chicago.

Over the years, though, there appeared growing dissatisfaction among gun industry people over that event. That unrest was centered around the severe weather that usually held sway in Chicago in February, the rip-off by unions, but most importantly around the fact that the firearms portion of the show was overwhelmed by the jock-oriented athletic products. Gun industry leaders decided to go it alone, to produce and hold their own trade show.

Predictions of failure were plentiful and dire, but under the stewartship of the National Shooting Sports Foundation and its dynamic Executive Director, A.H. "Rock" Rohlfing, this new event took wings. The site of the show was moved away from Chicago, and quickly assumed a pattern of rotation among various cities in the South and West — Kansas City, Atlanta, Houston, St. Louis, New Orleans, and the like. The "Ninth Annual" SHOT (Shooting, Hunting, Outdoor Trade) SHOW was held in January 1987 in New Orleans, and the overwhelming success of this decision by the gun industry is demonstrated by the fact that there were more than *one thousand* exhibitors. The concern now is that the Show is too big, with more floor space and more booths than anybody can cover in three days.

The U.S. firearms industry is experiencing traumatic times. Two of the great old names in the business have disappeared recently, with both Harrington & Richardson and Ithaca Gun Company failing. Others faded from the scene a bit earlier. Some are hanging on desperately.

Despite that, there *are* some good things happening. Du Pont, now the sole owner, continues to show strong support for Remington, which introduced more new products at that 1987 Show than ever before; Bill Ruger built a new plant in Prescott, Arizona to manufacture a new 9mm semi-auto handgun; Weatherby and Browning and others had excellent sales in 1986; a new company emerged which will manufacture the old H&R line of single barrels;

and the atmosphere was upbeat in New Orleans.

Each year I attend the SHOT SHOW to find out what's new, and here's what I found worth writing about at that 1987 edition.

Smith & Wesson had a new, modestly-priced .22 caliber, semi-automatic handgun, available in either target version, which has an adjustable rear sight and walnut grips, or a field version with fixed rear sight and checkered plastic grips. Both come with either 4 1/2-inch or 6-inch barrels. Lightweight (22 or 23 ounces), easy handling and quite accurate, it should be a winner. Features include an ambidextrous magazine release on the front strap, serrated trigger, a "cocked" indicator, and a magazine interlock which prevents firing unless the magazine is in place. Suggested retail is $189 for field model and $225 for target model. *Smith & Wesson, 2100 Roosevelt Ave., Springfield, MA 01101*

Federal Cartridge Company made a mid-year introduction of a new steel shot size in 12 gauge three-inch magnum. This hot load contains 48 pellets of F shot (a size between BB's and #4 Buck) which leave the muzzle at 1400 fps. Announced at the January S.H.O.T. show were five additional new steel shot loadings: 10-gauge magnums with F and T shot, 12 ga. three-inch magnum with T shot, 12 ga. short magnum with #3 shot, and 12 ga. "Hi-Power" with BB steel; and four new cartridges in the Premium line: 250-grain Nosler bullet in .338 Win Mag, 140-grain Nosler in 7mm Rem Mag, and a 120-grain Nosler in .257 Roberts (+P), plus a new 117-grain boattail (Sierra) in .25-06 caliber. With a muzzle velocity of 3150 fps, the new 7mm Rem Mag loading should become popular. Also new: 50-grain hollow point .22 Win. Mag; a 180-grain Soft Point in .30-06; three-inch Premium buckshot loadings of 000 and 1 Buck; and a new 124-grain 9mm Luger hollow point in the Nyclad line. *Federal Cartridge Co., 2700 Foshay Tower, Minneapolis, MN 55402.*

Alpha Arms created quite a stir a couple years back when it introduced Alphawood stocks, laminated, resin impregnated, and virtually impervious to weather conditions. Now it will stock other barreled actions with Alphawood, and accurize them with its patented pillar bedding system. First available will be for M70's, M700's, and M77's. *Alpha Arms, 1000 Spinks Dr., Flower Mound, TX 76051.*

Hornady added three new features to its Pro-Jector progressive reloader: automatic case ejector, auto primer shut-off, and improved auto indexing. Catalog features many new rifle and pistol bullets, as well as 78 loads of finished ammo in 22 calibers. *Hornady Mfg. Co., Box 1848, Grand Island, NE 68802.*

Sturm, Ruger & Co. had a new "MINI THIRTY" autoloading carbine, a modified version of the excellent Mini-14 Ranch Rifle. The big news is that this one is chambered for the 7.62x39mm cartridge, the Russian service cartridge called the M43 Russian short. Ruger says that performance is comparable to the .30-30, touting it as excellent for deer at modest ranges. Ammo is imported or manufactured by Norma, PMC, Lapua, Midway Arms and Hansen Cartridge Co., and the basic loading is a 123-grain .30-caliber bullet at 2340 fps muzzle velocity. For 1987, Ruger is also offering the M77 Ultra Light with a shorter (18 1/2 inch) barrel and iron sights. In .270, .30-06, .243 and .308 calibers. Weight: six pounds empty. *Sturm, Ruger, & Co., 49 Lacey Place, Southport, CT 06490.*

Remington Arms Company had 124 new products for 1987. Dominating their debut at the firearms seminar last November were items reflecting the Du Pont strength in synthetic materials, an array of innovative ammunition products, and a strong commitment voiced by the new Remington head man (Ernie Woodacre, Exec. V.P.) toward continued improvement both in products and customer service. Jack Preiser, Du Pont Director of Sporting Goods, also confirmed what had been rumored: that Remington was taking over the assets of Ithaca, and that a Remington version of the Mag-10 would be forthcoming.

Perhaps the biggest Remington news was a new auto shotgun, the M11-87 "Premier," in 12 gauge only for '87, which follows the S&W/Mossberg trend in that this one will shoot *any* 12 gauge shotshells interchangeably, from light field loads to three-inch mags. Retains the good lines of the old M1100 (which it will eventually replace), but has many internal changes which increase the durability by 50 percent. "Rem" choke barrels standard.

Remington also showed a new synthetic stock line built in the Remington plant, with both fiberglass/kevlar (FS) stocks and a new Du Pont synthetic stock made of Rynite (RS). Particularly catching my eye is a glass/kevlar stocked Model 7 which should be pure joy to tote and poison on deer. Weighs 5 1/2 lbs. with 18 1/2-inch barrel — in .243, 7mm-08, and .308 calibers — and in either .350 Rem Mag or .35 Rem from the Custom Shop. For the first time M700's will be available over-the-counter in the standard line in both the FS and RS stocks.

Quickly, other new items from Remington: 20-gauge "Rem" chokes; 20 ga. steel shotshells in three-inch mag (1 oz.); "Duplex" shotshells in steel (2x6's, BBx4's, and BBx2's); M7600 pump rifle in .30-06 now standard as a Carbine with 18 1/2-inch barrel; M700 Classic for '87 is in .338 Win Mag caliber; M700 with a "do-it-yourself" unfinished stock (about $300 suggested retail); new 100-grain loading for .257 Roberts at 2980 fps without the necessity of a +P rating; two new "XP-100" pistols — a .35 Rem version in the production gun, and a .223 Rem version from the Custom Shop which has a 15 1/2-inch heavy barrel. *Remington Arms Co., Du Pont, Wilmington, DE 19898.*

Redfield, Inc. had a new line of compact scopes: 2X-7X, 3X-9X, 4X-12X, 4X and 6X. All have the Written Lifetime Warranty. Also new: a mounting system 25 percent lighter than standard rings and bases. *Redfield, Inc., 5800 E. Jewell Ave., Denver, CO 80224*

Gold Medallion bore cleaner, which had attracted much favorable comment in the previous year, announced a clever little one-ounce "travel size" plastic container of the cleaner and conditioner. Good idea. *Gold Medallion, U.S. Products Co., 518 Melwood Ave., Pittsburgh, PA 15213.*

American Arms, Inc. unveiled a new line of shotguns with waterfowl and turkey hunters in mind. All feature non-glare parkerized barrels and receivers, come with slings, and have a five year warranty. There's a 10 ga. side-by double with 32-inch chrome line barrels (F&F), double triggers, suggested retail $550; a 12 ga. O&U with 28-inch chrome lined barrels fitted with choke tubes, single selective trigger, suggested retail $595; and two versions of a side-by double "turkey special" — 10 and 12 ga. magnums with choke tubes and double triggers. *American Arms, Inc., 715 E. Armour Rd., N. Kansas City, MO 64116.*

SKB shotguns were reintroduced by Ernie Simmons Enterprises, good news for the many shooters who had used them for years. O&U's in field and target versions (no side-by's for now), and three models of an autoloader which has a couple of innovative features: a magazine cutoff button, and an adjustment screw on the fore-end to allow using either regular light loads or three-inch magnums. *SKB Shotguns — Ernie Simmons Enterprises, 719 Highland Ave., Lancaster, PA 17603.*

CCI added a batch of new numbers to its Blazer line of ammo, the aluminum-cased cartridges which are becoming very popular, especially with non-reloaders. New for '87: .38 Spec. 125 gr. JSP,

.38 Spec. 158 gr. L-SWC, .357 Mag. 125 gr. JSP, .44 Mag. 200 gr. JSP, .44 Mag. 240 gr. L-SWC, .45 Auto 185 gr. TMJ, .45 Auto 200 gr. TMJ, and .45 Auto shotshell ammo. (TMJ is "Totally Metal Jacketed," a process that completely encases the bullet in copper — including the bottom.) *CCI, Box 856, Lewiston, ID 83501*

Speer Bullets had two new TMJ offerings in 45 Auto caliber, 185 gr. and 200 grain; and two new shotshell primers — #209 and #209M. *Speer Bullets, Box 856, Lewiston, ID 83501*

RCBS has such a complete line of reloading equipment it would seem difficult to find new items to add, but they do. This time: Rotary Case Trimmer Power Conversion, which motorizes your case trimmer by using any power drill; Vibratory Case Cleaner, which will clean up to 550 .38 Spec. or 190 .30-06 cases at a time; and a Primer Seating Depth Gauge. *RCBS, Box 856, Lewiston, ID 83501*

Weaver Scopes from Omark moved into full gear, with all these new scopes: V-9 3X-9X, K4 4X, V3 1X-3X, K2.5 2 1/2X, V10 2X-10X, KT15 15X, K6 6X, V7 2X-7X rimfire scope, and RK4 4X rimfire scope. Also new: a 12X-36X spotting scope, 8X24 binoculars, new line of rifle and shotgun scope mounts. *Weaver Scopes, Box 856, Lewiston, ID 83501*

U.S. Repeating Arms, which went into Chap. 11 reorganization at SHOT show time, 1986, was back in action, with a work force of almost 800 people by mid-year. New for '87 were: a 500-run limited edition Golden Anniversary M70 in .300 *Weatherby* caliber; more models stocked with Wintuff and Wincam synthetics; a M70 Lightweight, 22-inch barrel, in all calibers; a M94 in a Deluxe XTR model featuring semi-fancy wood, cut checkering and quality fit; M94 in .22 rimfire with laminated stock; M1300 "Waterfowl" pump with camo laminated stock; and a "Defender" pump with 18-inch barrel and pistol grip which can be converted to standard stocked, 28-inch barrel hunting shotgun. *U.S. Repeating Arms, 275 Winchester Ave., New Haven, CT 06511.*

Weatherby, which had a banner year in '86, had a new left-hand version of the Fibermark bolt action rifle. *Weatherby, Inc., 2781 Firestone Blvd., South Gate, CA 90280*

Leupold — an excellent-looking new 20X spotting scope, an expanded line of smaller binoculars, an 8X version of their compact scope, and a line of super-low rings. *Leupold & Stephens, Box 688, Beaverton, OR 97005*

Thompson/Center Arms added new calibers to its popular T/C Contender pistol: 7x30 WATERS, .30 M1 Carbine, .32 H&R Mag,

.32/20 Win., 9mm Luger, 6mm T.C.U., and 410 gauge. TCR single shot rifle now chambered for 10 rifle calibers and for 12 ga. slugs, all barrels interchangeable. T/C's excellent line of black powder rifles and pistols continues to expand. Lifetime warranty on all T/C firearms. *T/C Arms, Box 5002, Rochester, NH 03867*

Sierra Bullets introduced three new bullets designed for hunting performance with single shot pistols: 130-gr. 7mm SPT, an 80-gr. 6mm SPT, and a 135-gr. .30 cal. SPT. Also new: 150-gr. 7mm SBT Gameking, a 200-gr. .375 cal. FN Pro-Hunter, and a 90-gr. .32 Mag JHC Sports Master. *Sierra, 10532 S. Painter Ave., Sante Fe Springs, CA 90670*

Burris Scopes had three new Silhouette scopes in 10X, 12X, and 6X-18X powers; two new shotguns scopes in 1 1/2X and 2 1/2X; a parallax adjustable 6X Mini Scope, and a new "no drill," 'no tap" scope mount base for muzzle loaders. *Burris Company, 331 E. 8th St., Greeley, CO 80632*

Colt announced the Delta Elite, a new semi-auto pistol using the design of the Government Model but chambered for the new 10mm auto cartridge. Magazine holds 7 rounds. Available mid-1987. *Colt Industries, Box 1868, Hartford, CT 06102*

Bushnell added a new 2.5X-10X scope to its top-of-the-line Bausch & Lomb Balvar series, plus three B&L target scopes: 36X, 24X, and 6-24X. Also new: 10X Sportview target scope; two Compact scopes — 4X and a 2X-8X variable; two B&L handgun scopes in 2X and 4X; two "affordable" Sportview spotting scopes, a 20X-60X and a 15X-45X; a low-power variable Sportview scope — 1.5X-4.5X; and a Banner 2.5X shotgun scope. *Bushnell, 300 North Lone Hill Ave., San Dimas, CA 91773*

Daisy began its second *century* in the air rifle business by introducing a CO2 pellet revolver, the Power Line 44, a full-size replica of a .44 magnum. Swing-out cylinder and a six-inch barrel, but optional four and eight-inch barrels are available. Also new from Daisy are two new pellets: a round-nose and a pointed pellet, both .177 caliber. *Daisy Mfg. Co., Rogers, AR 72756*

Browning had an array of new guns, with the most newsworthy for me being a brand new auto shotgun, made in Belgium, called the A-500. Resembles a streamlined Auto-5, but is all new inside, complete with a short-recoil system which shoots all loads — 1 oz. target to three-inch mags — in any order without adjustment. And...Browning introduced two *16-gauge shotguns*, returning the "Sweet Sixteen" to the Auto-5 line, and adding a 16 ga. Hunting

Model to the Citori O&U line. Also new: an all-black version of the BPS pump called the Stalker; a left-hand A-Bolt in Medallion grade only (.270, .30-06 and 7mm Mag.); an A-Bolt Stainless Stalker and an A-Bolt Camo Stalker (laminated stock); a reintroduced M71 lever action in .348 Win caliber, and a Silhouette version of the Buck Mark .22 rimfire auto pistol. *Browning Arms Company, Route One, Morgan, UT 84050*

Nosler added two new rifle bullets to the Ballistic Tip line, a 120-gr. Spitzer in 6.5mm caliber, and a 100-gr. Spitzer in .25 caliber. And three new handgun bullets: a 115-gr. H.P. in 9mm; a 210-gr. JHP in .41 cal.; and a 250-gr. JHP in .45 Colt. *Nosler Bullets, Box 688, Beaverton, OR 97075*

Crosman's big news for 1987 was a new "world-class" pellet for .177 and .22 caliber rifles and pistols priced to sell at "one-fourth" the tab for comparable pellets. Five years and a million dollars went into perfecting this one, says Crosman, which is called the New Copperhead Pellet. *Crosman Air Guns, Rts. 5 & 20, East Bloomfield, NY 14443.*

Winchester/Olin, which pioneered the screw-in choke tube system with the Winchoke, unveiled a new, internal version which fits inside the barrels, out of sight, and will be standard on all "Winchoke" versions of the "Classic Doubles" — M23's and M101's. Winchester added 14 new steel shot loads for 1987, bringing its total to 35. New T-shot and BBB copper plated steel in 10 and 12 ga. magnums. Also, a new Super-Lite target shotshell in 12 gauge — 1 1/8 oz. of 7 1/2, 8, 8 1/2, or 9 shot; and two new center-fire loadings — 180-gr. .30-06 Silvertip boattail, and a 145-gr. 7x57 Power Point. *Winchester/Olin, 120 Long Ridge Rd., Stamford, CT 06904*

Mossberg had new "Accu-Steel" choke tubes designed for steel shot use, and cautions that it does NOT recommend use of steel shot with Accu-choke or Accu-choke II internal choke tubes. The Accu-Steel tubes can be used on these 12 ga. shotguns: Mossberg models 500, 712, 1000 and 3000; and choke tube barrels for Savage and Winchester (USRAC). The M712 autoloader, announced here a year ago, never got on track in 1986 but should be on line this year. The Speedfeed synthetic stock (it holds four extra shells) is now available for Rem 870 pumps as well as for Mossberg M500 and 3000 and S&W M3000. *O. F. Mossberg & Sons, Inc., 7 Grasso Ave., North Haven, CT 06473*

Tasco had a new Euro-Class line of scopes, with 30mm tubes instead of the 25.4mm (one-inch) standard, including 4X, 6X, 3-9, 3-12-1.5-6, and 3-9 powers. Equally important, Tasco has mounts to fit these tubes. Also new, the IR1X20P optical sight for pistols which Riley Gilmore used to win the 1986 Bianchi Cup. And, a new/old innovation giving a "post" reticle on demand. *Tasco, Box 520080, Miami, FL 33152*

Marlin unveiled a new "Midget Magnum," a .22 Mag lightweight, take-down bolt action rifle. This seven-shot, clip-fed repeater comes in a padded zipper case that floats, even with the gun inside, and a 4X scope is included. *Marlin Firearms Co., 100 Kenna Drive, North Haven, CT 06473*

New England Firearms Co. was a new firm founded in December as a result of an asset purchase of the former Harrington & Richardson Company. According to Pres. Paul Senecal they will shortly go into production of a full line of single barrel shotguns which will be called the "Pardner," and expanded upon that with other products as they see a need in the marketplace. *New England Firearms Company, Industrial Rowe, Gardner, MA 01440*

Sigarms, Inc. had a new/old President in the form of Ted Rowe, former President of H&R, and had on display at S.H.O.T. the excellent Sauer hunting rifles, and Sig-Sauer semi-automatic pistols. *Sigarms, Inc., 8330 Old Courthouse Rd., Suite 885, Tysons Corner, VA 22180*

Savage had an interesting new version of its pump shotgun. The M675, in 12 gauge only, comes with a "slug choke tube" and a quick-mounting open sight set, as well as three tubes for shotshells. *Savage Industries, Inc., Springdale Rd., Westfield, MA 01085*

Simmons had restructured its scope line into three levels: gold, bronze and silver, a la the Olympics and/or European trophy designations, and each scope has an attractive, appropriately colored plate on its side. Extensive line of scopes, as well as spotting scopes and binocs. *Simmons Outdoor Corp., 14205 S.W. 119th Ave., Miami, FL 33186*

Anschutz, widely acclaimed for its accurate rifles, surprised many of us by introducing a new single shot pistol designed for competition and for hunting. Unique left hand bolt; 10-inch barrel; chambered for .22 LR (five-shot clip) and at 9.85 ounces. Also new, two rifles — the Kadett, a five-shot .22 LR; and the Achiever, designed as the ideal first rifle for starting youngsters. *Precision Sales International, Box 1776, Westfield, MA 01085*

Beretta had expanded its "Sporting Clays" line of O&U shotguns to three — M686, M682 and M687L. Also new was the M1200 semi-auto shotgun, with "Beretta" quality but no engraving and a lower price. It's 12 ga. only, 28-inch Mod and 2 3/4-inch chamber. *Beretta U.S.A. Corp., 17601 Indian Head Hwy., Accokeek, MD 20607*

Charter Arms offered the "Bulldog Pug" as the latest in its line of moderately priced, lightweight revolvers. Chambering five .44 Spec. cartridges, it has a 2 1/2-inch barrel, and is available with a pocket hammer. Still in the line is one of the best survival tools available: the AR-7 Explorer Rifle, a .22 LR semi-auto which packs inside the stock — and floats. *Charter Arms Corp., 430 Sniffens Ln., Stratford, CT 06497*

Dan Wesson Arms, whose revolvers have been dominating the revolver class in silhouette competition, had a new revolver in chambered for the .32 H&R Magnum cartridge (also handles the .32 S&W Long and .32 Colt new police ammo). In either blue or stainless, it should be excellent for competition or small game. Also new, the DW in 45 Colt caliber, which should be a winner. *Dan Wesson Arms, 293 Main St., Monson, MA 01057*

May 1987

LONG LIVE THE GUNSMITH

A firearm is a thing of beauty and a joy, but frequently not forever. When a gun won't work it becomes something else again, often described in terms unfit for family consumption. Odds are great that you've witnessed *that* scene, one replete with frustration on the part of some hunter. He's surrounded by buzzing doves taunting him at spittin' distance, while he has parts of his autoloader scattered over two corn rows. He's watching a buck disappearing over the hill and wondering why his rifle didn't go bang when he pulled the trigger.

"What is WRONG with this #$*$# gun!"

He isn't really asking, since he already knows what's wrong with it. It won't shoot.

From my earliest experience with shooting I've had a soft spot for that mysterious man (you know *any* female gunsmiths?) who could fix a broken gun. He dealt in magic. He was my hero. He actually got paid for being around a whole raft of rifles and shotguns and pistols all day long, all week long. Most boys I knew had the same feelings, and most still do. Many of us had the urge to follow in the footsteps of those lucky firearms repair men, but for most that urge fell by the wayside. Judging from my mail, the fascination of gunsmithing as a way of life lives on.

How do you become a gunsmith? What's it really like? Can you make a living at it?

Just down the road from where I live is the gunsmith who does most of my work, and whose career I've followed for some quarter of a century. Ken Eversul is only 43, but he started working on guns while still in high school. He climbed the foothills and finally scaled the mountain. Along the way he learned to do, and did, virtually everything there is to do with a firearm. Stocks, barrels, chokes, cases, recoil pads, bluing, case hardening, stock bending... whatever. I took to Africa a .450-500 O&U rifle Ken built from a Browning Citori which would shoot into the same three inches from both barrels. Many police officers around the nation still use "Eversul" combat competition revolvers. His gunsmithing tools are in use in more than 60 countries, including Russia. Modest fortunes have been won by live pigeon shooters packing "bird guns" fine-tuned by Ken.

Except for the latter, he doesn't do much of any of that anymore. Now, more than 90 percent of his work is on fine (as in expensive) doubles. He is the only factory authorized gunsmith *in the world,* other than in the Brescia, Italy factory itself, for Fabbri shotguns, believed by many to be the best shotgun now being produced. Ken talked with me about his profession.

On How to Learn Gunsmithing: "Dad was an avid varmint shooter and experimenter, and some of his knowledge of guns rubbed off on me. I learned gunsmithing the hard and expensive way, by trial and error. Make a mistake, you repeat the job. Screw up a part you're making, and you make another one. You can learn general gunsmithing on your own, but it's time consuming, expensive and difficult."

Gunsmithing Schools?: "Probably the best way if you can't apprentice with a good gunsmith. I don't see how correspondence courses could get it done."

Gunsmithing Outlook?: "Not all that good. Investment in equipment is too large if you hope to handle most gunsmithing — $175,000 to $200,000, and the return on investment is low. One of our milling machines cost $25,000. I borrowed and took 20 years to pay it off.

"I think the best way to start for most people is on a part-time basis — general gun repair work done in your home or garage, or as a repair employee of a sporting goods store."

Changes and Trends?: "The business has changed drastically over the past couple or three years, and product liability is now the PRIME concern. Liability insurance for gunsmiths is very high, and I hate to see some guns even come through the door. Even if you never work on them you can end up in court. And even if you win in court, you lose. (Eversul has never had a suit against his business.)

"I've virtually eliminated all work that has much potential for liability involvement. Do NO trigger work except for known customers we judge as competent gun handlers and shooters. No work on autoloaders. Most of my work is on break-open guns — over and under and side/by rifles and shotguns.

"But there is a need for gunsmiths who will install recoil pads and scope sights, sight in rifles, do blue jobs, and find out why a gun won't feed, and in most communities there are men who fill that need. Most of them learned by trial and error, and do a decent job until they stretch their capabilities. More than 25 percent of our work on fine shotguns is to repair the damage done by other gunsmiths."

Most common repair problem?: "Cleaning dirty guns. No question. If hunters would keep their guns clean they'd eliminate most of their problems. The shell latches on autoloaders have always given problems, causing failure to feed. Recoil pad and scope attachment are regular items."

On Making a Living?: "If you've got enough money to build and stock a complete gunsmithing shop you probably don't need a job. If not, you can start on a part-time basis and build the business gradually, hopefully to go full-time as some point. You can attend a gunsmithing school, then gain experience by working for an established gunsmith. When you're on your own, try to devise something you can manufacture and sell to other gunsmiths and just to gun owners, small items which might not be profitable enough for big manufacturers to build. We've sold our specialized tools throughout the world."

On Gunsmithing as a Profession: "Very satisfying if you like to work on guns and like to deal with people who shoot, and can cope with the conditions mentioned above. If you expand beyond your ability to personally do all the work, a huge problem is to get competent help. When the two who work with me decide to hang it up (Harley Barrett and Harry Darby, both retired army and air force officers), I think I'll call it quits, too."

Brownells, Inc., of Montezuma, Iowa, is the leading supplier to gunsmiths in this country. Bob Brownell, who in April was awarded by the NRA its prestigious Professional Award for Public Service (only the third time it has ever been given), and who has done far more to advance the profession of gunsmithing than has anyone else, had this comment on the profession: "Our business continues to grow. Gun manufacturers who have gone out of business, and others who have discontinued many models, have created a greater demand for gunsmiths. With no factory to service the guns there's greater opportunity for gunsmiths.

"There are some good gunsmithing schools, and more on the way. For a man just beginning, it's best to start on a part-time basis. Working in a machine shop is excellent training. When they go full time, many want to set up shop in a tiny town out in the boonies, which is usually a mistake. Great place to live...but not many people or guns to work on. The ones who are doing great are in metropolitan areas or areas with shooting programs. The outlook for gunsmithing is very encouraging."

(For a list of gunsmithing schools, write to: Brownells, Rt. 2 Box 1, Montezuma, Iowa 50171)

October 1987

INVENTORY AND INSURE

A re your guns insured?
Are you *sure* about that!

I'm sure you can imagine the feelings I had a couple of decades ago when I stood among the smoldering, stinking remains of what had been my garage and storeroom and slowly began to wonder just what had been destroyed in that raging inferno.

Some things were obvious: an auto, a boat and trailer, five outboard motors, and the building itself, of course. But, just what all had been in that huge storeroom out back? Some guns, all the camping gear, a few cases of ammo and — what else? The items came to mind gradually, now and then, over the next few years.

The point is that I really had no idea what we had lost, and I quickly learned that insurance covered very little of it.

Inventory and insure!

That should be the motto of most outdoorsmen, but it is particularly appropriate for shooters where their guns are concerned. Do you really know how many guns you have, what and where they are, and how much they're worth? Are they insured?

Insurance is a funny game, and you can spell that "tricky." It is routine to hear that famous line, "I thought that was covered," and then to have the insurance agent point out the words in the policy which got the company off the hook. So what if he had to use a magnifying glass t'read it.

If you *believe* you have coverage on your firearms, verify that by getting it in writing from your company. Make them spell it out as to what is covered, where it is covered, and for how much. Do they need an itemized list of your guns. Some do and some don't. If they do, what information do they need. Do you need to notify the firm each time to acquire another gun, or is coverage automatic.

Sure, my guns are covered under my HOMEOWNERS policy!

Maybe. Most such policies cover household contents to a value of half the coverage on the house itself, which would normally be enough to take care of any guns you have. But a peculiar thing happened to most such policies in the past few years: they now have a maximum liability figure for firearms, at least for the "theft" provision.

You are absolutely covered to the maximum "household" limit if anything happens to your guns in your home, and to 10 percent of that if anything happens to them away from your home. And, no, we don't need an itemized list of your guns, Mr. Gresham, although you may send us one if you like. That is nice that you have so many nice guns.

Beautiful! A few years on down the line, when browsing through my policy for something else, I learned that a firearms maximum had been inserted, without any notice to me other than in the policy's fine print. In my case that maximum is $2000 for *theft* of guns.

My point is that you should be sure. Your homeowners policy coverage may be all that you need, but surprises aren't nice when it comes to insurance coverage.

One of the benefits of membership in the National Rifle Association is that with it you get, free, a modest amount of gun insurance. Even more important, you can buy additional insurance from the NRA at an excellent price...about $1.25 per $100 as of this writing.

For your inventory, and you should have one regardless of how many or how few guns you own, list a complete description of each. That will include: Manufacturer; Model; Serial Number; Gauge or Caliber; Type of Action; Barrel Length; and any other pertinent information about scope sights, mounts, chokes, choke attachments and the like. For your own information you might want to list when and how you acquired the gun, what it cost, what you think it's worth as of the inventory date, and any identifying data which might help in case the gun is lost or stolen.

Make at least three copies of that inventory listing. Keep a couple in *different* parts of your house, but put the other in a safe deposit box or give it to your attorney or to a friend to keep. And, if they want it, give a copy to your insurance company.

And, hey, do it now! Tonight. You hope never to wake to the crackle of flames, or to the dismaying sight of a forced window or door, but we can't count on that happy thought.

June 1987

Section Five

AMMUNITION

.270 .308 .358 Win.

We tend to take little things for granted, and nothing could be more true in this respect than the little, old .22 rimfire caliber. It *is* "old", having had its beginning way back in 1845, in Europe. What a career it has had, with no end in sight.

It *is* little, of course, with even the .22 Long Rifle cartridge stretching only an inch in length. And the .22 Short is, well, shorter. And only .22 inches in diameter. Tiny, but mighty in many, many respects.

Four billion is the figure most bandied about as the number of rounds of .22 rimfire ammunition made and sold in this country each year. "Over four billion" is the way most of the authorities put it, which figures out to quite a few for every man, woman and child in the United States. And that doesn't include the .22 rimfire ammo made in many other countries, some of which is imported and sold here.

Numbers like that make the .22 rimfire far and away the most popular caliber in the world. It has been for decades, and could well maintain that position forever. Amazing.

Any shooter worth his salt has his own, personal .22 rimfire experience (do you know any shooter or hunter who doesn't own a ".22"?), and mine began half a century ago with a single-shot Remington Improved Model 6 rifle. It still accounts for a few squirrels, a batch of sparrows and starlings, and a multitude of tin cans each year.

But the part I remember best from those years of yore was my efforts to maintain and replenish my supply of ammo, and my "summer schedule" will suffice for illustration. I would pick two gallons of green beans from Dad's garden, peddle them on our street for ten cents a gallon, and trade that twenty cents down at the hardware store for one box of .22 Shorts — 20 cents; 50 cartridges.

Today, light years later in terms of research and ballistic efficiency and inflation, I can buy a box of .22 Long Rifle ammo, the ultimate state of the art in rimfire ammunition, for not much more than a buck a box if I watch for the sales. At twice that it's a bargain. That low cost of operation is one of the reasons for the overwhelming popularity of the .22 rimfire. It's simply the best value there is in a firearm caliber. But that's only one of the reasons.

Add to that the fact that the ".22" has almost no recoil, makes very little noise, and is extremely versatile, accurate, and effective on varmints and small game, and it's easy to understand why this caliber is such a runaway winner.

For the record, which is a bit hazy on some dates, the French gun maker Louis Flobert produced the "Flobert Cap," as it became known, in 1845. That first .22 rimfire was followed a decade later by Smith & Wesson's new .22 Short, with the cartridge patented in 1854 and a revolver for it offered in 1857. The .22 Long came along in 1871 and the .22 Long Rifle in 1887.

A number of other .22's came and went through the years — the twin, the .22 Remington Special (RS). They're gone. Hanging on are the BB Cap, a very short cartridge similar to Flobert's original, designed for indoor or gallery use at very short ranges; and the CB (conical ball) Cap, essentially a beefed-up version of the BB Cap. Neither are manufactured in this country, although CCI makes what it calls a Mini-Cap CB which is a much more potent (727 fps/29-grain bullet) number than the original BB's and CB's.

CCI introduced an entirely new element into the .22 rimfire field in 1977 with its Stinger, a higher velocity cartridge which would function in rifles and pistols chambered for the .22 Long Rifle caliber. By using a longer case and a shorter, lighter bullet (32 grains compared to the 38-grain bullet in a regular .22 Long Rifle hollow point), this Omark firm produced a muzzle velocity of more than 1600 fps, appreciably greater than the 1200-1300 fps range of regular .22 L.R. ammo. Most ammunition companies now have their own versions of this ultra high velocity rimfire ammunition.

Why is the .22 rimfire so popular. It's ideal for teaching beginners to shoot, because of the light recoil, low noise, low cost, accuracy, and because of the availability of a wide array of rifles and pistols in all price ranges chambered for the caliber. It's the consummate "plinker," the perfect choice for shooting just for fun. The caliber is great for small game such as rabbits and squirrels, and for varmints such as crows, groundhogs, jack rabbits and prairie dogs. It is a superbly accurate cartridge, particularly in the match versions, and dominates target competition. Rimfire silhouette shooting is a fast-growing sport, attractive because such a range requires little space, and because shooting it is so inexpensive.

The .22 rimfire is not a toy!

Although it is manageable by youngsters, it has killed the largest animals. Grizzlies. Elk. The .22 rimfire, being the poacher's favorite tool, has killed thousands of deer, mostly at night in the glare of a headlight. Despite this, it is not a "big game" caliber, either legally or ethically. It is also, sadly enough, the favored tool of the professional hit man, being efficient and quiet, and very amenable to the use of a silencer at bullet velocities less than the speed of sound. The label on most .22 ammo boxes says it's dangerous within one mile. Believe it. It's also one of the very worst for ricochets, which makes the selection of a safe place to shoot doubly important.

The prominent surviving members of the .22 rimfire clan are the Short, Long and Long Rifle, and they are available in a wide array of offerings — hollow points, solids, shot cartridges, silhouette ammo, match ammo, pistol ammo, rifle ammo, high velocity, standard velocity, hyper-velocity. The Short and the Long Rifle are the important ones. The Long has little going for it.

In 1959 Winchester introduced a much more potent .22 rimfire, the .22 Winchester Magnum Rimfire (WMR). Although it has never reached the popularity predicted for it, the WMR is very much a part of the shooting scene today. Quite a number of rifles and handguns are chambered for it, and ammunition is produced by several companies. With a muzzle velocity of 1800 fps plus for its 40 grain bullet, the WMR substantially improves upon the performance of the .22 Long Rifle. The WMR cannot be used in firearms chambered for the .22 Long Rifle.

Herb Parsons, Winchester's famed exhibition shooter who died some years ago, told a favorite story about "twenty two" shooters. While driving the back roads of his native Tennessee he picked up a bare-footed youngster in ragged overalls who carried an old, single-shot .22 rifle. Great with kids and gifted with gab, Herb could get little more than a "yup" or a "nope" during the several miles along that dusty road before reaching the turnoff to the boy's home. When he stopped to let him out, Herb reached into the back seat and handed the youngster a 500-round carton of .22 rimfire ammo.

"He just stared at the box," Herb told me later, "and then briefly at me, before whirling and running away down the path. His eyes told the story, and conveyed the thanks."

Happiness was a kid with a .22 rifle and 500 rounds of ammo for it. It still is, and that's not all bad.

December 1985

GRANDPA'S GUN RIDES AGAIN

The cock pheasant burst from the hedgerow giving its unmistakable cackle, and the hunter swung the twin tubes of his graceful double past the outstretched beak and pulled the trigger. A typical scene, but there the "normal" ended. At the shot the man dropped to a crouch in order to determine the results of his effort, since his view was partially blocked by a cloud of smoke.

Grandpa's smoothbore was back in action!

Damascus! Before the turn of the century that was the magic word where quality shotguns were concerned. But it was a creature which required black powder shotshells, and the advent of smokeless powder headed all guns of such barrel construction toward obsolescence. Here's why.

Damascus barrels were constructed by winding alternating strips of iron and steel around a mandrel, then forge-welding them in that spiral. The method resulted in a pleasing pattern, with the finer and more graceful designs the hallmarks of quality, so much so that imitation Damascus patterns were sometimes applied to guns of poorer construction. Laminated and twist steel barrels fell into that category.

When properly made and cared for all, such barrels had adequate strength for use with black powder shells, but they could not handle the greatly increased pressures of smokeless powder. Some owners tried the new shells in Damascus, twist or laminated barrels, but the results often were disastrous. Even today some owners of these old guns use modern ammo in them, often with the same results — disastrous.

DO NOT SHOOT MODERN SMOKELESS SHOTSHELLS IN GUNS HAVING DAMASCUS, TWIST OR LAMINATED BARRELS!!!

Why? Again, because they develop much higher pressures than do black powder shells — 11,000 to 12,000 pounds per square inch as against perhaps half that for black powder.

"But I just use low brass, light loads in my old gun. No express loads or magnums."

No good! The lightest 12 gauge trap load available develops pressures almost as high as do the magnums, and pressures far, far greater than those from black powder loads.

As black powder shotshells faded from the shelves of gun stores the guns which used them were gradually relegated to the corner closet or to a couple of pegs above the mantel. Most of them have remained there for more than half a century. Some are junk and some are marginal, but others are magnificent.

Either for old times sake or simply because they are excellent shotguns, many owners of the good ones would like to use them for hunting now and then. For years they have written *Sports Afield:* "Where can I buy black powder shotshells?" And for years our answer was negative — none commercially available. But that changed back in the mid-1970's.

The news release announced it "Navy Arms is now manufacturing 12 gauge Black Powder Shotgun Shells specifically designed to be shot in any of the fine old timers. At last, you can shoot your favorite Damascus twist steel or soft iron barrel shotgun. It is time to get those great old favorites out of retirement and back into the field."

Loaded for Navy Arms in Germany, these shells were available only in 12 gauge, only in field loads, and only with 1 1/8 ounce of number 4 or number 6 shot. They were 2 3/4 dram loads, in plastic hulls with shot sleeves. List price was $3.50 for a box of 10, a bit more than twice the tab for modern smokeless equivalents. Cost might rule out these factory loads for trap, skeet or extensive "plinking," but should be no limiting factor for the man who wants to pop a pheasant, grouse, rabbit or squirrel now and then with granddad's favorite Betsy.

Navy Arms reported that their shells produce the same velocity as standard nitro-powder (smokeless) field loads but feature a lower pressure travel curve. The firm claims that "exhaustive tests have proven that they produce a fantastic pattern equal to or in many cases superior to their modern contemporaries. It is a marriage of modern technology with old time propellants."

Navy Arms is a division of Service Armament Company (689 Bergen Blvd., Ridgefield, N.J. 07657), and in its release announcing the new-old shells it made another point: "Great fun in any 12-gauge shotgun with 2 3/4″ chambers (which are standard on all modern 12 gauges), and can provide the shooter with a load of excitement, smoke and thunder, even from the most modern present day models."

The point is an obvious one easy to overlook, that you can shoot the black powder shells in any shotgun which is in good condition. Why should you? Well, most hunters won't, but I'll bet a nickel or two that many will simply because that's the nature of the beast.

We enjoy trying different things — or the same thing in a different fashion. Nostalgia is in, the bicentennial is here, and black powder is a part of both.

At the moment Navy Arms is out of the black powder shells, but President Val Forgett says he's negotiating with a new supplier and will have them again. Navy Arms sold 300,000 shells of the first batch.

CAUTION! Black powder is corrosive, and will cause your gun to rust unless it is cleaned immediately and thoroughly after it has been used. Repeat: Cleaned immediately — the same day. More on this down below.

Reload with black powder? Maybe!

Never at any time in history, since it ceased to be a necessity, has interest and activity in muzzle loading, black powder shooting been greater than it is today. Tens of thousands hunt, plink and compete with the front loaders, and the National Muzzle Loading Rifle Association itself has more than 17,000 members. The spring and fall meets of the NMLRA on its Friendship, Indiana grounds, incidentally, are events worth going out of your way to experience.

From these facts it is obvious that black powder can be handled safely, as our ancestors who survived to a natural death could have told us. Some who didn't, let's make the point, would now tell us that black powder can also be extremely dangerous.

"How do I treat black powder? Just as if it were a can of gasoline."

Charles Stone was talking, and his credentials consist of owning and operating one of the largest black powder shooting operations in the country. At his Neshanic Station Depot Antiques, Neshanic Station, N.J. he sells and shoots all types of black powder guns, sells all kinds of black powder rifle cartridges and shotshells, and stocks all components for black powder shooting. Including, of course, black powder.

"I treat black powder with respect," Stone continued. "I pour the powder only outside, alone. Black powder dust will float in the air, at a certain level if there is a heat barrier in the room."

Stone's concern stems from this fact: black powder is an explosive which will detonate when ignited even if unconfined. Smokeless powder, unconfined, will simply burn if ignited.

If you don't understand the significance of this difference, stay away from black powder. It will ignite (explode) very easily, even from static electricity at times.

The black powder shotshells sold by Stone at his Neshanic Station

Depot Antiques (in the mid-1970's the price was $6.00 per box of 25) are custom loaded for him by Thomas A. Mundy (Commercial Reloader and Bullet Caster, 69 Robbins Rd., Somerville, New Jersey), who lives just a couple of miles down the road. Although most of the three-quarters of a million rounds which he has loaded in the past five years were with smokeless powder, he also has extensive experience with black powder. Compared to modern machines which spew out smokeless shotshells in amazing numbers, Mundy's method of reloading black powder shotshells is primitive. His emphasis is on safety, avoiding any possibility of sparks or static electricity. Here's how he does it — for 12 gauge.

Thomas Mundy: "Can't run black powder through a regular reloading machine because of the danger of static electricity. I use paper hulls, and de-prime and resize full length with a Mec Shell Saver. Line up my primers and push the hull down over them with a dowel. Working from a small cardboard box containing not more than six or eight ounces of black powder at a time, I use an aluminum dipper to pour either 2 3/4 or 3 drams — never more — of powder into each hull. Push a 1/2-inch fiber wad down on the powder, by hand. Then, since the shells are all out and lined up, I just dip into each one 1 or 1 1/8 ounce of shot, and run each through a small reloading tool to crimp each case. I reload black powder shotshells on a limited scale, and very cautiously, but there's really nothing to it."

"The official industry position," one ammo official told me, "is don't shoot guns with Damascus, laminated or twist barrels, even with black powder. The reason is that the welds in the barrels do deteriorate with age, and from the inside out. Even if you get a Damascus gun which looks clean and good, it could be that the welds have deteriorated so that it won't stand even black powder."

The Sporting Arms and Ammunition Manufacturers Institute, this official went on to say, even supplies its members with a form letter to answer inquiries with this "no, don't do it" official position.

Beyond that official position, however, this man offered the thought that some of the Damascus guns, notably the Parkers, were better than some of the fluid steel barrel shotguns of that era. Condition of those guns today, of course, is the question mark, and he reports getting notice of six or eight accidents each year involving Damascus barrels and black powder shells.

If you're going to shoot one of the old timers, let a gunsmith check its condition beforehand. Some of them, I should point out, are reluctant to give their opinion, while others won't do so at all.

To repeat, black powder is extremely corrosive, and may cause barrels to rust in a matter of hours. Your must clean your gun the same day you shoot it.

The traditional method of cleaning black powder barrels is to scrub them with hot soapy water, rinse them with hot clean water, and, after the barrel is completely dry, to coat it with oil or a moisture-displacing lubricant. The bottom line is always, "Inspect it for the next few days just to be safe."

A newer method is to use specially-designed black powder solvents instead of the soapy water. Scrub the bore with brass brush and patches using the solvents, then with clean patches until the bore is dry. Then use an oil or moisture-displacent.

Charles Stone: "Black powder shooting is fun if you can take some of the drudgery out of it, and I no longer use hot water. On my personal guns I use nothing but WD-40. Spray it in and swab it out, with brushes and patches."

Navy Arms says its Black Powder Shotgun Shells will not always cause the actions of modern semi-automatics to operate properly, but that they work perfectly in all other models. Gearhart-Owen Industries, Inc., Moosic, Pa. 18507 is the only manufacturer of black powder in this country. Hodgdon Powder Co., Inc., Shawnee Mission, Kansas is another major source of black powder (imported from Scotland). Hodgdon has a Black Powder Data Manual which gives loading data for breachloading shotgun shells. Lyman (Rt. 147, Middlefield, Conn. 06455) has published a very good "Black Powder Handbook," but it contains nothing specific for black powder shotshells.

December 1975

THE FACTORY SHOTSHELL COMES OF AGE

T ighter patterns have been a continuing goal of ammunition manufacturers where waterfowl shotshells are concerned, and progress has been remarkable. How remarkable? Just consider that this fall you'll be able to buy over-the-counter duck, goose and turkey loads which the manufacturer claims have been giving 90 percent patterns at 40 yards.

And that, my friends, is indeed remarkable.

To obtain dense shot patterns it's necessary to minimize the effects of the factors which cause shot to disperse. The most important of these is the deformation of the shot which takes place before they leave the muzzle, so it is natural that the ammo makers have concentrated on preventing that.

Winchester took a giant step when it introduced the plastic shot collar in the early 1960's. This collar surrounded the shot charge and traveled with it down the barrel, minimizing deformation of the shot pellets which would be in contact with the barrel.

All companies now use some such shot protector in most of their shells, usually omitting it only in deliberate efforts to get wider patterns.

Winchester also introduced the first shell using a filler material in the shot charge. This granulated polyethylene powder (Winchester's trademark name for it is "Grex") filled the interspaces between the shot pellets, cushioning them and minimizing deformation against each other. This becomes of increasing importance with larger shot sizes. Buckshot loads are the ultimate example, showing the most improvement in patterns.

Winchester put the ingredients together several years ago and marketed a specialized waterfowl (and turkey) load which it calls the Super-X Double X Magnum. Available until this year only in the 12 gauge mags — short and three-inch, it carried 1 1/2 and 1 7/8-ounces of shot sizes #2 or #4 with the Grex filler. It has been generally acknowledged as being the finest long-range shotshell available.

Acknowledging the growing interest in the biggest legal gauge, Winchester has now added the 3 1/2-inch 10-gauge magnum in the Super-X Double X Magnum. It will contain 2 1/4 ounces of #2 shot in Grex — that's 1/4 ounce more than anybody else's 10 mag shells carry, with a folded crimp and a muzzle velocity of 1210 feet per second. Winchester claims 80 percent patterns or better.

And the three-inch 20-gauge magnum will be available in this same load, with 1 1/4 ounce of either #4 or #6 shot.

The harder the shot, the less it will deform passing through the gun barrel, which is essentially why steel shot gives such dense patterns. The "lead" shot used by all companies isn't really pure lead. It contains a certain percentage of antimony — the more antimony, the harder the shot.

For years Winchester has marketed a shell using shot coated with copper, which it calls Lubaloy shot. The coating makes the pellet more resistant to deformation, and these Super-X with Lubaloy loads have been some of the finest for years.

So...suppose we take shot pellets with a high antimony content, coat them with copper, use a shot protector and a cushioning filler. Just what would we have? Perhaps the ultimate in a long-range shotshell.

Federal Cartridge did just that, and is marketing a Premium line of 10, 12 and 20-gauge shotshells which include all the above ingredients. The shot are extra-hard, with a six percent antimony content, and they are copper-plated. The shells use a shot cup and a granulated plastic buffer material.

Federal reports that recent patterns tests with the 10-gauge magnums in the Premium line are running 90 percent at 40 yards.

Here are the four shotshells which will be available in this new Federal Premium Magnum line, which may be on your dealer's shelves by the time you're reading this (in time for the spring turkey seasons): 3 1/2-inch 10-gauge magnum with 2 oz. of 2's or 4's; three-inch 12-gauge magnum, 1 7/8 oz. of BB's, 2's or 4's; 2 3/4-inch 12-gauge magnum, 1 1/2 oz. BB's, 2's, or 4's; and three-inch 20-gauge magnum with 1 1/4 oz. of 2's or 4's.

Federal will also market in this Premium line 12 and 20-gauge Hi-Power and Field Loads which will have the copper-plated, extra-hard shot and the shot protector, but not the plastic filler. The Hi-Power 12's will be 3 3/4 drams/ 1 1/4 oz./ 2,4,6, or 7 1/2; and the Hi-Power 20's — 2 3/4 drams/1 oz./4 or 6 shot. Both are standard 2 3/4-inch length shells.

The Premium Field Loads: 12 gauge — 3 1/4-1 1/8-7 1/2, 8; 20 gauge — 2 1/2-1-7 1/2, 8.

With Federal's entry into the field, all three major ammo manufacturers will have excellent 10-gauge magnum loads this year. Winchester will make a running change from paper to plastic hulls, as the other two already are, which will make them feed well through the popular Ithaca Mag-10.

March 1977

A novice shotgunner is often confused by the array of shotshell loadings offered by manufacturers. Which shell should he use for what game? High brass or low brass? Field loads or express loads? What shot size? What powder loading? Yea, what brand? Let's take a look at this subject.

For openers, to simplify it to the extreme, here's a basic "Grits Guide" which won't lead you far astray. For doves, bobwhite quail, snipe, woodcock and crows — use light loads of #8 shot. For ruffed grouse — light 7 1/2's. For desert quail, Hungarian partridge, and chukars — heavy 7 1/2's. For ducks, pheasant, sage grouse, sharptail grouse, prairie chicken, rabbits and squirrel — heavy 6's. For small geese — heavy 4's. For large geese — heavy 2's. For turkey — heavy 4's. Where steel shot is required, use heavy loads of 4's for small ducks, 2's for big ducks, and BB's for geese.

For practical purposes we can divide shotshells into those two categories: light loads and heavy loads. Depending upon the manufacturer, these have a variety of labels. Light loads are generally referred to as "field loads" (Remington and Federal) or "upland loads" (Winchester). Heavy loads are more complicated, because all major manufacturers have more than one such entry.

Light loads are called "low brass" shells, a name derived from the fact that the metal rim at the base of the shell is narrow. Conversely, heavy loads are "high brass" shells — the metal rim is wider — most of the time.

For decades all high brass shells were simply "heavy" loads. Then came the magnums — three-inch sizes in both 12 and 20 gauges, and later the short or "baby" magnums that function in conventional length chambers. And, then, super magnums were developed.

Federal Cartridge Corporation now has four "heavy" loads: Hi-Power; Premium Hi-Power (shot are copper-plated); Super Magnum (a heavier charge of lead shot plus a buffer material to reduce shot deformation and improve patterns); and Premium Magnum (same load but with copper-plated shot). Remington heavy loads: Express; Express Magnum (heavier shot charges); and Nitro Mag (buffer material added). Winchester heavy loads: Super-X, Super-X Magnum (heavier shot charge plus a Grex buffer material); and Super Double X (about the same as Super-X, but with copper-plated shot).

Activ, which became active in producing shotshell hulls for reloading, and then loaded ammunition, in the early and mid 1980's, has a wide range of loadings. Its "super" shells are called Ultrashot, and its normal "long range" load is Bestshot. The Activ field hunting load is Gameshot, and its target loads are designated Amshot.

The point should be made that the shotshells available over the counter today are the best that have ever been offered. Manufacturers have made monumental improvements in the past few decades, especially in the areas of shot protection (shot sleeves and buffer materials), wads, and cases. Their efforts toward tighter patterns have, in some instances, tended to outstrip the abilities of the shooters to use them.

Patterns, in short, can be too tight. A shotshell (and gun and choke) which will put 90 percent of the shot inside a 30-inch circle at 40 yards, as some of the buffered loads will do consistently, is more efficiency than is really needed for ducks over decoys at 30 to 35 yards. If you don't need such performance, don't buy it. It costs more, and it makes the shooter less efficient — not more so — at bagging game.

If you do require such performance, these super loads are worth the money. They are excellent.

In buying shotshells, as in buying most products, you generally get what you pay for. The "discount" shells offered by some manufacturers cost less because they're worth less.

In addition to the regular lines, there are also specialty shotshells available. These include target loads for skeet and trap, which are some of the most efficient shells on the market, and which are very good for compatible game species such as doves, bobwhite quail, snipe and woodcock. Winchester, Federal, Remington and Activ all now have 1-ounce target loads in 12 gauge, which are excellent, low-recoil ammunition for these same bird species.

Another specialty shell is the "pigeon load," a 3 1/4-1 1/4 loading in 12 gauge favored by live pigeon competitors. This is essentially the same "light field load" offered by major manufacturers, but with harder shot (greater percentage of antimony in the lead, which increases cost and can improve patterns). Winchester and Remington also market an "international trap" loading, the same shotshell but with only 1 1/8 ounce of shot to comply with international trap rules. Both of these are available with nickel-plated shot, favored by many competitors. Activ has an International Competition load featuring nickel-plated shot.

Quite different are the "international skeet" loads from Winchester and Federal. These have no protective shot sleeves, the objective being to get wider patterns. Both have relatively soft shot, to further encourage deformation, and the Winchester loading is faster than normal (3 1/2 dram equivalent). Loaded with #9 shot only, both of these are good short-range choices for small game birds.

Back to the light load categories in the "Grits Guide," the choice is relatively simple. The Remington "ShurShot Field Load," the Activ "Gameshot," the Winchester "Upland Field Range" shell, and the Federal "Field Load" or "Premium Field Load" are all proper choices. Most of the target loads fit this "light load" category nicely.

Ah, to the heavy loads. Hunters should stick to the "standard" heavy loadings for most of their shooting. These are excellent performers at distances where a vast majority of the game is killed. Hi-Power, Super-X, Bestshot, and Express shells are examples.

The "super heavy" loadings are designed to deliver a heavier shot charge, the objective being to get sufficient pattern density at a greater distance than is possible with standard heavy loads. If your gunning calls for this performance, these will do the job if your shooting skill is comparably good.

My "Grits Guide" is just that — a guide, not a bible. I fine tune my choices to match shooting conditions. Where shooting distances are unusually long, especially where wind is involved, I use larger shot sizes. If Huns and chukars are flushing wild, for instance, I may switch to #6 shot; and drop to #4 shot for pheasants and sage hens under the same conditions.

Ducks, which vary widely in size and which are shot under varied conditions, call for more variety in shotshell selection. I frequently shoot teal with #7 1/2 shot to get good pattern density for these small birds. Short magnum loads of 4's are excellent for big ducks, especially for pass shooting. I often use this same load over decoys, going to a more open choke.

Ducks and geese are extremely hardy birds. That, plus the conditions under which they're shot, lends itself to cripple loss. That means that I don't worry about overkill with waterfowl. I try to use enough gun, and enough shot payload, to more than adequately do the job.

Steel shot is required for waterfowl hunting in some areas, and to get acceptable results hunters must switch to a larger shot size than would be the case using lead shot. This militates against the 20 gauge and favors the 10 gauge magnum, simply from the standpoint of payload and pattern density. Steel shot is available only in 20, 12 and 10 gauges, and in 16 gauge from Federal.

To get downrange performance with steel shot comparable to lead, you must use shot TWO sizes larger. The reason is that steel is less dense, and therefore ballistically inferior. When you jump two shot sizes, however, you lose pellet numbers and therefore pattern density. So, despite the fact that steel shot may give tighter patterns because the pellets don't deform as readily, hunters should use the tightest patterns they can get when using steel shot on waterfowl. Only in this way can you put the pellet count into your pattern which will give best killing effect.

For turkey, the "Grits Guide" listed heavy 4's as proper, a good all-around choice. Aiming for the head with lighter shot — 6's or even 7 1/2's — is preferred by many veteran turkey hunters. My choice for this tough bird is a 12 gauge loaded with the super magnum 4's, which will put a handful of shot into the head and neck out to 60 and 70 yards, yet which will still kill with body shots.

In 1987 Remington unveiled a "new" shotshell it calls the DUPLEX. It contains *two* different shot sizes, the idea being to give both pattern density with the smaller shot, and long range penetration with the bigger shot. In 12 gauge only (standard and magnum length), these are available in 2x6 and BBx4 in lead shot; and in those combinations plus a BBx2 loading in steel shot. I've used both on ducks and geese, and found them effective. I'm betting that the DUPLEX will be poison on wild turkeys.

What brand shotshell? All are good, but some may perform better in your gun than do the others. Only a pattern test on paper will reveal which is best for you.

Reloading? Never has it been easier, and more hunters are doing it than ever before, both for hunting and for clay targets. All three major shotshell manufacturers, in addition to the new Activ brand, sell reloading components. Ballistics Products, Inc. is a firm which specializes in components for hunting reloads.

For more shotshell information, you can contact: Federal Cartridge Corporation, Foshay Tower, Minneapolis, MN 55402; Remington Arms Company, Wilmington, DE 19898; Winchester, 120 Long Ridge Rd., Stamford, CN 06904; Activ Industries, P.O. Box 238, Kearneysville, WV 25430; and Ballistics Products, Box

488, Long Lake, MN 55356.

October 1982

BULLETS DO THE WORK

C ountless books and magazine articles have been written during the past few decades, by gun writers such as this one, on the respective merits of various calibers and rifles. A glance up from my desk brings into focus a bookshelf lined with imposing titles, most of them written by friends of mine who have my respect and admiration for the shooting and hunting knowledge they possess.

It has recently been brought to my attention that we may not be adequately emphasizing one of the most important aspects of the rifle-caliber-ammunition combination when it comes to big game hunting. That point is simply that it's what's up front that ultimately counts.

It is the *bullet* itself, in short, which does or does not perform satisfactorily on a particular animal when the final act is played.

For the purpose of this exercise we will assume that you and I have selected a caliber and a rifle which is appropriate and adequate for the game in question. We have sighted the rifle in properly, and when the magic moment arrives we have touched it off with finesse. The bullet speeds to the target and makes contact at the chosen aiming point.

Result? A quick, clean kill.

Not always. Not if the construction of the bullet itself is inadequate or improper for the task assigned it.

How should a bullet be put together? There is no one answer, and the problem is a complex one for the engineers who must cope with it. Not only must they take into consideration the size, anatomy, and construction of the game species on which the bullet will be used, but they must attempt to coordinate the manufacturing specifications of the projectile with the velocities to which it will be subjected.

It isn't easy.

How can you design a bullet to perform perfectly at a range of 50 yards when velocity is 3000 feet per second, and have it still perform perfectly out at 350 yards when the speed has dropped substantially? Perform perfectly on a lung-area shot at a thin-skinned whitetail and also on a shot through the shoulder blade of a big, tough bull elk?

Unless a bullet is built for a very specific use, it is obvious that its manufacturing specifications must be a compromise. That is exactly what most factory-loaded bullets are.

That isn't all bad. In most situations the commercially available loadings do an admirable job. But not always.

One of the most interesting experiences I've had in hunting I owe to a factory loaded bullet which didn't get the job done. It went to pieces, the jacket separating from the core and the core breaking up, on its way into the chest cavity of a lion. A second bullet entering from the opposite side did the same thing.

One or both of them might eventually have been fatal. They were not immediately so, however, and the big male got into dense vegetation. When we finally caught up with him some time later he decided to eliminate the source of his difficulties — me. He managed to approach to within 13 paces, very rapidly, before we were able to end the argument.

Less exciting, but even more intriguing, was the performance of 220-grain custom softpoint bullets loaded to factory velocity in a .300 Winchester magnum caliber. With it I shot a warthog which might have weighed about 50 pounds, a quartering shot which entered just forward of the hip on a line into the chest cavity. It literally blew up on entrance tearing a huge jagged entrance hole. The bullet core was recovered from the hip and the jacket from the stomach.

The most common failure in bullet performance involves the separation of the lead core from the bullet jacket. When that happens the whole package may not penetrate into the vital parts of the anatomy.

Manufacturers of all bullets, including those used in factory ammo, strive to avoid that separation problem. For most big game hunting, the ideal is for the forward portion of the bullet to mushroom while the base remains stable, and the whole affair should hold together. Various methods are utilized to achieve that.

The best known custom big game bullet had its origin 30 years ago, when a hunter named John Nosler became dissatisfied with bullets then available. The Nosler Partition Bullet was the result, and it has achieved a sound reputation among hunters around the world for good performance on heavy, tough big game.

The Partition is, as the name indicates, a two-part bullet. There is a front core and a rear core, the two separated by a partition which is a part of the jacket. The front portion mushrooms back to the partition.

"You can immediately spot a Nosler when you cut one out of an animal," an African professional hunter told me. "They all look just alike. Perfect performance."

Such complicated construction comes at a price, usually several times that of "standard" bullets. Many hunters consider them a bargain at any cost.

Reaching for a broader market, however, Nosler marketed a new bullet which it called the Solid Base, which is competitive in price with other bullets. Produced by the extrusion process, the base is quite thick and the thickness of the jacket tapers toward the nose.

Other custom bullets which have excellent reputations with reloaders on heavy big game animals are the Bitterroot, Barnes, Hornady, and Speer's Grand Slam. The Swift is a superb custom bullet, available at this time only in .375 caliber. Perfect performance may be one thing to one hunter and quite something else to another. Some prefer their bullets to "upset" upon contact to the point that they do not exit the animal, the point being that they expend all of their energy on and in it. Others prefer that bullet construction and velocity be such that it will go completely through most of the time, with the thought that such performance will give a better blood trail for tracking if that proves necessary. You pay your money and you make your choice.

One class of bullets is designed not to mushroom, of course, and that's the solid. Noted primarily for use on such game as elephant and cape buffalo, they are also useful on smaller quarry where a mushrooming bullet would be too destructive of meat or hide. Turkey, foxes, and coyotes come to mind.

Take an interest in the performance of your bullets on the animals you shoot from now on, if you haven't done so before. Become a "bullet digger." By retrieving those bullets, or the pieces of them, you could well find the key to future success.

December 1977

REDISCOVER THOSE LIGHT LOADS

old! Not as cold as the 21 below temperature which set west
Tennessee records that same winter, but still cold, and I was
grateful that the winds which had been whistling almost unimpeded
through our "summer" house, high on a hilltop outside Paris, blew
no more. Bundled and hip-booted, I stashed my gear in the pickup
and drove into town long before daylight.

The call had come late the evening before from my duck hunting
buddies: "You can't believe how many ducks are working the corn
fields down south. Field's are all flooded — just right, and tomorrow's the last day of the season. We'll meet you at the cafe."

Day was already breaking and ducks were overhead when we
slid the aluminum john boat from our pickup, which we had driven
down a farm road until overflow flood waters lapped at the tires.
The small outboard pushed us across the big field of bottomland
corn, now covered except for a few stalks here and there, until we
reached the timber on the far side. It took only minutes to locate
a natural blind upwind from the open water — a huge fallen oak
beneath which we pulled the boat. We were still stuffing shells
into magazines when mallards started working the dozen decoys
we'd tossed out.

A day to remember. The duck calls might not have been
necessary, but mallards in pairs and dozens rode the notes down
to us as if there were no tomorrow. The memory of that crystal
clear morning, brilliant sunshine reflecting from shining greenheads,
lingers on.

So does another fact. I was shooting a 20-gauge Model 12, using
light loads, and killed just about every duck I shot at graveyard
dead. I'm talking about real light loads — 7/8 ounce of #8 shot.
It wasn't from choice. Those quail shells were all I had in the house
when that late night call came.

In the fall of '84, a few decades later, I was again reminded that
it isn't always necessary to be shooting magnum shotshells to get
magnum performance. Okay, near-magnum performance. For a
week I gunned Sonnerup Manor in Denmark with Jon Liland,
shooting strong, high-flying, driven pheasants, and — again —
mallards, and all shooting was done with light loads. This time
it was 12 gauge, a one-ounce shotshell of #6 shot which is loaded
in England for Liland.

The solid, killing performance of this load on those big birds, including the high fliers, was impressive. The experience was another reminder that we can become overly obsessed with a shotshell burning a handful of powder pushing a huge payload.

Fred Kimble, the man who made choke boring in shotgun shooting a reality, was without doubt one of the finest wingshooters of all time. Much of his market hunting of ducks, during which he made some phenomenal runs, was done with a 9-gauge single barrel muzzleloader. In that big gun, however, he shot a modest 1 1/4 ounces of shot, the normal "express" load for our modern 12-gauge gun. We have other 12 gauge loadings in our U.S. factory repertoire, of course, which carry 2 ounces of shot.

All three major U.S. shotshell manufacturers — Remington, Winchester, and Federal — have introduced a light, one-ounce target load in 12 gauge in recent years, and competitors have generally been surprised at how well they score with the reduced payload. In 1985 Federal introduced a new shotshell called the EXTRA-LITE, a 12 gauge with a standard trap charge of 1 1/8 ounce shot, but at a slightly lower velocity which results in less recoil. Even more important has been the discovery by many upland bird hunters of just how good these excellent shotshells are in the field. Trap and skeet loads, as a general rule, tend to be the state-of-the-art where shotshell manufacture is concerned, which makes them superb on game birds as well as on clay targets.

Activ, the new Zigor Corporation shotshell manufacturing operation out of West Virginia, offers a wide range of selection, including 12 gauge one-ounce loads with either 2 3/4 drams or 3 1/4 drams of powder. Eley, the British maker of fine shotshells (now being imported and distributed by Mossberg), has a tempting array of English-style light loads with an unusual shot charge — 1 1/16 ounces. Even better, these are available in shot sizes from BB down to #8.

Don't confuse the term "light loads" with poor quality. It is generally axiomatic that you get what you pay for in most products, including shotshells, and high quality costs more. Trap and skeet shells, as a rule, are more expensive than are the so-called "game loads" or "field loads," usually because their ingredients are more expensive and/or quality control in the manufacture is more intense. Shooters should buy on the basis of their individual needs and requirements.

Why light loads? Recoil is reduced, which can contribute to

making a lighter load more effective for recoil-sensitive hunters. They can be less expensive. A one-ounce load is much more pleasant to shoot in the lightweight 12-gauge shotguns which have become very popular than are heavier charges, and such a one-ounce load is more effective in a 12 gauge than is a similar weight charge in a 20 gauge. The bigger tube gives better patterns. If you reload, you can save some 10 to 20 percent on the cost of shot alone by reducing your 12-gauge charge from 1 1/4 ounce or 1 1/8 ounce to one ounce.

Lighter isn't always better, of course. If you need that heavier load, use it. A good, heavy load will be more effective for distant shots than will a good, light load — provided both pattern equally well in your gun, and provided that you can shoot as well with either. The trick is to examine your own personal needs and shooting habits, then select your ammunition accordingly.

"Light" is a relative term, of course, and lighter in your case may simply be a switch to standard express loads for duck hunting from the magnums you've been using. Or to a trap load for doves from the express loads you thought you needed.

Lighter isn't always better, but it often is.

Sources for information on shotshell ammunition:
ACTIV INDUSTRIES, Box 238, Kearneysville, WV 25430
ELEY, O. F. MOSSBERG & SONS, 7 Grasso Ave., North Haven, CT 06473
FEDERAL CARTRIDGE CORP., 2700 Foshay Tower, Minneapolis, MN 55402
REMINGTON ARMS CO., Dupont Marketing Communications, Wilmington, DE 19898
WINCHESTER, East Alton, IL 62024

September 1985

HOMEMADE AMMO: NO MYSTERY

I have friends who give a slight shudder at the very thought of handloading their own ammunition, and I can identify with that — if I think back a few years. Time was when I thought that the whole process of reloading was somewhat akin to witchcraft, or at least closely related to operating a ham radio rig, which I didn't understand, either.

Most of us have a tendency to attribute mysterious qualities to things and processes which we don't understand, and for millions of shooters in this country the topic of reloading falls in this category. Nothing could be further from the truth. Making your own ammo is simple and uncomplicated. It is a clearly defined, mechanical operation that virtually anybody can learn — even master — quickly. I add the qualifier to get me off the hook, since there are always a few who only read the directions when all else fails. In reloading, that's too late.

Some time ago I was duck hunting with two old friends in the marshes of Louisiana when the subject of reloading arose. One of them, a cajun I hadn't hunted with for years, said, "Yeah, I reload my shells. Loaded four cases the other night in about an hour, maybe a little more."

That's *cases;* not boxes. He's retired, hunts every day, and saves one whopping amount of money by rolling his own ammo.

My friend, needless to say, isn't your average hunter, but he has lots of company out there across the land. There are many, many gunners who do use great quantities of ammo in hunting, plus thousands who can afford to shoot trap and skeet only because they reload. And more thousands who *would* shoot much more than they do if they did reload.

My cajun buddy has a "progressive" reloading tool. All that means is that, once the system is in operation, a fully-loaded shot-shell drops into the hopper each time he operates the handle on the reloader. It's a relatively expensive tool but, for him, easily justified because of the amount of shooting he does.

Near the other end of the scale is an old tool which has sat on my bench for a couple of decades. It's capacity is about four boxes an hour, and when all five in our family were trapshooting the tool stayed in use much of the time. All of our children could and did operate it well.

One event which gives a good perspective on reloading is a benchrest shoot. It proves the quality of handloaded ammo, since these guys are striving for, and getting, the best accuracy in the world — with reloads. And it shows how simple and uncomplicated the process is, since many competitors take their reloading gear right to the range, making adjustments on the spot.

Yep, I shifted from shotshells to metallic cartridges, but the same process applies. The key ingredients in either round are a case, a primer, powder, and a bullet or a charge of shot. That's all, folks. No mystery. The case (in shotshells, a "hull") is one from a factory round that has already been fired — hence, REloading, although unused factory brass and hulls are available for purchase. This re-using is where the savings comes in, substantial in either case, but more so for metallic cartridges. Rimfire ammunition cannot be reloaded.

Reloading tools now are available in a wider array than ever before, and you should choose one to fit your particular needs. If Henry Ford put autos on the streets of America, and Bill Weaver put scopes on hunting rifles, "Lee Loaders" have probably put more people to reloading than has any other brand. Although the line from Lee Precision, Inc. has expanded greatly to more sophisticated tools, still hanging in there is the basic, simple "Lee Loader" containing everything necessary to reload one caliber rifle or pistol cartridge. The price, in 1986, was $16.95.

On the opposite end of the scale, Hornady and RCBS have, in addition to basic presses, sophisticated progressive tools which cost several hundred dollars. Many other manufacturers offer excellent equipment, and a list of them is included at the end of this column.

The advent of required steel shot for waterfowling (and perhaps for everything) has increased interest in reloading on the part of duck and goose hunters, since factory steel shotshells are more expensive than are lead shotshells. You can reload steel shot, BUT special precautions are required. As a general rule, you CANNOT interchange the components which you would use for reloading lead shot. You must be meticulous in following all instructions; otherwise, pressures can be dangerously high.

Danger? Reloading, per se, is not dangerous. Smokeless powder is flammable but not explosive, and isn't nearly as dangerous as that can of gasoline stored in your garage for your lawn mower.

The one thing you should have, if you decide that reloading is for you, is discipline. Decide at the outset that you *will* read the directions — before all else fails. Switching types of powder can be disastrous, so always store powder in its original container. Keep records. Don't smoke while reloading, and don't allow anybody in the room to smoke. In fact, reloading is best done as a solitary activity since conversation isn't conducive to concentration.

Reloading manuals are the "bibles" for reloaders, and good ones are available for sale from: Hodgdon Powder Co., 7710 W. 50th Hwy., Shawnee Mission, KS 66202; Hornady Mfg. Co., Box 1848, Grand Island, NE 68801; Nosler Bullets, Box 688, Beaverton, OR 97005; Sierra Bullets, 10532 Painter Ave., Sante Fe Springs, CA 90670; Speer Bullets, Box 856, Lewiston, ID 83501; and from Lyman Products Corp., Rt. 147, Middlefield, CT 06455.

There are several excellent books on the market giving detailed instructions on how to reload, and most manufacturers of reloading equipment have booklets of their own. Ballistic Products, Box 488, Long Lake, MN 55356, is a good source of information and supplies for shotshell reloading, and has specific information on reloading steel shot.

For a look at the kinds of reloading equipment available, you might request a catalog from some of these manufacturers: RCBS, Box 1919, Oroville, CA 95965; Hornady Mfg. Co., Box 1848, Grand Island, NE 68801; Lyman, Rt. 147, Middlefield, CT 06455; C-H Tool & Die Corp., 106 N. Harding St., Owen, WI 54460; Ponsness/ Warren, Box 8, Rathdrum, ID 83858; Lee Precision, Inc., 4275 Highway U, Hartford, WI 53027; and MEC Inc., 715 South St., Mayville, WI 53050.

"Discover Reloading" is a 30-minute videotape which is available for sale from the National Reloading Manufacturers Association, 4905 SW Griffith Dr., Suite 101, Beaverton, OR 97005.

April 1987

SHOOTING STEEL SHOT

S hooting steel shot at waterfowl is no longer a question of "if;" now it's simply "how." That became true for most of the prime duck and goose hunting areas of the nation in the fall of 1987. Beginning then, all areas where the waterfowl harvest (ducks and geese — total) reaches or exceeds 20 per square mile had to use non-toxic shot. The rest of the nation was slated to be phased in progressively until the 1991-92 season, at which point no shotshells using lead shot will be legal for waterfowl anywhere in the United States.

Thirteen years ago I wrote for *Sports Afield* a comprehensive feature on the lead poisoning/steel shot topic. At that time there was immense controversy; there still is. But the required use of steel is a *fait accompli,* so here we address only the subject of what steel shot loads are available, and some considerations in using them to best effect.

Let me point out, for openers, that the steel shotshells being manufactured (and handloaded) today are light years advanced in performance over those available a decade ago, and I don't think the zenith in effectiveness has been reached. The rumor goes 'round that, since hunters must buy the steel loads which are available, ammo companies will no longer spend the R&D money necessary to advance the product further. Why try to make it better! Competition being what it is, I don't agree with that line of reasoning. In addition to the great progress made by ammo companies, a few dedicated, knowledgeable handloaders have evolved some very good steel shotshell products. Reloading steel shot, let me emphasize, is very different from reloading lead, and can be dangerous if not done properly. Steel is not nearly as forgiving of human error as is lead, which can lead to disastrously high pressures. Many of you will begin to reload steel now that you must use it. Learn to reload it safely.

Barrel Damage: Answers to this are a mixed bag, nothing clear-cut black and white. The extremes are easy. Don't use steel in your old, valuable, thin-walled doubles. Don't worry about using steel in pumps and autos made in the U.S. in the past couple of decades, or in doubles — side-by's or O&U's — that the maker approves for steel shot use. It's those in-betweens which give us the problems, and there is no pat answer.

Ammunition manufacturers hedge their bets with phrases like "it is unlikely," and "any significant performance problems," and "vast majority of modern shotguns do not exhibit any problems." Their caution is understandable. So is that of most gun makers when they speak of firearms made years ago, in light of the liability situation that prevails today.

The steel used in many older guns may have been very good steel, but often it was soft steel, and the barrels on many of those older shotguns, especially the better ones, were thin. I wouldn't use steel shot in such guns. Get the manufacturer's advice — if that manufacturer is still around, but expect to get an answer which isn't definitive.

Barrel damage, when it happens, usually occurs at the muzzle of tightly-choked guns, simply because the load of steel shot does not compress as does lead when squeezed through the choke constriction. In most cases such damage happens only after many, many rounds — more than most waterfowl hunters fire in many years, and is often limited to slight ringing (you can see a minor bulging around the barrel near the muzzle if you look down it in just the right light) which doesn't affect performance.

Barrel damage is most apt to take place when using larger shot sizes of steel, and the bad news is that most recent tests are showing that the larger shot sizes are much more effective at producing cleaner kills.

Chokes: For some time, despite my long-held belief that most bird hunters would be more successful with more open bores, I'd been bothered by the repeated assertion that hunters should use a more open choke when using steel than when using lead shot, the premise being that steel deforms less than does lead and therefore flies truer and gives more dense patterns for a particular constriction. Until a visit with Stan Baker, the Seattle shotgun specialist, I couldn't pin down the basis for my concern. It took him only minutes to get me on track (a point which later appeared in his article in *Shotgun Sports* magazine).

The potential trap is equating tight (full choke, for instance) patterns of lead and steel. The fallacy lies in the fact that there are many fewer pellets of steel shot in an "equal" load of steel than of lead shot. Here's why. We must use a shot two sizes larger in steel to get performance similar to that of lead: #4 steel instead of #6 lead; #2 steel instead of #4 lead. Fewer of the larger shot, obviously, can be put into a shotshell.

A valid comparison is to measure the number of shot in a tight steel pattern against the number in an equivalent lead load pattern, so let's do it. An 80 percent full-choke pattern using a 1 1/4 oz., #4 steel shotshell, heaviest available in a standard length 12 gauge, would put 187 pellets in the 30-inch pattern at 40 yards. Suppose we had gotten 187 pellets in our pattern when we used a short magnum of 1 1/2 oz. of #6 lead shot. That would be a 56 percent pattern, basically a tight improved cylinder, not the choice of waterfowlers for anything except for short range. An 80 percent pattern in that lead load, easily possible with the buffered, coated, hard shot now offered, would place 266 pellets in the pattern. A pattern of 266 lead vs. 187 steel. And remember that each #6 lead pellet is roughly equivalent in performance out at the target to each #4 steel, perhaps even better.

This example is not intended to downplay the effectiveness of modern steel shotshells on waterfowl, about which there will be more down below, but it is intended to caution you against falling into the trap of thinking that steel is as effective as lead. It isn't.

We face a complex dilemma in choosing the right choke. Because of the diminished pattern *density* of steel shot loads, as indicated by the example above, we may need the very *tightest* steel shot patterns possible in order to get the most effective killing performance. Steel shot *does* tend to give tighter patterns for a given choke constriction, but that's a moot point if we need even tighter patterns to give us effectiveness. One ammo maker even states that "full choke does not increase pattern density," which is at odds with other testing. As the choke constrictions tighten, it is true that the percentage *increase* in pattern density declines. We reach a point of diminishing return, but that doesn't mean that we're getting *no* return in the form of more density. At some point, of course, as is true with lead, results go the other way: the patterns become less dense.

Remember that how your barrel or choke tube is marked may have little to do with how tight your patterns are, which is equally true for lead shot as it is for steel. Only by patterning your shotgun can you really know how it shoots what.

Getting tighter patterns is a trade-off. The *potential* for barrel damage is greater, particularly with the large steel shot which are giving best performance. And, as is true with lead shot, hunters miss more birds with those super-tight patterns. Outweighing both of these is the possibility of increased crippling losses with less dense patterns of steel. For now, I'll use the most dense patterns I can get when I shoot steel shot at ducks and geese.

Forward Allowance: Much has been written about the necessity of *learning* to shoot steel shot, insofar as the distance you should lead a bird, since it has a higher muzzle velocity than does lead, and possibly a shorter shot string. It gets to the target faster at short ranges, thus you don't need to lead the bird as much; but then steel shot slows down faster than does lead after it passes a certain range, after which point you should give a bird more lead than you would with lead. Forget it! The variety of distances and angles and shot velocities make this whole premise border on the ridiculous. Lead ducks and geese the way you've always done, and you'll hit and miss the way you've always done.

Cost: Steel shotshells cost more than do lead, as a general rule (10 ga. steel is *less* expensive than lead in some areas). The difference should shrink as production increases to meet the increased sales. Why more costly, despite the fact that the raw material (iron) may be less expensive than lead? Part of the reason is that iron requires more processing, annealing to soften it to about 90 DPH hardness (lead is about 30 DPH, air rifle BB's about 150 DPH, and steel ball bearings about 270 DPH), and coating with a rust inhibitor. Tougher shot protectors required for steel are also more expensive to produce, and more powder is needed for the higher muzzle velocities.

Shot Sizes: Factory steel is available in shot sizes 6, 4, 2, 1, BB, BBB, T, and F in at least one loading in one gauge. For those unfamiliar with the bigger sizes, the dimensions (in fractions of an inch) of individual pellets are: #1 — .16; BB — .18; BBB — 19; T-shot — .20; and F-shot — .22. For comparison, #4 Buck is .24 inch.

Remember, the rule of thumb recommended by ammo companies is to use steel shot two sizes larger than the lead shot you formerly used — 4's instead of 6's, for instance, in order to get the same downrange energy. That's energy per pellet, keep in mind, which you will not have as many of in your pattern.

There has recently been much interest and enthusiasm for the bigger sizes — BBB's, T-shot and F-shot, and the success that avid reloaders have in their experimenting probably encouraged the offering of these in factory loadings. Both individuals and the companies have been pushing muzzle velocities to new highs in an effort to compensate for the inherent ballistic inferiority of steel, and there are now factory shells giving 1400 fps and more. In three-inch 12-gauge loads: Winchester has one at 1425 fps, Federal one at 1400 fps, and Remington another at 1375 fps, all substantially higher than comparable lead shot loadings.

Remington resurrected an old idea, improved it, and produced the "DUPLEX," a shotshell with two different shot sizes in the same shell. Early efforts in this direction simply mixed the shot, and weren't effective because the varying flight characteristics of the two sizes (the smaller shot slows down faster than does the larger shot) caused pattern disruption. In the new shells the bigger shot are loaded on top.

I used the DUPLEX loads in both lead and steel in the 1986-87 season, on both ducks and geese, and am favorably impressed. In steel, these shells will be available (12 ga. only) in BBx2, BBx4, and 2x6.

Gauges: Steel shot is available in many loadings in 12 gauge from the three major makers, several in 10-gauge magnum from

Winchester and Federal, and in very limited 20-gauge loadings from all three (Remington has only one 20-ga. load, a three-inch mag in 2, 4, or 6 shot size). In the fall of '87 Federal marketed the first (and only, to my knowledge) 16-gauge steel shot loads: magnum loads in #2 and #4 shot.

The 10-gauge magnum is in a class by itself when it comes to handling steel shot effectively, simply because of the payload of shot these 3 1/2" shells can carry. Federal offers one with 1 5/8 ounces of shot (F, T, BB, 2) at a sizzling 1350 fps at the muzzle. Winchester has a 1 3/4 ounce load (BB, 2) at 1260 fps; and a new loading with 1 1/4 ounce of copperplated T-shot or BBB's.

Shotguns chambered for the 10-gauge magnum aren't common, and the Ithaca MAG-10 autoloader has become increasingly popular. Remington, which bought some of the assets of the bankrupt Ithaca Firearms Company, plans to market a version of that "MAG-10." There are double barrels in this gauge on the market, including some new ones, and Stan Baker has been building 10-gauge O&U barrels for a few shotguns.

For most duck hunters, however, the 12 gauge will be the choice for waterfowling with steel, and there are excellent factory loadings available for it. If your gun will handle three-inch shells, use them. Strive for payload and high muzzle velocity, and a comparison look at ammo catalogs will sort these choices out. Using a 20-gauge, limit shooting to very modest ranges.

Reloading: Many manufacturers of reloading tools have made changes and additions to their presses with steel shot in mind, and there is certain to be greater emphasis in this direction. Two men who have done much experimenting with steel reloads are Tom Armbrust, of Ballistic Research; and L. P. Brezny, of Minnesota, and some of their comments and findings are of interest.

Armbrust: "I shot nine geese (snows and white-fronts) and three ducks in January using the three-inch Winchester Super Steel Magnum load of T-shot, and did not lose a cripple. The geese averaged two to four pellets per bird, and 75 percent of the T-shot completely penetrating the bird. The T-shot, with a muzzle velocity of 1350 fps is still moving 684 fps out at 60 yards, which is 39 fps faster than a #2 lead pellet at the same distance...The new Federal three-inch 12-gauge load of F-steel works well on large Canada geese for pass shooting.

"L.P. Brezny is measuring the pellet velocities downrange with an Oehler M33 Chronotach, and we have found it takes a steel pellet at least *three* sizes larger than lead to have about the same velocity past 40 yards. We've developed some 10-gauge Mag. Hyper velocity steel loads, 1 3/16 oz., that are running 1640 to 1865 fps, and once you reach the 1700 fps area, then down range velocity and energy are really increased. We're using the Super Sonic 1500 10-gauge wad, which has 12-gauge interior dimensions. A very heavy duty wad is needed to withstand the terrific setback of steel shot going from zero to 1700 fps in milliseconds."

Brezny: "Steel is outshooting lead at ultra long range, from 70 to 100 yards, in my penetration tests. It seems that steel can run almost 200 fps slower than lead and match penetration...penetrated 421 pages of a phone book. Lead T-shot, at same distance with 802 fps terminal velocity, 349 pages."

I do not advocate shooting waterfowl at extremely long ranges, but I include Brezny's data simply as information on downrange ballistic performance of individual pellets, both lead and steel.

Getting Ready: When you plan to hunt ducks or geese in steel-shot-only areas, prepare. First, find out if your shotgun will safely handle steel shot. If it is in that gray area, write the manufacturer and ask. Remember that you must give them a full description of the gun. When you decide which shotgun you will use, buy steel shot and pattern it. Find out what it will do in your particular gun.

Above all, remember that modern steel shotshells, used properly, will kill ducks and geese cleanly at reasonable ranges.

For more information about reloading steel shot you can contact: Ballistic Research, 1108 W. May Avenue, McHenry, IL 60050; Ballistic Products, P.O. Box 408, Long Lake, MN 55356; National Reloading Mfg. Asso., 4905 SW Griffith Dr., Suite 101, Beaverton, OR 97005.

July 1987

DAVE FACKLER'S BALLISTIC PRODUCTS

"I just got frustrated, sitting there in the hedgerows of North Dakota, banging away at geese and not getting them. Or not dropping the birds like I should even with the 10 gauge magnum. With my background, I figured I could produce a hunting load which would kill cleanly out to 80 yards with a 10 gauge. After a year of sketches and drawings and prototypes — driving Carol absolutely nuts, I finally came up with the Ballistic Pattern Driver. That wad will shoot. You can blow out anything from 1 1/2 to 2 1/2 ounces. It's roaringly successful."

Dave Fackler is a computer analyst and a man with a cause, and his quest for better shotshells for long-ranged wingshooting has drawn him into a very successful small business. His Ballistic Products, Inc. operation now caters to the needs of some 15,000 to 20,000 hunters throughout this country — and as far away as Australia, providing them with a modest array of loading components which are either difficult or impossible to get elsewhere.

"Mine is a classic case of being dragged into business," Dave told me during the NRA meeting in Kansas City one April. "I had no intention of anything except producing wads for me to use in goose shooting, and I really didn't care about anybody else. But it was ridiculous to build a $5,000 mold for me to have wads — and then stop."

Dave didn't stop. It was late 1974 when he finally had his BPD wad, and "used them on birds all over the place. They worked super! Killed birds cleanly at 80 yards with the 10 gauge magnum, and we could never do that before."

To take advantage of his investment, Fackler tried to market the wads through distributors, but that didn't work.

"Distributors don't understand the gun world," Dave explained. "They're second or third generation in the business. Maybe their dads and granddads understood it, but they don't. They had cases of my product but didn't know how to move it. And I kept getting letters from all over the place, guys wanting the wad and couldn't get it."

That put Ballistic Products, Inc. into the "mail-order" business.

"I asked a neighbor boy if he wanted to spend some afternoons mailing these things out," Fackler continued his tale, "and the whole thing just went absolutely crazy. Instead of mailing little packages, UPS comes with a huge van every day, and we ship by the tons."

Just what's so hot about the Ballistic Pattern Driver wad?

"It gives you good pattern control out at a distance," Dave explained, "and gives higher velocity, which is quite a help. By loading down to 1 3/4 ounces, you'll get 1400 fps."

How does a wad increase muzzle velocity?

"The BPD gives a very complete gas seal, which results in total burn of the powder. With slow burning powders you might not get a complete burn if you have a leaky seal. It's like an engine with leaky valves and piston rings — incomplete gasoline burn. Same thing happens with powder.

"You want a complete burn, but you want it to take place the whole length of the barrel, like a blow gun effect. You have a constant pressure behind the mass building up as the shot travels down the barrel. It's the length of time that pressure is behind the shot that builds velocity. Same principle that the pygmies use with their long blow guns, getting tremendous velocity because they're constantly putting pressure behind the dart."

You can handload better shotshells than factory loads?

"I shoot some factory ammunition because it's darn good. An ounce and three-quarter Federal Premium load is hard to beat. The work Remington has done with magnum loads, extra hard lead shot — that's good stuff. They're getting the message that there are a lot of guys out there willing to pay more for better hunting loads.

"I'm not putting ammo companies down. They do a good job, but it's mostly geared to target shooting. Even in many of their hunting loads, they use target wads. By reloading you can make up those weird and wonderful loads that nobody else will make for you. And even if some factory makes it, odds are good the average man on the street can't find it. I'll bet you'd have a time, right here in Kansas City, finding a 12 gauge load of 1 3/8 ounces of #5 shot, just for instance."

Fackler's wads — the Ballistic Pattern Driver — are designed to give better performance, primarily with heavy, long-range hunting loads, and not for ease of reloading.

"If I have problems loading it up before I pull the trigger, I don't care about that. I care about what happens after I pull the trigger. Most commercial factory wads and pistons and sleeves are designed for ease of reloading. All the crush section in them does is give you an adjustment area for the amount of powder and the amount of shot you're working with."

Ballistic Products, Inc. has become, in its owner's eyes, the "Sears & Roebuck" of the reloading world. "We are unique," is the way he put it, "The only service of its kind. We keep the quality high since, after all, shells are the least cost of any hunting adventure."

Beginning with only one product, that Ballistic Pattern Driver wad, this operation quickly expanded its line.

"We started shipping BPD's and people began requesting other items," Dave said. "Can you get me #2 copper plated shot? Fiber wads? This or that. I tried to help, and all of a sudden we had a whole garage full of stuff."

In addition to his original BPD for the 10 gauge, Fackler now offers a two-piece wad for the 12 gauge which consists of a gas seal and a shotcup, and patents have been granted or approved on both. Other items in his catalog (available for $1.00 from Ballistics Products, Inc., P.O. Box 488, Long Lake, MN 55356, which is a suburb of Minneapolis), include: lead shot, copper-coated shot and nickel-coated shot in an array of sizes from BB's down through 10's, plus buckshot and rifled slugs; a 12 gauge BPGS (gas seal); a 12 gauge magnum shotcup; hulls for reloading, in all sizes, both new and once fired; both fiber and felt cushion wads; ground polyethylene for shot buffering; waterproof hull marker labels ("nobody had one that would stick to the hull"); waterproof shell box labels ("same thing"); all reloading ingredients for all gauges from 10 down through 28 — for hunting loads only; 10 gauge shell boxes ("nobody else had 'em, so I had 'em made"); and a bandoleer for 10 gauge shells ("if you sit on shells they won't run through the action smoothly").

How about steel shot?

"By the time your column is in print I should have loading data available for steel shot. I'm working with Dupont and Hercules, running the loadings through and making sure they're correct. We're trying to get the 10 gauge wad just right. It's a lengthy process. We're selling steel shot now, but not the wads."

Fackler believes there's a lot of semi-foot-dragging going on in the shooting industry with regard to steel shot. That companies don't want to be caught with warehouses full of steel shot when and if that "wonderful solution" is finally found and "rammed down our throats."

"This fall all of Iowa is supposed to be steel; Michigan is already all steel; Minnesota has steel shot areas. Sooner or later the reloader must be able to reload steel shot, and do it safely. Steel shot runs your pressure up high, and reloaders are going to make mistakes with steel that they didn't make with lead simply because the margin of safety is much less," Fackler emphasized.

In addition to the mail-order catalog, Ballistic Products now has a manual titled "Reloading For Hunting: The Magnum Shotgun," which sells for $3.00 a copy; and should have available a steel shot reloading manual by the time you read this. In doing the R&D work on long range shotshell loads for five years, Dave Fackler has come to some definite conclusions — pending further research.

On steel shot: "doesn't kill as well as lead...round ball steel shot is only phase one, and better aerodynamic shapes for shot will extend effective range...buffering of steel shot is necessary to minimize the resonance, bell ringing effect which is absent in lead, which causes the solder in double guns to come unglued...states should not go 'all steel' just for ease of enforcement."

On long range waterfowling: his handloads will outshoot the aiming efficiency of the shotgun bead sight, so he's experimenting with optical sights and scopes...prefers speed over pattern in any compromise...average goose shooting distance is long ("70 yards in North Dakota is average, over decoys")...nickel plated shot is best killer. His favorite shot size in 10 gauge is #1. The 1 7/8 ounce load in 3" 12-gauge magnum is lousy, too slow, with 1 5/8 oz. load much better, he says, and #3 shot is excellent under 70 yards. Dave thinks .20 caliber buckshot (T shot) is excellent long-range shot size. Advises that high winds can be a big factor, necessitating heavy shot sizes. Very cold temperatures affect shotshell performance greatly.

Ballistic Products didn't sell primers or powder in the early days, but now does. They must be shipped to a federal firearms dealer, but his other items are shipped UPS directly to customers. The business is increasing some 25 percent each year, and Dave Fackler says, "That's all I can handle."

August 1980

BUCKSHOT FOR GEESE

B UCKSHOT! The very sound of the word conjures up a variety of meanings for various people, and in few instances will you find anybody completely unmoved by the term. To the deer hunter it's a pro or con thing, deploring the use of buckshot as an inefficient crippler, or praising it as a safe, deadly killer of bucks under proper conditions.

Buckshot! The "blue whistlers" from the pages of the "Wild West Weekly." In the twin tubes of a sawed-off double, the ultimate equalizer for the Dodge City sheriff taking on that whole rowdy gang.

Buckshot! The consummate, non-traceable tool for a hired gun.

But buckshot for goose hunting?

The very thought sends a shiver up the spine of most veteran wildfowlers, causes a glint in the eye of enforcement men where such goings-on are illegal, and a cry of anguish from those who say that hunting is already too dangerous. And, I must admit, the idea of shooting geese with buckshot didn't sit too well with me at first blush, and the verdict is still out.

But in this game of guns and shooting it doesn't pay to be overly obstinate, as pre-ordained "facts" fade into obscurity before the march of progress. Through rather embarrassing experience I've learned not to dismiss, out of hand, even the most far-out ideas. And buckshot for geese isn't all that far out.

To a Minnesota school teacher named Loyal P. Brezny, in fact, buckshot is the only way to go if you're after big geese at long range. By big geese he means the giant Canada geese, and by long range he's talking about distances to more than 100 yards. Now do I have your attention?

Before writing him off as a kook, consider that he has devoted two years to research and reloading and goose hunting, with the goal of finding out just how effective or ineffective various loads of buck are. In the 1978-79 season he recorded a total of 127 separate goose kills and, as he put it, "the end result is a strong argument in favor of buckshot by a wide margin."

The average killing range for these 127 kills was 70 yards.

Brezny is concerned with a particular kind of goose shooting: pass shooting along a firing line surrounding a refuge. "Hunting the ditch," as it is frequently called, waiting for a chance at geese leaving the refuge to feed in the surrounding countryside, or returning to the refuge.

"Few of us who hunt the ditch," Brezny explained, "wouldn't trade our #4 buckshot loads for a good decoy set, a deep pit, and a chance to connect on geese at 30 yards with a cup full of #2's. But the truth is that most hunters don't get a chance at such conditions. Hunting the ditch is, for the most part, free."

Working with his hunting partner and fellow teacher, Joe Polunc, Brezny first began to evaluate the performance of factory loads of coarse shot and buckshot. They found that beyond 65 yards, because of "low velocity and soft shot," penetration was poor. They then turned to handloading, using a reduced pellet load of harder buckshot to get the most velocity possible.

Since they found that the range limit for 12-gauge guns, even with handloads, was no more than 70 yards, they went to the 10 gauge magnum and developed four loads for this specialized brand of waterfowling: 1. a 2-ounce load of BB's; 2. a 40-pellet load of #4 buckshot; 3. a 34-pellet load of #3 buckshot; and 4. a 20-pellet load of #1 buckshot.

"We decided the BB load was acceptable for close range shooting out to 50 yards on big geese and 65 yards on smaller geese. The #4 buck load was a good medium-range load to 50 and 60 yards for any Canada geese. The #3 buck did well at 75 and 80 yards. And the #1 buck load," Brezny emphasized, "was reserved for the longer 100-yard shots giving a low margin of hitting potential. It put nine of its pellets into a three-by-four-foot pattern paper at 110 yards, with more penetration at that distance than that of a .22 caliber long rifle."

Using buckshot on geese at very long range immediately brings up the spectre of sky-busting — shooting at birds at such distance that only a miracle can produce a kill, and which is likely to produce cripples. But Brezny contends that the handloads they use are fully up to the long-range task.

"If a hunter can't hit or his loads don't kill at long range," he told me, "then he should stay within the limits of his gun and skill. But to chastise the long range gunner based on sportsmanship, or some individual's idea of reasonable range, whatever that is, is out of line. It's comparable to asking a big game hunter not to take that 250-yard shot because he might wound the animal. If a shotgun can do the job past 60 yards, there's no logical reason the hunter should stand around all day bird watching just because someone says they're out of range."

In the 1978 season Brezny personally killed 15 big geese at long range, averaging 4.4 shots per goose. This is a much lower average than conventional loads attain.

"Crippling exists in all waterfowling," Brezny admitted. "The best way I know to reduce it, short of not shooting, is to shoot at a specific target — no flock shooting, to shoot at a workable range, and to know the effective limits of your loads."

Loyal Brezny and Joe Polunc concluded the following from their experiences: 1. hunters who handloaded, and knew the loads from testing, had a major advantage over hunters using off-the-shelf shells; 2. hunters who used a variation of loads gained a definite advantage over the one-shot-size gunners; 3. 10-gauge gun gave a 20-yard increase in range, a point particularly evident in pattern testing at 85 to 110 yards.

"Don't misunderstand me," Brezny cautioned. "I'm not saying that buckshot is the final answer, because it does have drawbacks. It may be illegal in some states. In the hands of the indiscriminate shooter it can be a crippler and, even worse, dangerous, but the same argument can be levied against any type of shot under certain conditions."

So there you have it, something new to most goose hunters. To you it may be a cup of tea or a bowl of poison, but it's interesting. As soon as possible I hope to hunt a Minnesota ditch alongside Brezny and friends, to evaluate an unusual phenomena in the field of goose gunning.

October 1979

THE HOT RIMFIRES

W hen I was growing up in the foothills of Carolina quite a spell ago, one of our most important graduation days had nothing to do with school. It was the day we graduated from a "BB" gun to a "22."

Since then we've paved the roads and walked on the moon and seen a batch of other changes. But one thing remains the same. For today's space-aged youngsters with an outdoor bent one of the most memorable milestones is *still* that day they graduate — from a "BB" gun to a "22."

The most popular cartridge in the world is one of the oldest. The modern .22 rimfire really got under way in 1857 — 122 years ago, appropriately enough. That was the year that Smith & Wesson introduced its First Model revolver, chambered for the .22 Short cartridge. And that makes this number the oldest American, commercial, self-contained metallic cartridge, according to Frank Barnes in his *Cartridges of the World.*

Yankee ingenuity didn't sit still very long, and in 1871 it came up with a beefed-up version called the .22 Long. It was followed, of course, by the .22 Long Rifle cartridge, which apparently was developed by the J. Stevens Arms and Tool Company in 1887.

The trend then, as now, was to produce a "hotter" round. That continued over the years, with a variety of souped up, small-bore rimfires, but most of them have faded and gone. Nothing could overcome the enormous popularity of the rifles and pistols chambered for the .22 Short, .22 Long, and .22 Long Rifle cartridges.

In 1959 Winchester brought out an excellent .22 rimfire which it called the .22 Winchester Magnum Rimfire, a longer and more powerful version of the .22 Winchester Rimfire (WRF). WRF ammo is still available, but no rifles are now being manufactured for that cartridge.

Remington made a run at the souped-up, rimfire market not long ago with the 5mm Remington Magnum, which zipped a 38-grain, hollow point bullet from the muzzle at some 2105 fps, giving 374 foot/pounds of energy. That's impressive when compared to the ballistics of the .22 Long Rifle high velocity, a muzzle velocity of some 1255 fps for a 40-grain bullet, which give a muzzle energy of 140 foot/pounds. So are the stats on that .22 Winchester Magnum Rimfire — a 40-grain bullet, 1910 fps, and 324 foot/pounds.

The 5mm Rem Mag is on the way out. The .22 WMRF, a very good performer, hangs on, but its sales are insignificant when compared to the conventional .22.

So, for almost a century, the arms and ammo makers have fired and fallen back in their efforts to improve on the amazing .22 Long Rifle cartridge. Militating against their success was the fact that all of their advances required a new gun — one which would not digest the conventional Short, Long and Long Rifle ammunition.

But now there's a new kid on the block, and he is here to stay.

In the mid-1970's CCI shook shooters and industry alike when that firm unveiled a hot new .22 rimfire which it called the Stinger. Using a longer brass case, a shorter and lighter bullet, and a different powder, it gave a muzzle velocity "25 percent higher than other high velocity .22LR ammo." CCI says that the 32-grain bullet leaves an 18 1/2-inch barrel at 1687 fps, developing 202 foot/pounds.

But the best thing about this new one is that it can be used in any rifle or pistol chambered for the .22 Long Rifle cartridge.

In the Stinger, the good ole boys from Omark pulled a coup, a success, and it is understandable that the other manufacturers would not be far behind with their own versions. Winchester was the first to follow the lead, naming its entry the Xpediter, giving no ballistics, saying only that the 29-grain, hollow point bullet moves at "approximately 30 percent higher velocity."

Remington then announced the Yellow Jacket, with a 33-grain hollow point bullet that "leaves the muzzle at 1500 fps, or 245 fps faster than a regular, high velocity long rifle cartridge." Muzzle energy — 165 foot/pounds. It later came along with the Viper, a 36-grain (non-hollow point) bullet at 1410 fps.

Federal Cartridge now has the Spitfire, in two loads identical in specs to the Remington. The CCI Stinger ballistics now read a 32-grain bullet at 1640 fps, down a bit; and Winchester has dropped its hyper loadings completely.

These newcomers are not as accurate as is good, lower velocity .22 Long Rifle stuff — but then, very few cartridges are. They are sufficiently accurate for most hunting purposes, and they have found a pretty solid niche in the hearts of shooters.

When the Stinger, Xpediter and Yellow Jacket ammo first became available, I compared their affect on cans of Mr. Campbell's favorite tomato soup with the havoc wrought by conventional .22 Long Rifle and Long Rifle hollow point cartridges. The added destruction of the higher velocity loads was impressive. It still is.

May 1979

ACCURATE RIFLED SLUGS

S hotguns using slugs are required for deer hunting in some areas, but the combination has a poor reputation for accuracy. That stems in no small measure from the fact that most slug shooters use an upland or duck gun which has no sights except for that ineffective round bead out on the muzzle.

Some hunters have installed rifle sights, and even scopes, which greatly increases the effectiveness of the shotgun for deer. Then firearms manufacturers began offering "slug barrels" as optional equipment and followed with "slug shotguns." These were and are traditional, smoothbore barrels, but they are short and are equipped with rifle sights. Most are improved cylinder bore, which tends to give best accuracy. This was a great step forward, giving the slug deer hunter a short, quick-handling gun with good open sights.

Now, two new ingredients have advanced the state of the art in shotgun slug shooting. They are: 1. better slug ammunition; and, 2. rifled shotgun barrels in which to shoot them.

During the past few years shooting competitions have demonstrated the improvement which has taken place in shotgun slug accuracy. Two statistics from the most recent meet stand out: 1. Every winner used a relatively new, relatively unknown slug ammunition called the BRI Sabot; and 2. With one exception every winner used a *rifled* barrel on his shotgun. Most deer hunters, even those who use slugs, have probably never heard of either.

The slugs loaded by our three leading U.S. ammo makers are called Foster-type slugs (Karl Foster patented the rifled slug in 1931). In 12 gauge they weigh one ounce (Federal also has a 1 1/4 ounce loading), and are essentially short and fat, not the best shape from an aerodynamic standpoint.

These "Foster" slugs incorporate grooves around the outside perimeter, angled slightly, apparently designed to impart spin. Whether they do or not, or to what extent, probably depends upon the fit of that particular slug to a particular shotgun barrel. Both the slugs and shotgun barrels vary in size.

For some years the slug with perhaps the best reputation for accuracy has been the Brenneke, manufactured in Germany for more than half a century. It's widely used in Europe and has enjoyed some popularity in this country, where it is available in both loaded ammunition and as slugs for reloading from Dynamit Nobel of America.

The Brenneke weighs 1 1/8 ounce. It is basically cylindrical in shape, with a rounded, protruding point intended to give a forward center of gravity. It also has angled ribs or fins which compress inside any choke bore, according to Dynamit Nobel, although it cautions that "when using a screwed-in choke ensure that the screw connection is strong."

Stability of a slug in flight, according to Brenneke, is not achieved by spin as in the case of rifle bullets, but rather is imparted by the air flow past the base of the slug. It stresses that since the center of gravity of the Brenneke is well forward, it "travels like an arrow."

The newer BRI Sabot 500 slug is designed with similar premise in mind, but it depends for stability in flight on its most unusual shape as well as its weight-forward configuration, and on the "sabot" principle. This latter is a plastic covering which falls away from the slug after being fired. It's intended to give a better gas seal in the barrel, and to prevent deformation of the slug as it passes through the barrel and choke. (Remington has "sabot" ammo on the market for .30-06, .308 Win, and .30-30 Win which is called Accelerator, all loaded with 55-grain, .22 caliber bullets at much higher velocities than the normal ammo in those calibers.)

Perhaps the best description of the BRI Sabot 500 slug is that the shape is similar to that of a badminton shuttlecock. This hourglass-shaped bullet is .50 caliber, *less* than the bore diameter of a 12 gauge. The plastic sabot covering fills the space in between. It weighs 440 grains, slightly heavier than the one ounce slugs in most U.S. ammunition. Muzzle velocity of the BRI Sabot 500's runs about 1200 fps (my test rounds averaged 1170 fps), less than the 1500-1600 fps loadings of Remington, Federal and Winchester.

In addition to improved slug ammunition, the rifled slug barrels now available from several manufacturers have contributed greatly to slug accuracy. I used two such barrels from Hastings, of Clay Center, Kansas, for my testing, one with open sights and one with a low-power (1 1/3X) scope. Available only for Remington M1100 and M870 shotguns (but with barrels for other models coming soon), they are made in France.

How accurate are the new combinations? A news release arrived last week touting a new "first," a 100-yard minute of angle performance with rifled slugs. It was fired on Feb. 2, 1986 by Bob Sowash, VP of Ballistic Research Industries (BRI). He used the BRI Sabot in a Benelli slug gun equipped with a rifled barrel by E. R. Shaw. It was a three-shot group measuring less than one inch.

The release reminds me of another three-shot group I photographed, fired by "hermit" Buckskin Bill along Idaho's Salmon River with a .22 rimfire Marlin 39A rifle, at 170 yards, with open sights. The three shots formed a one-hole clover leaf.

"I knew I was gonna do it," Buckskin told me, " 'cause I kept gettin' closer." He had fired one three-shot group every morning for several years.

Despite that, this BRI release makes the good point that better accuracy with rifled slugs is here. Not "minute of angle" or anything like that on a consistent basis, but then that's performance not many bolt action rifles achieve.

The "world" slug championship in 1985 was won with a 5-shot group measuring 2 1/8" at 50 yards, also with a BRI/Benelli/Shaw shotgun. Scoped, of course. Many other shooters have gotten similar performance, or better, with the Sabot in rifled barrels. My results were almost as good, and included one 4" 3-shot group at 90 yards.

With iron sights, my groups doubled in size, but there was one 2 1/2" 4-shot group at 50 yards. Some iron sights, needless to say, are better than others. Using nothing but shotgun sights? BIG, wildly erratic groups.

The performance of Winchester, Remington, Federal and Brenneke slugs varied greatly from gun to gun. All will give solid deer-killing accuracy out to 50-75 yards IF decent sighting equipment is used (good iron sights, scopes, or one of the optical sights such as the Aimpoint), and provided that the hunter experiment with different slug brands in his gun to find which is best for it. The BRI Sabot fired in rifled barrels extends that effective range to a solid 100 yards or a bit more.

Rifled slugs, really, are not fun to shoot. From my M870 and M12 pumps, in 12 gauge, they are awesome in recoil from the bench. Gas-operated autoloaders took some of the bite out. Winchester, Federal and Remington slugs leaving the muzzle at 1500 fps plus deliver more recoil, of course, than does the similar weight Sabot slug at 1200 fps. They also deliver more energy at short ranges. Shotgun triggers are usually poor — heavy and creepy, which is marginally acceptable for bird shooting but not so for precision slug shooting. I replaced my M870 trigger with one made by Timney for Hastings, which was a great improvement. So would be barrel porting and stock recoil reducers insofar as bench testing is concerned, and I suspect that many hunters neglect "tuning" their slug gun simply because of the recoil.

For more information about the new BRI Sabot ammunition, contact: BRI, 2825 S. Rodeo Gulch Rd., Soquel, CA 95073; La Paloma Marketing, 1735 E. Fort Lowell Rd., Tucson, AZ 85719; or Hastings, Inc. (address below).

For info about rifled shotgun barrels, write: Hastings, Box 224, Clay Center, KS 67532; Mike Rock, 101 Ogden Ave., Albany, WI 53502; or E. R. Shaw, Thoms Run Rd., Bridgeville, PA 15017. For information about reloading rifled slugs, write: Ballistic Products, Box 408, Long Lake, MN 55356; or Ballistic Research Lab, 1108 West May Ave., McHenry, IL 60050.

November 1986

THE STRANGE CASE OF THE .280 REMINGTON

O dds are great that many of you reading this have little idea what the .280 Remington caliber is, despite the fact that it is one of the most versatile and effective big-game calibers on the scene. That's heavy praise, needless to say, in the face of the raft of excellent calibers available to the big-game hunter today, but it is a tribute voiced quite frequently by knowledgeable gun people. So, you rightly ask, why don't I know about it.

Enter that identity crisis. When Remington first announced the .280 Rem. caliber, way back in 1958, the real culprit in keeping this new one from ever getting off the ground was timing. Poor timing, that is, in that the .270 Winchester caliber was already off and running, with an established track record of good performance on game and a host of admirers touting its attributes. The .280 Rem. never caught up, and faded still further after that initial burst of "new caliber" enthusiasm.

Remington's factory ammunition for the new one didn't help. Although adequate, it wasn't initially loaded to get the full performance capability from the caliber, partially negating its marginal ballistic superiority over the .270 Winchester. That first chambering was for the Model 725 bolt action, but it was also offered at that time for both the M740 autoloader and the M760 pump. Those hunters who did load their own after buying a .280 Rem. found that they had a winner, but there just weren't enough of them to make the caliber a profitable one for Remington.

The Bridgeport firm did give it a chance. For a decade the caliber was offered in a succession of bolt actions, autoloaders and pumps, but in 1968 it was dropped from all except the M742 autoloader. in 1979, in a move to revive the .280 Remington, the firm decided to re-name it. More confusion. The first choice for the new designation was the "7mm-06 Remington," and my test Model 700 is so marked. It was almost a very suitable handle for the revived and revitalized (the new ammunition gave improved ballistic performance) caliber, but at the 11th hour another switch was made. Although based generally upon the .30-06 case, this caliber isn't *exactly* the same as the .30-06 case necked down to 7mm. Simply necking '06 brass down to 7mm to create ammo could be dangerous, and Remington felt that a 7mm-06 label might tempt shooters to do just that. The name was aborted before rifles so labeled ever reached the dealer shelves.

The name finally chosen, for which the M700 bolt actions were again chambered, and for which a factory 150-grain loading was offered, was the "7mm Express Remington." That, in the name game, might have been compounding a felony for confusion. There has been more than one occasion when 7mm Express Remington and 7mm Remington Magnum ammo has been switched, with interesting results. Not really any excuse for doing such a thing — except not reading the label. And, as if shooters weren't bewildered enough, Remington retained in the line the name ".280 Rem." for its 165 grain-round nose loading. Same cartridge case; different names.

In 1981 Remington unveiled its new semi-auto big-game rifles, the models Six and M7400, and among the calibers for which they were chambered was the 7mm Express Remington. That made for a very potent combination for hunters who prefer auto's, and they still enjoy modest popularity. Sales in the bolt actions were poor, and before you knew it there wasn't a Model 700 available in this caliber except through Remington's custom gun shop. In that year of 1983, when Remington dropped the caliber from standard model 700's, it also — guess what — renamed it. Back to square one! Back to the .280 Remington, where it probably should have been all along.

Look for the three-year "no bolt action" hiatus to be ending early in 1986. Remington will once again be chambering a Model 700 bolt action for this caliber. It's a tenacious, well-deserved effort to breathe life back into a fine caliber.

Why such a valiant, long-running effort to rescue a caliber? Beyond the business reasons is the fact that many shooters, Remington employees as well as outsiders, just hate to see such an excellent factory caliber fall by the wayside. It is worth the effort.

The 7mm caliber has long been known to offer appreciable ballistic advantages over most other calibers in "big-game" bullet weights. Sectional density and ballistic coefficient are two characteristics of bullets which are indicative of downrange performance, and 7mm bullets in the 150-to 175-grain range have the edge in both categories over similar weights in .270 or .30 caliber. A plus, for handloaders, is that there are many excellent 7mm bullets available from all manufacturers.

The positioning of the .280 Remington in the hunting scheme of things is simple. It's more potent than the .270 Win and the .30-06 and less potent than the 7mm Remington Magnum — but only a little more and a little less. It holds more powder than the .270 Win. and .30-06 and less powder than does the 7mm Rem. Mag, which should lead to more recoil and less recoil, respectively. As a practical matter, I can't detect much difference in the "kick" from my .270's and .280's. The 7mm Mag, perhaps my favorite caliber, does bounce a bit more, but I'm not very sensitive to recoil.

The reputation for accuracy of the .280 Rem. hasn't been all that good, except with the shooters who use the caliber. Such an anomaly could have stemmed from an isolated case or two which got into print once, and then gained credence from repetition. My Model Four shoots into two inches with factory ammo. I hunted in the Yukon last month with T. J. Vinet, whose Shilen-barreled, McMillan-stocked .280 Remington, with handloads, produces half-inch groups with regularity.

Remington manufactures a 150-grain, .280 Rem. round listed at 2970 fps muzzle velocity, and a 165-grain at 2820 fps (a round nose whose downrange performance lags badly), both from 24-inch barrels. Norma also offers two loadings: 150-grain soft point at 2871 fps, and a 170-grain PPC at 2707 fps. Neither Federal nor Winchester have the .280 Rem. in their ammunition lines. Many .280 Rem. enthusiasts wish Remington would offer a broader range of ammunition for the caliber, notably a 140 grain and a 160 or 165 grain in the "Core-Lokt" pointed soft points.

Add my name to the long list of shooters who like the .280 Remington and hope it doesn't go away as a factory number. Although it isn't a magic panacea for all big game, it is one of the best all-around calibers for all North American big game short of the big bears. It is at its best in a bolt action rifle, and I'm delighted that Remington is again chambering its M700 for the .280 Rem. Other manufacturers have, in the past, offered bolt actions in this caliber, but I know of none still in the line-up. And, given the past, checkered career of the .280 Remington/7mm-06/7mm Express Remington/.280 Remington, don't delay if you want one of the "new" M700's in this caliber.

(In 1986 Remington chambered for the .280 Rem. in a new M700 that is called the Mountain Rifle, perhaps the finest M700 the company has produced. With it, they introduced a fine new loading for the caliber: 140-grain Pointed Soft Point at 3000 fps muzzle velocity. Excellent combination.)

January 1986

Remington, which for a decade had been the innovator among factory arms and ammo manufacturers where new calibers were concerned, did it again in 1977. They introduced a new "super-8", the 8mm Remington Magnum. For some years Remington had progressively adopted one particular version of various successful wildcat calibers and made them standard items. Before, shooters who wanted such items as the .22-250, .25-06, 7mm Magnum, 6.5mm Magnum and .350 Magnum had only one route to take: have a custom rifle made for the particular caliber and then handload for it.

Many did just that! But many thousands more, frustrated either by finances or a disinclination toward reloading, longed in vain for those borings.

Then, along came Remington with over-the-counter rifles and ammunition for the .22-250, the 6mm Rem., the 6.5mm Rem. Mag., the 7mm Rem. Mag., and the .350 Rem. Mag. All were versions of successful wildcats. Their degree of success has varied greatly, from the immensely popular .22-250 and 7mm on down to the 6.5 and .350 magnums, which never really got off the ground.

The 6mm Rem., introduced initially as the .244 Rem. (ill-fated because its barrel rate of twist failed to stabilize hunting-weight bullets well), has never reached the popularity of the .243 Winchester, which was introduced the same year. But the 6mm Rem. still enjoys substantial success, and is even considered a slightly better case for reloading purposes.

"Somebody finally did it!"

That was the reaction of most of the gun editors assembled at the Hawkeye Hunting Club near Center, Texas that November, when Remington announced the introduction of the 8mm Rem. Mag. The reaction was an obvious one, since the "super eight" slot was one of the few voids in the ballistic scheme of things insofar as factory offerings are concerned.

Let's take a quick look at some of the numbers along the millimeter trail. At 6mm there is the .240 Weatherby Mag., plus the .243 Win and the 6mm Rem. At 6.5mm — the .257 Weatherby Mag. and the .25-06. Up a shade to 6.7mm — the .264 Win Mag. and the 6.5 Rem. Mag. The 7mm arena is well filled: 7mm Rem. Mag., .270 Win, .280 Rem., .284 Win, and 7x57. And later came the fine 7mm-08 Remington. The .30-caliber slot is loaded. In addition to all the standard .30 calibers, we have an excellent trio of 7.62mm magnums — .300 Win Mag., .300 Weatherby Mag., and .308 Norma Mag.

In the 8.6mm class, two fine calibers: .338 Win Mag. and .340 Weatherby Mag. In the 9mm — .358 Win Mag., .358 Norma Mag. and the potent .378 Weatherby Mag. Then, at the top, are the .458 Win Mag. and the .460 Weatherby Mag.

So, in slips Remington with this 8mm Rem. Mag., in a niche populated only by the dying .32 Winchester Special, and by the 8x57 Mauser. The latter, a good cartridge of little popularity in this country, is factory loaded only to modest performance in keeping with the many 8mm rifles in existence which wouldn't be safe with more powerful loadings.

The case is essentially identical to the .375 H&H Mag. case, necked down to accept the 8mm bullet (actual bullet diameter is .323″). Remington factory loads were and are with the 180- or 220-grain Core-Lokt bullets, and no other ammo manufacturer has loaded the caliber. By examining the tables, we see that the ballistic figures are impressive.

Remington points out that the loadings have sustained downrange velocities that produce exceptionally-flat trajectories and high remaining energies; i.e., that the 220-grain loading of the 8mm Rem. Mag. has greater downrange energy (200 yards or more) than 200-grain plus bullets in either the .300 Win Mag. or the .338 Win Mag. Remington continues that "the trajectory of the 8mm Rem. Mag. 220-grain load is flatter than the .300 Win Mag. 220-grain load, and roughly equal to the .338 Win Mag. 200-grain load despite the latter's lighter bullet."

Muzzle velocity of the 185-grain loading in this cartridge is 3080 fps, and of the 220-grain loading 2830 fps. This translates to muzzle energies of 3896 and 3912 foot pounds respectively.

The rifle to accept the new 8mm Rem. Mag. cartridge was the Remington Model 700 BDL with 24-inch barrel, and it's still available. Many custom gunsmiths have chambered for the caliber.

After shooting almost a box of ammo through the combination, I came to the obvious conclusion that this isn't a gun for plinking. But it is not an unpleasant rifle to shoot when considered under the umbrella of the Weatherbys and the other magnum calibers.

Knowing that the hunting public can be fickle where new offerings are concerned, I still guessed rather prematurely that this 8mm

Rem. Mag. would establish itself as a solid member of modern-day big game calibers. It didn't happen, but the 8mm Rem. Mag. is still excellent as a one-gun battery for the man who isn't particularly sensitive to recoil, especially if he is inclined to experiment with handloads.

With a proper 250-grain solid bullet in a handload, as the late Warren Page commented at that Seminar back in 1977, this new cartridge might be looked upon with favor as a one-gun battery for African game. I used it for just that a couple of years later.

It's no secret that no one big bore caliber-load can be all things to all people and places, and a comparison of the performance data for the 8mm Rem. Mag. with other numbers in the field demonstrates this well. The effectiveness of a bullet on game, apart from the construction of the bullet itself, depends largely upon the energy delivered at a particular range. And that energy is a product of bullet weight and velocity.

I've reviewed comparative energy figures for the magnums flanking the 8mm Rem. Mag., and examination of them is interesting. As an example let's look at the 175-grain 7mm Rem. Mag. vs. the 180-grain .300 Win Mag. vs. the 185-grain 8mm Rem. Mag. performances. At 100 yards the 8mm is on top, with 3132 foot pounds of energy, compared to 3095 for the .300 WM and 2718 for the 7mm. But at 200 yards the .300 WM has the edge, with 2654 foot pounds to 2494 for the 8mm and 2313 for the 7mm. The 7mm energy performance catches up with the 8mm at 300 yards, and the .300 continues to widen its lead. At 400 and 500 yards both the 7mm and .300 are out-performing the 8mm, with the .300 delivering 1614 foot pounds out at 500 yards, the 7mm 1372 foot pounds, and the 8mm 1170 foot pounds.

With the 220-grain loads, however, the 8mm starts out in front of the .300 and stays there out to 500 yards, although the gap narrows as the distance increases.

On the other end, the 8mm Rem. Mag. energy performance at all ranges with the 220-grain load exceeds that of the .338 Win Mag. in any of its factory offerings — 200-, 250- or 300-grain loads.

Keep in mind that all of the above calibers are potent numbers. To maintain a bit of perspective we might consider that the .30-06, which has taken all species of game on this continent and most of the African species, delivers 2347 foot pounds of energy at the muzzle with a 220-grain bullet, dropping to 1024 foot pounds at 500 yards.

A great plus for the 8mm Rem. Mag. in the years since its introduction is the array of excellent bullets now being offered to handloaders. Hornady, Speer, Barnes and Sierra have several 8mm bullet weights in their lines, and Nosler has a 200-grain Partition.

February 1977

7mm — THE EFFICIENT CALIBER

T he first 7mm caliber rifle that came into my possession did so without much effort or design on my part. Until that year most of my centerfire gunning had been with the .30-calibers — .300 Savage and .30-06, for the most part, and with the very good .257 Roberts.

Walter Womack of Shreveport, Louisiana, now retired but at the time one of the finest gunsmiths in the country, was the impetus behind that first acquisition. "You really should have a 7mm Remington Magnum," was his simple, opening salvo. "It's a good one."

When Walter spoke, I listened. Not only was he a premier builder of rifles, but he had the added advantage of being an experienced, competent big-game hunter, in addition to holding a national record or three for competitive rifle shooting. If my mentor said I needed a 7mm mag, so be it.

I had an old Springfield on hand, and in a few months it was transformed into a Womack Special in that 7mm Remington Magnum caliber, with a Douglas barrel and a Fajen stock. In the following decade it became my tool of choice, my companion on most of my hunts. We still get along famously.

That was in the early 1960s, soon after Remington introduced this caliber (1962). In the years since then my 7mm horizons have expanded, as has the array of 7mm choices available over the counter.

The funny thing about calibers is that they form personal connotations in the mind, usually different ones for different folks, but occasionally a common thread for most shooters. When the 7x57 (7mm Mauser) is on view, many of us recall that Bell used this "pip-squeak" to take a large share of the enormous number of elephants he collected in Africa. Of more recent vintage, the 7x57 reminds me of Bryan Smith, who retired in 1981 as a professional hunter in Zambia, after compiling a legendary record of accomplishment in several African countries. His reputation among his peers for marksmanship and cool-under-fire was widespread, and a bit amazing since those qualities are expected for professional "white hunters." That reputation extended to his clients, I might add, including a friend of mine whose angry, wounded lion was properly and neatly dispatched with Smith's 7mm, not too far in advance of the moment when my friend would have become a statistic. Although I was never fortunate enough to hunt with him, shortly before he retired Bryan showed me the Rigby bolt action in 7x57 caliber which was his "one gun," used always with solid bullets, and with a scope that seemed to be mounted a foot above the bore — European style. With it he collected camp meat and protected his clients, whether it was from elephant, buff or lion.

The 7mm choices now available in the American marketplace include the 7mm-08 Remington, the 7x57, the .280 Remington, the 7mm Remington Magnum, and the 7mm Weatherby Magnum. Another 7mm that enjoyed a brief spurt of modest popularity was the .284 Winchester, introduced in 1963, which is a short, fat cartridge designed to work through the actions of the Winchester Model 88 lever action and Model 100 semiauto. Quite a good caliber for its intended niche, it was virtually left an orphan when the M100 and the M88 were discontinued by Winchester. It is still available here and there, now and then, in factory rifles. The excellent Alpha Custom lightweight bolt action, which made its debut in 1983, is chambered for this caliber.

Let's take them one by one, beginning with that oldie from the fertile mind of Paul Mauser. His 7x57 has stood the test of time extremely well and is enjoying a resurgence of popularity in this country. More factory rifles are now chambered for this caliber than had been the case for decades.

There is one millstone around the 7x57 insofar as factory ammo is concerned. Since countless rifles of this caliber that began their careers as military weapons are still being used for hunting, many of them in questionable conditions, manufacturers of ammunition market only a very modest loading. Until last year the only factory fodder available was a 175-grain bullet at 2440 fps muzzle velocity, adequate for most deer hunting conditions but far short of what can be accomplished by reloading with lighter, more efficient bullets. Last year Remington dropped its 175-grain load in favor of a "140"-grain bullet, quite an improvement, but in deference to the old guns chambered for this caliber this cartridge is not loaded to its full potential.

That 140-grain bullet is in reality a 139-grain Hornady, the same very good bullet that is loaded in the Remington 7mm-08 cartridge. Now Federal Cartridge Corporation also has both 140- and 175-grain bullets for this caliber in its Hi-Shok line.

The 7x57, whether with factory ammo or handloads, has modest recoil and report, making it a particular favorite with those to whom these factors are important. When handloaded with a good spitzer bullet in the 150-grain class, to muzzle velocities in the 2600 to 2700 fps range, this caliber is excellent for all medium-sized North American big game.

In 1957 Remington did what has become a trend with this Bridgeport firm — introduced a factory version of a caliber that had long been the province of wildcatters. This time the number to be made legitimate was the 7mm-06, simply the .30-06 case that had been necked down to 7mm bullet dimensions by the experimenters. The dimensions of the new caliber were changed slightly, and to eliminate confusion with any other 7mm-06 wildcats this new factory round was labeled the .280 Remington.

It was, and is, a superior caliber. My first impression of it was impressive. In 1964 Sonny Gilbert and I were hunting with John Trumbo along the Missouri River breaks in Montana, and what Sonny's .280 Remington did to deer and antelope got my attention. He was using good 125-grain bullets in hot handloads, and they were very effective.

For all that, the .280 just didn't sell well, and in 1979 Remington "re-introduced" the .280 Rem as the — guess what — the 7mm-06 Remington. That's what the first press releases called it, and my sample Model 700 is so stamped. But a funny thing happened between the release and the first sales. The name was changed — to protect the unwary.

To avert possible liability problems, Remington decided at the eleventh hour to opt for the name 7mm Express Remington rather than 7mm-06 Remington. The reasoning was that handloaders might try to produce reloads for this caliber by simply necking down .30-06. brass to 7mm bullet dimensions, which could create potentially dangerous excessive headspace in rifles chambered for this caliber. These include either .280 Remington, 7mm-06 Remington, or 7mm Express Remington — all exactly the same caliber with the same dimensions.

Remington's new factory loading in the 7mm Express Remington used a different powder from that used in the .280 Remington and gave better performance. It gave (and still gives) a 150-grain Pointed Soft Point Core-Lokt 2970 fps muzzle velocity (the same bullet in the 7mm Rem Mag leaves the muzzle at 3110 fps). Now, Remington also markets a 165-grain Soft Point Core-Lokt in this caliber, but now it's back to the 280 Remington designation.

Whatever it takes to make the public aware of this caliber is probably worth it, but odds are slim that it will ever become very popular. The 7mm Express Remington designation was simply too confusing, too close to the 7mm Remington Magnum, which is why Remington made the switch *back* to the .280 Remington name. The fact is that this caliber may well be the most versatile of them all for North American big game.

The .284 Winchester, as indicated above, isn't likely to become a household caliber, which is a bit of a shame. It was an excellent caliber for that M100 semi-auto and the M88 lever action, two of the best pointing and handling such rifles ever to come along, and more's the pity that they aren't still around. Winchester is the only ammo company which produces cartridges for the .284 Win, with a 125 grain at a zippy 3140 fps, and a 150 grain at 2860 fps. Both are Power Point Soft Point bullets. The .284 Win can be handloaded to give superior performance in bolt action rifles, or in single shot's such as the Ruger Number One.

From the .280 Remington to the 7mm Remington Magnum is but a short step. What a winner this 7mm Remington Magnum has been! In a deer camp not long ago I checked the 13 hunters there and found that five were using this caliber. Two others were shooting the 7mm Weatherby Magnum, and one the 7mm Express Remington. It was a graphic example of the popularity of the 7mm's in general, and of the 7mm RM in particular.

There are many good 7mm bullets available for the handloader, and the 7mm RM can be made to perform with quite a wide range of bullet weights. The man who does not reload, however, would be hard put to find a better over-the-counter big-game combination than the 7mm Remington Magnum caliber paired with one of the many excellent factory loadings available.

The difference between the .280 Rem and the 7mm Rem Mag, according to the factory ballistic chart, is 140 fps with the 150-grain bullet. The slightly increased powder capacity of the latter case results in that edge in muzzle velocity and a bit better performance with heavy bullets, but with it goes more recoil.

The 7mm Weatherby Magnum? What's to say, except that it's

typically Weatherby: bigger case; more velocity; more recoil; excellent performance.

The latest addition to the 7mm line is the 7mm-08, and there are preliminary indications that Remington just may have another real winner in this one. Again, this is an adaptation of a wildcat that has been around for years: the 308 Winchester case necked down to take the 7mm bullet. The objective was to market a 7mm for a short-action rifle, as was true for the fading .284 Winchester.

The one factory loading available for the 7mm-08 has a 140-grain Core-Lokt bullet. For it Remington lists a muzzle velocity from a 24-inch test barrel of 2860 fps. What this adds up to, essentially, is virtually the same good performance we can get in the 7x57 with good handloads.

The first rifle Remington chambered for the 7mm-08 was the Model 788 bolt-action carbine with an 18 1/2-inch barrel. Even from this short tube handloaders can get 2900 fps muzzle velocity with 130-grain bullets, excellent for both deer and antelope. For use on black bear, strongly constructed 140- and 150-grain bullets are preferable. With these this little newcomer is adequate even for elk at modest ranges, with proper bullet placement.

Remington also chambers the Model 700 in both regular versions and the heavy barrel Varmint Special in the 7mm-08. There's a good chance that most other manufacturers will follow suit in their rifles. It's a good caliber — one that may well replace the old 7x57 in the hearts and gun racks of many hunters.

There you have the 7mm array now available from U.S. gun and ammo builders. Custom gunsmiths build a wide assortment of 7mm's, both factory numbers such as are listed here and wildcat variations. With bullets of good design, in the weight ranges most popular for big-game hunting in this country, the 7mm diameter is an extremely efficient one. In a caliber with adequate case capacity, it is excellent in retaining downrange velocity and energy and deserves the high esteem in which it is held by hunters worldwide.

March 1982

Section Six

GUN PEOPLE

"When you see me comin', better step aside; a lotta men didn't and a lotta men died."

Bill Jordan doesn't weigh 600 pounds, quite, but like the gorilla in that old joke, he can sleep just about anywhere he chooses. The reason is that William could be just about the deadliest man in the country in a gunfight, and it's a fact that this gentle giant from the bayous of Louisiana does things with a handgun that defy belief.

Bill wrote the book, literally, on combat pistol shooting, and the title he chose for his modest little volume says a ton: *No Second Place Winner.* In its eighth printing, it is either required reading or a textbook in virtually every law officer training program in the nation.

In 1980 I talked Bill into filming a segment for the "Sports Afield" television series with me, so many of you may have seen him perform. For eleven years with the NRA, and more years prior to that with the U.S. Border Patrol, Jordan gave shooting exhibitions throughout the U.S., but he came out of "retirement" to work with us.

"I haven't done this for five years," he cautioned, "so I'm probably rusty."

He wasn't! His quick draw was nothing but a blur, but on the tube we showed it in slow motion as well as in blinding speed. I should add that when his Smith & Wesson cleared leather, Bill knew what to do with it. From the hip, he shattered progressively smaller targets — down to aspirins, which I suppose could represent the middle button on a desperado's shirt.

"Speed is fine," he observed, "but accuracy is final."

He should know. His primary career consisted of some three decades with the Border Patrol, mostly along and across the Mexican border, dealing with smugglers and others who sought to enter the U.S. without benefit of immigration clearance. It was an era when this branch of law enforcement had more combat encounters than any state or federal force ever had, or has to this time. Jordan gained additional practical survival experience as a combat officer in the Marine Corps in the South Pacific in World War II, and later in Korea.

His retirement from the Border Patrol was followed by those eleven years as field representative at large for the National Rifle

Association, and it was during this period that he entered another avocation/vocation — magazine writer. For the past few years he has written a couple or three columns or articles each month on shooting and hunting for a number of "gun" magazines, but he recently decided that the chore had ceased to be fun, so retired… again, well almost. He'll continue to write one monthly question & answer column.

Lean and lithe, six foot, six inches tall and weighing more than 200 pounds, Bill has reached that three-score-and-ten plateau, and then some, but he's changed the rules. "I've changed that to four-score-and-twenty," he explained, with the stern look and dry humor for which he is noted, and I wouldn't bet against him reaching that goal. Watching the ham-sized hand of this 70-year-young man caress a pistol from a holster faster than the eye can follow, I find it difficult to doubt anything he has in mind. Bill was born in Louisiana in 1911, and "retired" back to his home state (Shreveport) where he still makes his home.

So did the jury (retire, that is) in a murder trial along about 1980, at which he was subpoenaed by the defendant to "testify." In a demonstration of reaction time, he faced a deputy already holding a cocked pistol. From a hands-up position, he drew and fired before the deputy could pull the trigger. After witnessing this, the jury deliberated 10 minutes, found the defendant not guilty, and bought 16 copies of Bill's book.

Safety, needless to say, is an integral part of Bill's performances, whether they're before live audiences or on radio and television. He didn't reach that three score and ten by being careless with guns, and regularly emphasizes that nobody should attempt any of his quick-draw feats with live ammunition. In his exhibitions, he uses wax bullets powered only by a primer — no powder at all, or just the primer alone if all that's needed is a "bang."

Less you get the idea that Jordan is one-dimensional when it comes to firearms, perish that thought. He attained the highest classifications in target shooting with all other arms — Class AA in both skeet and trap, and Lifetime Master with big bore and small bore rifle, as well as with pistol. Having hunted with him for both birds and big game, I can assure you that he is as proficient in sport gunning as he is on bullseyes. He has hunted extensively in Africa, as well as throughout this country and Mexico.

There may be a few pistol shooters who don't know who Bill Jordan is, but they know of him indirectly. The "Jordan holster," designed by Bill long ago, is worn by a majority of the uniformed enforcement officers in the nation, and by thousands of sportsmen who use handguns for plinking, target shooting or hunting.

In hundreds of exhibitions before sportsmen's groups and civic clubs, lectures at police academies here and abroad, and television appearances on such national programs as "I've Got a Secret," "What's My Line," "To Tell the Truth" and "Border Patrol" — on which he was consultant and in which he appeared in a number of segments, Bill Jordan has been a dynamic asset for the good guys, for those of us who like to own and use guns. His dazzling exhibitions of fast and accurate pistol shooting gained him access to vast audiences, but it was and is his wit, humor, slow drawl, and his intelligent, even-tempered espousal of the right to own and properly use firearms in today's society, which have converted many people to a pro-gun and pro-hunting status. For that we all owe him a round of applause.

Not that this articulate gentleman in the towering frame has gone unnoticed by his peers. In 1976 he was named the Outstanding Handgunner of the Year. Long before that the U.S. Border Patrol retired the badge Bill Jordan had worn, realizing that he had virtually become a legend in his own time.

So keep an eye out for lanky William. Watch for a tall stranger wearing a Texas hat, a Jordan holster, a southern drawl, and reflexes which make a cat seem awkward. And, if he looks your way, smile.

March 1981

MARGUERITE EVERHEART: SILHOUETTE CHAMP

"I can do anything I want, any time I want, when it pertains to shooting."

"My goal is to make the Olympic shooting team, and to win the Nationals again this year. I want to do it twice in a row."

"When I set my mind to it I can shoot smallbore like anything. I'll smoke 'em. One day my little brother picked up my rifle and ran nine chickens in a row, walked off and said, "Now that's how it's done." I got up and ran 10 and told him, "No, that's how it's done." He said, "I'm never going to beat you." I told him, "Don't worry, you will. You will one of these days — when I'm old.""

In mid-summer of 1984, on the NRA ranges at Raton, New Mexico, several hundred of the finest rifle shooters in the United States, Mexico and Canada tried to end one gunner's domination of the most difficult event in rifle competition. In the High Power "Siluetas Metalicas" Championship, one shooter had won the event twice in the previous three years, in 1981 and 1983, and finished second in 1982. Her competition included many world class shooters, among them the holder of a number of Olympic shooting medals.

That's right: HER! As in woman. Marguerite Lyn Everheart was in that year an attractive, poised, confident 23-year old college student who had blazed a meteoric path across the ranges of this challenging sport. In winning the crown in 1981 she set a new world record which still stood as she approached the 1984 matches.

What is it — this silhouette shooting? A piece of cake, no less. Just stand there with your deer rifle and knock down steel silhouette cutouts of birds and animals, shooting offhand, from your two hind legs, with no sling or other support of any kind. Four different targets: the chickens at 200 meters, javelina at 300 meters, turkeys at 385 meters, and the sheep out at 500 meters. That's 500 METERS — 546.8 yards — substantially farther than a quarter of a mile.

This shooting game is very difficult as I discovered some years ago when I saw the Nationals won with a score of about 60 percent. With that background, including a rather embarrassing personal "press" trial, I have followed the exploits of Marguerite Everheart with great interest and amazement. When she won the 1981 Championship with a world record score of 94X120 (78 percent), I considered that perhaps lightning had struck. When she finished second — the silver medal, so to speak — the following year, I was much impressed. Then, in October of 1983, in Reno, when she came from behind on the last day, running 10 straight pigs to overcome a five-target deficit, taking the crown again, I had to ask, "Who the hell IS this gal?"

After a long-running series of phone calls and letters, to her homes in Albuquerque and Soccorro, and to Eastern New Mexico State University in Portales, and to Ron Peterson's Guns in Albuquerque, where she worked when she wasn't shooting, hunting, fishing or studying, an interview was arranged. We met in Albuquerque on a cold, bright beautiful morning in February, after Marguerite had made the five-hour drive from Portales the previous evening. She brought along her seven-month-old German shorthair, who romped and ran over the gun club grounds during our photo session, and who then curled up and slept while I tried to find out what makes this winner tick.

Marguerite Everheart is 5 feet 6 inches, has hair that's "dishwater blonde," and hazel eyes that "change from blue to green, depending upon the light and my mood." She's the oldest of five children, having two brothers and two sisters, all of whom shoot. So does her father, who is the coach of the New Mexico National Guard shooting team.

"Mom's the only one who doesn't shoot. The rest of us shoot and hunt. We like to eat game meat. Birds or big game? There's more meat on big game, but I like 'em both. If I don't get to hunt I'm a grouch, and I haven't been deer hunting the past three years because of school and work and competition."

"I killed my first antelope when I was about 10 years old, and my best one is over 17 inches. I've hunted elk but haven't gotten one yet. I've killed deer, but missed one Boone & Crockett buck that Dad then killed."

Over the years the overriding trait I've found in shooting winners, be they after game, trap, skeet, live birds or X-rings, is confidence. They believe — yea, they KNOW they can handle the situation. They have mental discipline. Marguerite Everheart has these qualities in spades.

I had to ask, "You believe you can do anything?"

"Yeah, that's the way we've been trained. We set our mind to it, we can. From both Mom and Dad. They backed us in anything we wanted to do."

Marguerite is a bit old to be a second semester sophomore, which she was at the time of the interview.

"After I finished high school I laid out two years to work and figure out really what I wanted to do — and I'm glad I did. It's paid off in my shooting, and now I know what I want to do. I'm not going to waste four years of college. Now I'm doing so well I keep my advisors confused as to just what I'll be taking. I'll probably finish in two years with a double major, or a major and a couple of minors — business, accounting, math and maybe photography."

She began shooting silhouettes in May of 1979, and the natural question which comes to mind: why so good.

"I really don't know. I have some good coaches, and my family backs me. Some say it's just natural ability, but sometimes I wonder."

How about getting ready for a competition? Any special preparation?

"Oh, yes, mental and physical. I do a lot of mental work... concentrating. A lot of dry firing and practicing and stuff, and I try to visualize that I'm at a match and be consistent with everything. Calling my shots. And physically, try to keep the flab down, you know, so I can hold a rifle up for eight hours."

Marguerite shoots a Remington Model 700 rifle in .308 Win caliber, Canjar trigger, and after three years has just switched from a 10X scope to a 16X, both Weaver T-models. The rifle weighs 9 3/4 pounds, below the maximum of 10-2. Her trigger pull is set at 4 ounces or less; she uses a dot reticle in her scope. After an estimated 15,000 rounds through it, the barrel on this rifle is showing signs of wear.

"Yeah, because of that I used a custom bullet on the sheep last year. The barrel won't stabilize the 190 grain Sierra's I'd been using. At the Nevada State Match my spotter was Jack Hill, from California, and when we were sighting in early in the morning my bullets wouldn't stay on the rams. I couldn't hold a five-inch group, so we tried his bullets. With them, where I stuck it was where it hit — a three-inch group or something like that. He had enough to get me through the Nevada State and the Nationals, so I shot his bullets on the 500-meter targets."

Marguerite's Dad does her reloading if she can't get to it ("Everybody pitches in, ya know.") Even though her powder measure throws within 1/2 grain, she trickle weighs every load. ("I want to get all the error out and not wonder, 'Oh, gosh, is this lighter or heavier', so that's why I do it.")

"My spotter is extremely important," Marguerite told me. "Mine is usually my Dad or sister, my adopted Dad (Tommy Gatewood, Jr.), or some of the other guys. There are certain people I trust and some I don't. The spotter is supposed to take care of the wind, tell you where you hit, keep you under control, and without a good one I'd be dead sometimes. I just want to worry about the shooting, the shot, and let them worry about everything else.

As for aiming point, she tries to hold dead center most of the time, or where her spotter tells her to hold: "I've got it set so that where I shoot is where it hits. If you hold dead center all the time, when you get under pressure there's nothing to forget.

"When I'm shooting, there's a point where the dot will wiggle around, wiggle around and then finally it'll just stop, for maybe a second, and that's when I try to shoot. If I can't do it then I just start over again."

The road to shooting success for Marguerite Everheart has at times been a bit rocky, largely because of too many toos: too good; too young; and too female. A set of contest rules which seemed to be flexible from club to club plagued her from Junior Club competition on up, featuring such decisions as disqualification because she had won the year before, and rulings that she could not compete in open, women's and junior events in the same competition back when she was a junior, was a woman, and was proficient enough to compete in open competition. The discomforture of meet officials in such a situation is perhaps understandable, since it was unique. "If the clubs say there will be only one trophy per person," Marguerite explained, "that goes, because it's their range, which is fine by me."

"Resentment from other women?" Marguerite grinned. "Yeah, there's a good bit of that. Why? Because I'm shooting; because I'm good at it; and because they don't like their husbands hanging around me. The women shooters do have respect for me, and the guys just treat me like one of them. Some of the wives throw daggers all the time, but to the shooters I'm just another shooter."

It is obvious that the Everheart family is a close-knit one, "My mom, dad and uncle all went to the Nationals in Reno last year," Marguerite beamed. "It was the first time Mom had ever seen me shoot silhouette; the first time my uncle had ever seen me shoot at all, and he thought it was a blast, and it was the first time all year that Dad had coached me in a meet."

Marguerite won't ski because she doesn't want to break a leg. She's tried practical pistol competition just a bit, and she shoots on her university rifle team. Since silhouette shooting isn't an Olympic sport, she's trying to make the team in air rifle competition. She has competed in Canada (won the Canadian National Silhouette title in 1981), Montana, Mexico, Arizona, Nevada, Louisiana, Texas, Colorado and Ohio — and New Mexico. All of which stimulated me to ask, "Do you really enjoy it?"

"If I didn't like it," came the kind of answer I had become accustomed to expect, "I wouldn't do it!"

How about the future, goals on down the line? Just keep getting better? Keep winning every year?

"I'll never quit shooting unless something drastic happens," the confident youngster looked thoughtful. "After a while, after I finish school, I know that I'm going to get married, have some kids, and teach them to shoot. I'll never quit shooting."

And that should give rifle competitors, especially those aspiring to be champions in siluetas metalicas, something to think about over the next few decades.

[Postscript: Marguerite didn't win the 1984 matches; she finished second — one target out. Soon after that she did get married, and at the 1985 matches, with a tiny baby alongside on the firing line, all she did was win the top spot again. With a new world record — which broke her old one.]

July 1984

"IT'S A WEATHERBY!"

"It's a Weatherby" has, in a very short span of time, achieved a niche in the vernacular of shooters that is unique. It connotes far more than merely an identification of the gun manufacturer, and in the minds of most it conjures up immediate visions of a shootin' tool which will undress a deer at a thousand yards or move a charging elephant back a couple of paces.

In the minds of most, that is. There are others to whom Weatherby means other things. "That stock of his," one pundit put it, "is best suited for hanging on the wall of a French cathouse." And an African professional hunter drolly commented: "I do hope you didn't bring a Weatherby. We've had frightfully bad experiences with some of them."

High muzzle velocity, coupled with relatively light bullets which compliment such speeds, is the horse which Roy E. Weatherby has ridden to the top of his heap in some three decades. He mated his belief in such a combination to a distinctive new look for the rifle, and with hard work and his flair for promotion these two innovations became popular. So much so, in fact, that they are now almost commonplace in the market.

"I didn't invent high velocity," a 70-year young Roy E. Weatherby cautioned during an interview on September 4, 1980, his birthday. "Quite a few men were producing hot performers back in the 1940's, but they were custom jobs."

High velocity, admittedly a relative term, is now common among factory numbers available to shooters over the counter, but in the catalog ballistic listings the Weatherby calibers still have the edge. The laws of physics still being in force, of course, part of the price of that higher velocity is increased recoil. You pay for what you get.

Just how much punishment you'll get on the rear end of a Weatherby depends, first of all, on the caliber. Roy's magnums line-up runs like this: .224, .240, .257, 7mm, .300, .340, .378, and .460. All the designations are followed by W.M. (Weatherby Magnum), and the cartridges for them are decidedly not interchangeable with other rifles firing the same bullet diameters. Recoil from the .224 W.M., obviously, isn't as great as that from the .300 W.M., but I must add the observation that the punishment meted out to the shooter by Roy's biggie — the .460 W.M., seems to be a quantum leap upward from the next smaller caliber. As one strong man emphasized: "I'd rather the elephant get me than to pull the trigger on that damn thing again."

For the record, Weatherby touts the .460 W.M. as the world's most powerful caliber, with the factory 500-grain bullet leaving the muzzle at 2700 fps, giving 8100 foot pounds of muzzle energy. Also for the record, quite a number of little 'ole ladies in tennis shoes have used the .460 W.M. to kill a pot full of dangerous game.

The "Weatherby look" evolved from the flamboyant stock design which Roy finally settled on, the third time around, and for many years it was distinctively and instantly identifiable. It's a bit less so now.

"I made that stock, finally, with the flared pistol grip, the slantback on the fore-end tip, and then about 1950 I began using the first epoxy-type finish," Roy explained. "Now the whole world is using it. You can hardly tell our rifles from anybody else's. Some use the same stock as mine. My patent ran out on the nine-locking lug bolt feature, and on my cocking indicator, so other manu-facturers are now using them."

That shiny, flashy Weatherby look, achieved with rakish stock lines, white spacers, and that durable but glossy epoxy finish, would seem to be the last resort of a hunter wanting a gun to use rather than to hang on the wall. But experience has shown that this look popularized by Roy Weatherby is the look which sells best, and most manufacturers have fallen in line.

The background of Roy E. Weatherby and his rifles isn't complex. He grew up in Kansas an admitted "gun nut," loving shooting and gun designing. In the early 1940's he became interested in high velocity, and had rather spectacular success on deer with a .270 caliber using 100-grain bullets. The word spread, and Roy was soon making a few guns for friends — in his garage.

"I finally quit my job selling insurance — was making $800 a month, a lot of money back then — and rented a little place. Bought a Sears Roebuck lathe on time, a drill press, and I was in business. That was September of 1945, and I starved to death for years. Didn't know from day to day when the sheriff was coming to close me down."

"I studied velocities like you read a novel," Roy continued. "I just loved it. Couldn't buy a chronograph back then, so I built one. For years it was tough, but I kept going, thinking that my ideas were right."

Weatherby used any action he could get at first — Springfield, Enfield, Mauser, Winchester, Remington — for his semi-custom rifles, but later J. P. Sauer began to build his rifles in Germany using the FN action. Roy moved the operation to Japan in the late 1960's, when the German mark became too much more valuable than the dollar.

"I was the first one to begin having guns made in Japan," Roy told me, "and now everybody's doing it. When we re-tooled over there, we made some improvements in the old action, and I now think our Mark V action is the strongest in the world."

It was not until 1952 that Weatherby began to market ammunition for his calibers, so prior to that sales were generally limited to handloaders. Since then Norma has made the ammo for Roy, some of it using the excellent Nosler partition bullets. It commands a premium price.

"People sometimes wonder why they must pay more for 7mm W.M. than for 7mm Remington Magnum ammo," Roy laughed. "They should cost the same, but the difference is that Remington makes millions of rounds and we make hundreds of thousands. We're still a small company."

Small, maybe, but the worldwide aura of "it's a Weatherby" is out of proportion to that size. Some of Roy's elaborate, engraved, inlaid, and expensive rifles have been owned and used by some of the world's foremost public figures, resulting in exposure for Weatherby products which certainly hasn't hurt sales. The "Weatherby Award," created by Roy in 1956 and awarded annually since then, goes to "an internationally known big game hunter."

In addition to Americans, recipients have included hunters from Mexico, France, Iran, Denmark and Spain.

Weatherby fans are real fans. While talking with one of them some time ago in New Mexico, one who lived and hunted in Alaska for years, I casually mentioned that I'd just talked to Roy Weatherby. That was all it took.

"Man, I've got an old .300 Weatherby," Bob immediately launched his tale, "that I've shot a ton of game with. Great gun. And Weatherby really stands behind their rifles. Stock split once and they replaced it — no charge, even after I'd used it for years. Didn't expect that. Say, I remember one bear I shot..."

It's a Weatherby.

Roy semi-retired a few years back, and his son, Ed, took over the helm. Weatherby became the first to offer a factory rifle with a fiberglass stock (the FiberMark), and the rest of the industry soon fell in line. Today most companies have such synthetics in their line-up, and more are on the way.

For more information about Weatherby rifles, shotguns and other shooting equipment, write: Weatherby, Inc.; 2781 Firestone Blvd.; South Gate, Ca. 90280.

December 1980

THE MAN FROM BITTERROOT

In an age of assembly-line production, mass merchandising, and heavy accent on expansion, there exists in the field of bullet making an enigma. Hanging in there on the banks of Idaho's Snake River is a manufacturer who has no production line, who does no advertising, and who retains few dreams of expansion.

The "Man from Bitterroot" isn't really a manufacturer; he's a craftsman. Bill Steigers personally builds, with tender loving (hand) care, each of the bullets which bear the B.B.C. label. His is literally a one-man operation.

This B.B.C. isn't the British Broadcasting Company; it stands for Bitterroot Bullet Company, and has nothing to do with communications, unless delivery of a final message to a big game animal is what you mean. Thousands of hunters around the world believe, with religious zeal, that a "Bitterroot" can deliver that message better than can any other bullet.

They believe it enough to wait in line to gobble up Steigers' tiny output, and pay super premium prices. Like 50 cents to $1.00 and more for each one. That's just for the bullet, mind you, which must then be handloaded with components of the buyers choosing.

"I had no bullet failures."

"The Bitterroot bullet performance left nothing to be desired on 22 head of African game."

"I'm sold on your bullets."

Such comments are typical of many from the hundreds of letters which funnel in to the B.B.C. operation in Lewiston, Idaho. Calls and telegrams from many parts of the world to Steigers are common, reporting on the performance of his bullets. Most include detailed data as to range, where the bullet hit, damage to the animal, and weight of the recovered bullet.

One veteran gun writer, who has much experience at the reloading bench, the shooting range, and the hunting fields of several continents, summed up the sentiments of the B.B.C. fan club very simply: "The Bitterroot is the finest hunting bullet in the world."

After hearing such tributes for years, I began to wonder about the man himself. Who is Bill Steigers? Why is a Bitterroot better — if it's better?

Answers were elusive, so I began a correspondence with Steigers, and in the spring of 1978 we finally met to discuss his operation. Over a period of hours he told me of his background ("John Nosler and I have something in common; we were both truck drivers."), his competence in the bullet field ("I worked as a ballistician for another bullet company for nine years, mostly part-time. I've been a bullet-digger all my life. I'm not a machinist, much less a tool-and-die maker."), and above all his thoughts on bullet construction and performance.

Bill Steigers is retiring, but not shy; he is direct, but considerate; he has utter confidence in his product. He is also, of course, controversial, to be expected of one who believed that all other bullets left something to be desired, and who then proceeded to build a "better" one.

"The basic problem with most big game bullets," Steigers said, 'is that they break up. The core separates from the jacket. They go to pieces. It may kill the animal if conditions are right, but only wound if conditions are poor."

To keep his Bitterroot bullets together Steigers uses a much heavier jacket, and bonds the copper jacket to the lead core with solder. This is more expensive because copper is more costly than lead, and because the bonding is done by hand.

Steigers: "Many conventional bullets may start with a jacket thickness of .040 at the base, but when finished the sidewalls may be only .020 inches. The minimum for Bitterroots is .060 for the 7mm and .270 calibers, and .065 for the rest."

Gresham: "Most bullet jackets are thicker at the base and taper thinner toward the top. Yours doesn't?"

Steigers: "Basically not. I try to carry the full jacket thickness up to within about 3/8 inch of the top, then taper off. Once you get expansion, then the secret to high weight retention is to get the expansion stopped. The three things that govern bullet penetration are frontal area, how much resistance there is to that bullets passage, and the retained weight you have to drive that frontal area."

Stability of the bullet inside the animal, according to Steigers, is fully as important as is its stability in the air before making contact. He contends that the rotational velocity and gyroscopic forces necessary to accomplish this are much greater than those necessary to stabilize it *before* it reaches the target.

"When a bullet starts tumbling inside an animal," Bill explained, "it usually goes to pieces. It must remain point-forward to perform properly.

"If a Bitterroot bullet does not tumble there is no way it can break up and lose weight. High weight retention means good penetration, which means more tissue destruction and better killing qualities."

To achieve the high bullet rotational velocity necessary to achieve stability within an animal, Steigers recommends high muzzle velocities. He also contends that maximum pressures are necessary to get the best accuracy when using B.B.C. bullets (to cause the heavy base to upset and fill the bore).

Rotational velocity of the bullet can be increased by using a faster twist, of course, but that involves a new barrel. As Steigers put it: "Conventional bullets have been going to pieces for years. Rather than produce a better bullet, one that will withstand the present or increased rotational velocity that it would take to make the rifle-bullet combination better and more humane, manufacturers choose to keep the rates of twist as slow as possible and still maintain bullet stability...in the air."

Steigers believes that bullet failure is responsible for perhaps 10 percent of the big game animals which are wounded and lost each year, and is evangelical in his contention that use of better bullets would mean an enormous saving for the resource. He is realistic, however, about the limitations of bullet construction for universal use.

"You can't have your cake and eat it, too. A Bitterroot constructed heavily enough to perform ideally from a .300 Weatherby at short range cannot be ideal when fired from a .30-06 at 400 yards. You must have some compromise."

He also admits that bullets which disintegrate sometimes give spectacular results. "If a bullet hits a rib going into the lung cavity and goes to pieces, that type of performance will kill faster than the Bitterroot that stays in one piece when it goes through. But move a few inches to the shoulder and a conventional bullet may leave nothing but a nasty surface wound, maybe a broken shoulder, but no damage to the lung cavity."

The Bitterroot Bullet Company began operation in 1964, and Bill Steigers is the whole operation. He makes the bullets, fills the orders, and handles the correspondence. His annual output of some 25,000 bullets will not cause any major manufacturer to lose sleep.

"I regret I don't have the bullets everybody wants, but you're talking about 100,000 or 200,000 even on a limited basis. Out of the 17 bullets I list, I probably never have more than 7 or 8 in stock at any given time."

Bitterroots were off the market, for all practical purposes, from 1973 until last year, when Bill spent that time trying to tool up production machinery which would supply the demand without sacrificing quality. Now he's back in production, in a manner of speaking, at the same one-man, hand-crafted stand.

It goes without saying that Bill Steigers does not solicit business. Inquiries to the Bitterroot Bullet Company, P.O. Box 412, Lewiston, Idaho 83501 will get a printed postcard in return. The card lists the Bitterroot bullets which are available. A brochure, which contains actual photos of a dozen Bitterroots recovered from big game animals, giving details on the kill, will cost you 35 cents in coin or stamps plus a stamped, self-addressed envelope.

Steigers will answer requests for information about individual loading data, but only from his customers, if a stamped, self-addressed envelope is included, and only if the request format outlined in his brochure is followed. He really prefers that his customers (repeat: customers, only) call rather than write. "We can settle more problems in three minutes over the phone than we can in three hours of correspondence," was the way he put it. "I can spare the three minutes, but not the three hours."

The man from Bitterroot is understandably bitter about the 1968 federal gun control law, which he says has driven many small bullet makers out of business. That law permits interstate bullet shipments only to licensed firearms dealers. That's a minor problem for a big manufacturer who sells through dealers, but a major one for those who sell by mail-order directly to the consumer.

The hunter who wants to buy Bitterroots must arrange for a local licensed firearms dealer to receive his shipment, and must send a copy of that license to B.B.C.. I'm sure that such requirements will rid the nation of crime and violence.

Since Bill Steigers can't satisfy even the current demand for his Bitterroots, what's the answer for a hunter wanting better performance? What about the Nosler, the bullet with the widest reputation for top hunting performance at a premium price?

Steigers: "Some of the factory bullets are quite good, and there are some good custom bullets available. As for the Noslers, I have always admired John Nosler and his products. He has done a lot for the shooting game business, a lot in putting a better bullet on the market and conditioning the hunter's mind to use a better bullet."

Bill Steigers doesn't believe that his Bitterroots are the only good hunting bullets available. He only believes that they are the very best where terminal performance is the criteria.

September 1978

A BROWNING BY ANY OTHER NAME

T he "Gun That Won the West," and the gun used to trigger World War I, had something in common. Both were Brownings.

But you thought all along that it was a Winchester which tamed the wild frontiers of this expanding young nation, and it's certainly true that the lever-action rifle in question was sold under the Winchester label.

But John Moses Browning invented it.

Students of history may argue that it was a Fabrique Nationale .32-caliber Model 1900 which was used to assassinate Archduke

Franz Ferdinand and his wife in 1914, plunging the world into four years of war. They are right, of course.

But John M. Browning invented it.

"It's a Browning" was a comment which has, for as long as I can remember, connoted quality. It symbolized the epitome of craftsmanship, fully as much as "made in Japan" signified poorly made products — at one time. In today's era of Nikons, Sonys and Bushnells, and a lot of fine firearms produced by the Japanese, that made-in-Japan slur is no longer applicable.

But "it's a Browning" still is.

The "Browning" which made that reputation was and is the Browning automatic shotgun, the humpbacked model made in Belgium. It was the only Browning I knew of, as I grew up during the depression years, but I knew it only from a distance as the gun my Dad always called the best.

Way back then I never owned one of those, but finally came into possession of another 12-gauge automatic, a Remington Model 11. What I didn't know at the time was that it, too, was a "Browning."

Ithaca Model 37 "Featherlight" pump shotgun, Colt .45 automatic pistol, Winchester Model '97 pump shotgun, Stevens Model 520 pump shotgun, Colt Woodsman .22 automatic pistol, and the most popular lever-action big game rifle ever, the famous Winchester Model 94: all Brownings.

More than a hundred years ago this John Moses Browning began a career as an inventor of firearms which has never been equaled. There is little doubt that he was the greatest gun inventor the world has ever known, and it's unlikely that anybody will ever match his achievements.

Not long ago the company which bears his name (Browning, Route #1, Morgan, Utah 84050) celebrated the Browning Centennial year, and it is ironic that the genius of John Browning is so relatively unknown. Ironic, yet understandable, for such was the way this unpretentious man lived his life.

The Browning Automatic and the Browning Superposed, the former the achievement which the inventor considered his most difficult, and the latter his last one, are the two sporting firearms which have made the name a mark of quality to millions of shooters. But millions more who have used John Browning's inventions which were marketed by Winchester, Remington, Savage, Ithaca, Franchi, Colt, Fabrique Nationale, Breda and others have little idea of the man behind these guns.

The beginning of the bonanza of Browning firearms inventions took place in 1878 in Ogden, Utah Territory, when the 23-year old gunsmith invented his first rifle. It was a single-shot falling block model, the first of a flood of developments which in the next 48 years completely revolutionized the world's repeating arms.

John M. Browning and his brothers manufactured and sold several hundred of that first single-shot rifle, simply because he knew of no other way to get it on the market, but when he sold that patent to Winchester in 1883 a pattern was set. He preferred to sell his inventions instead of manufacturing them, and continued doing that throughout his life.

Winchester reaped the benefits for 19 years, buying all of the rifle and shotgun patents which Browning sold. They covered single shots, repeaters of both lever action and slide action design, and semi-automatics. Many were never manufactured, bought simply as protection against their acquisition by competitive companies.

The end of that Winchester era came in 1902, when John Browning severed his long relationship over a disagreement about the public acceptability of the autoloading shotgun. That breached the dam, and in the years that followed Brownings in disguise appeared as Remington's, Colts and a variety of other brand names.

The split with Winchester also brought about the first sporting firearm to be called a Browning, when Fabrique Nationale bought and manufactured under that name the "made in Belgium" automatic shotgun which created the Browning legend. It is still being produced today, although only in limited, high grade models, since most of the Browning production has been switched to Japan because of economic considerations.

Millions of Americans have had more than passing knowledge of John Moses Browning, but never associated it with a duck blind. They are the ones who used his fully automatic weapons in wars from the Spanish-American to Korea. Every American soldier since 1918 knows the B.A.R., the Browning Automatic Rifle, and most know the .30 and .50 caliber light and heavy machine guns — Brownings, that is — which were our dominate defensive and offensive weapons on land, water or in the air.

JOHN M. BROWNING: AMERICAN GUNMAKER is a fascinating book about this genius. Published by Doubleday & Company in 1964, it deserves a place on your bookshelf. It is available either through Browning dealers or directly from Browning, Route #1, Morgan, Utah 84050.

Many "Brownings" have become collector's items, fitting tribute to the frontiersman who was granted 128 patents covering at least 80 completely different firearms.

June 1978

STAN BAKER: THE SHOTGUN MAN

Stan Baker, the Seattle shotgun doctor, is an overnight success. It just took him a quarter of a century to reach that plateau.

The 6-4, 200-pounder, born in San Francisco is 1926, describes himself and his background in rather deprecatory terms. "I was a high school dropout. No formal education in anything, really. Basically a car nut, and kind of a drifter. Had auto body shops in Boise, Miami and a couple here in Seattle. Don't know exactly what made me get into the gun business."

Whatever it was that turned Stan to gunsmithing, serious shotgunners now say an "amen" to that twist of fate. Perhaps more than anyone else, Stan is the man now turned to by competition scattergunners in search of that elusive edge. And, increasingly, hunters who never pot a clay target or a live pigeon are figuratively beating a path to the cluttered Seattle shop where Baker began gunsmithing in 1956, and in which he still operates.

"When I rented that empty store and opened for business," Stan grinned, "I hardly knew the difference between a Springfield and an Enfield, but I borrowed a lathe from a friend and began. There was a fellow in Seattle at the time who built beautiful custom rifles. He never seemed to be in his shop, always had a big pocketful of money, so I decided that was the life for me. Custom rifles."

The fledgling gun builder soon discovered that there was no market for custom rifles built by Stan Baker.

"Nobody knew me, and my rifles weren't really that good. You gotta have a reputation that takes 20 years to build. And back then," he explained, "you couldn't get anybody to tell you anything about gunsmithing. Everybody was jealous. Today, you can get a copy of the Brownells catalog and learn as much about gunsmithing in an hour as I learned in 20 years."

With little market for his rifles, and bills to pay ("For years it was a question of paying this guy or paying that one, since there was no money to pay both bills at the same time."), the Stan Baker "custom rifle shop" began to take on any gun repair job. And to sell scopes and mounts, and then guns.

"General gunsmithing is a good education, but it's a tough way to make a living. To do well you must specialize, which I didn't realize until it was almost too late — about six years ago." Then, when I started turning down all repair jobs I thought I'd starve, but that's when I began making progress."

In the brief span of time since then, Stan Baker has become a familiar name to most skeet, trap and live pigeon shooters, and to many hunters. They know that this is the guy who can probably make their shotgun into a more efficient tool, and thus them into better performers.

Baker's limited repertoire of services includes installation of screw-in chokes, custom rechoking, forcing cone alteration, backboring, jug choking, changing point of impact, rechambering, bore work — honing and bringing it to proper dimensions, building of custom barrels and custom M1100's. Before visiting Stan and getting a full explanation, I didn't understand some of these procedures. Here's what I learned.

Screw-in chokes: This is an idea whose time has come, stimulated by Winchester's Winchoke. In 1975 Stan began installing his own version in any single barrel and in some doubles, and this has become his most popular job. Baker manufactures tubes in a wide array of choke constrictions, from .680 to .730, in .005 increments, plus a "skeet spreader" tube.

Forcing cone alteration: "The forcing cone is the short barrel section in which the chamber diameter is reduced to the bore diameter. In most shotguns it's short, a holdover from the days of inefficient paper wads when it was necessary to prevent gas escaping past the wads. Not needed now, and lengthening that forcing cone provides a more gradual transition, reducing recoil."

Backboring: "I guess it's a term I coined. It refers to boring out the barrel from chamber to the choke to increase its diameter. That puts in more choke by increasing the amount of constriction, which is really what choke is."

Jug Choke: "About like backboring, except that the diameter of the bore is increased only for a short distance behind the choke, not for the full length of the barrel."

Bore work: "One of our most valuable services is bore honing to remove pitting, tool marks and other imperfections. As for dimensions, bore diameters on shotgun vary widely, and many are undersized as compared with the 'standard' .729 of a 12 gauge. That's especially true of imported guns, and it causes excess recoil. The more enlightened manufacturers are now building them larger." Winchester's Super-X auto bore diameter is about .735, Ljutic's are about .740 as were the older Krieghoffs, and the new Remington Competition M870 is about .745 — about 15/1000 over standard bore size, which contributes to its recoil reduction. We can take the cheapest barrel and give it the dimensions — choke, bore, forcing cone — you get on the most expensive gun made."

Point of Impact and Pattern: "Many factory barrels are off several inches on their point of impact relative to where the barrel or rib points. They don't shoot where the shooter is looking, and he seldom has the vaguest idea where it's shooting. Same thing with pattern. Don't take for granted that you've got the choke marked on the barrel. I've found "full choke" barrels which had no choke in them at all. With the cost of shooting and hunting nowadays, I think it would pay for a guy to check things out a little. We can fix both point of impact and pattern to give a shooter what he wants or needs."

Stan makes unsingles for the shooter who has an O&U and wants a single barrel for it, with the barrel in the "under" position. He makes a similar conversion with the barrel in the "over" position which he calls the top single. These are for trap shooters, and they buy from Stan for a number of reasons. One is that unsingles aren't available for some O&U's, such as the M3200 and the Krieghoff. Neither are top singles available for some factory guns. Then, too, some competitors just don't like the factory versions of either unsingle or top single, as the case might be, and know that they can get one custom made from Stan with any special features they want — choke, barrel length, rib height, pattern and point of impact.

A rather recent addition to the array of Stan Baker offerings is a custom version of the Remington Model 1100 semi-automatic, which he calls "kind of an experiment." He lavishes on a tournament grade M1100 trap gun all of the refinements he can dream of, including screw-in choke system, back boring, lengthened forcing cone, ported barrel, recoil reduction unit installed in stock, tournament-tuned trigger, and other such niceties. Called the Eliminator I, it is priced at $1295.00. Stan also sells "Eliminator" barrels ($425.00) for the guy who already has an M1100.

Although most of Baker's work is for competition shooters, more and more hunters are discovering the advantages of his services.

"I like to work with hunters," Stan laughed, "because they usually accept the blame if they miss a bird. Trap shooters immediately start looking for the excuse — the gun pattern is wrong, a slow pull, the guy next door shuffled his feet, or something. But the fact is that the hunter might not have been at fault for missing. Many of them are discovering that there is a tremendous difference in gun barrels, point of impact, chokes and in ammunition. Some of the promotional ammunition is terrible."

"We're doing more work for skeet shooters, too," he continued, "now that they've learned they can break 100-straights with the .410 gauge. They take a look at the little gun and find it doesn't pattern as it should, isn't choked right."

Stan believes that the long forcing cone and the large bore diameter are the greatest contributors to recoil reduction, more effective than any device which can be added to the gun. His bottom line, however, is that it is the cumulative effect of all the refinements — proper forcing cone and bore dimensions, proper stock fit, efficient recoil pad stock recoil reducer — which can transform a shotgun from a demon into a delight.

If there is one trait which stands out above all else, where Stan Baker is concerned, it's his candor. Except for a rare "don't print that," usually to spare somebody's feelings, he discusses any aspect of guns and shooting with refreshing frankness.

The Remington Model 1100: "It's a piece of junk, but it's way ahead of whatever is in second place."

Backboring and recoil reduction and velocity: "Backboring does reduce recoil, and we're not sure why. You get something for nothing. Less recoil without losing velocity, which some say is impossible." What you lose in velocity the first few inches, through increasing volume, you must gain down the barrel by lessening friction. We invariably gain about 10 feet a second after backboring, using the same shells, which is really nothing but enough to show I haven't lost velocity."

His shooting ability: "Mediocre. A 22-yard handicapper. But you can be a chief mechanic at Indy without being able to drive the car."

Bulged and busted barrels: "Always because of an obstruction in the barrel, no matter what the shooter says. We get many of them to repair — cut off the damaged portion and rechoke the barrel."

Forcing Cone: "A necessary evil which is absent in rifles. Wouldn't need it if all shotshells opened up to the exact same length."

Gun Care: "Greatest thing hunters could do to keep their guns working? Clean 'em. Most never do. If they didn't do anything but hose them down liberally with WD-40 to wash out the gook, that would help."

Checking Point Of Impact: "Shoot half a dozen times at the center of the same big sheet of paper, at about 30 yards. That'll tell where the gun is shooting, not necessarily where it will shoot when you're swinging on game or a target with it."

Although Stan has taken down the sign which did hang in front of his store, people still come and he still does quite a retail business, mostly pistols. While Delmar Olson is presiding out front, machinist Art Berkler is making choke tubes, monoblocs and barrels; other craftsmen perform a myriad of chores; Baker's daughter, Maureen Jensen, handles the shipping and fills in at anything else; while Stan provides loose supervision and rigid quality control, and spends too much phone time on the calls which funnel in from around the country.

When Stan picked me up at the hotel, it was in an Auburn. At his home, where wife Kathy and a springer named Dixie rule the roost, are stashed a variety of other oldies in various stages of restoration, including a couple of Ferrari's, a Maserati, and a gull-wing Mercedes.

"Yeah, you might say that now I'm relatively affluent," Stan started over to answer the ringing phone one more time. "At least, the bank balance isn't a minus every month like it was for years."

For a brochure on Stan Baker services, write: Stan Baker, 10,000 Lake City Way, Seattle, WA 98125.

July 1982

BROWNELLS: MOTHER LODE FOR GUN OWNERS

T alk about a wish book! Had a Brownells, Inc. catalog been around when I was growing up, the big book from Sears wouldn't have been in the running. For anybody who loves guns and hunting and tinkering with firearms, the slick publication which springs forth each year from the unlikely locale of Montezuma, Iowa is a bonanza. Inside that front cover, on which is displayed an awesome array of gunsmithing tools, are pages and pages listing thousands of items, the stuff of which dreams are made.

Brownells is *the* source, for most gunsmiths in the nation, when it comes to supplies. And well it might be. It catalogs some 17,000 items, and at any one time about 99 percent of them are in stock. For those which aren't it's usually the fault of the manufacturers of those particular items.

Just leafing through the catalog gives me enough ideas for projects to last a lifetime. In addition to the basic gear such as screwdrivers for all purposes, micrometers, files, punches and that kind of thing, I get flashes of inspiration from Zip-Lock bags in a jillion sizes, do-it-yourself stock finishes, do-it-yourself bluing compounds, home tanning kits, bullets, brass, books, dyes, stains, epoxy, slings, sights and on and on.

The guy behind this amazing enterprise is an ebullient little man by the name of Bob Brownell, who was born in Sac City, Iowa, studied journalism ("didn't graduate...ran out of money"), ran a fishing resort in northern Minnesota, owned ("me and the bank") a service station in Montezuma, to which he added on a cafe and power shop and welding shop and a little garage, and found himself at the beginning of World War II with $18,000 worth of debts, and three children.

"Try paying off that when your customers could buy only two gallons of gasoline a week," Bob grinned as he recalled those times.

He ran his first advertisement in the American Rifleman in 1939 — for pistolsmithing. At that point he had no inkling of the huge mail-order business which lay farther down the road.

"Well, I had traded guns all my life, and fixed guns for people just for the hell of it, so I started doing pistol work in bed and ran that first ad." Bob had contracted a disease which kept him virtually bed-ridden for three years. "And about that time I read in a magazine that a company had developed a method of blackening spark plugs. I wrote them asking for some of the stuff, and they sent me 25 pounds, with instructions like you've never seen. Well, I polished a pistol and blued it in a bread pan on a kerosene stove, and I don't wish that on my worst enemy. But it worked — using that blackening compound. So I decided to sell it, wrote a little ad, and borrowed money from the bank to buy a barrel of the stuff. Some of the guys who bought from those first shipments 40 years ago are still buying from me."

During the War Brownell sent out mailers soliciting business, much of it for merchandise he didn't have, but it was in 1948 that he published his first real catalog. Now, about four decades later, he sells 50,000 of those Brownell "Wish Books" each year for $3.25 a copy, which the buyer gets back on his first order. They cost twice that to produce.

Those catalogs are the bibles by which gunsmiths around the country operate. They have confidence that a call to Brownell (or during "closed" hours to "Elly," the electronic order-taking machine), will in hours have a package headed their way bearing a Montezuma return address. They can depend on Brownell, knowing that only some one percent of their items will ever be backordered.

"I learned more about gunsmithing from Bob Brownell and his catalog and newsletters than I did from anything else," Seattle gunsmith Stan Baker told me a few years ago.

Stan's comment reveals the other side of Bob Brownell, the fact that he has been an immense cohesive and educational force over the past four decades in elevating the profession of gunsmithing to its present level of competence. He was and is a gunsmith; he taught gunsmithing; but most of all he encouraged and facilitated a massive exchange of gunsmithing ideas and techniques between practitioners of the art from throughout the nation.

"When I began trying to learn gunsmithing," Bob explained, "nobody would tell you the time of day. It was all black magic. It made me so mad; that's why I never keep a secret. I decided I was going to tell everybody whatever I learned. I wanted to make something out of this profession. That's been my life — to make gunsmithing a truly respected profession. And it's come true. We've now got the finest gunsmiths in the world in this country, bar none."

One of Brownell's most successful educational tools for 'smiths was and is his *Encyclopedia of Modern Firearms*. It is a service manual for gunsmiths, listing every part and giving schematic diagrams and instructions for disassembly and assembly of hundreds of firearms. It has sold more than 150,000 copies.

Bob's vehicle for sharing ideas and techniques of the profession is his "Newsletter," which he writes at irregular intervals and of which there have been more than 100. Many of them have been bound into two hardcover books *(Gunsmith Kinks* and *Gunsmith Kinks II),* and they are a treasure trove of information.

The letter is written in a humorous, folksy fashion as if it's directed to one individual, which it is: "I write it to Kjer Lyle, my old friend who encouraged me to start gunsmithing, and who isn't around any more. I use the letter to pass along tips from gunsmiths around the world. It's wonderful how they share their ideas. And it's amazing, Grits, how a guy who is either starving to death or busier than hell will take time off to make and send in beautiful, complicated drawings, complete detailed instructions. It's that spirit of cooperation that has brought us to this high level of professionalism."

There probably aren't more than 7,000 really professional, commercial gunsmiths in the country, according to Bob Brownell, so most of his customers are semi-professionals, or just gun owners who like to tinker, to do their own work. They've bought millions of dollars worth of the products which Brownell stocks and sells, plus great quantities of rust preventive and stock bedding concoctions which originated in the fertile mind of Bob Brownell.

"Our biggest selling product?" Bob pondered the question. "I guess it's Acraglas, our bedding compound."

The man now doing most of the actual running of this seven million dollar operation is Frank Brownell, the 48-year [in 1987] old son who has been with the operation for 24 years. A graduate of the University of Iowa with degrees in Journalism and Business, he has brought some new ideas to the business.

"He's doing it his way," Bob laughed, "and running it like it should be run. My way was wrong. He's brought in some great young people and gets all of them involved. He's organized."

But from Frank: "You know, Dad's a classic founding entrepreneur. He thought up the idea, put it together and made it work. He founded it. And here comes a young buck like me saying "Let's try something different." Not only did Dad let go; he let me try it. And I fell flat on my face. But together we make a good team, and we've become very good friends."

"Our philosophy," Frank continued, "is that all our customers are interested in is results. All they want is a box of supplies delivered to their doorstep three days after the order arrives here, which is why we keep our inventory so high. It's not the best way to manage an inventory from an economic standpoint, but we try to give our customers products, not excuses. As long as we can do that, the future looks great."

The Brownell Catalog is available for $3.25 from: Brownells, Inc., Montezuma, Iowa 50171.

October 1983

JOHN AMBER AND THE GUN DIGEST

Almost forty years ago an ex-Navy veteran who was working in a Chicago sporting goods store took over the reins as editor of a fledgling annual publication devoted to guns and shooting. Thirty years later he tossed those reins back, but in those intervening three decades John Amber made the *Gun Digest* the most respected and widely read annual in its field.

The 1979 Deluxe Edition of the *Gun Digest,* John's last, was 448 pages huge. The print run was more than a quarter of a million copies and, even at a healthy sticker price of $9.95 for this paper back, there won't be any copies left.

What manner of magic did the man called Amber weave to bring this publication to such prominence in the field of guns and shooting? One point is certain. He didn't do it by being tentative, which is perhaps one of the few words not in John Amber's extensive, erudite vocabulary.

"I told him I'd have to have a completely free hand in the selection of material, and the assurance that I could make each edition brand new," was the way John described his response to that first offer to edit the *Gun Digest.* Such firmness, plus an unflagging dedication to present the most innovative and in-depth treatment of the topic, have been the hallmarks of Amber's handling of this publication since that time.

"In those days after the war," John continued our talk, which took place during a New Mexico elk hunt, "there just wasn't much being published about guns, and all of us were hungry for any information. We had the shooting columns in the big three outdoor magazines, and the American Rifleman, but that was about all."

"Not only were there no magazines about guns and shooting except the Rifleman, there were virtually no books. Now, of course, we're inundated with such books — there's a gillion of 'em on the market, and there's been a proliferation of gun oriented magazines."

Odds are good that a goodly part of this change can be attributed to the success of Amber and his DIGEST. And any doubt about the magnitude of the change is easily dispelled by browsing through the newsstands and bookstores across the land, noting the wide choice of fare in both magazines and books which deal with guns and shooting.

"From the beginning," explained the man from Marengo (Ill.),

"I tried to make it appeal to all segments of the gun world — the handgunner, the rifleman, the shotgunner, the reloader, the gun collector, the casual plinker as well as the competitor — to everybody who likes guns and likes to shoot them. The formula worked, and I see no reason to change it. Ego speaking, of course."

As the DIGEST grew in size, Amber responded by running very lengthy, definitive, in-depth articles occasionally, mixing them in with both short and normal length features. Some of these ran to 15 and even 20 pages, and they frequently addressed a very narrow slice of the firearms-shooting field. Such diverse coverage provided a service which readers could not find elsewhere, and those readers reacted favorably.

"I think one of the reasons for our success," John said, "is the frank approach we've always taken. We call the shots like we see them. We criticize where we think it's needed. We don't pull any punches, and when you handle things this way I believe you establish a rapport and a credibility with your readers."

"We carry no advertising...and never have, so obviously have no obligation to an advertiser."

I asked John if he had detected any changes, over his thirty years at the helm, in the preference of readers where subject matter is concerned.

"No, I don't think there has been any change. As a matter of fact, I think that the desire for the type of thing we've been giving them has increased. They want more and more gun stuff — talk about them, describe them, dissect them, everything. That's what most of our readers want.

"About the only thing I started which got a few negative letters was the automotive coverage for sportsmen. Those guys obviously want nothing but gun coverage."

Amber brought the *Gun Digest* to a point where it's a virtual encyclopedia on guns and shooting, and a shelf filled with a couple of decades of this annual is just that. Individually or collectively, these books are excellent reference material both for the casual sportsman and for the serious student of shooting and guns.

More than half of the DIGEST is comprised of feature articles which span the gamut of topic matter, as witnessed by these random titles from that 1979 issue: "Art of the Engraver," "Handguns Now," "Gun Proof in India," "The Hunting Rifle Stock," "The Gatling Gun," "Crosswind Deflections," and "Let The Gun Talk," a superb story by the late Lucian Cary which was first published in 1941 in The Saturday Evening Post. The last half of the book is service oriented: Ammunition Tables; a listing of the firearms currently available, with suggested retail price; a great listing of books, periodicals and pamphlets about guns and shooting; and an excellent directory of the arms trade which lists the names and addresses of the suppliers of shooting equipment and related supplies. And much, much more.

John T. Amber was born in Freeport, Illinois in 1903, and during a 1979 interview said he didn't feel a day over 81. The facts didn't bear that out. At the time he had just returned from a hunting trip to Russia ("Enjoy the trip? Yes and no. Frustrating. They promised everything; delivered nothing. The hunting was good.") When I tried to call him a couple of months later, his wife Jean reported that he had just left Paris enroute to London. He seldom slowed down to wait for the world to catch up.

In creating the institution called the *Gun Digest,* John T. Amber became an institution himself. He died in 1986, one of the most knowledgeable men in the world on all aspects of firearms, shooting and hunting.

July 1979

THE MAN NAMED RUGER

V isualize a tall, courtly man with a drooping, bushy, handlebar mustache who looks a bit like Teddy Roosevelt. Consider that he is an authority on vintage automobiles. He designed and built one, in the grand class of the Bentley, under his own name. Listen to him talk about the great masters of art, pointing out his favorites among the Wythe's, Rungius', Bierstadt's and others which hang on his walls. Enjoy with him a conversation about books and authors, current or past. Finally, discuss firearms with him. You'll discover a romantic with a great love of history and an impressive knowledge of the world as it is and was. You'll have just met Bill Ruger.

A "legend in his own time" is an accolade which is bandied about rather frequently, more often bestowed than deserved. In the case of William Batterman Ruger, Sr., however, such a tribute is simply telling the truth. In an amazingly brief period of time, this 69-year old, Brooklyn-born New Englander has made a permanent impact on the firearms industry.

Let's emphasize the time frame, a remarkable aspect of this story. Only three decades ago a mention of Bill Ruger would undoubtedly have triggered a "Bill who?" response, even from knowledgeable shooters. Today, 27 years later, anyone interested in guns or hunting who doesn't recognize the Ruger label must have been in hiding. Ruger firearms have taken a well deserved place among the most popular, efficient, and respected firearms on the market. Such an improbable happening is a tribute to the vision, instinct and engineering ability of the man called Ruger.

When the company was started in January 1946, Ruger's financing partner was Alexander M. Sturm. Hence the name of the company, then and now, Sturm, Ruger & Company. Sturm died in 1951 at the age of 29, and in commemoration Ruger changed the color of the eagle trademark medallions set into the grips of the automatic pistols from red to black, an order which continues in effect today.

A .22 rimfire semi-automatic pistol was the first firearm marketed by Sturm, Ruger & Company. Plain vanilla in looks, but simple and innovative in design, this Standard Automatic was an instant success. So were most of the many guns to follow.

"I really got into the gun business more by accident than design," Mr. Ruger told me recently, "probably because I had these ideas for a .22 semi-automatic pistol design which could be produced by a relatively small company with relatively low start-up costs. No, we had no problems with it. If a gun is designed right, you never have any trouble with it. It will work well from the start."

From that modest beginning, the array of successful firearms introductions from the land of Ruger has run the gamut — single-action revolvers, double action revolvers, semi-auto big game rifles and rimfire rifles, both centerfire and rimfire bolt action rifles, over-and-under shotguns, single shot rifles, and military look-alikes in centerfire rifles. And more are on the way.

The most difficult Ruger gun design?

"I would say that our over-and-under shotgun seems to create more problems and puzzles," Ruger struggled to answer my question, "more urge to improve the design, than our other guns."

Nostalgic and traditional are two words which are appropriate when thinking about Ruger's firearms. He brought back the single-action "Peacemaker" revolver; the single shot, falling block rifle; and a classic bolt action rifle. All are superior to most of their predecessors, and to many of their contemporaries where they exist.

A key manufacturing technique which enabled Ruger to sell better products at lower cost, and still make money, was the use of precision investment cast parts of high-strength steel. His New Hampshire plant was the first gun factory in the world to do so.

All Ruger firearms were manufactured in Newport, New Hampshire and Southport, Connecticut, but there came into being a "Ruger West" in 1986 when Sturm, Ruger and Company built a small factory west of the Mississippi — far west of it, in Prescott, Arizona. It is the production facility for a new Ruger semi-automatic, 9mm handgun.

"There's a great reservoir of gun making skills in the West," Bill explained the project, "and I think we can take advantage of that."

Bill Ruger, Sr. enjoys the good life, but simple. He appreciates the finer aspects of art and engineering and the outdoors and good friends and good whiskey. He chooses his close friends with care, and can afford to surround himself with the best of the rest. That's not too shabby for a man whose first job, 45 years ago, was working in a machine shop for $20 a week.

He continues to pay his dues, to be a leader in the firearms field on all fronts, strongly supportive of pro-gun and pro-hunting organizations — with his endorsements and his money. He has testified before congressional committees on several occasions, an articulate, persuasive voice of reason countering legislation designed to restrict gun ownership and use, and urging adoption of laws which could bring sanity to the chaotic product liability situation which is strangling many industries and professions.

William Batterman Ruger may not be a man for all seasons, but he's the nearest to it that the American firearms industry has experienced for many decades.

Chronology of Ruger Firearms
1949: The Standard Automatic Pistol, .22 long rifle.
1951: The Mark I Automatic Pistol, .22 long rifle.
1953: The Single-Six Revolver, .22 long rifle (a Single-Six Magnum for .22 WRM in 1959).
1955: The Blackhawk Revolver, a single action .357 Magnum (1956 — .44 Mag; 1965 — .41 Mag; 1967 — .30 carbine; 1971 — .45 Colt with convertible .45 ACP cylinder).
1958: The Bearcat Revolver, a single action .22 long rifle.
1959: The .44 Carbine, .44 Mag caliber semi-auto rifle.

1963: The Super Blackhawk Revolver, .44 Mag.

1963: The Hawkeye Pistol, .256 Win caliber single shot.

1964: The Model 10/22 Rifle, a semi-auto .22 long rifle.

1967: The Number One Single-Shot Rifle, in many calibers.

1968: The M-77 Bolt-Action Rifle, in many calibers.

1971: Double Action Revolvers (Security-Six, Service-Six and Speed-Six) in .38 Spec and .357 Mag.

1972: The Old Army Revolver, .44 caliber black powder.

1973: The New Model Single-Six, New Model Blackhawk, and New Model Super Blackhawk, all with new, patented "transfer-bar" ignition system.

1975: The Mini-14 Rifle, semi-auto in .223 caliber.

1977: The Over and Under Shotgun, 20 gauge (12 ga. in 1982).

1980: The Redhawk Revolver, a .44 Mag. double action.

1982: The Mark II Automatic Pistol, .22 long rifle.

1983: The Ruger 77/22 Rifle, a bolt-action .22 long rifle.

1985: The Ruger Bisley, a single action target revolver in .44 Mag., .41 Mag. and .357 Mag.

1985: The Ruger XGI Rifle, a semi-auto .308 caliber.

1986: The Ruger GP-100, an all-new double action revolver which will replace all other Ruger double actions in the line.

1987: The Ruger P-85, a 9mm autoloading handgun.

March 1986

FAST AND FANCY SHOOTERS

F orty years ago I witnessed my first real exhibition shooting. Not "shooting exhibition," since I had seen quite a few of those performed over our bird dogs while growing up in the Carolinas. I'm talking about a sho 'nuf public demonstration of gun-wielding prowess, and I never quite got over the experience.

What I didn't know then, back in that winter of '46, was that my first taste was the *ne plus ultra,* the best there was. Maybe the best there ever was. In the four decades since, there has not been a more skillful shooter nor a more entertaining showman than was Herb Parsons, who died in 1959.

An incident from that exhibition stands out. After the show, as was his custom, Herb offered to shoot holes in coins as souvenirs for the audience, but added, "It's windy, so don't give me anything smaller than a nickel." The only coin in my pocket was a dime, which I handed to him when I reached the head of the line. He looked at the dime, cut his steel-blue eyes briefly into mine, then tossed the coin up and drilled a shot through the middle with his .22 Hornet. The dime is still on my key chain.

Mr. & Mrs. Adolph Topperwein, Charlie Flannigan, Dot & Ernie Lind, Annie Oakley, Capt. A. H. Hardy, Tom Hickman, Ed McGivern, Tom Frye, Doc Carver, Ken Beagle, Gus Perot, Wilbur Cox, Billy Hill — and Herb Parsons. They and other fine shots once toured the country thrilling big crowds with amazing shooting exhibitions. Most were representing arms or ammunition companies, but others were free lancers who performed for a fee. They had one thing in common: they were household names, and heros, to shooters throughout the land.

Where have they gone!

Herb Parsons, then a freshman in high school, saw Adolph Topperwein shoot, and forever after his goal was to become as good or better. Topperwein was his hero, and later helped train Herb.

Then Herb *became* a hero — to John Satterwhite, who tried to emulate the success of that legendary figure. He came close, and undoubtedly would have come closer had other considerations not reared their head. Things like making a living. Satterwhite shot International Skeet in the Montreal Olympics, won a batch of medals in international shooting competitions, set a few national records, and was on the *Sports Afield* All-American skeet team for a string of years. Not too shabby. He also learned to perform most of Herb Parsons' feats, and developed a crowd-pleasing line of patter which is eerily reminiscent of Herb's. Now a Sales Manager for Heckler & Koch, one of the largest gun manufacturers in the world, John recently came out of exhibition shooting retirement to perform at a Folk Festival in my home town, where I asked him the question: "Where have all the exhibition shooters gone?"

"Several reasons they're not around," Satterwhite quickly responded, obviously having pondered this matter at length. "One of the biggest, in my estimation, is that improvements in mass media — radio, television and especially magazines, made it unnecessary for arms and ammo companies to promote products with traveling exhibition shooters. They can reach more people quicker and cheaper through conventional advertising than by sending a man on the road."

"But that may be short-sighted," he added. "It doesn't replace the rapport developed in the one-on-one, face-to-face contact made by those exhibition shooters. They built great good will for the companies and their products, and good will toward shooting. It made shooting look like fun again — not the connotation of guns in alleys and crime and all the bad stuff."

John never saw Herb Parsons shoot, being only 16 years old when Herb died, but he studied the techniques of this shooting legend in every way possible. He virtually memorized the Parson film, "Showman Shooter," and visited Mrs. Parsons on two occasions to talk about her husband.

"She told me that, when Herb was little and the other boys would be out playing football, he'd be over in a coal pit throwing up chunks of coal and shootin' them with a .22 rifle, John told me. "She also told me that Herb knew the end was in sight for his 'occupation,' that he urged his sons to look elsewhere (both sons are now 'doctors,' one a physician in Ohio; the other, with a PH.D. in horticulture, a teacher at Texas A&M)."

Annie Oakley and Buffalo Bill Cody not only toured this country giving shooting exhibitions, but drew tremendous crowds in many other parts of the world. They were great "showmen" and excellent marksmen, but few who have studied the records believe they were as good as was Herb Parsons.

One of the crowd-pleasing acts performed by exhibition shooters was "drawing" a picture with .22 caliber bullet holes, the most popular artwork being an Indian head. Such memorabilia are now prized artifacts from that golden era.

Excellent shooters are still around, of course, and some do a bit of exhibition shooting. Bob Allen and his son, Matt, perform now and then, to promote shooting as much as to promote the Bob Allen line of shooting supplies, but Bob recently pointed out one of the problems emphasized by Satterwhite.

"There just aren't many places where we can shoot," the Des Moines expert said, "since much of our act involves rifles. The country has grown up. A .22 rifle bullet will carry more than a mile, and a center-fire even farther. Finding a safe location for our shooting isn't easy."

Shooting at aerial targets is the stumbling block, and these are the most crowd pleasing of all. Herb's biggie was throwing up seven clay targets and breaking them with seven shots from a pump shotgun, an unbelievably difficult feat. John learned to do that, and performed it for our slow-motion camera on the "Sports Afield" television series several years ago.

"I finally gave up on rifle shooting in exhibitions," John told me, "since it was just too hard to find a place to shoot."

John, Bob and Herb would shoot through the hole in a washer tossed in the air; hit the empty .22 caliber hulls in the air as they ejected them from a pump rifle; and keep a wood block bouncing with repeated hits from a rifle. Many of the old-time fancy shots also performed with pistols. Mrs. Adolph "Plinky" Topperwein was excellent. Ed McGivern was awesome with a double action revolver — putting six shots in a can tossed into the air, breaking five clay targets tossed into the air simultaneously, splitting a playing card tossed into the air. He was fast and and accurate, with perhaps his most famous performance that of putting five shots from a Smith & Wesson into a playing-card-sized group at 15 feet *in 2/5 of a second!* That was his best, but less than one-second groups like that were routine.

"Sure, there are some good shooters around now who could be great exhibition shooters," Satterwhite thought about it. "Keep in mind that a guy must be a great *shooter* before he can become a great *fancy* shot, and one of the tough things to find is a guy who can shoot and talk at the same time. Exhibition shooting is show biz. It takes training, which takes time and money, and gun companies aren't willing to foot that bill.

"Two current shooters who have great possibilities are Matt Dryke and Dan Carlisle (among the best in the world at international skeet and olympic trap), who came out of the service marksmanship training programs like I did. I hear both are doing some exhibitions, and I hope they continue and that other guys get into it. It's good for the shooting industry, and it's fabulous for spectators."

It is that. Satterwhite's performance at our Folk Festival was the consensus favorite among all of the exhibits and performances. As he said, mass media advertising would reach far more than the 20,000 people who attended the Festival, but for many years in many parts of the nation there'll be conversations that begin with, "Remember when that guy Satterwhite threw seven clay targets up and..."

January 1987

HUNTING

HOW TO HIT DUCKS

Poor timing is the culprit behind more inept shooting at ducks than is any other factor. The good news is that most hunters who suffer from this fault can improve their performance, often dramatically.

Wing shooting is perhaps my favorite kind of gunning, and duck hunting ranks near the top. It deals with decoys and dogs, blinds and boats, calling and camouflage. It is as varied as sculling a sneak boat on Merrymeeting Bay, wading a flooded Arkansas hardwood bottomland, or sitting in a blind just about anywhere. With that variety comes a wide range of gunning situations, each with its own peculiarities which need be considered if more than modest shooting success is to be achieved.

No matter which variety of duck gunning you're enjoying at the moment, rest assured that proper timing is important to all of them. And we can break timing down into two components: the time to make your shooting move; and the time to pull that trigger.

When ducks are working to decoys, let them keep coming as long as they're getting nearer to your blind. Hunters frequently rise to shoot as soon as the birds cross that nebulous "in range" mark, despite the fact that the ducks would undoubtedly have been much better positioned within scant seconds.

"Hey, they were in good gun range," is the response.

Marginal gun range — when the hunters began their shooting move. By the time they were up and in shooting position, however, the ducks had already begun to flare. The first shots were taken at that marginal gun range, at best, and subsequent shots were at out-of-range birds.

The shotgun is a short-range tool, and duck hunters should hunt with that in mind. Gear your techniques to the inherent capability of the gun.

In short, let the ducks keep coming as long as they will, and then ease quickly into shooting position. It's a great advantage to get that first shot off at birds still unaware of your presence, and most excellent duck shots do just that. They are fast, but they are fluidly smooth, in sharp contrast to the abrupt, jerky shooting moves of some gunners.

For each duck shooting situation, there is an optimum position for incoming ducks insofar as the duck hunter is concerned. There is one location in the flight path where the bird is easiest to hit, and it should be the hunter's goal to pull the trigger when the duck reaches that mark.

Other than making a move too soon, one of the most common mistakes is to let the bird get beyond that optimum point, which usually turns an easy shot into a difficult one. In the case of a passing bird, one that's crossing over the decoys out front or flying past overhead, the difficulty of the shot is magnified enormously when the duck becomes an outgoer instead of an incomer. Not only do the shooting angles become much more complex, but at that point the duck is presenting less vulnerable areas of the anatomy. The possibilities for crippling are much greater, in short, on going-away birds.

Timing will vary greatly, of course, depending on your shooting conditions. Mallards and pintails moving deliberately into a set of decoys is one thing; a flock of bluebills pouring past is quite another. The bottom line is that duck hunters should mentally prepare for the conditions under which they're shooting. Gear your thinking to making the right moves for that particular day. Steal a page from the olympic athlete whose preparation includes mental imaging — of soaring over the crossbar at a winning height.

Trigger timing? "It's what it takes for your brain to say to your trigger finger that you are at the right place: Shoot!" was the way Rudy Etchen put it in *Sports Afield* a decade ago. "Trigger timing is a terribly important thing. Your trigger-finger must hook up with your eyes and brain and gun barrel. You can't shoot every target or bird at the same speed."

Lazy eyes are responsible for the continued well-being of many game birds, including ducks. There is a tendency among most of us to focus our eyesight on the landscape out front, a general focus which has most things more-or-less in focus. That's as it should be most of the time. When you mount your shotgun to shoot, however, your eyes should be focused precisely on the target you've selected. Since the distance to that target is changing constantly, the focus of your eyes should change accordingly.

In many cases it doesn't. We watch a half dozen ducks approach, trying to see where each is in the pattern, trying to select one for our first shot while maintaining eye contact with the others. That requires a general eye focus, which isn't good enough for precise shotgun shooting. When you've selected a target, concentrate your eye focus on that bird. A conscious effort is required to follow-focus on that one duck as the distance changes, and practice is required in order to do it effectively, to have it become as nearly second-nature as is possible.

(For more on eye-sight and the effect on it of nutrition and exercise, read: "An Insight to Sports Featuring Trapshooting," by Dr. Wayne F. Martin, O.D., published by Creative Communications, 330 Dayton St., Suite 6, Edmonds, WA 98020; and "Bragg System to Better Eye-Sight," by Patricia Bragg, published by Health Science, Box 310, Burbank, CA 91503).

Organize! The better organized duck hunter is a more effective duck shooter. Not necessarily a better shotgunner, let me emphasize, but the duck hunter who has his act together has a better chance of hitting birds when the opportunities arise.

Ever shoot in a blind which is total confusion? Shell boxes, lunch pails, extra clothes and rain gear, spare duck calls — whatever, they're all in the way. I've been there, too, when that gear was mine. Most of it is desirable to have, but it shouldn't be in your way when you're shooting. When that magic moment arrives, the only gear you need, the only gear you should have at hand, is your loaded gun.

Odds are great that you will hit more ducks this fall if you chop half an inch, maybe more, off the stock of your duck gun between now and then. That's particularly true if your duck hunting calls for heavy, warm clothing, which most duck hunting does. The shotgun which mounts smoothly when you're in shirt sleeves, standing in the gun store, is awkward when you're wearing a bulky parka in the cramped confines of a duck blind. Consult a competent stock maker or shooting instructor, or just test your own gun under "duck shooting" conditions.

"How much do you lead a duck?" It's the question I'm asked most often by beginners, and it's the one with perhaps the least relevance to duck shooting success. It's axiomatic that you can't aim directly at a flying bird and hit it, unless it's flying directly toward or away from the gun. Beyond that, the techniques and opinions concerning "forward allowance," as the British tend to express it, are almost infinite. Sustained lead, snapshooting, swing-through — all are "systems" of gun pointing which are useful and effective for some gunners in certain situations. To the point, there is no answer for "how much" to lead a duck which is accurate for all shooters all of the time.

Experience is the only shortcut to becoming a good duck shot, to learning when to make your move, when to pull the trigger, how much lead to give, how to organize your gear. But keep in mind two points: 1. few ducks are missed by too much lead; and, 2. lifting your head from gunstock, at the shot, usually results in a miss.

Experience is the key. The more of it you have, the better duck shot you'll become, which is one more reason to hunt ducks at every opportunity this fall.

August 1986

SHOOT FOR THE SHOULDER

On an October morn in 1961 I learned a lesson about shooting big game animals. It took place on the Everson Bench in central Montana, where Henry Shipman had led me in search of the mule deer trophy I wanted.

We found him feeding in the wheat stubble, and in the half-light of that hazy day my 150-grain handload from the .30-06 went high. The buck dropped instantly, but was up and out of sight in a couple of seconds.

The mulie disappeared over the rim into a giant chasm known as The Sag, which slices through that dry land wheat plateau. Three hours, five shots and many miles later I locked my tag around his antler.

I had held for the lung area, and my first shot had gone too high to strike the lungs, but not high enough to break the spine. The bullet went completely through the buck damaging muscle tissue but no major blood vessels, so the blood trail was spotty. A partial ground cover of snow, and soft ground where snow had melted, made tracking possible, although very difficult and slow.

My additional shots at the wounded buck, always in a run as he broke from cover, seemed to have little effect, to the point that I believed I must be missing the deer. Not so. Four of the additional shots were "fatal" ones.

It was a perfect example of the phenomena of an animal's seeming immunity to further shock once it has been wounded. In such a condition they can absorb numerous good hits without going down.

Where should you shoot a deer? That "boiler room" area just behind the shoulder is the aiming point most recommended. It's quite large, contains the lungs and heart, and a bullet into it is invariably fatal.

But not always immediately fatal.

A lung-shot deer will frequently drop in his tracks, but not always. A heart shot deer will almost certainly run wildly for a short distance, sometimes as far as one to 200 yards.

Having your game animal move from the spot where shot is usually a disadvantage, one of three disadvantages of the "shoot 'em behind the shoulder" school of thought. It may, at best, put your trophy where it will be very difficult to retrieve. Wounded big game tends to run downhill, and in much deer and elk country the bottom line of downhill is the bottom of a canyon. There are situations, I admit, where it can be an advantage to have your buck run a distance after being hit, like toward the truck or horse.

The worst aspect of the scenario, however, is the possibility that the deer may be lost. Good blood trails from bullet wounds are the exception rather than the rule, and trailing a deer in dense vegetation without snow is extremely difficult. Losing one under such conditions is quite easy.

The other disadvantage to the traditional aiming spot is the penalty for being a bit too far back, which means a gut-shot animal. So what's the alternative?

Consider the shoulder shot.

I should have done so much earlier. Long before my experience with the Montana buck a friend of mine who had killed many, many deer touted me on the advantage of that particular aiming point. "They never go anywhere," was the way he put it. I should add that he was capable of putting the 180-grain bullets from his .30-06 just about where he chose.

A shot through that shoulder bone seems to do great damage to the nervous system of a deer or elk. It puts them down immediately, usually for keeps. In addition to the physical damage of breaking bones, the shock seems to be particularly severe.

A slight aim error with the shoulder aiming point isn't as apt to be as serious as with a lung-area hold. If the bullet wanders backward, it catches the lung section rather than the paunch. A bit forward it hits the neck. If the shot is a little high it can well smash the backbone, and a low shot often hits the heart, which is located quite low and between the front legs.

For some years I had toyed with the thought of writing this column. What triggered me to do it now was an account I read recently by John W. Spencer.

Spencer, formerly Regional Director for the U.S. Forest Service, unveiled his findings more than two decades ago in his chapter of "The Deer of North America."

With a .30-06, using 180-grain bullets, he killed 17 mule deer bucks, 4 bull elk and 3 buck antelope. All were killed with one shot through the shoulder, and only one moved out of his tracks. That bull elk went about 30 feet.

Switching to the .270 Winchester with 130-grain bullets, he continued his experiments with the shoulder shot. He shot 18 mule deer bucks and two antelope, all with one shot, and all were virtually instantaneous kills.

For the shoulder shot to be effective, the bullet used must have the velocity and construction to penetrate the shoulder blade and get into the body cavity. Most calibers in general use for deer would fit those criteria for mule deer or whitetail.

The case of elk is another story, since this is a much bigger animal with shoulder bones much more difficult to penetrate. Precisely where to draw the line on calibers which could be used with confidence for shooting elk through the shoulder is impossible to say, but I would tend to shy away from anything smaller than the 7mm magnum class, and that only with excellent bullets that will hold together.

Any bullet through the lungs will kill an animal, but the same is not true for a shoulder shot. Although a guide I know killed 15 consecutive elk with one shot each from a .243 Winchester — all lung shots, that light bullet is unsuitable for a shoulder shot.

Bullet construction makes a great difference. A caliber which might give insufficient penetration with bullets available in factory loading could be adequate when handloaded with such custom bullets as the Nosler Partition, the Bitterroot, Barnes, Swift, Hornady or Grand Slam.

One disadvantage of the shoulder shot is that it does destroy some meat, but that is a small penalty to pay for anchoring your game on the spot.

October 1977

T he mistakes which shooters make while out gunning, errors of commission, omission or judgment, must number in the thousands, since I can rapidly recall a few hundred to which I personally can lay claim. Over and over, however, a few choice ones crop up.

Such boo boo's can be serious, or just annoying. Some affect nothing more than the heft of your game bag, your satisfaction at the end of the outing, or your average on decoying ducks. Others may determine whether or not you get home from the trip at all.

Let's take a look at a few of these, which you can juggle to suit your own ideas of importance.

1. Get In Shape — And, then, stay in shape. It's probable that more game animals and birds owe their continued existence to the poor physical condition of hunters than to any other single cause.

2. Have Patience — Patience is the hallmark of big game animals, and the impatience of hunters is the reason those animals are so frequently able to achieve their primary goal: staying alive. Think patience.

3. Enjoy — Don't forget that the reason you're out there, shooting and hunting, is to enjoy the experience. Continually seek greater appreciation of the outdoors, and your hunts and shoots will grow more rewarding.

4. Sight It In — Yep, it still happens with regularity: hunters heading afield for big game without having checked their rifles since last season. Or, believe it or not, having ever sighted them in.

5. Pattern It — Many shotgunners have never patterned their shotguns. In no other way can they know the point of impact — where their shotguns shoot, nor what kind of coverage they're getting out where it counts.

6. Shoot It Year-round — It's impossible to become intimate with your favorite rifle or shotgun by using it only during the open season. Shoot it throughout the year. It's fun, and you'll become a much better shot.

7. Survival Kit — Take one along. Stock it for the junket at hand. "Survival" can mean an aspirin for that headache when you're on the shooting range, or a match to save your life if caught out in a winter storm.

8. Keep Swinging — Stopping your gun swing is perhaps the

leading cause of shotgun misses. Keep that muzzle moving after you've pulled the trigger.

9. Believe — Trust your senses of sight, hearing and smell when afield. Too many big game hunters dismiss such clues. If you think you saw, heard or smelled something, you probably did. Act accordingly.

10. Play Your Hunch — If your instinct tells you something, follow that advice. "I thought that buck might cross over down below, but..." Sad, familiar tale. Play that hunch.

11. Be Mentally Fit — Tune in to the shooting or hunting trip at hand, mentally preparing for what is to take place. When actually hunting, constantly play a game of "what if." Anticipate as many potential game confrontations as you can, taking into consideration your physical location and any other pertinent details. By doing so you'll minimize the number of times you must use that excuse line, "I was just surprised, I guess; I didn't expect that."

12. Choke & Length — Too tight and too long is the simple tale when it comes to shotgun choke and barrel length for the vast majority of shotgunners. Across the board, most wingshooters will take more game with the shorter barrels and the more open choke constrictions.

13. Equipment — The right equipment doesn't "make" the hunter, or shooter, but it helps a ton. Devote some thought to the kind of gear you need for your activities, and begin to accumulate the items you're missing, or replacing those which need upgrading. The right boots, for instance, might not make your next hunt successful, but the wrong ones are a cinch to make it either unsuccessful or unpleasant, often both.

14. Become a Naturalist — Not in the academic sense, of course, but the more you learn about the game birds and animals you hunt, and the non-game critters you encounter, the greater your satisfaction will be. There's little room in today's society, in fact, for the hunter who never knows, or cares, what species of ducks he's shooting. Respect wildlife.

15. Watch That Muzzle — Observance of one simple rule will make your shooting and hunting safe from gunshot. Never, even for a fleeting moment, allow the muzzle of your gun, loaded or unloaded, to point at anybody. A simple thing — but it's a rule which is violated frequently, even by experienced hunters.

16. Fit Your Gun — Man's anatomy is adaptable, and I don't have a particular fetish with precise gunstock fit, but I cringe when I

watch hunters with abnormal physical proportions tolerate factory gunstocks built for that mythical "average" shooter. Even those "average" gunners will often benefit from some fine tuning of their gunstocks, sometimes dramatically, but the improvement in marksmanship for the non-average gunner due to the proper stock change is usually enormous.

April 1985

I HUNT PIECES OF DEER

Some two decades or so ago my education in deer hunting took a giant step forward. It happened in Arizona, in the mountains along the Mogollon Rim, and the critters which flipped on the light were elk — not deer.

At the time John Hall was a biologist with the Arizona Game and Fish Commission, and as Information and Education chief for the same department I was tagging along with John on a casual big game survey up above the Rim. In addition to John's considerable other talents as a woodsman and hunter, he had an almost unbelievable ability to spot game.

"Did ya see those deer?" was a question I came to expect with frequency as we cruised along the back roads and trails. My answer was usually in the negative, despite the fact that John was driving and all I had to do was look. No matter what game species we happened across, odds were immense that John would see it first — if I saw it at all.

Let me emphasize that I am not blind, and wasn't at the time. To the contrary, at that point in time I had spent a substantial portion of my productive years in the out-of-doors, even lulling myself into a belief that I was a fairly competent outdoorsman. In that context it came as quite a shock to discover that my traveling companion had to serve as my seeing-eye dog.

The crowning blow took place as John and I were side-hilling our way on foot through a dense stand of timber, working toward a ridge from which we could glass several valleys. "See 'em?" Came the same old question, as John eased to a halt and peered up the mountain.

This time it was a whole herd of elk, and no I didn't see them, a fact which I laid on my leader with no little bit of frustration. "Right there," he gestured with patience, "about 75 yards up the slope. See the rump patches? There's a good antler sticking out from behind that biggest tree. A few of 'em are lying down. See the neck ruffs?"

Came the dawn! John Hall wasn't seeing elk. He was seeing pieces of elk. Rumps! Legs! Antlers! Ruffs!

That calendar portrait of a big buck deer or a huge bull elk standing broadside in a forest clearing is a stirring spectacle, a wondrous sight. The unfortunate fact is that such portraits have led countless hunters into expecting that same scene when the season opens. It doesn't happen that way with any frequency.

In the decades since that day on the mountain with John Hall I have taken that lesson to heart. Now I hunt pieces of deer, and my box score has shown a marked improvement. I'm confident that I now see many, many more animals during the course of a year's hunting than was formerly the case.

Odds are good that you can improve your chances in the same fashion, by taking a new mental approach to the task. The degree of that improvement will vary, of course, largely depending upon your geographical location, the character of your hunting terrain, and your present ability as a hunter. If you're already a "John Hall," forget it. You've got nowhere to go but down.

But if you're a normal deer hunter, which I consider is a better word than "average," then you can think your way to increased success. If you're a deer hunter who just never seems to be able to see deer, who seldom fills his tag, the degree of your improvement can be immense.

Let's first dispense with the obvious, that there will be a "calendar painting" situation now and then. The herd of mulies trotting across an open hillside, or one of whitetails feeding in an oat field. It is when the game is concealed, by timber or camouflage or light patterns, that your ability to sort out "pieces" is the key.

That limb which is just a bit too shiny evolves into a polished antler. The saplings down in the understory which seem to be out of character with the rest of the timber — legs of a motionless deer. An eye! There have been times when that bright, shining eye was the first evidence I had that a deer was there.

But a piece of a deer, for our purposes, is not necessarily a physical thing. Movement. A flick of a tail, a twitch of an ear, a subtly changing pattern of light and shadow as a big buck takes one deliberate step forward.

"Believe your eyes," was the way Lewis Rush put it. This Arkansas hunting buddy, a consummate hunter and woodsman, continued, "If you think you saw something, you did see something."

That one bit of advice has paid off for me in spades — in deer. At times what I saw was a bird or a squirrel, or a leaf movement triggered by an errant breeze, but then again it was that twitching ear or that flicking tail. Did that six-inch "twig" sprouting from the trunk of a massive oak really move? Five minutes of total immobility proved that it did, when the twig became the antler tip of a buck whose rack now hangs on my wall.

Of all the pieces, most important to me are light patterns, forms and lines. Deer woods are a constantly changing pattern of light, subdued or harsh, but always present. Any animal the size of a deer disrupts that pattern, and if you work at it you can literally see that disruption much of the time.

The horizontal back line of a deer is one of the surest giveaways to its presence in the woods. Woods, by and large, are vertical, and that horizontal form is out of place. Limbs can be horizontal, but most are without the form and substance of a deer's body.

LOOK for that horizontal line, for that form, for anything which is out of the ordinary in the forest. Look for legs, ears, tails, antlers, changes in light patterns, movements of any kind. Psych yourself into searching for these things, and the pieces will begin to fall into place in your deer hunting.

Let me make three other points which have been valuable to me. First, in most situations you can see better with binoculars than without them — even in dense timber. I am virtually a binocular freak because I know how glasses increase my success — as well as my enjoyment. I collect binocs like some guys collect guns. If I don't have a pair hanging around my neck I feel undressed. With my Bushnell's, Zeiss', Bausch & Lomb's, Leitz's, Tasco's and Leupold's I have looked *through* brush to spot deer on the other side. In open terrain they are, of course, that friend in deed.

Several years ago, using a favorite 10x40 Zeiss glass on a Montana hunt, I was searching a hillside across a canyon. It was a bare hillside except for isolated, stunted trees, each of which cast a patch of shadow at its base. Systematically checking those patches of shade for bedded down bucks, I noticed that one of the patches was "out of shape." That disruption from the ordinary happened to be caused by a bedded down doe, not a buck, but it does illustrate the value of being aware of anything out of the ordinary.

Second point: you can't see as much, particularly of the subtle things we've been considering, if you are moving. Act accordingly.

Third: keep constantly in your mind that the buck you're after is in no hurry. He is totally committed year-around to only two goals — to eat and to stay alive. (The only exception, of course, is that brief period of madness during the rut.) He can and will be the epitome of patience at deciding the safe, prudent course of action. Should he take another step forward, whirl and run, or remain completely motionless — for 15 or 20 minutes, as I've seen some do. Gear your hunting attitude to these thoughts.

October 1974

SHOTGUNS FOR DEER

W hen most big game hunters in this country think of deer, they think "deer rifle," but there are sizable areas where the tool of choice, or necessity, is the shotgun. There are some states, in short, which either allow or require the use of the scattergun for deer hunting.

"I just wouldn't use a shotgun on deer," goes the refrain I've heard on quite a few occasions from dedicated rifle shooters. But they would, if they hunted deer at all, in some states, or at some deer clubs which don't allow rifles even when the law does.

States which don't permit the use of breech-loading rifles (many allow muzzle-loading rifles) for deer hunting have safety in mind. Right or wrong, and there are proponents for both views, they believe that the shorter range of the shotgun makes it less hazardous than the rifle under the hunting conditions in that particular state. Those conditions, for the most part, involve heavy hunting pressure in restricted woodland habitat.

Use of the shotgun in the South is a different situation. There it is a tradition, and although you'll find an occasional "bear ball" (rifled slug, for the benefit of yankees) in the tube on a deer hunter's smoothbore, the name of this southern game is "buckshot." This tradition probably stems as much from convenience as utility. In the early days most families already had a shotgun, but few owned a center-fire rifle. As for the utility, in much of the deer habitat in the South the vegetative cover is dense, making "shotgun range" the rule rather than the exception.

Another condition which contributed to the utility of shotguns and buckshot was the use of hounds for deer hunting. When run by dogs, most bucks use the thickest cover as escape routes, and hunters learned to place their stands along these routes. Many of the shooting opportunities, as a result, were at fast-moving targets at short range in heavy vegetation.

Although there has been a substantial change in southern deer hunting tactics over the past few decades, involving a great increase in the use of rifles and a decrease in the use of dogs, the shotgun using buckshot is still very much a part of the deer hunting scene. The other side of the coin is that some states which require the use of a shotgun for deer also require the use of rifled slugs, prohibiting buckshot. Both safety and efficiency are touted as the reasons for this regulation.

It may come as a surprise to you, as it did to me, that only two states of the lower 48 prohibit the use of shotguns for deer hunting. The complexities of the regulations from state to state, and from county to county, make it virtually impossible to list those regulations nationwide, so check your own situation for what you can, can't or must do with regard to deer hunting. As an example of the variations, consider that in Connecticut it is the landowner himself who determines what "armament" (rifle, shotgun, muzzle-loader, bow) can be used on private land.

Some years ago I crawled foot by foot into a Kenya thicket after a wounded leopard, and the buckshot-stoked double which preceded me was a great comfort. Sheriffs and marshals of the old West found that their greatest ally in preserving the peace was a sawed-off shotgun loaded with blue whistlers. The police establishment, of late, has been rediscovering the efficiency of this tool.

I use these examples to make a point, one which cannot be emphasized too strongly. Virtually all of the above illustrations feature bar room distances — and less. The shotgun is a decent deer hunting firearm within its limited range, which is SHORT!

The inability or unwillingness to recognize this "short range" fact is the sad flaw in the use of the shotgun for big game. The only ethical tactic for deer hunters who use shotguns to pursue is to determine the effective deer range of their particular shotgun/load combination and then stay within it.

Now we get down to the nitty gritty. How effective is a rifled slug or a load of buckshot, and to what range?

Tough questions! In no other area of firearms data is there so much uncertainty, and there's a reason. There is virtually no consistency in the way different shotgun barrels perform with various buckshot and rifled slug shells. The only way — repeat, only way — you can know what your shotgun will do with buckshot or slugs is to test it extensively

Rifled Slugs: This is an awesome hunk of lead which at modest range is devastating to deer. The 12-gauge one-ounce slug, for instance, has substantially more energy at the muzzle than does the .30-30, and even the 20-gauge 3/4-ounce slug matches it. (The 410 gauge should not be used on deer.) The 1 1/4-ounce 12 gauge and the 1 3/4-ounce 10-gauge slugs even match the muzzle energy of the .270 Winchester cartridge.

For your guidance, the energy (foot pounds) delivered by that 1-ounce slug is 2364 at the muzzle, 1342 at 50 yards and about 950 at 100 yards. The 5/8-ounce 20-gauge slug: 1515 at the muzzle, 934 at 50 yards and about 600 at 100 yards. Federal markets a 3/4-ounce 20-gauge load which gives 1865 f/p at the muzzle, and 1175 at 50 yards; and a 1 1/4-ounce 12-gauge load giving 2695 at the muzzle and 1865 at 50 yards. The 170-grain .30-30 rifle cartridge, for comparison, has 1827 f/p at the muzzle and 1355 f/p at 100 yards.

Slugs are aerodynamically inefficient; consequently, they lose velocity and energy very rapidly. Repeat: they're effective only at short range.

They're effective if they hit a deer in a vital place, that is, and most hunters can't put them in that place without practice. The absence of sights on bird barrels makes slug accuracy difficult, and the use of scope sights, or slug barrels having rifle sights, improves accuracy substantially. It's more difficult to install a scope on a shotgun than on a rifle which has been drilled and tapped for a scope mount, but most gunsmiths can do it. Weaver (Omark Industries) makes a mount for Remington M1100 and M870 shotguns which can be installed by the owner in minutes. Receiver "peep" sights are available from several companies.

Using double barrel shotguns for rifled slugs is an iffy proposition. The barrels on your side-by or O & U may shoot rifled slugs to the same point of aim, but odds are great that they won't.

Buckshot: The buffered buckshot shells now available from all major manufacturers, which minimize deformation of the pellets, are much more effective than were the non-buffered loads. They give tighter patterns, which in turn give the multiple hits necessary for sure deer kills. At reasonable range.

You must test your shotgun with various buckshot brands and sizes to determine which will give you the best performance. There is no other way. Buffered buckshot tend to react to choke constrictions as do smaller shot, with tighter chokes giving tighter patterns; but, again, only testing will tell in your particular barrel.

Buckshot is available in sizes ranging from 000, which is the largest, with each buckshot pellet being .36 caliber and weighing 68 grains; to #4, the smallest, with each pellet a .24 caliber weighing only 20 grains. From these figures it's obvious why multiple hits are necessary for good results on deer. Use the largest size buckshot which will give you that kind of pattern density from your shotgun (16-gauge buckshot is available only with #1 buck, and 20 gauge only with either #3 or #2 buck.)

Test your gun for point of impact as well as for pattern. The use of a scope, or rifle sights, can be an advantage with buckshot just as it is with rifled slugs.

I consider 50 yards for buckshot and 100 yards for rifled slugs as maximum ranges for deer, and much closer than that is much better. When testing either, keep in mind that the same 12-inch lethal zone on deer applies just as it does with rifles. Neither buckshot nor rifled slugs will damage shotgun barrels, regardless of choke. Shotguns can be very effective on deer when used within their limitations. A Connecticut friend got his buck five consecutive years with six rifled slugs, with no shot more than 30 yards. Choose hunting techniques, or stands, which will give you only short range opportunities.

September 1983

Section Eight

HANDGUNS

"I told him at the time that it was a bad idea, that there just wasn't any market for it, which just shows what a prophet I was."

The man doing the talking during my visit with him in April of 1981 was Ted Rowe, President of Harrington and Richardson Arms Company. What he referred to was an idea broached to him several years earlier by one of his employees, a man named Warren Center. That idea was to produce an accurate, single shot pistol designed for hunting.

You know the rest. If the single shot T/C Contender isn't the most popular hunting handgun in the country today I'll be surprised. That's the name of the unique pistol which Warren designed, with the T/C part stemming from the names of the two partners who began the business — Ken Thompson and Warren Center.

In that April of 1981 I visited with Warren Center in the village of Rochester, New Hampshire, where his office and the factory are located. Seated at his cluttered desk which fairly shouts inventor, innovator, designer, the short gray-haired man chuckled at memories: "Ted wasn't alone in his thoughts about the pistol. Jack O'Conner said the same thing — thought we'd never make it."

Ken Thompson and Warren Center made it, for sure. In the dozen years since 1968, when the first T/C Contender emerged from the small plant, some 200,000 of these unusual handguns were sold, and that total has grown enormously since then. T/C offers the Contender in some two dozen calibers, and it has been wildcatted in a broad range of other numbers — .45-70, .444, and even a .577 caliber which really gets the shooter's undivided attention when it goes off. The Contender has become a favorite in the mushrooming sport of pistol silhouette shooting. Warren even offers a "shotgun" choke for it in .357 magnum and .44 magnum calibers, plus shot cartridges to match, which give "410 performance."

So just what is this handgun which has so caught the public's fancy? It is a top-break, long-barreled (10 or 14 inches) single-shot pistol which is beautifully made, is superbly accurate, and which has a most distinctive profile. Equally important, and perhaps more so, is the fact that the barrels of all calibers are interchangeable on the same frame.

"That interchangeability of barrels must have had something to do with the popularity," Warren Center pondered my question.

"Nobody had done it on a single shot pistol before, and all the other single shots fell by the wayside. Just by buying another barrel you've got a second gun with not too much money.

"Another thing that helped, I'm sure," he continued, "was this 'going back' in time movement — back to the 45-70, back to the single shot rifle or pistol. And you can put calibers in it that you can't put in a revolver, which must be a big factor. I never anticipated some of the big calibers they're wildcatting."

Thompson/Center Arms itself chambers the Contender for four wildcat cartridges (maybe more by the time this is in print) — the .22 K Hornet, the .30 Herrett, the .357 Herrett, and a new 7mm which has become popular with silhouette shooters. The pair of Herrett's were developed by the late Steve Herrett (as in Herrett's Stocks, Twin Falls, ID) and are shortened versions of the .30/30 case. T/C sells the dies for loading these hot ones, and they are a bit warm. Muzzle velocity of the .30 Herrett with a 110-grain bullet is 2,601 fps, and it's still going 2,000 fps at 100 yards. With the 125-grain bullet velocity is 2,273 at the muzzle. Stats on the .357 Herrett are: 2,365 fps muzzle velocity with 140-grain bullet, and 2,108 fps with 158-grain bullet.

A tremendous number of deer have been taken with the Contender in the last decade, plus a batch of bigger game. The top three sellers are .44 magnum, .357 magnum and .22 long rifle. Not that I necessarily advocate such an undertaking for the casual gunner, which I don't, but the experience of Larry Kelly (owner of Mag-na-port Arms) in Africa last year is an extreme example of what can be done with the handgun. Using a T/C Contender chambered for the JDJ .375 wildcat caliber, this veteran handgun hunter took almost three dozen head of big game, including elephant, buffalo and lion.

If squirrel hunting is more your cup of tea, the Contender is also chambered for the .22 long rifle rimfire. And, yes, it is also interchangeable with the center fire barrels, courtesy of a unique revolving firing pin which can be positioned for either rimfire or center-fire cartridges.

In May I took a Contender in .223 Remington caliber to South Dakota on a prairie dog shoot, and with the 4X scope atop the barrel it performed beautifully out to a hundred yards. Better than I did, if the truth be known, since it will shoot two-inch groups at that distance from the bench with the Frontier (Hornady) factory ammo I was using.

Warren Center was born in Massachusetts, hunted all his life, had a gun shop and built custom guns for a while, and worked for H&R from 1950 until 1966 when he quit to manufacture his single shot pistol. He wasn't quite sure it was the right move.

"I was 50 at the time," he explained, "and figured maybe this isn't the right thing to do at my age. But I did it and I haven't been sorry."

Ken Thompson had a going business making castings for a number of firearms companies, but was looking for a product to make and market when Warren's pistol came to his attention.

"What I really wanted to do," said Warren, "was to sell the pistol to him and keep the job at H & R, but he wouldn't agree to that. He said that if I didn't join him he wouldn't make the gun. Frankly, I didn't think the pistol would set the world on fire, but I didn't figure I had that much to lose. I could always go back to tool making."

It's obvious that Warren Center, who was the 1980 recipient of the "Handgunner of the Year" award, didn't find it necessary to return to tool making. Now, 750 people are busy producing his products. But he didn't stop with the Contender. In 1970 he designed a black powder rifle called the "Hawken" which became very popular, and followed it with the "Patriot" black powder pistol which met with like success. Then in 1973 came another rifle, the "Seneca," and the following year a .54 caliber "Renegade."

On the drawing boards when I visited Warren in 1981 was a single shot, top lever, break open rifle.

"No," he grinned. "I don't mind if you just mention that we're working on something like this. Probably be a year before we have it on the market, but I'm sure we'll start getting letters."

[Thompson Center did get that new TCR single shot rifle on the market a year or two later, and you can read about it in another chapter of this book.]

(T/C Contender pistols retail for about $200, with additional barrels less than $100. For more information, write Thompson/Center Arms, Rochester, New Hampshire 03867.)

September 1981

THE AMAZING HANDGUN SILHOUETTE SHOOTERS

Many riflemen in this country would hesitate to shoot at a deer at a range of 200 yards. The terrain they hunt doesn't lend itself to such distances. And odds are good that most of them will be surprised to learn that there are thousands of shooters in the U.S.A. who can smoke a target *smaller* than a deer at that distance — with a *handgun*.

And do it every time!

"I just missed out on the shoot-off," Benny Mobley, a hometown buddy of mine told me last week, as he bagged the milk and bread I'd just bought at his neighborhood grocery around the corner from my house. "There were six guys in it. Oh, yeah, they were all straight."

What he means by "straight," of course, is that all of these finalists in the Louisiana Silhouette Handgun Championships went through the program without a miss: 60x60 — on targets out to 200 meters. Lanny Russell won it when he toppled another bank of five targets clean, eliminating the other finalists. Oh, yes, for the tie-breakers the "50-meter" chicken targets were used — shot at 200 meters.

Hey, wait a minute! Nobody can hit anything with a pistol at more than bar room distances. Don't you read the papers! Or listen to television. The only thing a handgun is good for is causing accidents in the home and shooting up friends and lovers at spittin' range. Right?

The 1986 International Handgun Metallic Silhouette Association (IHMSA) championships were held in Idaho Falls in August, and there were 1,146 competitors on the line. They came from most states from coast to coast and many foreign countries — France, Norway, Brazil and Canada, among others. In this "world series" of handgun silhouette, the match consists of 80 shots, and in the unlimited class 33 shooters were perfect — 80x80! Benjamin Cook, using a Remington XP-100 in .308 Win. caliber, won the shoot-off in which they used tiny .22 rimfire targets set out at 150 and 200 meters.

Who *are* these guys!

Handgun silhouette shooting is a fast growing shooting sport. Like all silhouette shooting, it is popular because it's fun, and much of that joy stems from the sight and sound of a steel target being knocked over by a speeding bullet. It's the carnival shooting gallery reincarnated — and then some.

Siluetas Metalicas was a rifle shooting game which eased into Arizona from Mexico more two decades ago. It grew rapidly in popularity in this country, being a competition in which any hunter and his big game rifle could compete with honor, since everybody missed many (or most) of the targets, which were positioned out to 500 meters — 547 yards. Still very popular, it's growth has slowed under the listless, unimaginative stewardship of the National Rifle Association.

Rifle silhouette's key problem is that it doesn't have an "Elgin Gates," the man who started IHMSA, Inc. and who is its continuing President and guiding force. Begun in 1976, it now has some 41,000 members.

Silhouette shooting, including the handgun variety, is simple in concept. Competitors shoot at a metal silhouette target of a bird or animal, and score a "hit" if they knock it over. A hit which doesn't topple the target is a miss.

In IHMSA bigbore handgun silhouette there are four kinds of matches: Production; Unlimited; Revolver; and Standing. Most of those perfect scores are shot with unlimited guns from the "prone" position, in which the shooter lies on his back with feet pointed toward the target and braces the pistol barrel against the side of his leg or thigh.

It's an odd position, true, (not well suited for self-defense, needless to say, or for hunting, although there are possibilities even here), but it is a tremendously accurate way to shoot a handgun. It is also an excellent method of demonstrating the capability of the handgun itself in the hands of competent marksmen.

Specifications as to allowable handguns are rigid. "Production" class guns must be just that: over-the-counter handguns with maximum barrel length of 10 3/4 inches which weigh no more than four pounds; "Unlimited" class: anything goes, within a 15-inch barrel length (and sight radius) and 4 1/2 pound weight. The "Standing" and "Revolver" matches are both shot with pistols which comply with "Production" class rules, and a revolver must have a cylinder which works.

There are four kinds of handgun silhouette targets: a chicken (11"x13") at 50 meters; a javelina (14"x22") at 100 meters; a turkey (19"x23") at 150 meters; and a ram (28"x32") at 200 meters. The normal match, for each class, may consist of 40, 60 or 80 shots, divided equally among the targets.

Since the targets must be knocked over to count as a hit, bullet energy out at the target is a prime consideration. Most popular calibers are the .357 Maximum, .357 Super Mag (developed by Elgin Gates, and said to be the genesis of the .357 Maximum), and .44 Magnum; several calibers designed specifically for benchrest shooting — 7mm TCU, 7mm IHMSA, and 7mm International; and rifle calibers adapted to handguns, among them the .308 Win., the .375 Win, and the .30-30 Win.

The most popular handguns in silhouette shooting are the T/C Contender single shot, the Wichita bolt-action single shot, the Remington XP-100, the Ruger Super Blackhawk single action revolver, the Dan Wesson revolver, and the Smith and Wesson revolver. Lon Pennington, of Colorado, has won the Revolver match at the Internationals four years in a row with a .357 Super Mag in a Dan Wesson pistol, by all odds the most popular firearm in this event (22 of the top 25 places at the 1986 matches). His 1986 score was 80x80, the only straight. He also won the Production event in a shoot-off with four others who had perfect scores (including a lady from France), using a T/C Contender in 7mm TCU caliber; he won the Standing event with the same handgun with 63x80, a couple of targets ahead of second place.

The goal of silhouette shooters is to find an accurate caliber/gun which will give enough impact to topple targets yet with the least recoil possible, and the search for such combinations has contributed greatly to the development of better handguns and better ammunition. The amazing scores they now shoot with regularity bear this out.

Shortly after IHMSA was organized, the NRA began a handgun silhouette program. In addition to matches which are similar to those under the IHMSA banner, NRA also has a "Hunter Class" which is fired on targets half the size of IHMSA targets and at half the distances. Pistols used must be production guns in certain production calibers, with barrel length/weight maximums at 10 inches and 3 3/4 pounds. This is the only match under either IHMSA or NRA in which telescopic sights may be used. Both IHMSA and the NRA conduct .22 rimfire silhouette matches (maximum range is 100 meters), and the NRA also has an air pistol program (maximum range is 25 meters).

It isn't necessary, of course, to shoot perfect scores in handgun silhouette to be competitive. Just as in trap and skeet, there are classes in which shooters compete against others of like ability.

For more information, contact: IHMSA, Inc., P.O. Box 1609, Idaho Falls, ID 83401; and, NRA, 1600 Rhode Island Ave., Washington, D. C. 20036.

February 1987

A t a gathering for gun writers in December of 1986, Smith & Wesson officials outlined the state of the industry insofar as handguns are concerned. Some of the points were items that are general knowledge, but there were a few surprises.

Item: the overall sale of handguns in the U.S. had been down since 1982, but purchases of autoloading pistols had been rising since 1983. Item: from two to seven million women, according to S&W research, will buy a small handgun in the next few years. Item: S&W had a gap in its product line when it considered the growing popularity of auto's, and the size/weight/cost/recoil considerations involved in a handgun for the lady.

Enter the S&W Model 422, the jewel in Smith & Wesson's line-up of new products for 1987. It's a semiautomatic pistol, .22 caliber, chambered for the .22 Long Rifle cartridge only, and it meets the parameters established by the Springfield firm in filling the vacant niche: light in weight; relatively small; virtually absent of recoil; and moderate in price.

For several months I put the M422 through its paces, and was very favorably impressed. For openers, it works, which is the first consideration when examining a semi-auto. Out of the several hundreds rounds put through the pistol there were only two "jams," when the empties hung up in the slide, but that occurred when I was shooting the pistol while holding it upside down. After that, however, even in that far-fetched attitude, recycling was normal.

I tried a variety of ammunition — standard and high velocity, silhouette and match grade, and found little difference in the performance from batch to batch. If anything, accuracy seemed to be a bit better with run-of-the-mill ammo, and was very good with several brands of "silhouette" cartridges.

Just how accurate one of these pistols can be is beyond the scope of this test, since I didn't install a scope for the shooting. My iron sight groups don't inspire fear in the hearts of competitive pistol shooters, but at 30 feet a quarter was in trouble, and out at 40 yards coffee-cup groups weren't unusual. From a bench rest, of course.

The trigger pull on my sample is very, very good — crisp and moderately light in weight. If the same is true of production pistols which reach dealer shelves then S&W deserves congratulations.

My M422 has a 4 1/2-inch barrel, adjustable rear sight, and

has black nylon grips. With the 10-shot clip magazine empty, it weighs 21 ounces on my postal scales. With a six-inch barrel, which is available, add an ounce of weight. Fixed sights is another option. Overall dimensions: 5 1/2 inches by 7 1/2 inches with the short barrel.

The market for which S&W has especially targeted this new automatic consists of four groups: 1. new shooters; 2. young shooters; 3. women shooters; and 4. families. I expect they have a winner with these categories, but I'm also betting that the M422 will be very popular with many other shooters, those who are not necessarily young, new or female. It's a good-shooting, nice-looking lightweight which will fit into many outdoor activities.

The designer/engineers at Smith & Wesson put much thought into this one, giving it a full house of useful features. The slide stays open after the last shot in the magazine is fired. The pistol won't fire unless the magazine is firmly in place. The slide release is on the left side in the "thumb" position, and the safety is immediately behind the slide release. The magazine release is in a recess in the front of the grip strap, handy to operate with either hand, and the front of the trigger guard is contoured for two-hand shooting. The rear sight is a square notch, and the front a serrated ramp sight.

Smith & Wesson continued in its line the Model 41 semi-automatic, of course, and the M422 is not designed to compete with it. Despite the fact that it is not on the same quality plane of the M41, however, I think that this new offering may be a better all-around choice for most sportsmen.

S&W has field and target designations for the M422 — both available in either barrel length. Field guns have fixed sights and synthetic grips; target guns have an adjustable rear sight and walnut grip panels. Suggested retail prices are $189 for the field version; $225 for the target model.

That price is for the package, the box which contains not only the pistol, but also a cleaning kit, a bottle of Rem Oil, a box (50 rounds) of Remington HV ammunition, and two targets. The combination is a nice touch, particularly for the markets for which this M422 is intended.

The history of .22 rimfire semiautomatic pistols in this country since World War II is dominated by very few entries. I recall with fondness the High Standard HD-M I bought shortly after returning home from the service and used for many years, until somebody skilled at breaking and entering decided he liked it, too. The HD-M, used in large numbers by the armed forces in training programs, was excellent. The Colt Woodsman was *the* semi-auto for a long time, but it disappeared from the scene.

Since 1950 Bill Ruger's .22 auto pistol has been the standard with which most shooters identify. The first firearm this innovator placed on the market, it is still (in the Mark II version) the dominant such gun out in the field.

The new S&W 422 is in the same price ballpark as the Mark II, with which it will be competing. Shooters are fortunate — or will be when S&W is able to supply the demand — to have two such excellent guns as these from which to choose. There are many differences between them, but one of the most apparent is weight. The Mark II weighs about 36 ounces, courtesy of its virtually all-steel construction, compared to 21 ounces for the M422. S&W made extensive use of aluminum in building this one, which reduced weight enormously, but the barrel, slide and the magazine are made of steel. Most shooters know that poorly designed, badly produced, or damaged clip magazines are a major source of malfunctions in any type of semi-auto firearm. The clip on the M422 seems to be almost a copy of the tried and proven magazine which S&W has long used in its Model 41.

The new pistol feels good, looks good, is a shooter, and the price is right. It's encouraging to see this old-line firearms manufacturer design and market such an innovative, exciting product. For more information, write: Smith & Wesson, Box 2208, Springfield, MA 01102.

June 1987

THE BIG HANDGUN: 44 MAGNUMS

Some years ago I was much impressed with the handgun exploits of Tom Mix, and of the other assorted cowboy heros of the silver screen. What got my attention wasn't so much the blinding speed with which they dispatched villains at spittin' distance, but instead their uncanny ability to drop a badman from the saddle at very long range with every pop of the pistol.

It's safe to say that the screen writers and directors took a liberal helping of literary license in depicting such prowess, but since 1956 many of those shooting feats have been possible, even practical. That year marked an epic development in the field of handgun cartridges, the introduction by Remington of the .44 Remington Magnum caliber. A quarter of a century later, it is still the most powerful commercial handgun cartridge available, and it is primarily this caliber which has given respectability to shooting achievements which were seldom attempted before its introduction.

The genesis of any new firearm development is interesting, and that of this .44 Magnum is well documented by author Roy G. Jinks in "History of Smith & Wesson." Enter Elmer Keith, the little man with the huge hat, from Salmon, Idaho, who has gained a well-deserved reputation during decades of gun writing as Mr. Big Bore. For years he advocated the use of heavy loads in the Smith & Wesson .44 Hand Ejector revolver, and in the early 1950's Elmer urged the factory to build a handgun strong enough to handle loads similar to those he had developed. Smith & Wesson did just that, and prevailed upon Remington to develop a cartridge that would be called the .44 Magnum.

The new Smith & Wesson chambered for this caliber was designated the Model 29, and when the third such revolver came off the production line on January 27, 1956, it was sent to Elmer Keith, called by Jinks "the father of big bore handgunning." The new cartridge was called the .44 Remington Magnum, and the handgun/cartridge combination was an immediate success. It still is.

At the time of the debut of the .44 Remington Magnum, the most potent handgun caliber available over the counter was the .357 Magnum, still one of the most popular numbers with both hunters and law enforcement personnel. But, in one full swoop, the .44 Magnum doubled the performance of the .357 Magnum, a quantum leap in handgun power.

Such performance doesn't come without a price, of course, and in the case of the .44 Magnum the man behind the gun must cope with substantial recoil. Punishment on the rear end of a handgun chambered for this biggie, in fact, was far beyond what most of the early users expected. Most of them had made the transition from .38 Special to .357 Magnum with little difficulty, but that giant step to the .44 Magnum plateau was something else again.

The .44 Magnum is still not a plinker's cartridge, but in the past couple of decades a great number of shooters have learned to live with it and like it. Longer barrel lengths, more weight, different grips, barrel porting, new handgun designs — all have contributed to the increasing popularity of this powerful caliber.

It's not only powerful, however; it's accurate. A few years ago several of us were sighting in rifles before a New Mexico elk hunt, when handgunner Skeeter Skelton sat down at the bench and squeezed one off with his Super Blackhawk. Center of the bullseye at a hundred yards. Well, the .44 Mag isn't that accurate, not for me, but it is good enough that it's become a favorite with silhouette competitors, who must combine accuracy with enough knock-down punch to topple heavy targets out at 200 meters.

Yep, that is 200 meters, a handgun range which would make even Tom Mix happy. And we're not talking about an occasional hit at that distance, since the silhouette competitors shoot perfect scores with fair regularity. It's true that some of them employ rather specialized firearms and shooting positions to achieve such results, but their accomplishments certainly are indicative of the potential of the .44 Magnum cartridge in an appropriate handgun.

The .44 Magnum has become reasonably popular as a law enforcement/self defense caliber, with an undeniable assist from "Dirty Harry," but it's for hunting that it is most popular. In the big .44, handgun big game hunters found a far more efficient tool than they had prior to its introduction. Let's look at the numbers.

The hottest factory handgun before the .44 Mag was the .357 Magnum, which gives a muzzle velocity of 1235 fps with a 158-grain bullet from a four-inch barrel. The .44 Magnum gives a 180-grain bullet 1610 fps muzzle velocity. That translates to 1036 foot pounds of energy at the muzzle, almost twice the 535 foot pounds of the .357 Magnum.

With a 240-grain bullet, favored by many big game hunters, the big .44 has 1180 fps and 741 foot pounds out front, and this from a four-inch barrel as shown in the Remington ballistic charts. Most handguns used for hunting have much longer barrels, with correspondingly improved performance.

To keep things in perspective, we might note that this same .44 Magnum load gives 1650 foot pounds when fired from a 20-inch rifle barrel, and still has more than 1000 foot pounds at 100 yards, where the handgun performance is down below 600 foot pounds. By comparison, the .30-30, which some consider marginal for deer, gives 1827 foot pounds at the muzzle and 1350 at 100 yards.

The .44 Magnum handgun market in the U.S.A. is dominated by half a dozen models manufactured in this country. The Smith & Wesson Model 29 (and the stainless steel version — the M629) is still very popular. Others finding most favor are the Ruger Super Blackhawk, a single-action revolver; Thompson/Center Contender, a single shot; the Dan Wesson, a double-action revolver; the Ruger Redhawk, a double-action revolver; and the Mossberg Abilene, a single-action revolver.

Two other .44's which are produced in the U.S.A., and which are beginning to find their way to dealer's shelves, are the Sterling Arms X-Caliber, a single shot; and the Interarms Virginia Dragoon, a single-action revolver. Several .44's of foreign manufacture are imported and sold.

The T/C Contender has been a phenomenal success, and the most popular factory caliber in this single shot is the .44 Magnum. Ruger's Super Blackhawk has been a favorite with hunters since its introduction in 1963 (a regular Blackhawk in .44 Magnum was produced in 1956, the year the .44 Magnum caliber was unveiled), and continues to be extremely popular. The Dan Wesson and the Ruger Redhawk are big, heavy, high quality double-action revolvers which handle the .44 Magnum caliber well. The Abilene is a super smooth single-action which is very accurate. Shooters now have an excellent array of .44 Magnum handguns from which to choose. Here are the details.

Smith & Wesson Model 29 and M629 Stainless: 6-shot, double-action revolver, available with four, six, or 8 3/8-inch barrels (M629 in six inch only). Weight — 48 oz. for the M629. (Smith & Wesson, 2100 Roosevelt Ave., Springfield, Mass 01101)

Sturm Ruger Super Blackhawk: 6-shot single-action revolver, available with barrel lengths of 7 1/2 or 10 1/2 inches. Weight — 48 and 51 ounces. (Sturm, Ruger & Co, Inc., Southport, CT 06490)

Sturm Ruger Redhawk: A massive 6-shot, double-action revolver of completely new design. Stainless steel only. Barrel length — 7 1/2 inches. Weight — 52 ounces. (Sturm, Ruger & Co. Inc., Southport, CT 06490)

Thompson/Center Contender: Innovative single shot handgun which features barrels interchangeable for length and caliber. Barrel lengths — 10 or 14 inches. Weight — 43 ounces to 56 ounces. (Thompson/Center Arms, Rochester, N.H. 03867)

Dan Wesson: Another excellent, massive 6-shot double-action revolver with the unique feature of readily interchangeable barrels. Barrel lengths — 4, 6, 8, and 10 inches. Weight: From 48 to 69 ounces. (Dan Wesson Arms, Inc., 293 Main St., Monson, MA 01057)

Mossberg Abilene: An excellent single-action 6-shot revolver. Barrel lengths of 4 5/8, 6, 7 1/2 and 10 inches. Weight with the shortest barrel is about 48 ounces. (Mossberg, 7 Grasso Ave., North Haven, CT 06473).

Sterling Arms X-Caliber: A single shot similar to the T/C Contender. Barrel lengths 8 and 10 inches (interchangeable). Weight — 52 oz. with eight-inch barrel. (Sterling Arms Corp., 211 Grand St., Lockport, N.Y. 14094)

Virginia Dragoon: Single-action revolver. Barrel lengths — 6, 7 1/2, 8 1/2 and 12 inches. Weight — 52 oz. with 7 1/2-inch barrel. (Interarms, 10 Prince St., Alexandria, VA 22313)

February 1983

HANDGUNS FOR HUNTING

Curt Earl and I made a run for it, up and around the hillside in the mountains near Safford, Arizona, trying to intercept an elusive herd of "pigs." We had been hunting javelina for a couple of days without success, enjoying the great weather of February, and this time the luck was on our side.

When we peaked out over the ridge we could see movement in the brush across the canyon, but I couldn't find anything shootable through my scope. Then Curt, a few yards to my left, began touching them off, and at the fourth shot grunted, "Got 'em!"

The interesting thing about the javelina boar that met destiny that Spring morning is that he was done in with a handgun, and all that way back in the early 1950's. Curt rolled him over with a .357 Magnum revolver. At a guesstimated range of somewhere between 35 and 50 yards.

Despite what we hear from anti-gunners, most of the network commentators, and all of the liberal newspapers, handguns *are* good for something. Good for more than just shooting friends and relatives, as we hear over and over, and for causing accidents. As was true for Curt and his javelina, handguns are of great use to a few million sportsmen for hunting.

There are, we should make the point, more than *four million* people in the U.S. who *do* hunt with handguns.

Some of my fondest memories revolve around crisp, quiet

mornings in the squirrel woods of Louisiana, where I live. The gun I use most often is a scope-sighted .22 rimfire or a shotgun, but my greatest satisfaction comes from outings where my choice is a .22 rimfire pistol. Usually with open sights; sometimes with a scope.

I don't kill as many squirrels with a handgun, but they mean more. I learned to hunt to the capabilities of the tool, my gun, my handgun, in my hands. I'm no Bill Jordan or Bill Blankenship or Skeeter Skelton, but by using techniques anybody can learn I seldom went hungry for bushytail gumbo.

Many of the shots I take when hunting squirrels with a handgun are from a sitting position, back braced against a tree trunk, using both hands. With elbows braced against my knees, I can give a squirrel fits at modest ranges.

That's the key to any kind of hunting, but it's especially applicable to handgun hunting. Know what the gun can do in your hands, and take advantage of all techniques which will make you more efficient.

Some hunters have taken handgun hunting to the ultimate. With the short gun, they've killed the biggest and most dangerous game in the world — elephant, lion, Cape buffalo and leopard. For such hunting to be ethical, the hunter must use the specialized equipment capable of cleanly killing such game, and must become sufficiently proficient with it.

Two hunters who have done just that are Larry Kelly and J.D. Jones, both of them long associated with handguns and handgun hunting. Larry is the man behind Mag-Na-Port, and has been a driving force for recognition of the short gun as a suitable hunting firearm. He is the founder of the Handgun Hunters Hall of Fame, and made the first award in 1984 to Bob Good, President of The American Sportsman's Club.

J. D. Jones is the founder of Handgun Hunters International, and publishes "The Sixgunner" for its members. Not only has he handgun hunted extensively and successfully throughout this continent and in Africa, as has Larry Kelly, he has developed some outstanding wildcat handgun calibers, and markets the most popular custom handgun bullets (JDJ bullets) on the market for really big game.

J. D. doesn't equivocate when it comes to handgun hunting of big game: "If a guy cannot learn to handle shooting big bore handguns, he ought to stay the hell at home or use a rifle. Most real handgun hunters, those who go with just a pistol, are pretty proficient. It's the ones who take both rifle and pistol, and say they'll use the handgun if they get a good enough shot, who won't ever become good with a handgun. They should stick to rifles."

Both Larry Kelly and J. D. Jones are recipients of the annual "Outstanding Handgunner Award."

It's true that some monster handgun cartridges have been developed for use on really big game, but you don't have to go quite that far to get into handgun hunting. That favorite .22 rimfire is excellent for squirrels and for cottontails. The .22 WMR is even better.

The same two rimfires can be used on small varmints such as prairie dogs, but hotter calibers are much more fun and much more efficient out at varmint ranges. Some of the excellent ones are the .22 Hornet, .222 Remington and .223 Remington.

For big game in the deer class, nothing less than the .41 Magnum should be considered in a factory caliber, despite the fact that many bucks have been taken with the .357 Magnum. The .44 Magnum is even better, and quite suitable for other big game animals — elk and moose for instance — under good conditions, at close range. With proper bullets the .44 Mag will handle anything on this continent and much African game.

But there are even better calibers, such as the rifle calibers for which handguns are now being chambered. Three favorites are the .30/30, .35 Remington, and the .45/70. Others are the .30 Herrett and .357 Herrett, both developed by the late handgunner and grip-maker Steve Herrett. And there's the series of hot wildcats developed and built by J. D. Jones.

For hunting with a .22 rimfire caliber, chose the handgun action you prefer: single or double action revolver, semi-automatic, or single shot. All will do the job well.

For big game and varmint hunting, either the revolver or the single shot should be the choice. There are excellent double action revolvers available from Smith & Wesson and from Dan Wesson, and both single and double actions from Ruger.

The most popular single shot pistol, and one of the most popular hunting handguns, is the Thompson/Center Contender. It is chambered for a wide array of calibers, from .22 rimfire up to the hot wildcats, and barrels can be interchanged to give great versatility. With one frame and three barrels, for example, you can have a .22 plinker, a .223 Rem varmint pistol, and a .45/70 heavy game gun.

Handgun hunting isn't for everybody, but it's a satisfying challenge for those willing to devote much time and effort into becoming proficient.

The address of Handgun Hunters International is P. O. Box 357 Mag, Bloomingdale, Ohio 43910.

Section Nine

OPTICS

Section Nine

OPTICS

H unting squirrels with a rifle is one of my favorite brands of fall sport, but last year I found myself in a situation which prompted thoughts of switching rather than fighting. At that moment I would gladly have traded my rifle for a scattergun.

There was nothing wrong with the rifle, let me add. Scoped as it was, under proper shooting conditions, it would shoot groups the size of a squirrel's head at reasonable ranges.

My problem on that October morn, however, was that shooting conditions were not proper. A storm front was moving in, with heavy cloud cover and wind. In that Alabama hardwood bottomland, beneath a dense canopy of oaks and gum trees, the light level was very low.

As wildlife so frequently does in advance of a weather front, the squirrels turned it on. On several occasions I could see half a dozen at one time, and hear a couple more giving that inimitable, staccato bark. It was fete day in that bayou bottomland for the bushytails, and it seemed as if the world had turned to squirrels.

Delightful experience, but it would have been a bit more satisfying had I been able to see the squirrels in my scope. Light conditions were so poor that I simply couldn't follow the bouncing bits of fur with any degree of success. Only by silhouetting them against the dark sky did I have a slim chance of having the crosshairs in the right place when the gun went off, but during that wild hour or so the squirrels were seldom motionless long enough for that. Just exactly how many I killed and how many shots were fired is classified information, but I will hint that I could have doubled my bag without approaching the limit. That morning was a classic instance of a situation where bigger is better when considering scopes for .22 rimfires.

Most scope sights used on rimfire .22's have tube diameters of either 3/4 inch or 7/8 inch, while those used on center-fire rifles are typically "one-inch" scopes. The latter, with their correspondingly larger objective lens, are substantially superior in performance.

The scope I was using that dark morning in Alabama was a good 7/8-inch model which is sold as a ".22" scope, and in most situations it is entirely adequate. Under those abnormal conditions, however, I am confident that a good one-inch scope would have increased my success.

Manufacturers market scopes for .22 rimfire rifles in 3/4-inch and 7/8-inch tube sizes, rather than the one-inch size, as a concession to cost and to scale. The "big game" scopes sell for two to three times the price of a .22 scope, and most rimfire shooters are content with the smaller tubes. As for scale, a big one-inch scope can appear out of proportion on a small rimfire rifle, and the individual must decide for himself whether or not performance takes precedence over aesthetics.

Most 3/4-inch and 7/8-inch scope sights are relatively inexpensive, and are tremendous values, far superior to open sights. A giant step toward encouraging their use on .22 rimfire rifles took place some years ago, when rifle manufacturers began grooving their receivers to accept the clamp-on rings which normally are furnished with the scopes.

Now another trend is under way. Scope manufacturers have noted the increasing number of rimfire riflemen who are willing to pay the price for the better performance offered by one-inch scopes, and a number of them now offer one-inch scope rings which clamp into the grooved receivers of most .22 rimfire rifles. It is an excellent system affording virtually instant installation by the owner. Adapter bases are also available for .22 rifles which don't have the dovetail receivers.

In recent years scope manufacturers have offered more and more one-inch scopes designed for rimfire use, and there are now a host of "compact" big game scopes — short and light — which can be adapted very nicely to .22 rimfire purposes.

When a big game scope programmed largely for ranges of a hundred yards or more is used for .22 rimfire hunting a potential problem exists. It is aim error caused by parallax.

A scope can be adjusted to be parallax-free at only one distance, and manufacturers have selected 100 or 150 yards as that distance for their one-inch "big game" scopes. With such adjustment the parallax-induced error at big game ranges, on big-game size targets, is insignificant.

Such potential error is magnified at shorter ranges, and may be as much as half an inch or more at 25 yards for scopes adjusted parallax-free at 100 yards. Perhaps more important, focus may be impaired at short distances.

The solution is simple. Major scope manufacturers will reset their scopes to be parallax-free at any desired distance (35 to 50 yards is a good choice for rimfire shooting), at either no charge or a small service fee. When reset for shorter distances, keep in mind, potential parallax error is much greater at longer ranges.

Other considerations play a part in choosing a rifle scope. Image brightness, relative brightness, exit pupil, light transmission, objective lens aperture, twilight factor, field of view, magnification, resolving power, eye relief, and relative light efficiency — if you care to delve into each of those goodies, be my guest. It is fascinating.

If not, you can take it from me that, as in boxing, a good big scope is far superior to a good little scope.

March 1987

BILL WEAVER: HENRY FORD OF SCOPE SIGHTS

About 50 years ago a young Kentucky shooter, unhappy with the very few, high-priced telescopic sights then available, decided to make his own. Bill Weaver did just that, and the world of shooting has never been the same.

The desire of that 23-year old for a more reliable scope sight, mounted low on the barrel, and his ingenuity in fulfilling that desire, began a revolution in sighting equipment that continues to this day. Whereas a scope-sighted rifle was a rarity at that time, today more than 70 percent of all center-fire rifles are fitted with a scope immediately after purchase.

Bill Weaver did for scope sights what Henry Ford did for automobiles. Both produced good, efficient, innovative products at prices most people could afford.

Although Bill Weaver hand crafted that first scope sight in his Newport, Kentucky machine shop for his own use, he quickly realized that it had potential for general sales. It went on the market in 1932 or 1933 for the first time, as the Weaver 3-30, a 2 3/4X power glass with crosshair reticle. As advertised in the September 1933 issue of the American Rifleman, the price was $19...complete with mount.

To appreciate the magnitude of this, consider that other domestic scopes on the market at the time were selling for $45 to $60. It also helps the perspective to remember that one dollar per long day was not an unusually low pay scale for many wage earners back then.

The young man from Kentucky soon became a Texan. In 1934 he loaded up a truck with the best of his equipment, two assistants, and drove to El Paso, and there the company prospered. From that modest beginning it grew to a bustling firm with more than 400 employees.

Bill Weaver realized his dream. Using assembly-line, mass production techniques, coupled with in-house manufacture of virtually all of the parts, he turned out millions of good telescopic sights which were within the financial reach of most shooters.

None of it would have been possible, of course, without this amazing man's many talents. Most people who knew him and his operation put it simply: "He was a genius."

Bill Weaver not only designed the scopes he built, he designed the intricate machine tools needed to put them together. And then he built the tools.

The list of scope sight innovations for which Bill Weaver is responsible is almost endless, but a few stand out. The K4, a 4-power model introduced in 1946, became one of the largest selling scopes in the world. In 1950 Weaver's Model KV, offering either 3-power or 5-power, was the first variable. And in 1954 Weaver pioneered the first nitrogen-filled scope, a start toward eliminating the monstrous problem of scope fogging.

The W. R. Weaver Company was sold to Olin in 1968, and Bill Weaver died a few years later. But the man's contributions to better sighting equipment go on and on. Late in 1976 Weaver announced a new line of silhouette/varmint/target scopes called the T-Models. They included a new, patented internal adjustment system called Micro-Trac, which became standard on all Weaver center-fire scopes, and which became a landmark feature of the line.

Just as Bill Weaver had a hunting itch for a better scope long ago, so did the Weaver R&D team react with Micro-Trac to a new, modern need. Silhouette shooters require scope adjustments which can be changed repeatedly with exact results, and Micro-Trac had that repeatability in spades.

Three of the top four scores at the 1977 National Silhouette Championship were shot with T-scopes, including a new national record of 77. In 1978, three scores of over 180 were fired, including an incredible 88 — all with Weaver Model T's.

The scope sight is by all odds the most efficient rifle sight of them all, and to Bill Weaver must go the credit for making it standard equipment on most big game rifles. He designed many of them, and produced millions, but he also made another contribution.

Bill Weaver's success stimulated the competition which led to the situation which riflemen now enjoy, a thriving industry which offers a staggering array of scope sights to fit any need.

[The W. R. Weaver Company fell by the wayside in the mid-1980's, finally ceasing operation. The Weaver scopes and Weaver scope mounts, however, were bought by Omark, Inc. and, made in Japan, they are still quality and still on the market.]

February 1979

BINOCULARS: SUPERB HUNTING AID

In 1894 Zeiss began manufacture of the first prism binoculars, but the significance of that epic event continues to elude many hunters. Almost a century hasn't been time enough for the message to sink in: that the right binocular, properly used, is one of the most valuable tools for the sportsman with a gun.

It isn't that use of and respect for binoculars isn't widespread, because that is indeed the case. My point is that use of binoculars by hunters should be almost universal.

Two vignettes, repeated frequently over the years, leap to mind. In one the big game hunter is using his riflescope to scan the distant hillside for game, then he zeros in with it to identify a movement. I cringe to consider that the movement might be me. The other is the hunter who says, "Nope, I don't need binoculars; I've got good eyesight." Or, "Can't use binoculars in this thick cover."

In the first instance, using a riflescope to search for game is terribly inefficient. Using it to identify an unknown "animal" is dangerous, violating the cardinal gun safety rule of never pointing a gun at anything you don't intend to shoot.

No man's eyesight, of course, is in the same league with a pair of good binoculars. And there is seldom, if ever, a geographical situation in hunting where a good glass would not be advantageous.

For most people the pairing of "binoculars" and "hunting" conjures up the image of a big game hunter in our western wide open spaces, and it's an accurate one as far as it goes. Sitting and searching is one of the most profitable uses of his time for the man after mule deer, elk, antelope, sheep and goats. A typical tactic for the western guide is to ride or walk to vantage points along a ridge, and scan the valley below and the hillside beyond with binoculars. It is an extremely successful method of operating.

The point should be made here is that these western hunters are searching for game with binoculars, as opposed to identifying animals already spotted or evaluating a particular animal for trophy qualities. Glasses are obviously valuable for the latter uses, but a point some non-western hunters miss is that they are also extremely useful for finding game.

One quick glance, let me add, doesn't usually get the job done. Several years ago, on a sheep hunt high above Idaho's Middle Fork, five of us spent 45 minutes glassing one basin before we saw the four rams which were bedded down in full view. Feel free to take a second look. Perhaps the angle of the sun will have changed enough to give a tattle-tale shine from the antler of the buck lying under the juniper. A whole herd of antelope has a way of just appearing, where there were none when you looked minutes before.

It is a misconception to think that binoculars are of no use to the man who hunts deer in the woods, the thickets and the brush. With them he can actually look into and through those thickets and brush, to a degree which must be experienced to be believed.

Let me belabor a point which has been made here before. When you are looking for a big game animal in heavy cover, with or without the aid of binoculars, look for the pieces. Gear your senses to respond to a leg, a rump patch, the twitch of an ear, the shine of an antler, a movement, a changing light pattern, or a horizontal line where none should be in a vertical forest.

Binoculars and birds make a happy pair, too. Use the glasses to check ponds and creeks for ducks, to pin down the exact field the geese are using, to identify ducks before they're in range (quite helpful with point system bag limits), to follow the flight of the covey of chukars that flushed wild. We use them to mark down crippled waterfowl which fall at a distance, and to locate flight lines of doves and crows.

In eastern Washington geese fly from the rivers and lakes to feed in the snow-covered fields during the winter, and friends of mine hunt them successfully with the aid of binoculars. From vantage points they spot the dark geese in the snow-covered landscape, drive as close as possible, crawl the rest of the way, then jump-shoot the birds.

The value of the binocular was driven home one morning when they forgot the glass. But without it they finally located a flock of birds a couple of miles away, so they tell it, and made their long ride, creep and crawl. When they rose from behind a terrace with guns at ready their flock of "geese" had become a herd of sheep. So much for eyesight.

Since the first Zeiss prism binocular arrived those many years ago, the conventional binocular has been of that *Porro prism* design, in which the objective lenses are farther apart than are the eyepieces. But in the mid-1960's a new *roof prism* design became available which has the same straight tube look of the early "field glasses."

Both the Porro prism and the roof prism designs are excellent, but the latter permits a reduction in the size of the binocular. For that reason it has become increasingly popular with hunters, a trend which is certain to continue.

Two focusing mechanisms are generally available, but the center focus far exceeds the individual focus model in popularity. The choice isn't critical for most hunting situations, but the center focus is handier for close-in viewing such as bird watching. The I.F. system does have the advantage in that its focus is less apt to be changed accidentally, which does happen frequently with the C.F. model when you're just carrying it. Some hunters prefer to focus that I.F. binoc at about 100 yards, which puts everything within "big game" distance sufficiently in focus to be practical.

One valuable innovation developed by Bushnell is Insta-Focus, a rocker-arm arrangement which permits very rapid focusing

How about those numbers? What does 8x30 mean? And 382 ft./1000 yards?

That 8x30 means a magnification of 8 power, and a diameter of the objective lens of 30mm. The latter combination — 382ft./1000 yards — means that the binocular has a field of view of 382 feet at 1000 yards distance. Magnification, the diameter of the objective lens relative to the power, and the field of view all are factors which the hunter should consider when buying a binocular.

Let's examine magnification first. The practical range for hand-held use is from 6 power to 10 power, and my personal binoc arsenal spans that range. My favorite on the low end is a Bushnell 6x25 Custom Compact which is three inches high, weighs 11 ounces, and has a 420-foot field of view. It is an ideal glass for heavy cover, and fits nicely into my shell bucket on duck and goose hunts. At the other end are two veteran pairs of 10x40's: a Leitz Trinovid and a Zeiss, both roof prism binoculars which are superb for long range viewing.

The 10X power is too high for some people to handle comfortably, and for them an 8X or 9X is preferable. The 7X is perhaps the best choice for an all-around binocular.

The more you practice with your binocular the better you'll be able to use it. Experiment with various methods of holding the glass until you discover which one is best for you. Where the situation permits, a sitting position with elbows braced on the knees is one of the steadiest.

The diameter of the objective (front) lens determines the light gathering power of the binocular, provided that the power remains the same. Thus a 7x50 glass would gather more light than a 7x35, making it better for conditions where the light level is low.

We can get a relative indication of the light gathering power of various binoculars by multiplying the power by the objective diameter: 6x25 = 150; 7x35 = 245; 8x30 = 240; 7x50 = 350; and 10x40 = 400. Keep in mind that under bright daylight viewing conditions this isn't important, since just about any binocular gathers more light than the contracted pupil of the human eye can utilize. It is under the low level light conditions of early morning and late afternoon, frequently prime game times, that light gathering power can be significant. It doesn't come without cost, since such glasses are usually bigger and heavier.

Sometimes they're worth it, and then some. Hunting Desert Bighorn in Mexico a decade ago I got my first taste of a real specialty binocular which was invaluable. Jorge Belloc, my guide, used a pair of 15X60 Zeiss glasses which literally lit up the mountainsides, and from a sitting position Jorge could hold them steady. I had to have a pair, and do. Although they weigh some 3 1/2 pounds, they are a superb aid at finding game at great distances. Zeiss offers a tripod adapter for this biggie, and I frequently use it on my spotting scope tripod.

Field of view is self-explanatory. There are some binoculars on the market now which have tremendous fields of view, but most quality glasses have a field of view that is fully adequate.

The super miniatures deserve mention. They're a fallout from the roof prism design which permits the barrels to be hinged, and when folded for carrying some of these are smaller than a package of cigarettes. For a couple of years I've been using several of these, and seldom go anywhere without one of these shirt-pocket jewels along.

These ultra miniatures don't replace larger binoculars. Because of their small size they are much more difficult to hold steadily, and for that reason aren't practical for prolonged viewing sessions. Within their limitations, however, they are amazing. And when you reach the top of the ridge after a hard climb that miniature binoc in your pocket is much more valuable than that standard size glass you left hanging over the saddle horn.

In binoculars, as in most products, you get what you pay for. But beyond that you can be assured that the values available in glasses today exceed anything we've known before. Actual suggested retail prices range from about $50 to more than $1000. With minimal care most of them will give many years of service, thus the prorated cost is moderate no matter what you spend.

April 1977

CHOOSING A BIG GAME SCOPE

N ot many years ago it would have been proper to begin an article like this with a substantial discussion of "scopes vs. iron sights," but that is no longer necessary. There are a few obvious hunting situations where open sights or aperture sights are preferable to glass, but the overall superiority of scopes as aiming devices has long been acknowledged.

What about rain or snow? Won't that mess me up using a scope? Isn't a scope mighty slow?

Those considerations continue to crop up with regularity, so let's cover them rapidly and move on. There are violent weather conditions which make scope use difficult, or even impossible, but they are rare. Lens covers can cope with just about any rain other than a deluge, and certainly with snow. And, speaking of lens covers, remember that you can make a very serviceable one by cutting a section from an old inner tube. The price is right, good enough to take several along on your hunt in case you lose one.

Somewhere along the line in the distant past the myth got started that a scope sight is "slow." By that is meant that it takes more time to get off a shot with a scope than it does with open sights. Perhaps it began back when scopes were not as efficient as they are today, when the fields of view were small and the view through the tube dim. That situation disappeared decades ago, of course, but the myth lingers on.

Under virtually all conditions the scope sight is the fastest of them all. The primary reason this is true is that the scope puts the sight and the animal in the same plane of view. The shooter has no need to "align" anything. He just places the scope reticle on the target and pulls the trigger.

The older we get, and the less agile our eyes become, the greater the superiority of scopes over open sights. Not only can we *see* better with the scope sight at any age or eye proficiency, but the scope eliminates the requirement of aligning three objects — rear sight, front sight and target — at varying distances from our eye, a task which becomes increasingly difficult as the years go by.

Shooters have a tremendous choice of excellent telescopic sights from which to choose, both manufactured in this country and "made in Japan." That latter label is now largely a mark of distinction, rather than the slur it once was, whether applied to cameras, autos, electronics — or scopes. German scopes are also excellent, and are beginning to make their move in the U.S. market now that models have been designed to appeal to American tastes. No matter which scope you choose, if you stick to the reputable, established brands you can hardly go wrong. Most have incorporated into their current units all of the advances in technology which are available. The search for perfection goes on, of course, and each year finds manufacturers introducing new innovations. Get copies of the catalogs from the manufacturers. Not only will they permit you to compare, but some contain a great amount of information about scopes and their use.

It's true that the optimum amount of magnification in a scope sight depends upon hunting condition, low power for short ranges in the thick stuff and higher for longer distances in the open, but there's a unit which makes such consideration almost academic. It's the variable scope, which gives you a choice of magnifications with a twist of the knob.

I prefer variables for all hunting, simply because it makes my rifle (and me) more versatile. Let's look at their pro's and con's.

Time was when variables had problems. Their more complicated mechanisms were less reliable, less rugged than fixed power scopes. Resolution throughout the power range was not as good. Parallax was a problem. Shifts in point of impact from one power to another were often substantial. And, variables were more expensive.

They're still more expensive, but dollar for dollar you get more for your money.

In pure terms, variables are still less rugged, usually offer a tad less resolving efficiency, and do often give a slight change in impact from one end of the power range to the other. In terms of hunting efficiency, however, those points are meaningless. That's not only my opinion, but that of all of the major scope manufacturers with whom I checked.

If you know that all your hunting will be under one set of conditions, buy the fixed power which best suits your needs. It costs less, and is marginally "better." If all your hunting is in heavy cover, buy a 2 1/2X; for average conditions, a 4X; and for open country, a 6X. If you're getting a scope for varmint hunting where long shots at small targets are the rule, the higher powers offer an advantage. In any case, you need not feel "undergunned" by having a fixed power scope.

If you want versatility, however, don't hesitate in going with a variable. If your fixed power choice would be a 2 1/2X, buy a 1 1/2X-4X or 1 1/2X-5X variable — something in that low power range. Replace a 4X choice with a 2X-7X or 2 1/2X-8X, and a 6X with a 3X-9X. Good variable scopes are now very reliable, withstanding the recoil of the heaviest calibers exceedingly well, and the early problems with parallax and shifts of impact have been eliminated for all practical hunting considerations.

There once was an old wives tale which said you could see your target better in poor light conditions with a low power scope than with a high power. 'Tain't so — for hunting conditions. Just as with binoculars at daylight and dusk, or in dark cover, you can distinguish detail much better with higher magnification.

Why this is true isn't important to most hunters, but if you want a few lines for the hot stove league, here they are. That old wives tale apparently sprang from the now-discredited "relative brightness" figure, which has been discontinued by scope manufacturers, the one which said that at low power more light comes through so you can see better in the dark. The trouble with that is that the eye can't utilize all that extra light, since it will dilate to only some 5mm or 6mm under poor hunting light conditions, and to about 7mm in the dark. Quantities of light beyond what the eye pupil at that size can accept are wasted, and even the highest magnification big-game scopes transmit more than enough.

But the resolving power of low magnification is better than that of high, so you'll see detail better. Right? Again, nope, that isn't true. As Al Akin, of Bushnell, explains it: "The average human eye can resolve about 60 seconds — one minute — of light, and even at the maximum 9X all good 3X-9X variables resolve much better than that...about twice that, in fact."

Al is a testimonial for variable scopes. After being a vital cog at Bushnell for 27 years, and being privy to all the data relative to scope efficiency and reliability, he has variables on all of his two dozen rifles.

The original crosshair reticle was progressively joined over the years by a variety of other options: post, post and crosshair, center dot, dot and crosshair, lighted dot, crosshair and/or post, tapered crosshairs, and the "plex." The latter was originated by Leupold as the Duplex, a crosshair with the outer sections heavier than the center portions, and all manufacturers now have their versions of this reticle.

The "plex" is the most popular reticle for big game hunting, and that popularity is well deserved. One scope maker offers only that reticle, but others still have conventional crosshairs, posts, and dots. For big-game hunting, my favorite is the plex type.

"Rangefinders" are now available in some scopes. Most work on the principle of fitting an animal between two lines in the scope, by rotating the power ring, after which you can read the range on an indicator in the scope tube. Then, by knowing the trajectory of your bullet, you determine how much to hold over at long range.

There is now, also, an additional innovation for some of these scopes. After determining your distance, you dial in that distance on the scope, after which you may then just aim directly at the spot you wish to hit, with no holdover.

"Rangefinders" and "distance dialing" are considerable engineering achievements, and they're fun to play with. Rangefinders are geared to the "average" size of a deer (shoulder to brisket measurement), and adjustment must be made for animals not that size. Fit an elk body between the lines, and the distance would be the scale reading plus one-third. For antelope, three-fourths the scale reading.

Silhouette shooters have proved conclusively that aiming directly *at* the target is more accurate than holding over (or under), and their needs for scope adjustments with precise repeatability have stimulated vast improvements in scope adjustments. Despite the integration of these improvements into hunting scopes, via the distance dialing arrangement, I cannot generate much enthusiasm for this feature in my own hunting. The good ones do work, if you do your part.

Rangefinders and distance dialing are not needed except for long-range shooting, and the calibers competent to kill cleanly way out there have quite flat trajectories. The 150-grain 7mm Rem Mag., sighted in for 250 yards, is only about 6 1/2 inches below the point of aim at 350 yards. In the exceptional circumstances when I shoot at distances greater than that, I simply aim at a spot somewhere between the back line and the middle of the chest cavity, depending upon how many football fields away I guesstimate the animal to be. Having said that, simply and smugly, I must confess that there have been occasions when I longed for distance-estimating help from somewhere.

Scopes with rangefinders and distance dialing can be used conventionally, as a scope without those features, so don't hesitate to buy one with them if that's your inclination. They're fun to play with, and just might help you pot that trophy of a lifetime. If you do get one, however, practice with it until the mechanics are second nature.

Knowing that I always use the maximum power on my variable when time and circumstances permit, I had a friend of mine shoot three five-shot, 50-yard groups at various power settings with a M70 in .243 caliber. At 2X, T.L. Miller's group size was 1 3/8 inches; at 4X it was 1 2/8 inches; and at 7X it dropped substantially to 5/8 of an inch. An open sights group ran 2 7/8 inches. Using a scope on a M1100 shotgun cut the rifled slug group size in half from that of the standard shotgun sights.

THE RETICLE RIDDLE

"I like a post," Pete told the group of us, in a hunting camp in New York state during a discussion of scopes for deer rifles. "In the woods up here you can see a post long before and after you can see crosshairs."

"Sure can," chimed in Jim, "whose .308 Sako with an old 1 3/4X Lyman Alaskan we were examining. "I like that post. Just sit that buck on top of the post and...*pow!*"

Although a post reticle isn't one of my favorites, that discussion brought back memories of a moment forever etched in memory. It happened in Kenya in the late 1960's, in a leopard blind where we had waited for hours as daylight waned. As that light disappeared a very big leopard appeared, sprang swiftly into the bait tree and began to feed.

I tried to see the medium crosshairs in the 4X scope, thought I did, but obviously didn't. At the shot the big cat hit the ground and vanished with one leap into the dense vegetation. We never saw him again.

If! If the reticle in my scope had been...something different, would it have made a difference? Post? Dot? Heavy crosshairs? How about an illuminated dot at the center of the crosshairs, which wasn't in existence back then. Would any of them have meant a trophy leopard rug in my den rather than a record-sized memory in my mind?

The probable answer is yes. The shot was an easy one — 40 yards, from a sitting position, with a forked-stick rifle rest. The rifle was very accurate, and in the preceding days I had taken numerous game animals out to several hundred yards without difficulty. A heavy post or heavy crosshairs very probably would have enabled me to kill the leopard. But the flip side of that, however, is that such a heavy reticle would have made unlikely or impossible the long-ranged performance that took those other trophies.

Therein lies the dilemma of the reticle riddle. As in the selection of a caliber or a scope power, the choice of the aiming device within a riflescope is a compromise. The fine crosshairs which are ideal for prairie dogs way out yonder are almost useless on deer in the timber at daybreak and dusk. A heavy post which might work well on a buck in heavy deer woods, conversely, completely covers a small varmint at long distances.

European scopes have traditionally tended toward very heavy reticles, with one of the favorites being a "three-legged" crosshair, one with the top leg missing. There are many variations of this: three heavy legs plus a thin top leg; a heavy post with a thin horizontal "hair;" three heavy legs which don't quite meet in the middle; and three heavy legs plus a finer mid-section. A simple, heavy post is also widely used.

The primary reason why hunters in many parts of Europe prefer such heavy reticles is because of hunting conditions. Much of their hunting is in dense, dark forests, very early or very late in the day, and even at night, and under such conditions a very prominent reticle is a must.

In this country a simple crosshair was the standard for many years, and with refinement it became available in fine, medium or coarse dimensions. Varmint and target shooters using higher magnification scopes preferred very fine crosshairs. The simple "dot" reticle had its day in the sun, with both hunters and target shooters, and it retains a measure of popularity with both. The post reticle became available and popular, and it still is in some quarters.

What we shooters have done over the years in the selection of a scope reticle is try to pick the best for our particular brand of gunning. We compromised.

Compromise! That's exactly what scope manufacturers have now done, going largely or entirely to an innovative reticle which is generically called the "plex." First designed and used by Leupold (the DUPLEX), it is a crosshair which is heavy toward the outside, but which has a thinner portion in the center. It goes far toward giving the best of both worlds — a heavy aiming framework for bigger animals in poor light, and a more precise one for smaller targets or big game at a distance.

A similar solution has been around for many years — a crosshair tapered from heavy on the outside to thin in the middle, and there are versions of this still on the market. To that Leupold has added the dot (the Leupold Dot), which seems to float on almost invisible crosshairs in the middle of the viewing area.

At one time Bushnell had an innovative "Command Post" reticle, a crosshair with a post which could be flipped into position as needed. Rumor has it that this will be brought back. The firm now markets a reticle in which, with a twist of a knob, a lighted red dot will appear at the center of the crosshair. Tasco and Simmons have "light on demand" aiming point models. All are similar to the lighted dot aiming point in the optical sights now popular in practical pistol shooting competition. Burris has a "Fine Plex" in addition to a regular plex, and a "Post Crosshair."

Apart from the range-finding reticle arrangements in some scopes, regular scope reticles can be used as rough rangefinders. Dots cover so many inches at a hundred yards; the thin section opening of a plex reticle subtends a definite distance; the lines in both the thin and the thick sections of such reticles blot out "X" inches at various distances. Most manufacturers give such statistics in their scope specifications. Study, experience and practice are the keys to making use of this possibility of estimating distance to an animal.

The search for a better reticle is never ending, and the solutions can be complicated. The Shepherd Scope features a series of aiming circles, aligned vertically, bigger ones at the top and smaller ones toward the bottom. By fitting the animal in the proper circle, according to the instructions, you have compensated properly for that particular distance, and you just use that circle for aiming.

To sum up, for every occasion there's a perfect reticle. Dots are great for some target and varmint shooting; poor for big game in the timber. Medium crosshairs are very effective in most shooting situations, and fine ones are excellent for long-ranged varmint shooting. The lighted aiming point works. For all-around shooting the plex is best, which is why it has become the standard of the industry.

April 1986

TASCO: ROAD TO RESPECT

S hortly after World War II a man named Dave Bushnell made a move which would eventually change the American perception of "made in Japan." He began importing Japanese-made rifle scopes, during a period when the above label signified poor quality. The scopes sold because they were inexpensive. They quickly became severe competition for Bill Weaver, the "Henry Ford" of scope sights, and his low-end, solid-quality line eventually fell victim to whatever combination it was — lower labor costs, U.S.-financed state-of-the-art production lines, better quality, trade barriers or whatever — which made the Japanese scopes a better buy in the view of American hunters.

You know the rest of the story. Japanese industry, ingenuity and dedication, coupled with massive infusion of economic aid from America, and guidance as to the preferences of U.S. buyers, brought the Japanese optics industry to the top. Bushnell prospered and still does, as their scopes and binoculars, and other Japanese optical products, gradually went from poor to better and finally to good. Nikons and Canons, for instance, now dominate professional photography.

Dave Bushnell did not have the Japanese connection exclusively to himself very long. Other entrepreneurs ventured into the water, and most went through the same growing pains as did Bushnell. Then the few became many, and hunters were again faced with the problem of sorting out the good from the bad. Some forgettable names cropped up and most dropped out just as quietly. One which didn't fade away was a small Miami firm with the coined name of Tasco.

Tasco is George Rosenfield is Tasco. A combat navigator-bombardier in World War II, son of a Boston produce dealer, George was influenced by wife Estelle to abandon any thought of following in his father's footsteps ("She didn't like the thought of me going to work at one or two o'clock in the morning.") He started Tanross Supply Company, a wholesale fishing tackle and hardware distribution firm, but soon began to buy binoculars from a New York importer. There he discovered an industry which he felt had great growth potential. George "retired" to Florida, sold the tackle and hardware business, shortened the name to Tasco, and in 1953 began his travels to the Orient to seek out manufacturers of optical products.

"You're using a Tasco?"

No respect! Serious shooters didn't eat quiche or use a Tasco scope. Rosenfield, like those who went before, had his quality problems. The general perception of his scopes in the early years was of a product which was "cheap" as well as inexpensive. You bought a Tasco scope or binoc if you couldn't afford anything else, or for your wife or youngster, or an enemy. That reputation may have been a bum rap, but most probably was semi-justified.

My personal experience with the brand wasn't none, but it was slim. Ten years ago I tried a Tasco mini-binocular and a 3X-9X variable scope. The binocular was mediocre. The scope was very "bright" and, although the adjustments left something to be desired, I used it on a 6mm Rem M700 to kill my biggest antelope. Until last fall that was my only exposure to George Rosenfield's grab-bag of goodies.

What a difference a decade makes!

"It's as good as any I've ever tested," Don McGuffie told me over the phone. "I'll bring you the targets and data. I'm sure the one flier is my fault. I was on low power and the crosshairs pretty well covered the half-inch aiming dot."

I should be so lucky with my fliers — one inch out. Don is a friend who shoots bench rest, and I call on him when I really need a scope wrung out beyond hunting accuracy. When he straps a glass to one of his .222 Rem. benchrest rifles, the quality tale gets told.

Don used Tasco's best 3X-9X variable, the World Class Wide Angle Zoom. With a 40mm objective lens, it is 12 5/8 inches long and weighs just 11 1/2 ounces. Field of view at 100 yards: 15 feet at 9X and 43 1/2 feet at 3X. Positive, click adjustments are 1/4 inch.

I asked Don to test the scope through the power range, shooting it at 3X, 5X, 7X and 9X, since one of the faults of earlier variables (and some present ones) was a shift in point of impact with a change in power. Four shots fired at 4X, 5X, 7X and 9X grouped into one-half inch, which is much better than the accuracy capability of most big game hunting rifles. A fifth shot, at 3X, was that flier Don mentioned — one inch out. When Don ran the "around the clock" test of the scope adjustments — right, down, left and up, the point of impact came back to within 3/8 inch of the first shot, within the grouping ability of even Don's bench rest rifle. He was impressed with both the brightness and the performance, and with the wide range of adjustment capability: about seven feet both horizontally and vertically, which makes zeroing possible with just about any rifle and mount.

That kind of performance is impressive, and so is the Tasco guarantee on all World Class (top of the line) optical products. It says simply that the scope will be repaired or replaced at any time during the owner's lifetime if it fails to operate properly, or is ever damaged, even if it's the owner's fault.

I hunted antelope with George and his crew one fall, and met with him the following spring in Miami, where all but a dozen of his 200 employees work. He had just returned from one of his frequent trips to Japan, where that other dozen operate, and was filled with enthusiasm and new ideas.

"We began as simply an importer," he explained, "but now we're far beyond that. We have our own engineers and designers who develop products, and have developed a rapport with manufacturers in the Orient over a 30-year period to produce the products. Our goal is to offer the best at popular prices, and that requires market research and quality control as well as product design."

How far has Tasco come in 30 years? In terms of sales, to a whopping $50 million dollars plus last year. In terms of market: to 60 countries around the world. Product? Riflescopes (hunting, silhouette, target, pistol, optical, shotgun, rimfire, air gun, range-finding, trajectory-compensating), telescopes (spotting, compact, zoom, rubber-coated, camouflaged) binoculars (full-sized, mini, roof prism, porro prism, rubber coated, zoom, zip focus, wide angle, camouflaged), tripods, window mounts, shoulder mounts, shooting glasses, sport glasses, fishing glasses, scope mounts, and scope-guides.

Respect?

Probably not nearly as much as is deserved, but improving. Tasco products have been used by NASA, the U.S. Marine Corps, the U.S. Navy, and many governmental agencies in this country and others around the world. They're featured by top quality European distributors, who move much of Tasco's foreign sales (about 20 to 25 percent of total sales) right there in the lair of quality optics. They travel incognito under such brand names as Weatherby, Colt, Savage and Marlin. They're made in Japan — and Korea, Hong Kong and Taiwan (where production is just beginning on what George calls "probably the best production and testing facilities of any in Japan").

"We're getting there, but I want everybody to know just how good our scopes are," said Sheryl Rosenfield. She's the daughter of the founder, the Executive Vice President of Tasco, and is a sharp, hard-driving businesswoman who is impatient to have Tasco acknow-ledged as being top drawer. "We've got the sales and we have excellent products, and fully expect to soon have the image of quality as well as of value."

She's probably right. The Tasco line is extensive. I can nit-pick a few items (the shooting glasses are too small, the window mount is poorly designed, etc.), but my experience with the 1985 products indicates that George Rosenfield sells scopes and binoculars which are indeed excellent in quality as well as in value. For a catalog, write: Tasco, 7600 NW 26th St., Miami, FL 33122.

July 1985

SPOTTING SCOPES

"There he is!" Jonathan Adams stared across the canyon on the Mescalera Apache Indian Reservation, zeroed in on a light blob among the green trees. He eased his binoculars into position, then borrowed my more powerful 10X40's, but finally shook his head. "Can't tell how big, but from his color he looks young. Wish we'd brought the spotting scope."

But we hadn't, and even the 10-power binocs couldn't evaluate that bull elk at 1,000 yards. As it turned out, Jonathan called the bull across the canyon to within less than a hundred yards of where we sat, and the six-pointer was young, with antlers too slender for trophy consideration. Had the elk not responded to the call, however, we would have had a long, difficult stalk to get within "evaluating" range.

With a spotting scope the task would have been simple.

Remember the bewhiskered sea captain, legs spread and braced against the pitch and roll of his ship's deck, who unlimbered a brass telescope, extended it full length, and immediately determined that the sail low on the horizon belonged to "Black Bart" — or some such pirate of note. Good show. Especially since the point of view scene we as an audience got — camera looking through the scope — was rock steady.

Spotting scopes are useful primarily because they offer higher magnification than is available in binoculars, but that comes with a price. Most of us, sea captains notwithstanding, can't hand hold a spotting scope with any degree of success. We must place it on a tripod, a unipod, a window mount or something similar, or brace it over a rock or termite mound, padded by a jacket.

For the hunter or shooter, a spotting scope is a specialty tool for which he may have no use. If his activity calls for one, however, nothing takes its place. Such is the case with competition rifle and pistol shooters. They rely on specific knowledge of where each shot is going to make any adjustments necessary to keep their bullets in the black. Unless they're using a high magnification scope sight, which in itself will often reveal bullet holes at 100 yards, that flow of information most often comes through a spotting scope.

At a recent metallic silhouette pistol competition I watched shooters rely on their spotters — using spotting scopes — to feed them data after each shot. Of most interest to me was the nature of that info, especially for those who weren't missing any targets (there were several possibles that day). Those shooters wanted to know exactly where on the target their bullets were striking, and the scope watchers could tell them.

Evaluating trophy quality of individual game animals is, of course, an obvious use of the spotting scope. In the minds of most it is associated primarily with open, high mountain hunting — for sheep, goats and the like. But it is really useful for a far broader range of hunting activity, and odds are good that more and more such precision tools will be found in backpacks and saddlebags now that spotting scope offerings have become so varied. The improved manufacturing techniques and materials which have revolutionized scope sights, binoculars and cameras are beginning to be applied to spotting scopes. Not only are they better, but some of them are amazingly small and light.

Hunters routinely rely on spotting scopes when after sheep, goats, antelope, caribou and grizzly, but rather seldom for other species. In the case of mule deer hunters, they're often missing a bet. On many occasions I've been able to put a "yes" or "no" or "maybe" label on a buck at long range, by using a spotting scope, eliminating miles of unproductive riding or walking. Or, on the other hand, heading me toward a potential trophy. Much mule deer terrain lends itself to such evaluation.

So does some whitetail country. One club in Louisiana has raised deer stands — platforms on stilts — in oat fields which may be a mile or more in length. Members frequently use spotting scopes from those stands. On at least one occasion, from one of those stands, Ham Hamilton watched a cougar through his 20X scope for quite a while, providing a thrill which demonstrates one of the fringe benefits of such scopes: it's just fun to have the close-up view of wild game — and birds — that's difficult or impossible to get in any other way.

As is true of most products, spotting scopes are available in a fairly wide range of options. First of all, you'll notice that optical technology has eliminated the need for the super long, telescoping tubes of yesteryear by using the same prism arrangements which distinguish modern binoculars from the older "field glasses." Also, there are now on the market new spotting scopes which employ the mirror lens principle used in some camera lenses, providing higher magnification in a shorter tube.

The simplest spotting scope is a fixed power scope, with its only moving part being a focusing ring. Next is the scope on which the eyepiece is interchangeable, giving you a choice of power. Last is the zoom, which gives a continually varying power range with a mere twist of a control.

As for magnification, higher isn't always better. If mirage is a problem, as it frequently is under hot conditions, you'll get more definition at lower power than at the high ranges. Then, too, as magnification increases, the field of view decreases, which can be a problem in locating a game animal through the scope under hunting conditions. Variable power scopes help with both of those problems. They can be adjusted to get the best compromise between magnification and mirage. And, a hunter can also use the lowest power setting (maximum field of view), to locate an animal, and then increase the magnification while keeping the game centered.

A few spotting scopes have an external aiming device, similar to sights on a rifle, which help in getting zeroed in on an animal. One option available from many manufacturers, preferred by competition shooters, is the 45-degree eyepiece, which permits the shooter to look through the scope without moving from his shooting position.

The vast improvements in spotting scopes is reflected in two Bushnell Spacemaster scopes of mine. The 10-year old is fixed power with interchangeable eyepieces, is 16 1/2 inches long and doesn't miss weighing three pounds by very much. The newer one, about three years old, is 12 1/2 inches long and weighs 41 ounces, and it's a 20X-45X zoom. The newest Spacemaster, as shown in the current catalog, is 12 inches long and weighs only 37 ounces. These latter specs are almost identical for the Weatherby Sightmaster (20X-45X zoom).

For a couple of years I've been using a small, lightweight (9 1/2 inches and 19 ounces) Bushnell scope called the Stalker. It's a good one, a fixed power 20X. The new Stalker has interchangeable eyepieces (10X, 15X and 20X), and is a bit shorter and lighter than mine.

If you don't choose a variable, which I prefer, a 30X is a good all-around power for a hunting scope, Zeiss has an excellent mirror lens spotting scope in that 30X. It's 8 1/2 inches long, weighs about two pounds, and is armor coated with rubber. Spotting scopes can be used on camera tripods, but most spotting scope manufacturers offer short-legged tripods designed for shooting use. Bushnell has an excellent window mount for scope or camera, which also works pretty well on tree limbs under half an inch diameter. Tasco has a similar mount with a two-inch C-clamp capability. Redfield offers an ingenious, tiny tripod for its new mirror scope which can be used either as a tripod or on a car window. There are also holders which can be screwed into a tree trunk or limb. Gun stocks, designed or modified, can be used with spotting scopes just as they are with cameras, but they're awkward if you're also carrying a rifle.

Buying a spotting scope is a compromise, as is true for just about any product. Variable power scopes are generally more expensive and heavier. Lighter weight scopes are more difficult to hold. Weight isn't a consideration in competition shooting, but often is under hunting conditions. Before making your choice, evaluate your own spotting scope needs and study all the literature available.

February 1984

INDEX

DID YOU BORROW THIS COPY?

You should have your own copy of this excellent reference work. The easy-reading style of Grits' writing makes this a book you can get comfortable with, again and again.

Treat yourself! Get your own copy of GRITS ON GUNS. If you already have a copy, consider giving one to a friend. It's a gift that'll rate at the top of any shooter's list.

Send me _____ copies of GRITS ON GUNS at $25 plus $2.95 shipping and handling. (For standard hardcover edition). or _____ copies of the deluxe, limited edition at $40 plus $2.95 shipping and handling.

Name _____

Address _____

City _____ State _____ Zip _____

MC _____ Visa _____ Card Number _____

Exp. Date _____

Signature _____

Cane River Publishing
P.O. Box 4095
Prescott, AZ 86302

_____ I don't need another copy of GRITS ON GUNS right now, but please notify me when you bring out other books by Grits so that I can have the option of being one of the first to order new releases.